Enduring Nations

Enduring Nations

Native Americans in the Midwest

Edited by
R. DAVID EDMUNDS

University of Illinois Press
URBANA AND CHICAGO

Library of Congress Cataloging-in-Publication Data

Enduring nations : Native Americans in the Midwest /
edited by R. David Edmunds.
p.   cm.
Includes bibliographical references and index.
ISBN-13 978-0-252-03330-8 (cloth : alk. paper)
ISBN-10 0-252-03330-2 (cloth : alk. paper)
ISBN-13 978-0-252-07537-7 (pbk. : alk. paper)
ISBN-10 0-252-07537-4 (pbk. : alk. paper)
1. Indians of North America—Middle West—History.
2. Indians of North America—Middle West—Government relations.
3. Indians of North America—Middle West—Social life and customs.
I. Edmunds, R. David (Russell David), 1939–
E78.M67E63   2008
977.004'97—dc22   2008006402

For Scooter, Sunny, Mingo, Quanah,
and Airedales everywhere.
May your days be full of long walks,
unwary cats, and lots of dog biscuits.
Give 'em hell, gang!

Contents

Illustrations

Enduring Nations

Introduction

A People of Persistence

R. DAVID EDMUNDS

At the beginning of the twenty-first century, most Americans do not associate the states that once comprised the Old Northwest with Native American people. When quizzed about the regions in which Native Americans played a major role, Americans invariably refer to the Desert Southwest, the Great Plains, the northern Rockies, or Oklahoma. Residents of Michigan, Wisconsin, and Minnesota readily acknowledge that Indian people still occupy reservation lands in their states, but with the exceptions of disputes over hunting and fishing laws, and concern over the impact of Native American gaming, most non-Indian citizen of these three states relegate modern Native Americans to the fringe of modern society: ethnic communities to be tolerated and endured, but not major contributors to the development of contemporary societies and economies in the twenty-first century.[1]

For non-Indians living in the lower Great Lakes states, Native Americans usually are incorporated as part of the romanticized folklore of the past (local place names or legends) or are envisioned as exotic folk to be encountered on summer fishing trips or other vacation excursions to northern Wisconsin or Minnesota. Most residents of Ohio, Indiana, or Illinois are unaware of the Indian people living in their midst or that these people and their forebears played a major role in the history of the region and the American nation.

Yet the demographics of the region refute such assumptions. In 2000 the six states (Minnesota, Wisconsin, Michigan, Ohio, Indiana, and Illinois) that border the western Great Lakes contained almost 250,000 Native American people, and this enumeration includes only those individuals who listed themselves as solely Native American, not the many others who identified themselves as multiracial, or "part-Indian." If people who identified themselves as of mixed descent are included, the numbers swell to over 460,000. Since Native American people in the Midwest have a long history of intermarriage with non-Indians, the latter figure probably is more accurate. Indeed, census reports indicate that 17.4 percent of all Native Americans in the United States currently live within this region.[2]

Tribal people have shaped the region's history. As Alan Shackelford (chapter 1) illustrates, during the pre-Columbian period the Midwest, and particularly the confluence region of the American Bottom, hosted a succession of Native American cultures that fostered hunting, gathering, horticulture, and trade networks. These societies skillfully adapted to changing environmental patterns, and in turn may have altered the ecology of the region itself. Although the pre-Columbian settlement of Cahokia is sometimes touted as a "pre-historic American Indian city," Shackelford argues that its population was considerably smaller than previous estimates of twenty thousand to thirty thousand residents, but that the complex of mounds and religious centers there exercised considerable influence throughout the Illinois and Mississippi valleys. Moreover, he points out that the Illinois occupancy of the region and their subsequent alliance with the French during the fur trade era "was but another in a long series of adaptations to new peoples and environments" (p. 31).

With the exception of the Meskwakis (Foxes), most of the midwestern tribes forged close alliances with the French and participated readily in the fur trade. Indeed, pelts supplied by the Great Lakes tribes formed the basis of the northern fur trade throughout the late seventeenth and eighteenth centuries, and French traders and coureurs de bois formed liaisons with native women, producing growing mixed-lineage populations that often served as intermediaries between tribal and French colonial governments. Moreover, as Richard White and others have so ably illustrated, in the Great Lakes region the two cultures (tribal and Creole French) often blended so harmoniously that residents of the region lived within a "middle ground," a cultural amalgam in which individuals subscribed to values from both sides without questioning whether these traits were indigenous or European. During the first two-thirds of the eighteenth century tribal people from the Great Lakes played a major role in the colonial warfare that flared incessantly during these years. Warriors (and their families) often voyaged hundreds of miles to Montreal, Niagara, or Fort Duquesne, where they joined French campaigns against the British frontiers. Meanwhile, Indian people in Illinois, Indiana, and Michigan also assisted the growing Creole French population in these regions to produce wheat, corn, and other crops that were shipped downstream to Montreal or Louisiana.[3]

During the American Revolution, some tribal people in Wisconsin and Illinois sided with the Americans, but most Native Americans in Michigan, Indiana, and Ohio supported the British. Supplied by British agents at Detroit, war parties of Shawnees, Miamis, and Wyandots repeatedly scourged Kentucky, keeping American settlements in the Bluegrass State under virtual siege through most of the conflict. Indeed, from the tribespeople's perspective, they and the British won the Revolutionary War in the West, and they were dumbfounded at American claims to the region in the immediate postwar period. Indian determination to retain their lands in Ohio led to the border warfare of the early 1790s, in which the Northwestern tribes twice devastated American armies (Harmar's Defeat in 1790; St. Clair's Defeat in 1791), before falling to Anthony Wayne at Fallen Timbers (1794). The resulting Treaty of Greenville (1795) opened much of Ohio to American settlement and set the stage for further American penetration and settlement of the region. Fifteen years later the Shawnee Prophet and Tecumseh attempted to rally the tribes for a last concerted defense of their midwestern land base, but by 1810 it was too late. American settlers had flooded into the region in such numbers that they now outnumbered the tribespeople, and Native Americans themselves were divided over whether they should oppose or attempt to cooperate with the new American government. Although many tribesmen fought with Tecumseh and the British during the War of 1812, others, such as the Shawnee chief Black Hoof, attempted to form an alliance with the Americans. Tecumseh's death and the Indian defeat at the Battle of the Thames (1813) effectively removed any European assistance for the tribesmen, and in the two decades following the Treaty of Ghent (1815) the Americans forced the tribes to sign treaties ceding much of their land in the region.

Most of the chapters in this volume center on the two centuries that have passed since the midwestern tribes mounted the last concerted military defense of their homeland, and the chapters' authors concentrate on issues or themes associated with tribal people during this period. A persistent question, one that plagued Native Americans in the early nineteenth century and that continues today, is the relationship of Native American leaders to the federal government. Indian leaders long have "walked a fine line" between attempting to protect their people's interest and acquiescing to the demands of federal Indian agents. Most have tried to select facets from the jumble of federal policies thrust upon them and to manipulate these policies on their people's behalf. Obviously, some have been more successful than others, but Thomas Colbert (chapter 3) argues that Keokuk, while overshadowed by the more historically famous Black Hawk, worked diligently for his people's welfare. Rejecting Black Hawk's militarism, Keokuk used his friendship with federal agents to secure temporary reservations for the Sauks and Mesk-wakis in Iowa, and to secure federal funds to sustain the tribe during the removal period. Like many other Native American leaders during these (and more recent) decades, Keokuk sometimes used his position as a government "money chief" to benefit his friends and relatives. Yet his leadership enabled the Sauks and Meskwakis to persist, and if they suffered during the removal period, they fared better than many of the other tribes who were removed from their homelands east of the Mississippi.

So did most of the Ottawa and Ojibwe people in Michigan. As Gregory Dowd (chapter 7) illustrates, several circumstances (the Depression of 1837, a proximity to Canada, and non-Indian misgivings over the injustice of American Indian policy) combined to retard, if not thwart, the removal of the northern Michigan tribes west of the Mississippi. Dowd's chapter also offers insights into the role that rumors played on the American frontier. Because of their experiences, Native Americans readily believed rumors that Indian removal was part of a larger American plot to spread disease and foster their extermination, while non-Indians' assumptions about Indian "character" and their fears of potential hostilities caused American citizens to project their own doubts about themselves (Jacksonian society) upon tribal people.

Black Hoof and Jean Baptiste Richardville sought an accommodation with the federal government. Like Keokuk, Shawnee chief Black Hoof also has been eclipsed by the more famous Tecumseh, but the old Shawnee chief was a faithful ally to the Americans. During the War of 1812 he served the American cause, leading "Loyal Shawnees" against Tecumseh and pro-British Indians. Following the war, Black Hoof was temporarily praised and feted as an "honored guest" by white Kentuckians, and he hoped to use such good will to safeguard Shawnee lands in Ohio. Enlisting the support of Quaker missionaries, Black Hoof urged his people to embrace yeoman agriculture, but white pressure for their lands in Ohio reached such a pitch that the Shawnees eventually were forced to abandon their homelands for new territories in Missouri and Kansas. Yet as Stephen Warren (chapter 4) points out, Black Hoof's leadership and the lessons learned by the Shawnees in negotiating with the federal government served them well in forging a new Shawnee nation in the West.

Jean Baptiste Richardville manipulated "the system" more successfully than either Keokuk or Black Hawk. Bradley Birzer (chapter 5) illustrates that during the removal period, Miami métis Richardville used his business acumen to obtain large tracts of land "in fee simple" for members of his family, and for other influential Miamis. Although title to these "personal reservations" rested in the hands of Richardville and a handful of other relatively wealthy Miamis, these leaders then offered haven to those Miamis opposed to removal, essentially establishing new, privately held reservations for many Miamis within their old homeland. Like other Indian leaders in Illinois, Indiana, and Ohio, Richardville could not indefinitely postpone the removal of his tribe, but his private lands became a sanctuary for those who refused to emigrate; moreover, they also became a magnet that attracted Miamis who became discontented with the new lands in Kansas and who then returned to Indiana. Indeed, many members of the large community of Miami people still resident in Indiana are descendants of Miamis who sought refuge on Richardville's lands during the 1840s and 1850s.

Richardville exemplifies another important facet of the Native American experience in the Great Lakes region during this period: the emergence of large numbers of métis people who served as role models to other members of their tribe, and who also served as intermediaries between tribal communities and the federal government. Prior to the removal period, much of the commerce in the region was dominated by métis traders and merchants who functioned as members of tribal societies, but who also envisioned themselves as a people somewhat removed from more traditional tribal members. Many of the métis, both male and female, continued to meet their tribal kinship obligations, but they also participated in the Creole French or Anglo societies that emerged around regional trading centers, or in the American Bottom. Many incorporated European clothing into their wardrobes, were educated in parochial boarding schools, spoke French and/or English (in addition to tribal languages), and considered themselves to be a socioeconomic elite within the Great Lakes region. Obviously, these people were part of both tribal and European societies, but their particular identity was malleable, transcending their affiliation with either or both camps.

Questions of identity intensified after large numbers of Americans arrived in the Great Lakes region. Although both their Creole French neighbors and "full-blood" kinsmen readily accepted the métis, there was no place for people of mixed lineage and heritage within the American socioeconomic system. Newly arrived Americans subscribed to racially polarized categories: individuals were "white," "black," or "Indian." In response, some métis, such as Richardville, initially seemed to jump back and forth across the color line, but by the late 1840s he was forced to accept his role as a spokesman for the Miami people, and thus he became, at least in the eyes of the Americans, indelibly part of the Native American community.[4]

Other métis, particularly a group of well-educated young women, challenged the American system. Rebecca Kugel (chapter 8) indicates that a small but influential group of young métis women, educated in Protestant mission schools, refused to accept the American categorization that they were fit only for domestic service and sought positions as teachers and missionaries, economic positions that accorded status to women in nineteenth-century American society. These women argued that racial definitions meant nothing in their case, since they were sophisticated, young Christians whose education and accomplishments mirrored or even surpassed the accomplishments of Anglo-American women in the region. Their strong sense of identity enabled many of them to initially thwart the racial polarization, although by the end of the nineteenth century many of their children and grandchildren were forced to accept the American categorization.

Susan Sleeper-Smith's biographical analysis of Frances Slocum (chapter 6) provides an interesting case study in the ongoing malleability of Native American identity in this region, and it illustrates that although some Indian people became more "white" in an effort to remain in their homeland, once they embraced such a racial category, it proved difficult to reassert their "Indianness." Sleeper-Smith also addresses another ongoing issue that confronts Native American communities in the Great Lakes and in other regions: is Native American identity a genetic trait, or is it a subscription to a certain set of cultural values accepted by other members of the tribal community? Certainly, Frances Slocum, a former "white captive" among the Miamis, lived most of her life as an accepted member of the Miami community, yet she emphasized her Anglo-American lineage as a buffer against removal. In the twenty-first century, similar questions of Native American identity continue as one of the most critical issues facing modern tribal communities.

As the chapters written by Kugel and Sleeper-Smith suggest, women have always played a major role in defining the identity of Native American people in the Great Lakes area; several other authors have examined their contributions to tribal economies and social welfare in the region. Lucy Eldersveld Murphy (chapter 2) indicates that Sauk, Meskwaki, and Ho-Chunk (Winnebago) women dominated the mining of lead in the Dubuque-Galena region of the northern Mississippi Valley, and that the production of this commodity rivaled or even surpassed the fur trade as a source of income for these tribes. The entrance of American miners into the region during the 1820s ended the women's mining activities, but Murphy's chapter offers some interesting insights into an economic role rarely associated with Native American (or other) women.

Focusing on the Native American experience in the twentieth century, Melissa Meyer (chapter 12) illustrates that traditional patterns of social welfare utilized by Anishinaabe (Ojibwe) women to care for kinspeople and other members of the tribal community have continued into the present, although they have assumed new forms in modern times. Through oral traditions and interviews with contemporary Anishinaabe women, Meyer shows that throughout the twentieth century, women have continued to contribute to the community's economy. Moreover, traditional women's responsibilities, such as providing for the elderly, ill, indigent, or children, also continue to be addressed, although modern Anishinaabe women now seek to remedy these problems through a host of new institutions such as church mission societies, hospital auxiliaries, state or private welfare agencies, colleges, and tribal governments. Meyer argues that tribal women see their participation in such activities as a "responsibility" to their people, rather than as an assertion of feminist "rights," and that these modern obligations have precursors within traditional Anishinaabe society.

Obviously, the Anishinaabe women discussed in chapter 12, as well as other tribal people, have masterfully adapted many facets of their tribal cultures to changes forced on them by the dominant American culture, yet at no time have demands for such adaptation been more stringent than in the twentieth century. First isolated (and almost abandoned) on reservations, then relocated to major urban areas, and finally offered new opportunities for enlarged tribal sovereignty, Native Americans in the Great Lakes region, like Indians elsewhere, have admirably endured a "rollercoaster" of changing federal Indian policies in the twentieth century. In chapter 9, Brenda Child, focusing on Ojibwe survival strategies during the Great Depression, chronicles how Ojibwe families placed many of their children in federal or religious boarding schools during these dark years in an effort to ensure that their children would have access to adequate, food, clothing, and medical care. Meanwhile their parents sought employment through federal work programs such as the Indian Civilian Conservation Corps (CCC), which not only employed many Native American laborers but also cut roads, erected telephone lines, and reforested many of the Ojibwe reservations. Like the boarding schools, the Indian CCC camps also provided their residents with food, shelter, medical care, and a minimal wage when other employment was unavailable. As Child points out, Ojibwe participation in these programs often was not their first choice, but it allowed Ojibwe families to persist during the depths of the Great Depression.

Perhaps the period of greatest adjustment was the 1950s, when many Indian people were sent into major urban areas through the federal government's "relocation" program. Prior to that decade, most Native Americans in the Great Lakes region (and elsewhere) had resided in rural areas and rarely had visited distant large cities. During the 1950s, however, in an effort to force Indian people to "join the mainstream of American life," federal Indian agents encouraged Native Americans to move to several large midwestern or western cities, get "regular jobs," and find housing apart from reservation communities. Indian agents initially paid for their relocation, helped them secure employment and obtain housing, and then encouraged them to cut their reservation ties.[5]

James LaGrand (chapter 10) investigates how new Indian residents adapted to urban life in Chicago during the 1950s and illustrates that many fared remarkably well. Yet he argues that instead of following federal directives to blend into the non-Indian society, Indian people in Chicago sought out "Indian work" from a limited number of companies; they also congregated in Native American neighborhoods, particularly the "Uptown" region on the city's north side. Housing conditions in this region were often crowded, but urban Indians preferred to live close to one another, and social agencies strengthened these neighborhoods by establishing Indian Centers in their midst. Unfortunately, however, some of the social problems that plagued reservation communities reappeared among Native American enclaves in Chicago, but the new residents formed urban Indian communities that have nevertheless "emerged as a viable part of Chicago's multiethnic, urban society" (p. 208).

During the final two decades of the twentieth century, enlarged interpretations of Native American sovereignty have provided many tribes with an opportunity to pursue new economic enterprises. Indian gaming is the most visible form of this new activity, but tribal entrepreneurs have expanded economic ventures into other venues that also promise to benefit their communities. Focusing on the Menominees, Brian Hosmer (chapter 11) examines the effect of this new tribal capitalism in the Great Lakes region and argues that the Menominees' development of a lumber industry during the first half of the twentieth century provided precedents for gaming and other economic activities of more recent decades. Hosmer compares the similarities and difference between lumbering and gaming, how both industries have affected tribal politics, and how Menominees have continued to adapt their daily lives to the demands of the marketplace. Although he offers no "blanket endorsement" for such tribal enterprises, he does point out that resources generated from such activity may "provide opportunities to preserve who, and what, they [the Menominees] are" (p. 235).

The chapters included in this volume focus on several themes that are important to understanding the history of Native American people in the Great Lakes region. First, far from being peripheral to the historical development of the states that border the western Great Lakes, Native Americans played major roles in the region's history. During the pre-Columbian period they developed adaptive strategies that later enabled them to successfully bridge the political and cultural differences between themselves and French and British colonists. In the colonial period they participated in the great colonial struggle for control of eastern North America, often pursuing their own agendas amidst the diplomatic and military maneuvers of the Europeans. During the first decade of the new American Republic they temporarily prevented the American settlement of Ohio, and in these years the continued influence and military power of tribal people remained a central focus or concern for federal officials. As late as the War of 1812 political control over much of the Great Lakes region remained in Indian hands, and only after the death of Tecumseh did federal officials clearly gain hegemony over the region. In retrospect, Native American people were the primary actors in the history of the Great Lakes region until the 1830s.

The chapters in this volume also illustrate that Native Americans are an adaptive people. During the colonial period they readily embraced the socioeconomic system of the Creole French, combining tribal and European values to create a uniquely successful blend of both cultures. In contrast, the Anglo-Americans who gained control over the upper Midwest following the War of 1812 assumed that Native American people would disappear, either through their assimilation and absorption into American society or more probably through their removal west of the Mississippi. Yet Native Americans in the region again adopted new strategies that allowed them to retreat into the northern fringes of the Midwest, or, like the Miamis of Indiana, they "hid in plain sight" within the confines of American society. And even those people dwelling on the reservations of northern Michigan, Wisconsin, and Minnesota adapted tribal ways to new political and economic conditions, ensuring that tribal values and traditions would continue. Into the twenty-first century, growing numbers of tribal people have also adapted to life in urban centers, facing new challenges but retaining their strong sense of Indian identity.

Issues of identity have often been contentious in the Great Lakes region, and they form a focal point shared by many of these chapters. "Being Indian" has long been a malleable quality, but many tribal people, through their marriage with non-Indians and through their ability to combine indigenous and European ways of life, have stretched the boundaries of Native American identity. Individuals such as Jean Baptiste Richardville, Frances Slocum, or the young métis women discussed in chapter 8 certainly enlarged the conventional definition of the term, and their lives offer insights into the continued evolution of such a designation. Indeed, the experiences of these Native Americans of mixed lineage, or of Native Americans who functioned successfully in both tribal and "non-Indian" worlds, offer a precursor of Native American identity in the twenty-first century. Not only do recent census figures indicate that over half the people who identify as "Native Americans" in the Midwest now are of mixed lineage, the proclivity for intermarriage is accelerating. Demographers argue that if current trends continue, by 2080 almost 90 percent of all Native American people in the United States will be of less than one-half Indian by lineage.[6]

Several of the chapters also illustrate that Native American leaders in the Great Lakes region have learned to "manipulate the system." Although faced with an imbalance of power, nineteenth-century chiefs such as Keokuk, Richardville, and Black Hoof used "loopholes" within the administration of federal Indian policy to protect their people, retain their homelands, and obtain adequate compensation when these homelands were finally surrendered. Participating in the marketplace and achieving an adequate balance between individual profits and communal values have engendered criticism of some leaders (particularly Richardville and Menominee administrators), and undoubtedly these tensions will continue. Yet the marketplace also offers opportunities. In the twentieth century leaders among the Menominees and other tribes used the special legal status accorded to tribal governments to establish economic enterprises that have provided for, and hopefully will continue to benefit, their tribal communities. Gaming remains the most publicized facet of this new entrepreneurship, but possibilities await in other venues.

Four chapters focus on the role of Native American women in this region, a topic that has drawn increased attention from scholars during the past quarter century. For years historians generally ignored the contributions of native women, but since the 1970s they have reexamined the influence of women in tribal society and have illustrated that in the Great Lakes region, as elsewhere, Indian women have always formed the very warp onto which the fabric of tribal society is woven. Certainly, throughout the historic period and into the twenty-first century, Native American women in this region have contributed to their tribe's economy, cared for their families, and provided guidance and assistance to tribal communities. Obviously, their sense of responsibility to the welfare of their communities has been a focal point of their identity, and their adherence to these obligations continue.

Finally, the tribal people of the Great Lakes region are a people of persistence. Although many tribes were forced to cede their homelands in the rich agricultural regions of southern Wisconsin, southern Michigan, Ohio, Indiana, and Illinois, tribal people still live in these regions. Many may be of mixed lineage, and some lack federal recognition, but they proudly cling to their tribal heritage and trace their ancestry back to the late eighteenth century, when they still held sway over vast tracts of what is now fertile farmland. Others reside in crowded "Indian neighborhoods" in major cities such as Milwaukee, Minneapolis, Detroit, and Chicago, but even in the midst of these concrete canyons they have survived and retained a strong sense of "being Indian." To the north, amidst the lakes that dot the forested "north country," tribal communities still occupy reservations that now serve as their homelands. Although many of these reservation communities are sorely lacking in economic assets, they remain "wellsprings of Indianness," places where tribal people who have left the region seeking employment opportunities periodically return. These reservation communities, along with the urban neighborhoods and the less formal associations of tribal people in the lower Midwest, will remain. Tribal people continue to believe that they were placed in or brought to this region by the Creator of the Universe. They have weathered many changes, but they still occupy their homelands. They believe that they, like the Great Lakes themselves, will endure.

Notes

1. A note on tribal nomenclature: the authors of the chapters featured in this volume differ among themselves over the use and spelling of tribal nomenclature. In some instances, for example, the same tribal group or community has been referred to as "Ojibwe" or "Aninshinaabe"; "Ottawa" or "Odawa"; "Winnebago" or "Ho-Chunk"; "Sioux" or "Dakota," etc. The editor generally has used the term utilized by the authors within their chapters, with other or optional nomenclature supplied in parentheses—for example, Winnebago (Ho-Chunk).

2. "The American Indian and Alaska Native Population: 2000" (Washington: U.S. Census Bureau, 2002), 5–6, available at http://www.census.gov/prod/2002/pubs/c2kbr01.15pdf.

3. See Richard White, *The Middle Ground: Indians, Empires, and Republics in the Great Lakes Region, 1650–1815* (New York: Cambridge University Press, 1991).

4. See R. David Edmunds, "'Unacquainted with the Laws of the Civilized World': American Attitudes toward the Métis Communities in the Old Northwest," in Jacqueline Peterson and Jennifer S. H. Brown, eds., *The New Peoples: Being and Becoming Métis in North America* (Winnipeg: University of Manitoba Press, 1985), 185–93.

5. See Donald Fixico, *Termination and Relocation: Federal Indian Policy, 1945–1960* (Albuquerque: University of New Mexico Press, 1986).

6. Russell Thornton, *American Indian Holocaust and Survival: A Population History since 1492* (Norman: University of Oklahoma Press, 1987), 236–37. See also Russell Thornton, "Health, Disease, and Demography," in Philip J. Deloria and Neal Salisbury, eds., *A Companion to American Indian History* (Malden, Mass.: Blackwell Publishers, 2002), 76–80.

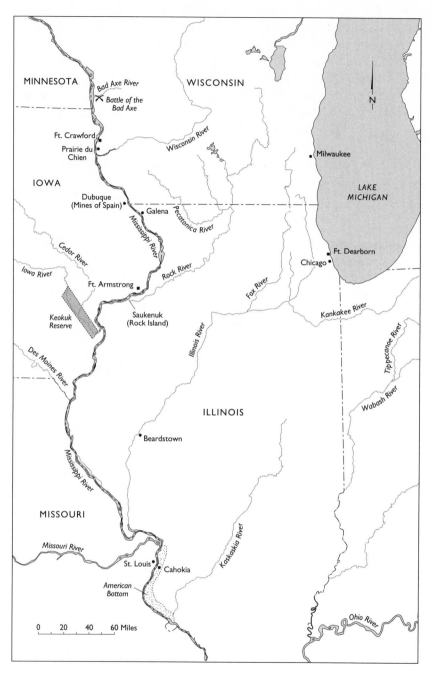

The Upper Mississippi Valley

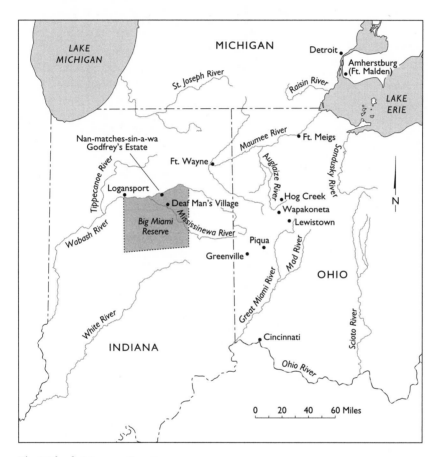

The Wabash-Maumee Frontier

The Western Great Lakes

1. The Illinois Indians in the Confluence Region

Adaptation in a Changing World

ALAN G. SHACKELFORD

For the Illinois Indians the appearance of Frenchmen in their country during the summer of 1673 signaled profound change. Though the Illinois leaders who met Marquette and Joliet may not have understood the exact nature of the opportunities and dangers implicit in establishing relations with the newly arrived Europeans, they were quite aware the meeting portended change in their world.[1] The Illinois already were in the midst of adjusting to a "new world" of prairies and bison when the Europeans arrived in the Midwest. Within a century, the Illinois would find themselves sharing the heart of their country with a relatively large and commercially prosperous colonial population. Once a dominant power in the region between Lake Michigan and the Mississippi Valley, the Illinois would find their hold on the northern and southern peripheries of their territory threatened by intensified colonial warfare. In addition to the warfare, the introduction of Old World diseases and the loss of women of childbearing age through intermarriage with French men would lead to the dramatic decline of Illinois population during the seventeenth and eighteenth centuries.

In the historiography of colonial and Native North America the Illinois often have been depicted as native accommodationists. Of the various Indian peoples inhabiting the western Great Lakes area and the upper Mississippi Valley, a region the French referred to as the *pays d'en haut,* none were as cordial to Europeans as the Illinois. Early in the colonial history of the Illinois Country, Illinois women and men intermarried, creating a métis population that would become an integral part of the region's Creole society. Apart from the métis portion of French Creole society, Illinois villages quickly integrated themselves economically and socially into French colonial Illinois. Notably, the largest French colonial communities in the American Bottom, the flood-plain of the Mississippi River bottom opposite modern St. Louis, began as Indian villages in which French traders and missionaries took up residence. Even when the Illinois and Creole communities were physically separate, the two maintained close relations based on kinship and shared economic and strategic interests. When France ceded the region to Britain following the Seven Years' War, the Illinois remained aloof from the Indian uprising often referred to as Pontiac's Rebellion. Instead of becoming associated with indigenous resistance movements, the Illinois carefully cultivated peaceful relations with Spanish and British authorities on both sides of the Mississippi. More than a decade later, during the American Revolution, most Illinois communities readily accepted George Rogers Clark's offer of neutrality in the conflict between the Americans and the British. Frequently historians credit this close colonial relationship to the demographic collapse and "cultural crisis" experienced by the Illinois during the seventeenth and eighteenth centuries.[2] Unquestionably, the Illinois declined in population and influence under both the French and British, but their history illustrates other important facets of the American Indian experience during this watershed period.

In an article entitled "The Indians' Old World," Neal Salisbury has urged historians to consider how North America's pre-Columbian past may have shaped the colonial experiences of both Native Americans and European newcomers. By placing the colonial encounter in a broader temporal context, scholars can better understand long-term processes and patterns that had their origin prior to the coming of Europeans, yet had critical influence on the character of French and Indian relations in the "New World."[3] This chapter will examine the Illinois Indians' ability to adapt to new environments and will illustrate that their relationship with the French had important anteced-ents in the precolonial period. When the French encountered the Illinois, they met a people who themselves had recently migrated into a new country in order to take advantage of opportunities presented by a rapidly changing natural and social environment. In the face of this new environment and its new opportunities, Illinois society and economy had proved adaptive and flexible. In sum, the Illinois were well practiced at meeting the challenges presented along a cross-cultural frontier when the first Europeans made their appearance in Illinois country in 1673.

At the time of their initial contact with the French, the Illinois were a loose association of as many as twelve separate tribal communities, including the Cahokia, Chepoussa, Chinkoa, Coiracoentanon, Espiminkia, Kaskaskia, Maroa, Michigamea, Moingwena, Peoria, Tamaroa, and Tapauro. By 1700 Euro-American observers identified only the Peoria, Kaskaskia, Tamaroa,

Cahokia, and Michigamea tribes, the others having been absorbed by these groups, foreign Indian tribes, or French colonial communities. When the French first heard of the Illinois from native intermediaries, they were reported living around the southern shores of Lake Michigan. But later, when the French had direct contact with the Illinois and their neighbors, the Illinois reportedly occupied approximately sixty villages in the Mississippi and Illinois valleys. The Illinois were closely related in terms of language and culture to the Miamis, who at the time of French contact lived just north of them in southwestern Wisconsin. The close cultural and linguistic affiliation between the Illinois and Miamis caused the earliest French observers difficulty in discerning between the two groups. That their languages were similar suggests that the division between the two people emerged shortly before the appearance of the French in the western Great Lakes. Notably, the location of the Illinois and Miamis near the Mississippi Valley made them the westernmost Central Algonkian people encountered during the period of initial contact with Europeans.

The location of the early historic Illinois-Miami speakers placed them on a cross-cultural frontier between Siouan-speaking peoples associated with the Prairie Peninsula (the grassland region stretching from central Illinois westward through eastern Kansas, Nebraska, and South Dakota) and Central Algonkian–speaking peoples associated with the Great Lakes and Ohio Valley. This location and the historic processes associated with it gave the Illinois and Miamis a unique appearance among the Central Algonkian peoples encountered by the French in the Midwest. The French readily noted the differences between the Illinois-Miami speakers of the prairies and the Central Algonkian Ottawas, Fox, Sauks, Potawatomis, and Kickapoos, whom they encountered around Lake Michigan. In terms of subsistence strategies, settlement patterns, and in certain facets of material culture, the Illinois-Miami speakers closely resembled their Chiwere Siouan neighbors (the Iowa, Missouria, and Otoe) to the west. Yet language and certain elements of social organization still reflected a close historic relationship between Illinois-Miami speakers and other Central Algonkian peoples living in eastern Wisconsin. The diverse linguistic and cultural affiliations of the Illinois-Miami speakers encountered by the French in the seventeenth century suggest historic Illinois and Miami communities were the product of a dynamic, late prehistoric/protohistoric frontier.[4]

The territory the Illinois inhabited in the seventeenth century stretched southwest from the southern shores of Lake Michigan to the Mississippi Valley, as far south as the mouth of the Arkansas River. How and when the Illinois came to occupy this region has long been obscure. This uncertainty is somewhat surprising since the southern portion of this region has long been a focus of interest for North American archaeologists because of its rich record of pre-Columbian antiquity.

Most historians of North America are aware that Mississippian Cahokia, located in the American Bottom, was the site of a populous pre-Columbian community.[5] Today this site, containing North America's largest prehistoric earthwork and an excellent interpretive center, has made great strides in bringing America's pre-Columbian past to public consciousness. Indeed, discussions of Mississippian Cahokia have become a required component of the formula that dominates the publishing of American history textbooks.

But most students of North American history, including many historians of early America and Native America, are oblivious to the Mississippian and Woodland communities—settlements without monumental earthworks— that contemporaneously occupied the northern portions of what would become the Illinois country. Equally invisible to historians are the native communities that occupied the region before Cahokia's emergence and following its decline. This is particularly ironic since during the past four decades the area has served as a focal point for the development of new archaeological techniques. This "new archaeology" has provided greater insight into pre-Columbian diets, health, and mortuary practices. Improvements in older archaeological methods such as ceramic analysis and radiocarbon dating have also provided far better diagnostics for cultural shifts and enabled scholars to develop a temporally broad cultural chronology reaching back more than twelve thousand years. In addition, new approaches to studying settlement patterns and material assemblages have furnished insights into the various political and social organizations of the many communities that made the American Bottom home. Today, archaeologists know that over a period of more than twelve thousand years this region attracted a succession of Native American populations, and that their communities participated in some of the most important social, political, and technological developments occurring in pre-Columbian North America.[6]

Unfortunately, some historians have used prehistoric Cahokia in an ahistorical manner. Instead of envisioning Cahokia as part of an evolving, dynamic Native American prehistory, the noteworthy Mississippian community has been singled out to establish that Native North Americans are not doomed to "simplicity," whether barbaric or noble. It is also has been used to contrast a prehistoric "cultural" zenith with later historic Indian communities degraded through the deleterious effects of the Columbian exchange and European colonialism. Yet these rhetorical uses of Cahokia as a symbol of late prehistoric North America do little to illuminate how the course of late prehistory shaped native experiences of the creation of the "New World."

Throughout much of the pre-Columbian period, Native Americans used the major rivers flowing into or through the Confluence Region, the portion of the Mississippi River where it is joined by the Illinois, Missouri, and Ohio rivers, as avenues of travel and transportation. Beginning with the expansion of Paleoindian populations eastward from the Great Plains circa 10,000 B.C., rivers brought new peoples into and through the Confluence Region. Patterns of Paleoindian debris suggest the Mississippi Valley's initial human inhabitants left homes on the Great Plains and followed the Missouri and Arkansas rivers eastward. Paleoindians followed the Illinois and Ohio rivers from the Mississippi Valley into the Great Lakes and the Appalachian Mountains.[7] Following the initial dispersal of Paleoindians through the continent, these waterways continued as avenues of transportation. Later, during the Early Woodland period (700 B.C.–A.D. 200), groups followed these same rivers from the Great Lakes and upper South back into the Confluence Region, where they intermingled and created new, regionally unique cultural traditions.[8]

During what Robert Hall has called Illinois' two prehistoric cultural climaxes, the Middle Woodland (200 B.C.–A.D. 400) and the Mississippian (A.D. 1050–1350) periods, the region played conspicuous roles in interregional interaction networks that connected much of North America east of the Rocky Mountains.[9] Though low intensity interregional exchange had occurred across the Confluence Region at least since the Late Archaic period (1500–700 B.C.), during the Middle Woodland and Mississippian periods vital routes of communication and transport linking communities in the Great Plains, the Great Lakes, and the Southeast Woodlands intersected in the Confluence Region. Exotic raw materials, craft items, decorative and symbolic motifs, and ideas were transferred into and through the communities of the American Bottom and the lower Illinois Valley.[10]

Yet the future home of the Illinois Indians was not merely an oft-traveled crossroads. American Indian groups repeatedly came into the region and settled there. A significant factor making the region attractive to a succession of communities throughout the pre-Columbian period was the diversity of environmental zones that bordered the Mississippi and Illinois Rivers. Different ecological zones thinly paralleled the main channels of the rivers. The valley floors of these rivers were patchworks of wetlands, prairies, and forests in a variety of growth stages, depending on contours in elevation and the severity of recent flooding. Deciduous forests dominated by climax growth of oak and hickory trees blanketed the heavily dissected uplands immediately adjacent to the river valleys. The forests gave way to prairies in transitional parklands that were biotically rich because of the overlapping forest and grassland environments. Finally, this forest-prairie transition zone gave way to tree-studded grassland prairies where floral and faunal resources were relatively less diverse.[11] The Native Americans who occupied the Prairie Peninsula from the Late Archaic period forward all practiced diversified subsistence strategies that made major river valleys particularly attractive locales for settlement.

The most famous and historically significant prehistoric community found in the Prairie Peninsula was that of Mississippian Cahokia. Today Mississippian Cahokia is most noted for the presence of the largest extant pre-Columbian earthwork, Monks' Mound. But Monks' Mound and the more than one hundred other mounds in its vicinity were once part of a complex ceremonial precinct that stood at the heart of a Mississippian society that extended over much of the adjoining floodplain. Once celebrated as an "urban center" with a population of between twenty and thirty thousand inhabitants, archaeologists have recently reduced their estimates of pre-Columbian Cahokia's population to between nine and fifteen thousand. Though Mississippian Cahokia was not the population center it once was thought to have been, it does appear to have been an important religious and political center for a larger, more dispersed Indian population. The extensive Mississippian population of the American Bottom was dependent on maize agriculture and lived in hamlets and villages scattered along the most elevated ridges within the floodplain. The monumental scale of mound construction at Cahokia is believed to reflect the ability of its priests to create an inclusive civic and religious identity that integrated the inhabitants of the American Bottom's countryside into a larger sense of community. Cahokia's influence over the American Bottom appears to have endured little more than two centuries, emerging between A.D. 1050 and 1100, and appearing in decline by A.D. 1275. Though Cahokia was once thought to have been the center of an extensive political and economic empire, it is now clear that its most important influence on the outside world was cultural. Notably, much of this influence, while manifested throughout much of the Mississippi Basin, occurred following Cahokia's decline.[12]

The decline of Cahokia and the abandonment of the American Bottom was the beginning of a wider, prolonged demographic shuffling and cultural transformation occurring throughout the Prairie Peninsula. Though it once was assumed that Mississippian Cahokians were the ancestors of the region's historic inhabitants, archeologists now discount any meaningful continuity between the residents of Cahokia and other neighboring Mississippian sites, and Indian people occupying Illinois during the Historic Period.[13]

Not only did Cahokia collapse as a polity and a community, but between A.D. 1300 and 1500, the adjoining portion of the Mississippi Valley between the mouths of the Missouri and the Arkansas rivers was largely depopulated.

Evidence of late prehistoric occupation of this region in any form, whether as large aggregated Mississippian towns or smaller, scattered Woodland hamlets, is sparse. As a result, regional specialists have come to refer to this stretch of the Mississippi Valley and the adjoining uplands as the "Vacant Quarter."[14]

The disappearance of Mississippian communities in the interior of North America is often associated with the introduction of Old World epidemic diseases introduced by sixteenth-century Spanish *entradas;* however, the decline of Middle Mississippian communities in the Midwest preceded the introduction of foreign contagion.[15] Indeed, Cahokia's disappearance in the middle of the thirteenth century demonstrates that New World calamities are not needed to explain all historical change experienced by Mississippian communities. A number of hypotheses have been forwarded to explain Cahokia's collapse and the subsequent depopulation of the central Mississippi Valley. A changing environment has been posited as a possible impetus for Middle Mississippian decline. Some scholars suggest human environmental overexploitation depleted the soil and timber resources Mississippian economies depended on.[16] Others argue that the onset of drier, cooler weather associated with a Pacific climatic episode reduced the productivity of Mississippian agriculture, making large, complex societies less economically sustainable.[17] Some anthropologists believe that Mississippian chiefdoms were structurally unstable and vulnerable to historical change associated with chiefly succession and warfare. Recently, the dean of Cahokian scholars, Timothy Pauketat, has argued that for too long archaeologists have overlooked the possibility that Cahokia's decline was essentially a human-authored, political event. He suggests that the kinship alliances upon which the authority of the Cahokia elite depended made the priestly polity susceptible to factionalism. Internal political dissension and an associated loss of prestige by Cahokia's priests and chiefs may have caused the ceremonial center's collapse.[18]

Not all of the Illinois country was sparsely occupied following Cahokia's collapse. For at least a century following Cahokia's demise, Middle Mississippian communities continued to exist to the north of the American Bottom in the Illinois Valley and in the upper Mississippi Valley. When they disappeared, neighboring communities of the Oneota material culture tradition persisted, particularly along the northern margins of the region, between the southern end of Lake Michigan and the Mississippi River. Oneota communities, though influenced by their one-time Middle Mississippian neighbors, differed from them significantly. Their settlements were generally smaller and did not exhibit the social stratification and hierarchy visible in many settlements of the Middle Mississippian tradition. Oneota subsistence resembled Middle Mississippian subsistence in its diverse utilization of horticulture, hunting, fishing, and collecting naturally occurring plant foods. But compared with most Middle Mississippian subsistence systems, which were focused upon floodplain agriculture, those of the Oneota were not as dependent on agriculture or a single ecological niche; Oneota subsistence was far more reliant on the broad diversity of food resources. As a result, Oneota people regularly relocated their settlements in order to capitalize on seasonal and environmental variability in food resources.[19]

But a changing environment transformed Oneota subsistence during the fourteenth and fifteenth centuries. During this period the Oneota people underwent a bison revolution, one occurring centuries before the introduction of horses from the Old World attracted large numbers of nomadic hunters westward onto the Great Plains. The climatic changes associated with the Pacific climatic episode made the Prairie Peninsula home of the Oneota more hospitable to flora and fauna associated with the Great Plains. Key among these changes was the eastward migration of large herds of bison into and across the Prairie Peninsula. The Oneota adapted to the appearance of these new animals by making bison hunting integral to both their economic and social lives. Soon Oneota peoples were moving westward across the Mississippi River onto the grasslands of Iowa and Missouri, and eventually across the Missouri River into eastern Kansas, Nebraska, and the Dakotas. Not all Oneota communities abandoned their region of origin, and many remained near the southern shores of Lake Michigan. From this location they conducted annual bison hunts on the prairies of northern Illinois, southern Wisconsin, and eastern Iowa, while maintaining access to the fishing waters and trade routes of the Great Lakes. Oneota settlement and subsistence patterns now embraced the part-time occupation of permanent villages, generally near lacustrine or riverine environments, where gardens and fields were cultivated. But on different occasions during the year, Oneota communities temporarily abandoned their permanent villages. In the summer, Oneota communities moved onto the prairie en masse in order to conduct a communal bison hunt. During the cool months of late fall and winter, village communities also often dispersed into smaller kin-based bands in order to hunt prey seeking shelter and browsing in river and stream valleys.

Thus the Oneota tradition played an important transregional role during the fourteenth and fifteenth centuries. As archeologist Dale Henning indicates, the Oneota culture was a "bridging culture" linking the culture areas of the Great Plains and the eastern woodlands across the Midwest's Prairie Peninsula.[20] Not only were Oneota settlement and subsistence patterns a blend of practices from the two major environmental-culture areas on its eastern and western borders, but Oneota communities were also vital conduits for the transfer of people, ideas, practices, and materials between the Great Plains and eastern woodlands.

This dynamic pre-Columbian frontier environment pulled Illinois-Miami speakers westward from the central Ohio Valley onto the Prairie Peninsula. When Marquette and Joliet first explored the Illinois country, they did not encounter any Winnebagos, Iowas, Otoes, and Missourias, historic ethnic groups thought to have descended from the Oneota communities occupying the region in the late pre-Columbian period.[21] The Winnebagos at that time were living near Green Bay in eastern Wisconsin and the latter three tribes were established on the prairies of Iowa and Missouri. Instead, the French explorers encountered the Central Algonkian–speaking Illinois. French missionaries and traders had extensive experience dealing with Central Algonkian–speaking Sacs, Foxes, Kickapoos, Mascoutens, and Potawatomis whom they previously had encountered near the Winnebagos in the vicinity of Green Bay. All of these Central Algonkian groups had recently relocated to Wisconsin from Michigan or northern Ohio shortly before the arrival of the French in the region.[22]

But in terms of subsistence and settlement strategies, the Illinois and Miamis more closely resembled their Iowa, Missouria, and Otoe neighbors to the west than their linguistic cousins residing near Green Bay. Although the Illinois and Miami peoples were thoroughly adapted to life on the Prairie Peninsula when the French first visited them, they shared with their fellow Central Algonkians located to the west of Lake Michigan an origin in what is modern Ohio. Together with the Shawnees, the Illinois and Miamis were affiliated with the late-prehistoric Fort Ancient tradition of the central Ohio Valley.[23] Thus the close linguistic and cultural relationships shared between the various Central Algonkian ethnic groups encountered by the French west and southwest of Lake Michigan have their roots in shared historical relationships reaching back to late pre-Columbian Ohio.

Historians traditionally have argued that the migration of Central Algonkian peoples from their ancestral homes in Ohio to the western Great Lakes and the upper Mississippi Valley resulted from upheavals caused by European colonialism. When the French first entered the western Great Lakes, they described a region dramatically affected by the wars of the Five Nations or the Iroquois, often referred to as the "Beaver Wars." These wars, waged by the Five Nations against the Native allies of New France, drove a number of Native communities to the region west of Lake Michigan (modern Wisconsin). Indeed, the first French missions and trading posts in the western Great Lakes were established to maintain relations with refugee Huron, Ottawa, and "Fire-Nation" (Mascouten) communities who had fled their homes to the east.

But the Beaver Wars of the seventeenth century were not the beginning of social, cultural, and demographic tumult in the region. As David Brose writes, "Late prehistoric times along the southern coast of Lake Erie were indeed dark."[24] Archaeological evidence from the sixteenth century indicates that both nutritional stress and violent deaths associated with warfare were common among late fifteenth- and sixteenth-century inhabitants of northern Ohio. The onset of the Little Ice Age made agricultural endeavors in northern Ohio increasingly risky. In addition, the expansion of Iroquoian-speaking peoples from the east threatened communities already experiencing economic difficulties. As a result, there was an out-migration of peoples from the southern shores of Lake Erie into Fort Ancient communities along the central Ohio Valley. Close cultural relationships had existed between these peoples prior to this diaspora, so the migrants joined groups with whom they were already acquainted and perhaps related.[25] This process of multiethnic fission and fusion presaged the multi-tribal communities Europeans would later encounter in the western Great Lakes. This phenomenon is often attributed to the social disruptions caused by Old World diseases and colonial wars, but social and cultural plasticity predated the deleterious effects of colonialism. The fluid sense of ethnic identity and flexibility in social organization readily apparent in colonial-era Native American communities of the Midwest are evident in the archaeological remains of their late-prehistoric forebears.[26]

The demographic movement and cultural exchange between the Prairie Peninsula, the southern shores of Lake Erie, and the Ohio Valley also predated the Wars of the Five Nations. Oneota peoples of the Prairie Peninsula and Fort Ancient peoples of the central Ohio Valley interacted with one another shortly after the turn of the fourteenth century.[27] This transfer of people, practices, and ideas appears to have occurred across central Indiana. The distribution of late prehistoric Oneota and Fort Ancient artifacts in Indiana reveals a pattern of interaction stretching from Madisonville, a Fort Ancient site in southwest Ohio, to Oneota communities located around the southern tip of Lake Michigan.[28]

It is this late-prehistoric pattern of cross-cultural interaction that explains the movement of Illinois-Miami–speaking peoples out of the central Ohio Valley to the region around the southern shores of Lake Michigan, most probably during the second half of the sixteenth century or opening decades of the seventeenth century. Prior to their movement into the Mississippi and Illinois river valleys, the Illinois briefly made their homes near the southern shores of Lake Michigan and in the upper Illinois Valley. When the Ottawas and Hurons first told Jesuit missionaries about the Illinois, they located them in the general neighborhood of Lake Michigan and the upper Illinois Valley.[29] Some of the names the Illinois used to denote themselves and names assigned to them by other native groups reflect the Illinois' protohistoric location near Lake Michigan. The Michigamea tribe of the Illinois took its name, meaning "big lake," from its residence near this body of water. Moreover, neighboring tribes referred to the southern portion of Lake Michigan as the "Lake of the Illinois."[30]

The movement of the Illinois and Miamis into the region around the southern shores of Lake Michigan displaced the Siouan-speaking Oneota peoples who had occupied the region. This displacement provides a chronological framework for the migration of Illinois-Miami speakers into the region. The Huber phase, the final Oneota presence along the southern shores of Lake Michigan, abruptly disappears from archaeological records during the first half of the seventeenth century. Coinciding with the Huber phase's disappearance is the appearance of Danner- and Keating-style pottery in the region. Both styles of pottery possess strong affinities to Fort Ancient Madisonville phase ceramics.[31]

The disappearance of the Huber phase and the appearance of Fort Ancient–derived pottery correspond with the oral tradition of a war between the Illinois and Winnebagos, sometime between 1620 and 1650. When the Illinois entered the region, the Winnebagos were at war with the Ottawas, Algonkins, and Nippissings, who were then acting as middlemen in the fur trade, carrying beaver pelts from native communities of the western Great Lakes to French settlements in the St. Lawrence Valley. Thus the Winnebagos found themselves isolated from the emerging New World trade. The Illinois sought to broker a peace between the warring parties, perhaps hoping to assert themselves as intermediaries between the Winnebagos and New France's indigenous trade partners. Despite their diplomatic efforts, and perhaps because of them, the Illinois soon found themselves embroiled in war with their Winnebago neighbors. The broadening of the conflict to include the Illinois was disastrous for the Winnebagos. The Illinois utterly defeated the Winnebagos, killing many and taking most of the survivors captive. The few Winnebagos who escaped fled north, seeking refuge near the Menominees who lived between Green Bay and Michigan's Upper Peninsula.

The defeat of the Winnebagos had significant consequences on the prairies west and southwest of Lake Michigan. The Winnebago previously had prevented the Illinois and Miamis from occupying this region. With the Winnebagos vanquished, the Illinois and Miamis were now free to move west across southern Wisconsin and northern Illinois toward the Mississippi Valley. Thus when the French first journeyed to the country in 1673, they found many Illinois communities located not near Lake Michigan but on the prairies adjoining the Mississippi Valley.[32]

The motivation for the Illinois-Miami exodus from their Ohio homeland, first to the region near Lake Michigan and then onto the prairies of Illinois, remains uncertain. Historians long have speculated that they were forced from Ohio by other native groups, primarily the Five Nations of the Iroquois.[33] This interpretation is consistent with many historians' assumptions about the unsettled state of affairs in the Great Lakes–Ohio Valley region during the seventeenth century. But this analysis contains several flaws. In retrospect, the Illinois appear to have relocated to the Prairie Peninsula prior to 1650, when the Beaver Wars devastated the eastern Great Lakes and Ohio country. The first refugees to enter the *pays de Illinois* probably were the Petuns, allies of the Hurons.[34] The presence of these displaced peoples from the east seems to have initiated the first Illinois clash with the Five Nations. The first recorded Iroquois incursion into the *pays des Illinois* occurred in 1653, when a small group of Iroquois raiders, in pursuit of fleeing Foxes, were almost destroyed by the Illinois.[35] Yet these early skirmishes did not signal a general Iroquois invasion of Illinois territory. Intense hostilities between the Iroquois and the Illinois did not begin until some twenty-five years later.[36]

Some scholars interpret the presence of Illinois villages in northeastern Missouri as evidence that the Iroquois had driven them westward from Illinois territory proper,[37] but there is no documentary or archaeological evidence to suggest that these villages were actually outside the *pays des Illinois*. They were located near the mouth of the Des Moines River not far from the confluence of the Illinois and Mississippi Rivers. The placement of these villages was consistent with Illinois settlement strategies observed elsewhere in the region. The villages were located near a diverse set of subsistence resources and rivers that provided natural routes of transportation and communication between the Mississippi Valley and Lake Michigan. Settlements along the Mississippi Valley had better access to French trading posts and missions at Green Bay and Chequamegon Bay than did those in the Illinois Valley.

The Illinois communities visited by Marquette and Joliet in 1673 did not appear to be intimidated by the Five Nations. Although the French had clashed with the Iroquois in the St. Lawrence Valley and were well aware of the Iroquois' military prowess, they made no mention of the Illinois anticipating or fearing an attack from the Five Nations. Indeed, in 1673 the Illinois villages still remained unfortified; they were not surrounded by palisades.[38] In addition, the sudden appearance of the French took the Illinois by complete surprise, suggesting the villagers did not rely on scouts or sentries and did not feel threatened.[39] The conflict between the Iroquois and the Illinois was not initiated until 1679, six years later.[40]

In retrospect, it seems more probable that the Illinois' migration from Ohio to Lake Michigan and then to the Prairie Peninsula predated Iroquois expansion. The Illinois were drawn to the prairies by the assets and attractions of the region, not forced out of Ohio by the Five Nations. Their new environment altered Illinois life and encouraged new cultural patterns that transformed the Illinois into prairie people: hunters more dependent on new food sources than were their Algonkian-speaking neighbors, who still resided in more forested regions that enshrouded the Great Lakes region and upper Ohio Valley.

Access to bison herds on the prairies transformed Illinois life. Like most Algonkian-speaking tribes, the Illinois had pursued their subsistence through a variety of activities, including gardening, hunting, fishing, and foraging. The gardening complex of the Illinois was similar to that found throughout the late prehistoric and early historic Eastern Woodlands and included corn, squash, and beans. Although the Eastern Woodlands Indians were horticulturists, they also collected wild plant foods such as seeds, nuts, berries, and tubers. But what made Illinois and Miami subsistence unique compared with that of closely related Central Algonkian peoples living near the Great Lakes was their growing reliance on bison hunting, which became so important that it shaped the seasonal regimen of residential mobility practiced by the tribe. Large communal bison hunts were conducted in the summer months after fields and gardens had been planted. During these hunts, most able-bodied community members abandoned their permanent villages and together ventured upon the upland prairies in pursuit of large herds of bison. After the hunt, the Illinois returned to their permanent villages so that they could harvest their crops in late summer and early fall. Hunting was also important during cold-weather months, but the Illinois utilized different techniques in this season in order to pursue a wider variety of game. During late fall, Illinois villages broke into extended family-groups and scattered along river valleys to hunt deer, elk, and bison, sheltering there from harsh winter conditions.[41]

Their original subsistence strategies were similar to those followed by other Indian tribes of the western Great Lakes, but the Illinois appear to have made choices similar to those made earlier by Oneota groups, such as the predecessors of the Iowas, Otoes, and Missourias. The Illinois eschewed life near the shores of Lake Michigan and chose to move onto the prairies where bison could be encountered more frequently and in larger numbers. The Illinois and Miamis both utilized fish, but unlike the Winnebagos, Menominees, and others who chose to live along Lake Michigan, they were less than avid fishermen. Most early observers of the Illinois noted the importance of bison meat to the Illinois diet. Moreover, the summer hunts conducted between the planting and harvesting of crops were as much festivities of community solidarity as subsistence activities. The early French so associated bison with the Illinois Indians that the animals were often referred to as "les boeufs ilinois," or Illinois beefs.[42] Though bison roamed in small numbers as far north as the prairies of southwestern Wisconsin and as far east as the western slope of the Appalachian Mountains, they were found in large herds on the upland prairies adjacent to the rivers of the Confluence Region. Unlike many of the Illinois' northern and eastern neighbors, who made distant westward expeditions to hunt bison, the Illinois had access to large herds in areas adjoining their permanent summer villages.

There is evidence that the Fort Ancient progenitors of the historic Illinois and Miamis glimpsed the possibilities of large-scale bison hunting even before they left their homes in Ohio for the western prairies. During the sixteenth century, the forefathers of the Illinois in Ohio maintained close ties with Siouan-speaking Oneota peoples inhabiting the prairies of Illinois and Wisconsin. Cross-cultural interaction in the form of visits, trade, and perhaps intermarriage between these peoples was frequent. The large numbers of Oneota-style hide-scraping tools and bison bone artifacts found at some late Fort Ancient sites in Ohio suggest that Illinois-Miami speakers journeyed west to hunt with friends and allies before they decided to relocate there themselves. Siouan influences on Miami and Illinois hunting appear to have been profound. The use of large communal, summer hunts was probably introduced to the Illinois and Miamis by their western neighbors. The Miamis and the Illinois also formed specific men's societies charged with policing hunts, a practice they probably learned from Siouan Oneota peoples. Thus the westward migration of the Illinois did not require them to drastically change their subsistence strategies. They continued to practice traditional methods of hunting, gathering, and foraging while placing greater emphasis on hunting bison.[43]

Though the Illinois may have come to the prairie to hunt bison, they also found improved growing conditions for their gardens and fields. The Confluence Region had been home to some of the earliest gardening complexes developed in the Eastern Woodlands (circa 1000 B.C.).[44] Compared to the western Great Lakes, the Confluence Region had a longer growing season. More growing degree days provided critical insurance to a population somewhat dependent on its garden produce to provide winter food stores.[45] The loess-covered bluffs and alluvial bottomland ridges of the Mississippi and the lower Illinois Valleys provided well-watered and well-drained settings for Indian gardens. In addition, the frequent seasonal inundation of floodplains kept climax forest growth at bay and made those locales easier to clear for agricultural endeavors. Moreover, the wide bottomlands of the lower Illinois

Valley and the American Bottom provided an abundance and diversity of edible plants, fish, freshwater mussels, and waterfowl.[46]

Though the Illinois exploited plant foods in the Confluence Region much as their predecessors had, they also could count on a new faunal resource not available to Native Americans in the region prior to 1500. Bison, like the Illinois themselves, did not move into the Confluence Region until the sixteenth century, when large numbers of the animals migrated east of the Mississippi River for the first time.[47]

Trading opportunities also may have drawn the Illinois westward, since the Confluence Region provided an ideal hub for a far-reaching riverine network. When Jesuit missionaries first collected detailed information about the Illinois, they reported that the tribe was renowned as warriors and traders. The Jesuits reported that the Illinois actively traded with the Ottawas, bartering slaves to the latter for goods of European manufacture. In 1667 groups of Illinois traveled to Chequamegon Bay at the southwestern end of Lake Superior in northern Wisconsin to trade directly with the French.[48] Moreover, archaeological evidence indicates the Illinois had begun to incorporate some European trade goods, particularly brass kettles and other metal objects, into their daily lives, well before French explorers or missionaries ever entered the *pays des Illinois*.[49]

The Illinois seemed to have been more interested in commerce than warfare. During the middle decades of the seventeenth century, the Illinois made peace with traditional enemies such as the Dakotas and Winnebagos in order to secure safe passage to French trading posts on Lake Superior.[50] Trade relations with communities to the south along the Mississippi River and to the west along the Missouri and Arkansas rivers were also cultivated. Ceramics manufactured by native groups in the lower Mississippi Valley and the lower Missouri Valley are common in ceramic assemblages from Illinois archaeological sites and suggest intensive exchanges between the communities of these regions.[51] The Michigamea tribe of the Illinois maintained a particularly important relationship with the Quapaws in northeastern Arkansas. The Michigameas established summer camps near Quapaw villages on the Black and Arkansas rivers, joined with Quapaws on summer hunts, and provided the Quapaws with European trade goods. The Michigameas continued in this relationship until 1686, when the French established Arkansas Post and replaced the Michigameas as the primary source of European merchandise.[52]

The tribes with whom the Illinois most frequently warred were groups to the south of the Quapaws, such as the Chickasaws and Natchez, and particularly those in the Missouri Valley, including the Pawnees, and sometimes the Iowas, Missourias, and Otoes. Illinois conflicts with the Chickasaw and

Natchez tribes may have been spurred by trade rivalries, since the Chickasaws served as middlemen for English traders in the Carolinas, while the Natchez maintained their own "French connection" with lower Louisiana until relations between the tribe and the French soured in 1730.[53] In contrast, Missouri Valley tribes like the Pawnees, Iowas, Missourias, and Otoes were for the most part isolated from independent access to European trade goods. The Illinois generally maintained a mixed relationship (sometimes war, sometimes trade) with the Iowas, Missourias, and Otoes, whose proximity made them potentially valuable trade partners and allies. But the Pawnees, who lived farther west, bore the brunt of Illinois slaving raids. The Pawnees were not targeted as potential rivals but as a convenient and vulnerable source of slaves for the Indian slave trade that thrived in French communities in Canada and Louisiana.[54]

The Illinois were jealous of their roles as middlemen in the commerce between the French and other tribes, and they were willing to risk angering the French in order to protect those roles. In 1680 when Robert Cavelier sieur de La Salle announced his intention to build a fort in the central Illinois Valley, the Illinois vociferously opposed the plan. They believed the post would threaten their control over the trade between the French and other tribes in the Mississippi and lower Missouri valleys.[55] During the early eighteenth century the growth of the French settlement in the lower Illinois Valley and the American Bottom eventually diminished the Illinois' dominance, but the tribe continued to play an important role in the region's trade through the middle decades of the century. French traders depended on Illinois guides and traders to introduce them to the tribes to the west, while Illinois traders used their connections with the Osages and Caddos to import significant numbers of horses into both European and Indian settlements in the Midwest. In addition, Illinois hunters continued to supply European inhabitants of the American Bottom with turkeys, bison, and venison.[56]

Ironically, the same factors of environment and geography that earlier had drawn Illinois tribespeople to the Confluence Region also made it attractive to French settlers. The French were quick to capitalize on the region's productive environment and its strategic location astride important routes of communication and transportation. French farms in the American Bottom were so productive that the area became the "breadbasket of Louisiana," supplying wheat to New Orleans. Commerce to, from, and through the Confluence Region served as a vital part of French Louisiana's economy. It also served as a crossroads, helping to bind French settlements in New France with those in Louisiana. The economic and strategic importance of the Confluence Region and the American Bottom, long a factor in the development of pre-Columbian societies, continued.[57]

By attempting to understand the prehistoric world in which the Illinois originated, as well the colonial one to which they contributed, historians can transcend the anachronistic depiction of the Illinois as merely dispensable and superfluous colonial proxies. Events and conditions preceding European contact markedly affected how the Illinois and other Native Americans experienced and interacted with the colonial "New World." In many cases, their interaction with the Europeans was but another in a long series of adaptations to new peoples and environments. By placing the colonial experience of the Illinois in a broader temporal and cultural context, historians can perceive them as agents of historical change—a people using their own historical experiences to meet the opportunities and challenges of a dynamic world. American history does not begin with European contact. Native American people had a history prior to 1492. The "New World" of the Europeans was shaped by an American "Old World" that had a viable history of its own.

Notes

1. Reuben G. Thwaites, ed., *The Jesuit Relations and Allied Documents* (Cleveland: Burrows Brothers, 1896–1901), 59:129–37.

2. For an example of this interpretation of Illinois history see, Clarence Alvord, *The Illinois Country, 1673–1818* (Urbana: University of Illinois Press, 1987), 223; Emily Blasingham, "The Depopulation of the Illinois Indians," *Ethnohistory* 3 (1956): 193–224, 361–412; Raymond E. Hauser, "The Illinois Indian Tribe: From Autonomy and Self-Sufficiency to Dependency and Depopulation," *Journal of the Illinois Historical Society* 69 (1976): 135.

3. Neal Salisbury, "The Indians' Old World, Native Americans and the Coming of Europeans," *William and Mary Quarterly* 53 (1996): 435–58.

4. Charles Callender, "Illinois," in *Handbook of North American Indians: Northeast*, ed. Bruce Trigger and Wilcomb Washburn (Washington D.C.: Smithsonian Institution Press, 1978), 673–80.

5. Although a number of historians have conflated the archaeological site of Cahokia with the Illinois and French settlement of Cahokia, the two are in fact quite distinct, being separated by more than seven miles and lacking any historical association. Daniel Richter writes of Pontiac being killed "within sight" of the mounds of Cahokia, but the Ottawa warrior was actually killed in the vicinity of the Creole town of Cahokia; see Daniel K. Richter, *Facing East from Indian Country* (Cambridge, Mass.: Harvard University Press, 2001), 210.

6. For brief surveys of pre-Columbian Indian life prior to the Mississippian period in this region, see Thomas E. Emerson and Dale McElrath, "Interpreting Discontinuity and Historical Process in Midcontinental Late Archaic and Woodland Societies," in *The Archaeology of Traditions,* ed. Timothy R. Pauketat (Gainesville: University of Florida Press, 2001), 195–217; Andrew C. Fortier, "Pre-Mississippian Economies of Southwestern Illinois, 3000 B.C.–A.D. 1050," *Research in Economic Anthropology* 19 (1998): 341–92.

7. David G. Anderson, "The Paleoindian Colonization of Eastern North America: A View from the Southeastern United States," in *Early Paleoindian Economies of East-*

ern North America, ed. Kenneth B. Tankersley (Greenwich, Conn.: JAI Press, 1990), 185–90.

8. Thomas E. Emerson and Andrew C. Fortier, "Early Woodland Cultural Variation, Subsistence, and Settlement in the American Bottom," in *Early Woodland Archaeology,* ed. Kenneth B. Farnsworth (Kampsville, Ill.: Center for American Archaeology Press, 1986), 483–84.

9. Robert Hall, "An Interpretation of the Two-Climax Model of Illinois Prehistory," in *Early Native Americans,* ed. David L. Browman (The Hague: Mouton, 1980), 401–62.

10. For Hopewell exchange, see Mark F. Seeman, *The Hopewell Interaction Sphere* (Indianapolis: Indiana State Historical Society, 1979). For Mississippian exchange, see John E. Kelly, "Cahokia and Its Role as a Gateway Center in Interregional Exchange," in *Cahokia and the Hinterlands,* ed. Thomas E. Emerson (Urbana: University of Illinois Press, 1991), 61–82.

11. William P. White, Sissel Johannessen, Paula G. Cross, and Lucretia S. Kelly, "Environmental Setting," in *American Bottom Archaeology,* ed. Charles J. Bareis and James W. Porter (Urbana: University of Illinois Press, 1984), 15–58; April A. Zawacki and Glen Hausfater, *Early Vegetation of the Lower Illinois Valley,* Illinois State Museum, Reports of Investigations no. 17 (Springfield, 1969).

12. For good descriptions and discussions of Cahokia, see Thomas E. Emerson, *Cahokia and the Archaeology of Power* (Tuscaloosa: University of Alabama Press, 1997); George R. Milner, *The Cahokia Chiefdom: The Archaeology of a Mississippian Society* (Washington, D.C.: Smithsonian Institution Press, 1998); Timothy Pauketat, *The Ascent of Chiefs: Cahokia and Mississippian Politics in Native North America* (Tuscaloosa: University of Alabama Press, 1994).

13. For an example of attempts to link the Illinois Indians to preceding Mississippian cultures, see Donald E. Wray, "The Illinois Confederacy and the Middle Mississippian Culture in Illinois," *Illinois Academy of Science Transactions* 36 (1943): 82–86.

14. Charles R. Cobb and Brian M. Butler, "The Vacant Quarter Revisited: The Late Mississippian Abandonment of the Lower Ohio Valley," *American Antiquity* 67 (2002): 625–41; Stephen Williams, "The Vacant Quarter and Other Late Events in the Lower Valley," in *Towns and Temples along the Mississippi,* ed. David H. Dye and Cheryl Anne Cox (Tuscaloosa: University of Alabama Press, 1990), 227–338.

15. Ann F. Ramenofsky, *Vectors of Death: The Archaeology of European Contact* (Albuquerque: University of New Mexico Press, 1987); Marvin T. Smith, "Aboriginal Depopulation in the Postcontact Southeast," in *The Forgotten Centuries: Indians and Europeans in the South, 1521–1704,* ed. Charles Hudson and Carmen C. Tesser (Athens: University of Georgia Press, 1994), 257–75.

16. Neal H. Lopinot and William I. Woods, "Wood Overexploitation and the Collapse of Cahokia," in *Foraging and Farming in the Eastern Woodlands,* ed. C. Margaret Scarry (Gainesville: University of Florida Press, 1993), 206–31.

17. David A. Baerreis, Reid A. Bryson, and John E. Kutzbach, "Climate and Culture in the Western Great Lakes," *Midcontinental Journal of Archaeology* 1 (1976): 39–58.

18. Timothy R. Pauketat, "Refiguring the Archaeology of Greater Cahokia," *Journal of Archaeological Research* 6 (1998): 71–72.

19. Dale R. Henning, "The Oneota Tradition," in *Archaeology on the Great Plains,* ed. W. Raymond Wood (Lawrence: University of Kansas Press, 1998), 348.

20. Ibid., 345.

21. These are not the only historic ethnic groups associated with the Oneota cultural tradition. Sites associated with Dhegihan-speaking Siouan groups in the western Prairie Peninsula as well as sites associated with Sioux-proper–speaking peoples in Minnesota are also associated with the tradition. Neither of these groups, though, is a likely candidate for having occupied the prairies of western Illinois and southern Wisconsin in late prehistory.

22. Richard White, *The Middle Ground: Indians, Empires, and Republics in the Great Lakes Region, 1650–1815* (Cambridge: Cambridge University Press, 1991), 14.

23. David S. Brose, "Late Prehistoric Societies in Northeastern Ohio and adjacent Portions of the South Shore of Lake Erie," in *Cultures before Contact,* ed. Robert A. Genheimer (Columbus: Ohio Archaeological Council, 2000), 96–122.

24. David S. Brose, "Penumbral Protohistory on Lake Erie's Southern Shore," in *Societies in Eclipse,* ed. David S. Brose, C. Wesley Cowan, and Robert C. Mainfort Jr. (Washington, D.C.: Smithsonian Institution Press, 2001), 61.

25. Ibid., 59–60.

26. Theodore Binnema notes that Native American communities on the late prehistoric and protohistoric northern Great Plains exhibited a similar ethnic diversity and flexibility. Theodore Binnema, *Common Ground and Contested Ground: A Human and Environmental History of the Northwestern Plains* (Norman: University of Oklahoma Press, 2001), 12–16.

27. Penelope Drooker, *The View from Madisonville: Protohistoric Western Fort Ancient Interaction Patterns* (Ann Arbor: Museum of Anthropology, University of Michigan, 1997), 317–32.

28. Ibid., 46–47.

29. Thwaites, *Jesuit Relations,* 18:231; 23:225–27; 42:221.

30. Dan F. Morse, "The Seventeenth-Century Michigamea Village Location in Arkansas," in *Calumet and Fleur-de-Lys,* ed. John A. Walthall and Thomas E. Emerson (Washington D.C.: Smithsonian Institution Press, 1992), 57; Thwaites, *Jesuit Relations,* 55:97.

31. Larry Grantham, "The Illini Village of the Marquette and Joliet Voyage," *Missouri Archaeologist* 54 (1996): 1–20; James A. Brown and Robert F. Sasso, "Prelude to History on the Eastern Prairies," in Brose, Cowan, and Mainfort, *Societies in Eclipse,* 214.

32. Some Illinois are identified as residents of villages around the Jesuit missions in the vicinity of Green Bay during the seventeenth century. But these Illinois appear to have been visiting their close kinsmen the Miamis as well as coming north to treat and trade with the French.

33. For instance see: Raymond E. Hauser, "An Ethnohistory of the Illinois Indian Tribe, 1673–1832" (PhD diss., University of Northern Illinois, 1973), 11; Wayne C. Temple, *Indian Villages of the Illinois Country,* Illinois State Museum Scientific Papers, vol. 2, part 2 (Springfield, 1966), 12–13; White, *Middle Ground,* 1–49.

34. Thwaites, *Jesuit Relations,* 55:235.

35. Nicolas Perrot, *Memoire sur les Moeurs, Coustumes, et Religion des Sauvages de l'Amerique Septentrrionale* (Montreal: Comeau and Nadeau, 1999), 119.

36. For the Beaver Wars, see Jose Antonio Brandao, *Your Fyre Shall Burn No More: Iroquois Policy toward New France and Its Native Allies to 1701* (Lincoln: University of Nebraska Press, 1997); George T. Hunt, *The Wars of the Iroquois: A Study in Intertribal*

Trade Relations (Madison: University of Wisconsin Press, 1940); Roland Viau, *Enfants du Neant et Mangeurs d'Ames: Guerre, Culture, et Societe en Iroquoisie Ancienne* (Montreal: Boreal, 1997).

37. Eric Hinderaker, *Elusive Empires: Constructing Colonialism in the Ohio Valley, 1673–1800* (Cambridge: Cambridge University Press, 1997), 13.

38. Callender, "Illinois" 674–75; Hauser, "Ethnohistory of the Illinois," 261.

39. Hunt, *Wars of the Iroquois*, 147.

40. Ibid., 145–61.

41. On summer buffalo hunts, see Pierre Deliette, "Memoir of De Gannes concerning the Illinois Country," in *The Western Country in the Seventeenth Century*, ed. Milo M. Quaife (Chicago: Lakeside Press, 1947), 93–103. On deer hunting by the Illinois, see Melvin B. Anderson, ed., *Relations of the Discoveries of La Salle from 1679–1681* (Chicago: Caxton Club, 1901), 69.

42. Bacqueville de la Potherie, *History of the Savage People Who Are Allies of New France*, in *The Indian Tribes of the Upper Mississippi Valley and Region of the Great Lakes*, ed. Emma Helen Blair (Lincoln: University of Nebraska Press, 1996), 366–67; Thwaites, *Jesuit Relations*, 269; Annie Heloise Abel, *Tabeau's Narrative of Loisel's Expedition to the Upper Missouri* (Norman: University of Oklahoma Press, 1939), 71.

43. Drooker, *View from Madisonville*.

44. See the various essays in Bruce D. Smith, *Rivers of Change: Essays on Early Agriculture in Eastern North America* (Washington, D.C.: Smithsonian Institution Press, 1992).

45. For Jesuit comment on the growing season of the Illinois, see Thwaites, *Jesuit Relations*, 51:51.

46. James A. Brown and Robert F. Sasso, "Prelude to History on the Eastern Prairies," in Brose, Cowan, and Mainfort, *Societies in Eclipse*, 207.

47. John W. Griffin and Donald E. Wray, "Bison in Illinois Archaeology," *Transactions of the Illinois State Academy of Science* 38(1945):21–26; Paul W. Parmalee, "The Faunal Complex of the Fisher Site, Illinois," *American Midland Naturalist* 68(1962):399–408.

48. Thwaites, *Jesuit Relations*, 59:127.

49. Thomas Emerson and James Brown, "The Late Prehistory of Illinois," in Walthall and Emerson, *Calumet and Fleur-de-Lys*, 107.

50. Thwaites, *Jesuit Relations*, 54:191.

51. John A. Walthall, "Aboriginal Pottery and the Eighteenth Century Illini," in Walthall and Emerson, *Calumet and Fleur-de-Lys*, 169–70.

52. Morse, "Seventeenth-Century Michigamea," 55–58.

53. Daniel H. Usner Jr., *Indians, Settlers, and Slaves in a Frontier Exchange Economy: The Lower Mississippi Valley before 1783* (Chapel Hill: University of North Carolina Press, 1992), 65–76.

54. Russell Magnaghi, "The Role of Intertribal Slaving on the Great Plains in the Eighteenth Century," in *From the Mississippi to the Pacific: Essays in Honor of John Francis Bolton*, ed. Russell Magnaghi (Marquette: Northern Michigan University Press, 1982), 43–53.

55. Moyse Hillaret, "Declaration faite par devant le Sieur Duchesneau," in *Decouvertes et Etablissements des Francais dans l'Ouest et dans Le Sud de l'Amerique Septentrionale* vol. 2, ed. Pierre Margry (Paris: Maisonneuve, 1876), 108–9.

56. Andre Penicaut, "Relation de Penicaut," in *Decouvertes et Etablissements des Francais dans l'Ouest et dans Le Sud de l'Amerique Septentrionale* vol. 5, ed. Pierre Margry (Paris: Maisonneuve, 1883), 489–90.

57. Carl J. Ekberg, *French Roots in the Illinois Country: The Mississippi Frontier in Colonial Times* (Urbana: University of Illinois Press, 1998); Nancy M. Surrey, *The Commerce of Louisiana during the French Regime, 1699–1763* (New York: Columbia University Press, 1916).

2. "Their Women Quite Industrious Miners"

Native American Lead Mining in the Upper Mississippi Valley, 1788–1832

LUCY ELDERSVELD MURPHY

On the Fourth of July 1828, lead miners at the Sugar River Diggings looked up from their work to see an intruder watching them intently. A white man, teamster Esau Johnson of Blue Mounds, happened upon these mines located about twenty miles southwest of modern Madison, Wisconsin, while out hunting stray cattle with Thomas P. Clark. Johnson later recalled that the mines were located near a Winnebago (or Ho-Chunk) village led by a man named Spotted Arm. He wrote, "There was a parsel of Indians digging. I went to one hole that certainly was forty feet deep. Two Indians were there on top and two squaws down in the hole . . . digging."[1] Indians—probably elderly men—who were stationed at ground level lowered tin pails attached to ropes; Native women filled the pails with lead ore, and, Johnson later wrote, "the Indians then halled [*sic*] them up . . . catching hand under hand." The quantity of ore they had extracted impressed Johnson; he recorded, "They certainly had over one hundred thousand lbs."[2]

When Johnson and Clark rode up to the Indians' camps, according to Johnson, "Their Chief Old Spotted Arm came . . . hollowing [*sic*] that he could have been heard half a mile or more" and told the two men to leave. After Johnson explained that they were hunting cattle and not trying to take over the Indians' mines, the suspicious Spotted Arm told the two where to find the lost beasts but was unable to prevent them from touring the Indians' lead-smelting grounds. The teamster noted, "They had fifty-two Furnaces in blast makeing [*sic*] Lead . . . along a Spring Brook where the Bank was four or five foot high."[3]

American Indian lead mining has received little notice in either scholarly literature or popular culture. The pervasive images of Native Americans in the eighteenth and nineteenth centuries portray them hunting, warring, or even farming. But by the time Esau Johnson stumbled upon the lead mines near Spotted Arm's village in 1828, indigenous people had been mining substantial quantities of the mineral for more than six decades. Sauk, Meskwaki, and Ho-Chunk (Winnebago) women dug lead (also known as *galena*) in what are now the states of Iowa, Illinois, and Wisconsin. The work was seasonal—an occupation of summer—and was part of women's economic patterns that combined activities such as growing crops, tending children, cooking, processing furs, producing maple sugar, and making clothing, mats, and baskets. Protected by men and assisted by elderly men and children, these women were clearly the central workers in the Indians' lead production process.

Mining for lead was extremely important to the Meskwaki (or Fox), Sauk, and Ho-Chunk (Winnebago) Indians because they used it to diversify their production and to avoid the vulnerability of relying on furs alone to purchase imported products such as guns, blankets, clothing, food, cookware, traps, and so forth. Besides being a commodity they could trade to Euro-Americans, lead could be made into ammunition for their own use and was traded to other Indians.

Unfortunately, it is difficult to catch more than a glimpse of Native American women lead miners in any one source. The primary reason, of course, is that written records from this period tend to reflect the viewpoint of the white men who wrote them, writers with a tendency to ignore women and their roles. When they mentioned "Indians," as Esau Johnson did, they tended to mean "Indian men." Another reason, however, is that Native American men such as Spotted Arm tried to protect the women miners from observation and abuse by outsiders and potential interlopers.[4] Furthermore, if these women left letters, interviews, or memoirs, the author has yet to find them. Nevertheless, a variety of sources provide a handful of details about their mining activities, the function of mining within the Indians' economies, and the roles that Native women played in mediation with white immigrants and visitors in the lead region.

* * *

For at least four thousand years, Native Americans had dug lead in the Upper Mississippi Valley and traded it as far away as the present states of Ohio, Alabama, Mississippi, Georgia, and the province of Ontario. Archaeologists who uncovered lead objects and subjected them to trace element analysis found that Indians used lead from this region to make ornaments such as beads, buttons, pendants, and bird effigies. Native people sometimes ground it and used the powder to make sparkling paint for items such as masks. Some ancient indigenous cultures used the galena objects for personal adornment of the living, and some made it into grave goods and paint for mortuary purposes.[5]

During the seventeenth century, when the French learned about the Upper Mississippi Valley lead mines, fur traders in the Illinois country accepted lead along with furs in exchange for trade goods, and they apparently taught Indians to smelt ore and to make molds for crafting objects out of melted lead.[6]

The French colonial presence encouraged Native production of lead, but another factor also spurred this increase. Indians readily adopted firearms, perhaps the most significant item available from traders. Indians valued these weapons because the technology both enhanced men's ability to hunt and increased their military prowess. Indeed, wars with the Iroquois in the late seventeenth century had demonstrated that tribes without guns could be devastated by tribes who used them. Although Indians depended on Europeans for gunpowder, they could make their own musket balls with lead, so Native demand for galena increased with Indian hunters' participation in the fur trade during the eighteenth century. Furthermore, both international wars and local intertribal conflicts stepped up demand. In other words, men's activities as hunters and warriors stimulated women's activities as miners. Both Indians and Euro-Americans needed galena for ammunition and bought it from Native miners.[7]

By the middle of the eighteenth century, midwestern Indians had been in contact with European traders for a century, exchanging furs, food, moccasins, and many other items for guns, kettles, hoes, blankets, beads, and similar products. From the late 1730s onward, French Canadian officials insisted that the indigenous people participate in this trade, threatening to rekindle the genocidal Fox Wars, which had ended in 1737, if they did not. Colonial wars disrupted trade, however, and by the end of the Seven Years' War, it was clear that midwestern Indians were dissatisfied with limited and unreliable access to trade goods, particularly guns, powder, and bullets.[8]

Indians in the region were, in the mid-eighteenth century, already digging substantial quantities of lead for themselves and to trade to Europeans and neighboring Indians. A French official recorded in his diary in 1754 that he "sent ten Frenchmen to the mine to make musket balls with the sixty Sakis working there."[9] Two of the Native lead mines appeared on a French map of the region published in 1755.[10] In 1766 a traveler commented, "So plentiful is lead here that I saw large quantities of it lying about the streets in the town belonging to the Saukies, and it seemed to be as good as the produce of other countries."[11] This Sauk village was famous as a market center, attracting customers from hundreds of miles away.[12] Archaeological evidence suggests that the Ho-Chunks (Winnebagos) also became involved in mining during the late eighteenth century.[13]

During the 1780s, when the American Revolution had again underscored the vulnerability of trade and the need for firearms as defensive (as well as offensive and hunting) weapons, an opportunity to expand lead exports presented itself to the Meskwakis living along the Mississippi River. It is uncertain whether the Indians recruited Julien Dubuque to market their lead, or whether he persuaded them that a partnership would be mutually beneficial. Most likely, it was a combination of the two.

A French Canadian born in 1762 near the St. Lawrence River, Dubuque moved to Prairie du Chien about 1783 after serving an apprenticeship as a clerk in the fur trade of Mackinac Island. According to tradition, Dubuque married a Meskwaki woman, although her name has been lost to posterity. In 1788, a council of Meskwakis granted Dubuque usufruct rights to an area of land containing lead deposits "trouve par la femme Peosta" (found by the woman Peosta). Was Peosta the bride? No one knows for certain. In any case, Meskwaki leaders signed a statement permitting Dubuque to use the land; it noted that the locals called Dubuque "la petite nuit," the Little Night.[14]

Dubuque and his Indian wife established what grew into a large farm and trading post on the west side of the Mississippi near the Meskwaki village and lead mining operation. He called his estate "the Mines of Spain," to curry favor with the Spanish colonial government of Louisiana, of which Iowa was a part during Dubuque's early tenure.[15] A trader in the western Great Lakes region and upper Mississippi River valley before 1809 recorded the three economic activities at the Mines of Spain: "Dubuque seems to be the owner of [the lead] mines, and trades and farms there." He added, "I have never seen a man in any of the Indian nations . . . who could manage Indians as well as him."[16] Whether Dubuque was "managing" the Indians or vice versa probably depended on one's point of view. Nevertheless, the local Indians seem to have been generally very fond of him: a generation later the Sauk leader Black Hawk referred to Dubuque as "our relation."[17]

Dubuque served as a middleman, linking Indian miners with markets in St. Louis and perhaps elsewhere. Although he gained a reputation as a miner, he probably did little or no digging himself. He had about ten French Canadian employees who did a variety of tasks for him, including farm and fur trade work, and they also may have done some mining.[18] Most of the lead he exported, however, was brought to him by local Indians.

Native lead mining was principally carried out by Indian women, although children or elderly men might help out. A visitor in 1818, for example, observed the Meskwaki lead mines near the Mississippi River and remarked,

"The women dig the ore, carry it to the river where they have furnaces, and smelt it."[19] This work was strongly sex-typed, as another's comment, "The warriors and young men, hold themselves above it," makes clear.[20]

During the eighteenth and early nineteenth centuries, the Indians used mining techniques that were best described by a white miner who in 1830 watched them from the east side of the Mississippi, envying their mines, as they worked near modern Dubuque, Iowa: "There were often fifty or a hundred boys and squaws at work, on one vein. They would dig down a square hole, covering the entire width of the mine [and] leaving one side not perpendicular, but at an angle of about forty-five degrees, then with deer skin sacks attached to a bark rope, they would haul out along the inclining side of the shaft, the rock and ore."[21] Indian miners also used European pickaxes, hoes, shovels, crowbars (some of them made out of old gun barrels), Indian-made baskets, and, later, tin pails. They broke up mineral deposits by heating the rocks with fire and then dashing cold water on them.[22]

Many of the miners who brought lead to trade at the Dubuque estate lived at the nearby village, which was known by the name of its principal chief, Acqua or Kettle. One observer described the town: "Corn fields stretched along the bluffs, up the ravines, and the Coule valley. . . . About seventy buildings [were] constructed with poles, and the bark of trees . . . Their council house . . . was ample in its dimensions, and contained a great number of [fireplaces]."[23] A list of all the items found on Dubuque's estate at the time of his death in 1810 demonstrates that Meskwaki miners exchanged their lead in small quantities at the Dubuque horse mill for wheat flour, and that they brought their smelted slabs to a post in or near Dubuque's cellar to trade for goods such as jewelry, gunpowder, and probably other items.[24]

Indian women who married the French Creole workers laboring at the Dubuque estate seem to have maintained a traditional material culture and passed this to their children. White settlers found the Métis children's graves after 1832 and thoughtlessly dug them up. One related that "their graves were mostly distinguishable by palings being placed around them. Many of these bodies were found quite entire, with little trinkets about them, such as pieces of silver, wampum, beads, knives, tomahawks, etc."[25]

After Dubuque died in 1810, his St. Louis creditors tried to take possession of the property, but the Meskwakis prevented this, explaining to the U.S. government agent "that they had given that mine to Mr Dubec [sic] during his life, after which it was to revert to the nation." To enforce their will, they burned all the buildings and refused to allow interlopers to move in.[26]

Native women continued to mine for lead through the 1820s. Meskwakis mined along the western shores of the Mississippi (from which whites were excluded until 1832) and around the Fever River. Ho-Chunks (Winnebagos), and to a lesser extent the Sauks, mined between the Rock and Wisconsin rivers, east of the Mississippi.

Mining had become an increasingly important part of the Indians' economies. From the 1780s onward, they had intensified their lead mining as they reduced their hunting in response to diminishing populations of fur-bearing animals and conflicts with western Indians such as the Dakotas. In 1811, for example, Sauks and Meskwakis sold four-hundred thousand pounds of lead to traders, a sizeable amount in a year that the United States imported about four-and-a-half times that quantity (1,837,702 pounds) of lead from overseas.[27] This quantity was in addition to the lead they traded to other Indians or used themselves. Their U.S. agent reported that same year that they had sharply reduced their participation in the fur trade, writing, "They have mostly abandoned the chase, except to furnish themselves with meat, and turned their attention to the manufacture of lead."[28]

One government trader who arrived in September 1811 later recorded, "The Indians had made large quantities [of lead] during the year and had it all on hand. . . . From ten to fifteen canoes, carrying 2000 pounds, were at the landing daily. I was kept from morning to night weighing and paying in goods, no opposition within five hundred miles."[29] Ten years later, in 1821, another agent commented that mining was so important that he could not see how "the major part of the Foxes and some of the Sauks could exist without those mines."[30] The Meskwakis at "Dubuks mines" would probably "raise 6 or 800,000 [pounds] of minral [sic]" during the summer of 1826, about twice the quantity produced in 1811.[31] In 1889, a Ho-Chunk (Winnebago) man named Cugiga (Spoon) Decorah reminisced to his interviewer about the lead mines, emphasizing the intensity of mining: "Our people once owned the lead mines in Southwestern Wisconsin. I have seen Winnebagoes working in them, long before the Black Hawk War. There were a good many at work in this way, nearly all the time in summer. . . . They made lead-mining their regular work."[32]

Decorah also remembered that the Indian miners traded the lead to other Indians: "Some dug lead for their own use, but most of them got it out to trade off to other Indians for supplies of all sorts. . . . Every fall and spring hunters would go down to the mines and get a stock of lead for bullets, sometimes giving goods for it and sometimes furs."[33] Similarly, in his autobiography, Black Hawk discussed lead mining as part of the summer hunting and gathering activities, after which Sauks exchanged with one another the products they had collected.[34] Apparently very few whites were aware that the Indians had Indian customers for their galena; most accounts do not mention it.

It would be tempting to accept white observers' views that the Indian women were oppressed victims of lazy and arrogant men who forced them to work in the mines.[35] However, Indian lead mining appears to be an adaptation of indigenous gender roles in which women had some control over the management of their own production and the allocation of resources. In farming and maple sugar making, and in other types of women's production, women organized their own work routines and controlled the resulting food and crafts.[36] Similarly, women seem to have had some influence in determining mining techniques and access to the mines. After 1788 (and perhaps earlier) the only whites who were permitted regular access to the mines were those who were accepted as bridegrooms by the local women and their families.[37]

Men served in support roles to women miners. Esau Johnson noted the men raising containers of lead that women had filled, and he also observed Spotted Arm's efforts to drive off the white intruders and to guard the miners. Other accounts not only note Indian men on patrol against trespassers, but they also comment that elderly men and children assisted women in mining.[38]

Sources do not clearly indicate whether men worked with women at smelting (the purification of ore by melting it in carefully constructed temporary furnaces), but it seems likely that men were involved in this capacity because native mining organization resembles that of maple sugar production. Lead mining was a seasonal occupation, as was sugar making. Men chopped wood and kept the fires going when women boiled maple sap into sugar; similarly, men probably chopped wood for the smelting fires, and may have smelted some ore until white traders began to process it themselves.[39]

Archaeological studies of more westerly Indians suggest that making musket balls was sex-typed as men's work. Tragically, lead working probably contaminated the surrounding soil, causing some children to suffer from lead poisoning.[40] Sauk, Meskwaki, and Ho-Chunk (Winnebago) Indians probably sex-typed musket-ball making in the same way, and they, too, may have contaminated their soil and exposed their children to lead poisoning.[41]

Before the 1820s, virtually all of the traders were the husbands of Indian women living in the mining region. Although the Indians made every effort to prevent white intrusion into their region, they needed to market their lead and so required traders to purchase the mineral, just as fur traders had long exchanged blankets, cloth, jewelry, guns, and other products for pelts.

These men became husbands as part of a traditional Native assimilation process, probably dating to the precontact era. Immigrants could become kin through marriage or, less frequently, adoption. As family members, strangers became obligated to their neighbors; this served as a means of regulating conduct. If outsiders rejected this assimilation process, they were viewed with suspicion and could expect no cooperation from Indians because their rejection would be seen as evidence of bad intentions. Native customs allowed polygyny as well as divorce, making Indian matchmakers suspicious of the European who protested that he was already married or preferred a long courtship to make sure of compatibility. Like the husbands, young women whose marriages were arranged might take comfort in the possibility of divorce. The social and economic pressure combined to persuade traders to compromise on their own culture's marriage taboos and marry local daughters (sometimes qualifying these as "country marriages" in their correspondence with outsiders). From the Indian point of view, economic relationships then became personal.[42]

We should not assume, as contemporary observers often did, however, that families casually delivered their daughters to total strangers. One set of letters clearly reveals that family members carefully investigated a man's character before proposing a marriage. After 1822, when the U.S. government forced the Indians to allow whites into the lead region, Horatio Newhall set up a smelting establishment near the mines previously worked by the Meskwakis of Old Buck's band. Old Buck and his family camped within a mile of Newhall's furnace during the winter of 1827–28. Newhall wrote to his brother in March 1828, "Himself & sons often visit me in town. And I have made me a Dictionary of the most common words in their language so that by the help of this I can understand them tolerably well. I have been at his lodge twice."[43] After careful observation, visiting, and evidence of Newhall's character, courtesy, respect, and desire to communicate, Old Buck and his family proposed a marriage. "He wants me to marry his daughter," Newhall wrote, "because he says, I am a great man."[44] Newhall apparently declined this offer.

The concern and intervention of another Native parent is evident in the memoir of a lead trader who married a Sauk-Meskwaki woman named Pasoquey in 1811. George Hunt, working for the U.S. government, took a stock of goods to the lead mines at "Tete Mort," about nine miles south of present-day Dubuque in Iowa, and made friends with his Sauk neighbors. The match between Pasoquey and Hunt linked him with his most numerous customers, and was, of course, in the best Indian tradition. An older Sauk woman named Shequamy, probably Pasoquey's mother, camped near the storehouse and trading post the newlyweds shared with Hunt's employees: two army veterans and a Métis interpreter.[45] In this way, Shequamy could keep an eye on Hunt and give support and assistance to Pasoquey, who was soon pregnant.

But Shequamy also protected her son-in-law Hunt and seems to have saved his life. One morning when she "went out early . . . to procure bark to stretch fur with," she discovered a hundred Ho-Chunk (Winnebago) warriors preparing to attack Hunt and was able to warn him in time for him to prepare his weapons. Shequamy then retreated to a Sauk hunting camp two miles away—probably taking Pasoquey with her—and sent warriors to try to protect him. They failed to prevent the attack, but Hunt escaped and Shequamy gave him a shot gun, blankets, and other provisions, and sent her son Cashinwa to guide him and a fellow survivor several hundred miles overland to Fort Madison.[46]

Although it was very common for families to arrange a young woman's marriage, sometimes the women themselves took an active role. The Sauk-Meskwaki woman Mawwaiquoi's marriage began as a spiritual quest, however, not an economic endeavor or diplomatic mission. A message came to her in a dream, or vision. Probably she had fasted, as young Indian people were taught to do, to seek guidance from the spirit world about their future lives. "In her dreams," an early writer related, she "had seen a white (man) unmoor her canoe, paddle it across the river, and come directly to her lodge. She knew . . . that in her dream she had seen her future husband." Perhaps fearful, Mawwaiquoi visited a United States fort (possibly Fort Edwards) looking for this man; she recognized him in the post's surgeon, Dr. Samuel C. Muir, a Scotsman. He had studied medicine in Edinburgh, and was said to be "a man of strict integrity and irreproachable character."[47]

Mawwaiquoi convinced Muir that they should marry; they spent many years together and had five children.[48] Soon after they met, Muir left the army, apparently in response to official disapproval of the Muirs' interracial marriage. By 1829, he became a lead trader, establishing a post on the island opposite Acqua's village on the Mississippi River. After she married Muir, Mawwaiquoi probably did not mine for lead but instead helped her husband with the lead trade. Later, Muir and Mawwaiquoi moved to Puck-e-she-tuk at present-day Keokuk, Iowa, and then to Galena. One of Galena's early historians recorded that Muir treated Mawwaiquoi "with marked respect. She always presided at his table, and was respected by all who knew her, but never abandoned her native dress."[49] The family moved from Galena back to Puck-e-she-tuck, where Muir died in the cholera epidemic of 1832, leaving "his property in such condition that it was wasted in vexatious litigation." Mawwaiquoi was "left penniless and friendless, became discouraged, and with her children . . . returned to her people."[50]

* * *

Intensification of lead production meant an increase in the commercial value of Native women's work (mining), while men's military and police roles expanded. Since Euro-American men like Muir and Dubuque were more interested in trading than mining lead, the Indians continued to specialize as producers. They maintained an active role as miners and continued to control the region and its trade. As long as Indians could mine and sell galena, they were less vulnerable to fluctuations in their ability to produce furs and to changes in the fur market. They had a commodity that other people wanted, both in and outside the region. Moreover, they produced a commodity they themselves used for ammunition, a necessity they otherwise would have had to purchase.

After 1822 government officials forced the Indians to allow whites into the lead region. Initially Indians, blacks, and whites lived and worked together peacefully in the Fever River (later called Galena River) region. In 1823 the population in the region included about 11,400 Indians and seventy-four whites and blacks. For a while, white and black men and Indian women mined separately, but near one another.[51] Underlying tensions sometimes were resolved with Native humor. One observer remembered: "The Indian women proved themselves to be the best as well as the shrewdest miners. While Col. Johnson's men were sinking their holes or shafts, in some instances the squaws would drift under them and take out all the mineral or ore they could find. When the men got down into the drift made by the women, the latter would have a hearty laugh at the white men's expense."[52]

During the 1870s, the author of a community history interviewed some of these early miners. They described the community about 1823 as containing approximately eight log cabins in the immediate vicinity of "the Point"—later called the town of Galena, "but the river bottoms, ravines and hillsides were thickly dotted with the wigwams of the Sacs and Foxes, who . . . were engaged in hunting and fishing, and supplied the whites with a large portion of their meats, consisting of venison, game, fish, etc. The squaws and old men, too old to hunt, raised most of the mineral which supplied the furnaces."[53] Indian and white boys fished and prospected together.[54] As the Indians continued to mix mining with other production, the Anglophones (that is, English-speakers) proved to be customers for Indian hunters. This brief period of co-resident but separate Indian and Anglo mining was relatively calm, probably because the number of Anglos remained fairly small until the middle of the decade.

Unfortunately, the lead rush accelerated from the mid-1820s through the Black Hawk War of 1832, when about four thousand whites and about a hundred blacks arrived in the region seeking wealth and adventure. In twos and threes they spread out across the hills, throwing up shacks or tents wherever they found deposits of mineral. They founded towns with names such as Galena, Mineral Point, Hardscrabble, and New Diggings.[55] The Indians' objectives in mining were at odds with the newcomers; the former tried to maintain their families and communities in their increasingly constricted homeland, but the white and black lead rushers came to Fever River to find adventure and wealth and go home, not to cooperate with Indians. As Anglo immigration increased, so did confrontations between Indians and lead rushers.

Although young and middle-aged Indian men might prospect, smelt, and guard the mines, the actual mining itself in Native communities continued to be done by women. Native and Anglo gender roles seem not to have influenced each other: Natives maintained their traditional division of labor, and Anglos continued to think of mining as men's work. These different gender roles prevented Native Americans and Euro-Americans from mining together. Whites did not hire (or marry) Indian women to mine for them, and Native men would not have done the work. Although collaboration might have made good sense, Indian women miners neither hired nor married white or black miners.

There were good reasons for the women to avoid the Anglo lead rushers. Native women may have viewed men who mined lead as assuming women's roles and effeminate: not likely husbands. More important, male miners' encounters with Indian women during the 1820s were increasingly exploitative and violent, treatment that Indian men protested vehemently. For example, mining boss Moses Meeker wrote that (in about 1823), "Indians . . . offer[ed] lewd women to the whites for whisky, which too many of the young men accepted to their sorrow."[56] By the mid-1820s, Ho-Chunk (Winnebago) leaders were complaining to their agent that "some of the white people are insulting to the Indians and take liberties with their women."[57] The 1827 Ho-Chunk (Winnebago) Revolt, discussed below, was partly provoked by the kidnapping of Ho-Chunk women, when drunken whites lured the women aboard a vessel ascending the Mississippi bound for Fort Snelling. Indian men responded by attacking the boat as it descended the river.[58] A few months later, a white miner in Galena knocked down an Indian woman and stomped on her head, killing her. An Indian agent who happened to be nearby observed the woman as she was dying and reported the incident to the local authorities, who did nothing.[59] Court records and newspaper reports indicate that white and black men in the mining area also sometimes abducted, enslaved, and beat black women and girls. In addition, some white women were abused and abandoned by husbands addicted to alcohol and gambling.[60] It is little wonder, then, that many Indian women avoided contact (let alone mining) with the Anglophone miners.

By 1826, conflict between Indians and whites in the lead region was ready to erupt into violence. In spite of the best efforts of Ho-Chunk (Winnebago) patrols, hundreds of Anglo miners were trespassing on Indian lands, destroying Indian villages and cornfields, driving away the game, and appropriating Indian lead deposits. Ho-Chunk leaders repeatedly warned both miners and U.S. government officials that trouble was likely if the intrusion did not stop. But the government-appointed Superintendent of the United States Lead Mines, Lieutenant Martin Thomas, gave permission to the Anglo miners to work on the Ho-Chunk (Winnebago) lands, telling them that they should "remain there until blood is spilled," to force a confrontation he knew would result in Indian land cessions.[61]

In 1827, the Ho-Chunk (Winnebago) Revolt reflected the Indians' outrage at the miners' incursions, the abuse of Indian women, and (false) reports that Ho-Chunk prisoners at Fort Snelling in Minnesota had been murdered. On June 24, members of the Prairie La Crosse band attacked a Creole family who had taken in a retired U.S. soldier, killing two men (including the soldier) and seriously injuring a child. Six days later, about sixty Indians attacked two keelboats, the crew of which had kidnapped several women the day before. Three Indians and two whites were killed.[62] As a result, Martin Thomas's objective was achieved, and the Ho-Chunks (Winnebagos) were forced to cede their lead lands.

Spoon Decorah was about nineteen at the time the Indians were forced from the mining region, and six decades later he remembered: "When the whites began to come among the mines, the Big Father said to his Winnebago children: 'I want this land and will have my own people to work it, and whenever you go out hunting come by this way, and you will be supplied with lead.' But this agreement was never carried out. . . . Never was a bar of lead or a bag of shot presented to us. . . . No, we never saw any of our lead again, except what we paid dearly for; and we never will have any given to us, unless it be fired at us out of white men's guns, to kill us off."[63]

The lead rush was also partially responsible for causing the Black Hawk War five years later. As a sympathetic official recalled in his memoir, the Anglos' intrusion on Indian lead lands "was the egg out of which the Black Hawk War was hatched."[64] Whites traveling from southern Illinois and Missouri into the lead region passed the Indian town at Saukenuk and coveted the attractive fields and townsite, returning later to invade the community and provoke the Sauk villagers, including Black Hawk. A decade of tension had already angered Indians throughout the mining area and its periphery, so there was substantial sympathy and even encouragement for Black Hawk and his followers, who attempted in 1832 to return from exile west of the Mississippi. Unfortunately, the United States responded with disproportionate violence, and hundreds of people were killed.[65]

* * *

Before the dramatic increase in Indian mining in the late eighteenth century, the only major commercial product available to Native Americans in this region was furs. But a variety of circumstances limited their ability to produce these pelts, including species population fluctuations, bad weather, war, and scarcity of weapons and ammunition. However, once they increased their galena production, Indian people could make their own musket balls and shot. Moreover, the mineral provided an alternative commodity that was nearby, enjoyed a constant demand by both whites and Indians, and could be used to purchase a wide variety of items. By intensifying lead production, the Indians diversified their economies and reduced their vulnerability to dependency. But once non-Indian frontier adventurers and the United States government realized the potential of the upper Mississippi Valley mineral deposits, the indigenous people again became vulnerable. These intruders seized the resources Native American women and their families had developed and the mineral production they had commercialized. By 1832, the Indians were forced to leave the lead region.[66]

Notes

1. Esau Johnson Papers, Group C, 1–2, Karrmann Library, Wisconsin Room Archives, University of Wisconsin–Platteville. The two modern reservation communities of Ho-Chunk/Winnebago people disagree on the proper term to use in regard to tribal nomenclature. In 1994 the Wisconsin Winnebago Tribe officially changed its name to the Ho-Chunk Nation, and people residing on the reservation in Wisconsin refer to themselves as "Ho-Chunk-Gra." In contrast, the Winnebago Tribe of Nebraska, residing on the tribal reservation near Winnebago, Nebraska, continue to refer to themselves as "Winnebagos." The editor has decided generally to use both terms in this essay.

Both the author and the editor recognize that the term "squaw" is highly objectionable, and obviously have refrained from using it except when it is included in a direct quote and has been retained to illustrate the particular perspective or "mindset" of the contemporary observer who is being quoted.

2. Ibid., 2.

3. Ibid., 2.

4. Henry R. Schoolcraft, *Travels through the Northwestern Regions of the United States* [1821] (Ann Arbor: University Microfilms, 1966), 343; Giacomo Constantino Beltrami, *A Pilgrimage in Europe and America* (London: Hunt & Clarke, 1828), 164.

5. John A. Walthall, *Galena and Aboriginal Trade in Eastern North America* (Springfield: Illinois State Museum, 1981); Ronald M. Farquhar and Ian R. Fletcher, "The Provenience of Galena from Archaic/Woodland Sites in Northeastern North America: Lead Isotope

Evidence," *American Antiquity* 49, no. 4 (1984): 774–85; John A. Walthall et al., "Galena Analysis and Poverty Point Trade," *Midcontinental Journal of Archaeology* 7, no. 1 (1982): 133–48; John A. Walthall et al., "Ohio Hopewell Trade: Galena Procurement and Exchange," in David S. Brose and N'omi Greber, eds., *Hopewell Archaeology: The Chillicothe Conference* (Kent, Ohio: Kent State University Press, 1979), 247–50.

6. Dean Anderson, "Documentary and Archaeological Perspectives on European Trade Goods in the Western Great Lakes Region" (PhD diss., Michigan State University, East Lansing, 1992), chap. 7; Janet Davis Spector, "Winnebago Indians, 1634–1829: An Archeological and Ethnohistorical Investigation" (PhD diss., University of Wisconsin, Madison, 1974); Karl J. Reinhard and A. Mohamad Ghazi, "Evaluation of Lead Concentrations in 18th-Century Omaha Indian Skeletons using ICP-Ms," *American Journal of Physical Anthropology* 89 (October 1992): 183–95; Reuben Gold Thwaites, "Narrative of Spoon Decorah," *Collections of the State Historical Society of Wisconsin* 13 (1895): 458–59; Kristin Hedman, "Skeletal Remains from a Historic Sauk Village (11RI81), Rock Island County, Illinois," in Thomas E. Emerson, Andrew C. Fortier, and Dale L McElrath, eds., *Highways to the Past: Illinois Archaeology* 5, nos. 1 and 2 (1993): 537–48; Phillip Millhouse, "A Chronological History of Indian Lead Mining in the Upper Mississippi Valley from 1643 to 1840," unpublished paper, collection of the Galena, Illinois, Public Library, 1–5; Jeanne Kay, "The Land of La Baye: The Ecological Impact of the Green Bay Fur Trade, 1634–1836" (PhD diss., Geography Department, University of Wisconsin, Madison), 175–76; Walthall, *Galena and Aboriginal Trade,* 20.

7. Millhouse, "Indian Lead Mining," 1–5; Kay, "The Land of La Baye," 175–76; Thwaites, "Narrative of Spoon Decorah," 458–59.

8. Kenneth P. Bailey, ed. and trans., *Journal of Joseph Marin, French Colonial Explorer and Military Commander in the Wisconsin Country, Aug. 7, 1753–June 30, 1754* (published by the editor, 1975).

9. Bailey, *Journal of Joseph Marin,* 57.

10. "Partie Occidentale de la Nouvelle France ou du Canada," map reproduced from an engraving in the collection of Historic Urban Plans, Ithaca, New York, in the possession of the author.

11. Norman Gelb, ed., *Jonathan Carver's Travels through America, 1766–1768* [1778] (New York: Wiley, 1993), 75.

12. Ibid., 74.

13. Jeanne Kay, "Land of La Baye," 176.

14. There are several copies of this agreement, which differ slightly. In some, the mine was found by the woman Peosta; in others, by the wife of Peosta. Peosta is spelled several different ways. M. M. Hoffman, *Antique Dubuque* (Dubuque, Iowa: Telegraph-Herald Press, 1930), 79–83; William E. Wilkie, *Dubuque on the Mississippi, 1788–1988* (Dubuque, Iowa: Loras College Press, 1988), 81.

15. Wilkie, *Dubuque on the Mississippi,* 81; Reuben Gold Thwaites, "Notes on Early Lead Mining," *Collections of the State Historical Society of Wisconsin* 13 (1895): 271–92; Thomas Auge, "The Life and Times of Julien Dubuque," *Palimpsest* 57, no. 1 (January/February 1976): 2–13.

16. William Arundell, "Indian History," *The Miner's Journal,* Galena, October 30, 1830, typescript copy, State Historical Society of Wisconsin, Madison, 3.

17. Donald Jackson, ed., *Black Hawk: An Autobiography* [1833] (Urbana: University of Illinois Press, 1990), 150.

18. Julien Dubuque Estate Inventory, 11 June 1810, P. Chouteau Maffitt Collection, Missouri Historical Society, St. Louis; Wilkie, *Dubuque on the Mississippi,* 93; Hoffman, *Antique Dubuque,* 83.

19. Edward Tanner, "Wisconsin in 1818," *Collections of the State Historical Society of Wisconsin* 8 (1879): 288.

20. Schoolcraft, *Travels,* 344–45.

21. Lucius H. Langworthy, "Dubuque: Its History, Mines, Indian Legends, Etc.," *Iowa Journal of History and Politics* 8, no. 3 (July 1910): 376.

22. Schoolcraft, *Travels,* 343–44; Moses Meeker, "Early History of the Lead Region of Wisconsin," *Collections of the State Historical Society of Wisconsin* 6 (1872): 281.

23. Langworthy, "Dubuque," 372–73.

24. Julien Dubuque Estate Inventory, 11 June 1810, P. Chouteau Maffitt Collection, Missouri Historical Society.

25. Lucius Langworthy, "Early History of Dubuque," *Iowa Journal of History and Politics* 8, no. 3 (July 1910): 375.

26. Nicholas Boilvin to Secretary of War William Eustis, 7 July 1811, in Clarence Edwin Carter, *The Territorial Papers of the United States* (Washington: Government Printing Office, 1943), vol. 11, 168.

27. Nicholas Boilvin to William Eustis, 11 February 1811, typescript, Wisconsin Room, Karrman Library, University of Wisconsin, Platteville; Schafer, *Wisconsin Lead Region,* 253. In most years, the United States imported between 1.6 million and 3.6 million pounds of pig and bar lead. This does not include imports of lead for paint, generally another 1 million to 2.8 million pounds. See ibid.

28. Boilvin to Eustis, 5 March 1811, Karrmann Library.

29. George Hunt, "A Personal Narrative," *Michigan Pioneer & Historical Collections* vol. 8 (1885), 662–69, and vol. 12 (1887), 438–50. Quote is from vol. 8: 668.

30. Thomas Forsyth to John C. Calhoun, 18 August 1821 [the letter is dated 1822, but content makes clear it was 1821], Thomas Forsyth Papers, Draper Manuscripts, State Historical Society of Wisconsin, Microfilm, 4T104.

31. George Davenport to O. N. Bostwick, 29 January 1826, Chouteau-Papin Collection, Missouri Historical Library; Nicholas Boilvin to William Eustis, 11 February 1811, type-script copy, Wisconsin Room, Karrmann Library, University of Wisconsin, Platteville.

32. Thwaites, "Narrative of Spoon Decorah," 458.

33. Ibid.

34. Jackson, *Black Hawk,* 93.

35. Schoolcraft's comment, "as is usual among the savage tribes, the chief labour devolves upon the women," was echoed in an article by M. M. Ham: " . . . the working of the lead mines was given over almost entirely to the squaws, for the Indians consider it beneath their dignity to labor at mining or any thing else. All manual labor was cast upon the women. . . ." Schoolcraft, *Travels,* 344–45; Ham, "Who was Peosta?" *Annals of Iowa* 3rd. ser. 2, no. 6 (July 1896): 470–72.

36. A good starting place for studying Native gender roles is Nancy Shoemaker's an-

thology *Negotiators of Change; Historical Perspectives on Native American Women* (New York: Routledge, 1995).

37. Thwaites, "Notes on Early Lead Mining," 286–88; Joseph Schafer, *The Wisconsin Lead Region* (Madison: State Historical Society of Wisconsin, 1932), 35.

38. For a more detailed discussion of Indian men's activities in the lead region, particularly as police patrols, see Lucy Eldersveld Murphy, *A Gathering of Rivers: Indians, Métis and Mining in the Western Great Lakes, 1737–1832* (Lincoln: University of Nebraska Press, 2000), 125–33.

39. Jackson, *Black Hawk,* 92; Thomas Forsyth to J. C. Calhoun, 24 June 1822, Draper Manuscripts, State Historical Society of Wisconsin, microfilm, 4T133; Thwaites, "Notes on Early Lead Mining," 282.

40. Archaeological studies of Omaha Indian skeletons buried in the eighteenth century in present-day northeastern Nebraska, where there were no lead mines, found that men had higher concentrations of lead in their bones than did women, suggesting that Omaha men made musket balls, ingesting some of the galena in the process. Probably they bought the lead in bulk from Indian or European traders. Some children's skeletons contained nearly incredible quantities of galena. Children absorb much higher percentages of the galena they ingest than do adults. Reinhard and Ghazi, "Evaluation of Lead Concentrations."

41. A study of a Rock Island village site, probably Saukenuk, is currently being undertaken by anthropologists from the University of Illinois at Urbana-Champaign and should yield better information on these issues.

42. See Sylvia Van Kirk, *Many Tender Ties: Women in Fur-Trade Society, 1670–1870* (Norman: University of Oklahoma Press, 1980); Jennifer S. H. Brown, *Strangers in Blood: Fur Trade Company Families in Indian Country* (Vancouver: University of British Columbia Press, 1980); Jacqueline Peterson, "The People in Between: Indian-White Marriage and the Genesis of a Métis Society and Culture in the Great Lakes Region, 1680–1830" (PhD diss., History Department, University of Illinois at Chicago Circle, 1981); Jacqueline Peterson and Jennifer S. H. Brown, eds., *The New Peoples: Being and Becoming Métis in North America* (Lincoln: University of Nebraska Press, 1985). Also see Tanis C. Thorne, "'For the good of her people': Continuity and Change for Native Women of the Midwest, 1650–1850," in Lucy Eldersveld Murphy and Wendy Hamand Venet, eds., *Midwestern Women; Work, Community, and Leadership at the Crossroads* (Bloomington: Indiana University Press, 1997); Nancy Oestreich Lurie, *Mountain Wolf Woman, Sister of Crashing Thunder: The Autobiography of a Winnebago Indian* (Ann Arbor: University of Michigan Press, 1961).

43. Horatio Newhall to Isaac Newhall, 1 March 1828, Horatio Newhall Papers, Illinois State Historical Library.

44. Ibid.

45. Hunt, "Personal Narrative," 8:667–68; Thomas Forsyth, "half-breeds," Draper Collection, 2T22. Forsyth lists her as both Pasoquey and Sawssoquoe.

46. Hunt, "Personal Narrative," 8: 668–69 and 10: 438–44.

47. *Jo Daviess County* [1874], 234; Thomas Forsyth, "half-breeds," 2T22a.

48. Isaac R. Campbell, "Recollections of the Early Settlement of Lee County," *Annals of*

Iowa, 1st Ser., 5 (1867), 889–90. Also see Peterson, "People In Between," chap. 2 ("Women Dreaming"), especially pp. 61–62 on vision quests.

49. *Jo Daviess County* (1878), 235.

50. Campbell, "Early Settlement of Lee County," 890; quote is from *Jo Daviess County*, 235.

51. Thomas Forsyth to Thomas L. McKenney, 28 August 1824, "Letters Received by the Office of Indian Affairs," Prairie du Chien Agency 1824–42 files, microcopy 234, roll 696; Joseph Street to James Barbour, 8 January 1828, ibid.; Helen Tanner, *Atlas of Great Lakes Indian History* (Norman: University of Oklahoma Press, 1987), 139; *History of Jo Daviess County, Illinois* (Chicago: Kett, 1878), 243; Meeker, "Early History," 280–81.

52. Meeker, "Early History," 282.

53. *Jo Daviess County*, 243.

54. Ibid.

55. Consolidated Returns of Mineral and Lead Manufactured, 1827–1829, Historical Collections of the Galena Public Library, Galena, Illinois.

56. Meeker, "Lead Region," 290.

57. Thomas Forsyth to William Clark, 10 June 1828, Draper Manuscripts, 6T84.

58. Ellen M. Whitney, ed., *The Black Hawk War Papers*, 3 vols. (Springfield: Illinois State Historical Library, 1970–1973), 2: 793n3; [Marie G. Dieter], *The Story of Mineral Point, 1827–1941*, [1941], reprint (Mineral Point, Wisconsin: Mineral Point Historical Society, 1979), 18.

59. Joseph M. Street to the Secretary of War, 15 November 1827, typescript in the William Clark Papers, State Historical Society of Wisconsin, Madison.

60. Galena *Miners' Journal* 13 September 1828, p. 2, col. 2; "Louisa I. Holmes vs. Roland R. Holmes, 1832, in J. Daviess County Court Records, Galena Public Library, on loan to the Karrman Library, University of Wisconsin–Platteville; "Sally George vs. Alexander George," 1832, ibid.; "Dunkey vs. William Morrison, 1832," ibid. "Leonard Bryant and Mary Bryant vs. Alexander Neavill & Elias Griggs," ibid.

61. Esau Johnson Papers, Group C, pp. 2–3, Group B, p. 71; Edward Langworthy, "Autobiographical Sketch," 353; "Extract from Mr. J. Connolly, Indn. Sub Agent Fever River Galena," 23 June 1828, "Letters Received by the Office of Indian Affairs," M234, Roll 696; Subagent John Connolly to William Clark, 12 February 1828, ibid.; Joseph M. Street to Unknown, 15 November 1827, ibid.; Thomas Forsyth to William Clark, 20 July 1827, Forsyth Papers, Draper Manuscripts, 4T:277.

62. Thomas Forsyth to William Clark, 28 July 1827, Forsyth Papers, Draper Manuscripts, 6T66; John Marsh to Lewis Cass, 4 July 1827, Carter, *Territorial Papers*, vol. 11, 1096; James H. Lockwood, "Early Times and Events in Wisconsin," *Collections of the State Historical Society of Wisconsin*, 2(1856): 157–68; Thomas L. McKenney, *Memoirs, Official and Personal* (Lincoln: University of Nebraska Press, 1973), 127–32.

63. Thwaites, "Narrative of Spoon Decorah," 458–59.

64. McKenney, *Memoirs, Official and Personal*, 132.

65. John W. Spencer, "Reminiscences of Pioneer Life in the Mississippi Valley," in J. W. Spencer and J. M. D. Burrows, *The Early Day of Rock Island and Davenport* (Chicago: Lakeside Press, 1942), 14–17. Also see Jackson, *Black Hawk*; Cecil Eby, *"That Disgraceful Affair," the Black Hawk War* (New York: Norton, 1973); Anthony F. C. Wallace, *Prelude to*

Disaster (Springfield: Illinois State Historical Library, 1970), and Roger L. Nichols, *Black Hawk and the Warrior's Path* (Arlington Heights, Ill.: Harlan Davidson, 1992), 88–89.

66. John McNeil, Pierre Menard, and Caleb Atwater, Commissioners, report, 7 August 1829, "Letters Received by the Office of Indian Affairs," Prairie du Chien file, roll 696. Also see "Articles of a Treaty at Prairie du Chien . . .," 1 August 1829, in Charles J. Kappler, comp. and ed., *Indian Treaties, 1778–1883* (Mattituck, N.J.: Amereon House, 1972), 300–303. At the same time, the U.S. government purchased rights to the region held by the "United nations of Chippewas, Ottawas and Potawatamies," although few, if any, of these Indians lived in the region.

3. "The Hinge on Which All Affairs of the Sauk and Fox Indians Turn"

Keokuk and the United States Government

THOMAS BURNELL COLBERT

In the early 1830s, when relations between the Sauks led by Black Hawk and whites on the Illinois frontier gravitated toward conflict, Thomas Forsyth, the former American agent with the Sauk and Meskwaki tribes, stated that Sauk chief Keokuk "is a sterling Indian, and he is the hinge on which all the affairs of the Sauk and Fox [Meskwaki] Indians turn."[1] And Keokuk did in fact have a great effect on the ensuing Black Hawk War. He succeeded in keeping most of his fellow Sauks and Meskwakis out of the fighting, and the United States government declared him principal chief for a confederated tribe of Sauks and Meskwakis. Consequently, artist George Catlin, who toured the West painting Indians, would write, "There is no Indian chief on the frontier better known . . . than Keokuk."[2]

By the late 1830s Keokuk had become an important and well-known Native American. However, his reputation and legacy has been one of varying appraisals and continuing controversy. To some he was an admirable Indian spokesman and leader. To others, he betrayed his people by selling their land to the United States and misusing tribal funds for his own gratification. Part of this disparity of opinions is based on a comparison of Keokuk with his great rival, Black Hawk. Not only did the followers of Black Hawk generally disdain Keokuk's authority and many of his actions, they were later joined by white historians who envisioned Black Hawk as a noble Native American leader trying to save his culture and home from the destructive and acquisitive forces of American society. These historians interpreted Keokuk as a self-seeking sycophant to whites, especially the government of the United States.[3] Moreover, Black Hawk had dictated a widely read autobiography. He has also been the subject of several biographies. In contrast, no book-length account of Keokuk exists. Therefore, in an effort to evaluate an important facet of Keokuk's life, this chapter will focus on Keokuk's relationship with the federal government.

Keokuk was born in 1780 or 1781 (although some writers have said as late as 1788) in the central Sauk village of Saukenuk, located at modern Rock Island, Illinois. His father remains unknown, but his mother, Lalotte, was a woman of mixed Sauk and French ancestry. As an adult, Keokuk was a large, strong man who excelled in dancing and athletic events. Contrary to the statements of his detractors, especially Black Hawk, he distinguished himself as a warrior, particularly in confrontations with the Sioux. In addition to his bravery, he also was an eloquent orator and skilled diplomat. As a result of his abilities, while yet a young man he became the "guest-keeper" at Saukenuk. In that capacity the tribe provided him with the resources to host visitors, a function that made his lodge the center of social activity. Keokuk also entertained whites who visited the village, and these experiences helped him to hone his diplomatic skills.[4]

Keokuk's rise to power came during the War of 1812. Unlike Black Hawk, a war chief who sided with the British, Keokuk and many Sauks opted to remain neutral. However, in 1813 when they heard that an American military force had attacked Peoria (on the central Illinois River), the Sauks at Saukenuk prepared to abandon their village until Keokuk, still a young warrior, spoke to the Sauk council and chastised them for their fear. Since Black Hawk was absent fighting Americans on the Detroit frontier, Keokuk vowed that he would lead a war party to defend Saukenuk. Keokuk's oratory swayed the council, and they named him as their war chief, a role that only members of the Fox clan, of which Keokuk was a member, could hold. The American threat failed to materialize, but Keokuk retained the title of war chief, a fact that perplexed and angered the war chief Black Hawk when he and the so-called British Band returned to Saukenuk later in the year.[5]

With his new status, Keokuk became a spokesman for the tribe with the United States government. His first major venture into tribal diplomacy came in 1816 when, with Black Hawk and other Sauk and Meskwaki chiefs, he journeyed to St. Louis to formally end hostilities with the United States. They signed a treaty of peace and reaffirmed the controversial treaty of 1804 in which the Sauks and Meskwakis had agreed to relinquish land east of the Mississippi, including Saukenuk.[6]

In 1821 Keokuk returned to St. Louis, where he met with Indian agent William Clark in response to Clark's demands that the Sauks surrender two warriors accused of murdering a Creole-French settler, and that the Sauks also release four prisoners taken in a raid against the Otoes. Keokuk informed

Clark that the Sauks would *voluntarily* surrender the two warriors accused of murder, but they would never accede to government *demands* for them. Clark wisely accepted Keokuk's counsel and "asked" for the two warriors. In response, Keokuk surrendered the two Sauks and freed the four Otoes. Clark later wrote he agreed to Keokuk's suggestions to "enhance the worth and popularity of Keokuk," whom he envisioned as a rising young chief who would seek peace and friendship with the United States. Much to the relief of Keokuk, who feared a tribal backlash over the incident, the arrested warriors were later released by Clark for lack of evidence. Additionally, Clark and subagent Thomas Forsyth gave the Sauk delegation gifts and publicly praised Keokuk, which also enhanced Keokuk's reputation among his people.[7]

Keokuk thereafter became a frequent visitor to St. Louis. In 1822 he signed a treaty that ended the federal government's "obligation" to maintain a government "factory" (trading post) for the Sauks and Meskwakis. More important, land disputes arose over the boundaries between white settlement and tribal lands, and Keokuk and other tribal leaders appealed to Clark to send them to Washington, D.C., to argue for their land rights. Clark at first demurred, but increasing Sauk and Meskwaki hostilities with the Sioux threatened peace on the frontier. Therefore, Secretary of War John C. Calhoun approved the trip. In 1824 Keokuk journeyed to Washington, where he argued for Sauk, Meskwaki, and Ioway rights to lands in Missouri, stating that although the Osages had sold lands in that state to the government, it was not theirs to sell. It belonged to the Sauks and Meskwakis by right of conquest. Calhoun evidently agreed, for he drew up a new treaty paying these tribes for the disputed lands in Missouri and establishing a "Half-Breed Tract" in extreme southeastern Iowa, an area set aside for mixed-blood individuals. Calhoun also promised the Meskwakis that federal officials would keep whites away from their lead mines in northeastern Iowa. On the other hand, Keokuk and Calhoun reached no resolution on warfare against the Sioux. Once the negotiations ended, the Indians received gifts and toured the cities of New York, Baltimore, and Philadelphia. Already disposed toward peace with the Americans and desirous of their largesse, Keokuk was impressed with the size, wealth, and population of the United States. Following the trip he became more fully convinced that the only prudent political position was for his people to ally with the Americans.[8]

In a further effort to foster peace among the frontier tribes, Clark and Governor Lewis Cass of Michigan called for a council of all regional tribes at Prairie du Chien, Wisconsin, in 1825. Keokuk and his entourage arrived last, paddling up the Mississippi in full war regalia and singing war songs. Keokuk remained militantly defiant to the Sioux, but he responded to Clark's pleas for peace and assured the agent that he shared in his "great wish" for a peaceful settlement. After days of haggling, the Sioux agreed to a series of intertribal boundaries suggested by Keokuk and his allies. The Sauks, Meskwakis, and Sioux then signed a "firm and perpetual peace," pledging not to hunt on each other's territories. Although the peace would not last, Keokuk had again exhibited his ability to please American officials and defend his people's interests through diplomacy.[9]

By 1827 Keokuk faced new difficulties in maintaining good relations with American officials. The Sioux had trespassed on Sauk hunting lands, and Black Hawk wished to retaliate. Keokuk, fearing that a Sauk raid would spark a larger conflict, told Forsyth of Black Hawk's intentions. In response, Forsyth threatened to arrest Black Hawk, and he informed the Sioux of the old war chief's intentions. Since he had lost the element of surprise, Black Hawk abandoned his plan. Meanwhile, Keokuk served as a scout for the army in several skirmishes with the Winnebagos (Ho-Chunks) (Red Bird's War), and in gratitude General William Atkinson presented Keokuk with a silver-studded saddle and bridle—possessions Keokuk valued for the rest of his life.[10]

During the next two years Keokuk endeavored to maintain the peace with the United States. In 1829 Clark wanted to remove all the Indians except for the Kickapoos from Illinois. In addition, fur trader George Davenport convinced Keokuk that the Sauks needed to move to Iowa, since whites were finally preparing to fulfill the Treaty of 1804, which gave them access to all Sauk lands east of the Mississippi. In response, Keokuk sent most of his followers across the river into Iowa, but he stayed at Saukenuk in an attempt to counteract the influence of the militant Black Hawk.[11]

In the summer of 1829, federal officials convened another general council at Fort Crawford (Prairie du Chien, Wisconsin) to discuss the purchase of Indian mineral lands on the upper Mississippi. Again Kekuk made a dramatic entrance. Since the Winnebagos (Ho-Chunks) in attendance were still angry over their recent conflict with the United States, Keokuk and Meskwaki chief Morgan arrived at a timely moment with two hundred of their warriors, began a war dance, and informed the Winnebagos (Ho-Chunks) that thirty American warships supported by four hundred additional Sauk and Meskwaki warriors were en route up the river. The report was false, but it cooled the tempers of the Winnebagos (Ho-Chunks). However, when the talks commenced, the Sauks and Meskwakis refused to sell their mineral lands. In fact, Keokuk remonstrated that William Henry Harrison, who had negotiated the 1804 treaty, had cheated them. He also protested that the Half-Breed Tract had not yet been surveyed and settlers were already cutting timber there. In addition, he noted angrily that the Sioux continued to violate the Treaty of

1825 by hunting on Sauk and Meskwaki land. In all, while Keokuk and Morgan cowed the militant Winnebagos (Ho-Chunks), the two chiefs refused to give up more land.[12]

Although some Sauks accepted Keokuk as a champion of tribal interests, Black Hawk and his followers continued to denounce him as an accommodationist. He was unable to prevent obdurate Sauks from returning to Saukenuk in 1830 or to keep some young Sauks from seeking the war path. Early in 1830 several Meskwakis were killed by a mixed party of Sioux, Winnebago (Ho-Chunk), and Menominee warriors; Black Hawk clamored for vengeance. Fearing that a general war was imminent, Clark met with Keokuk and his advisers at St. Louis in March 1830. Clark urged the Sauks and Meskwakis to form closer political bonds, and he promised to end the liquor traffic that seemed to plague their villages. Although Keokuk was a heavy drinker, he agreed that the liquor trade should be curtailed, but when Clark then proposed that the Sauks sell more land, pay their debts to traders, and start farming like white settlers, Keokuk protested. In turn, Keokuk complained that the Sioux continued to plague the Sauks and Meskwakis by not honoring intertribal boundary lines established in 1825. He asked Clark for permission to return to Washington to plead the Sauk and Meskwaki case before the president. Clark refused and a disgruntled Keokuk returned to Iowa.[13]

The difficulties with the Sioux continued, leaving the Sauks and Meskwakis caught between the American hammer and the Sioux anvil. The Sauks were distraught over the enforcement of the 1804 treaty in which they had agreed to relinquish their lands in Illinois to the Americans, and they were especially resentful that they would have to abandon Saukenuk. In addition, they had become increasingly indebted to American fur traders at a time when more and more good hunting and trapping lands were being lost to settlers. Moreover, the Sauks and Meskwakis now contested with the Sioux and other regional tribes over game-rich lands to the north and west.

As tension between the tribes increased, Clark summoned Keokuk back to St. Louis in June 1830. Accompanied by two hundred Sauk and Meskwaki warriors who crowded into Clark's office and onto surrounding grounds, the usually conciliatory Keokuk charged that the recent deaths of the Meskwakis should be blamed on American officials since they had asked for a meeting with the Meskwakis, and then they had informed the Sioux, Winnebagos (Ho-Chunks), and Menominees that the Meskwakis were en route to Prairie du Chien. To "cover the deaths" of the Meskwakis, Clark gave the Meskwakis about $1,000 worth of trade goods and secured an agreement from Keokuk and other leaders in attendance to assemble for another peace conference at Prairie du Chien.[14]

When Keokuk and the Sauks and Meskwakis met with Clark and other tribespeople (including the Sioux) at Prairie du Chien later that summer, Clark called for a new treaty of peace among all the tribes. He also sought to purchase more Indian land. The Sauks and Meskwakis refused to sell any of their mineral lands, but they did agree to relinquish enough land to create a neutral buffer zone between themselves and the Sioux. The region, a strip of land forty miles wide in northern Iowa, was split into two equal areas, with the Sioux to the north and the Sauks and Meskwakis to the south. Both sides could hunt in their respective zones but neither could live there. Keokuk agreed to the plan, but he questioned its effectiveness. He warned the Sioux, "If a Sioux comes out of their neutral ground on my land, I shall think that he has come there to kill me; and if he sees my track on his land, he may know that such is my purpose in regard to him." He later informed his people that he had signed the agreement only to maintain good relations with the Americans.[15]

Yet Keokuk's problems continued. In the spring of 1831, officials ordered Black Hawk and his followers, who had reoccupied Saukenuk, to leave the village. Black Hawk refused, and General Edmund Gaines, accompanied by a small contingent of troops, arrived at Rock Island in June and prepared to drive the Indians back across the Mississippi. Black Hawk defiantly proclaimed his right to reside at Saukenuk, but Keokuk partially defused the situation, convincing about fifty Sauk families to leave. Clark duly informed Gaines that "in justice to Keokuk and other real chiefs and principal men . . . they have constantly and zealously cooperated with the government's agents in furthering its views, and in their endeavors to effect the removal of all their people from the ceded land." On June 25, 1831, Governor John Reynolds arrived with fourteen hundred Illinois militiamen. Gaines and Reynolds then forced Black Hawk to sign an "Articles of Capitulation," in which he and his followers agreed to move west of the Mississippi, to cease their contacts with the British in Canada, to grant the United States the right to build roads and forts on their land, and to follow the leadership of Keokuk and other civil chiefs. The agreement also stipulated that if Keokuk could not control dissident Sauks, he was obligated to inform nearby military authorities.[16]

In July 1831, a Sauk and Meskwaki war party killed several drunken and weaponless Menominees near Fort Crawford. The fort's commander demanded that the attackers be handed over for trial, but Keokuk refused, explaining that the lives of the Menominees were in retribution for the earlier killings (1830) of the Meskwakis. He also complained: "Why do you not let us fight? You whites are constantly fighting. . . . Why do you not let us be as the Great Spirit made us, and let us settle our difficulties?" As for the accused offenders, he stated that the warriors would have to surrender on their own. His reply elicited much praise from his warriors, but despite his public bombast,

Keokuk then journeyed to the Menominees and Winnebagos (Ho-Chunks) and talked peace.[17]

Tensions temporarily diminished, but Black Hawk and his followers endured a miserable winter (1831–32) in Iowa, and in April 1832 Black Hawk led about one thousand men, women, and children back to Illinois. War erupted. Keokuk pointed out the foolhardiness of Black Hawk's action and kept most of his followers out of the conflict. When the fighting began, Keokuk traveled to Fort Armstrong at Rock Island, stating that reports of his intention to attack the fort were false and that he would do his best to keep the majority of the Sauks and Meskwakis on the west side of the Mississippi. For Black Hawk, the conflict culminated on August 2, 1832, with the Battle (or Massacre) of the Bad Axe. Hundreds of Sauks, including many women and children, were killed. Black Hawk and many of his cohorts became prisoners of war.[18]

In September 1832 General Winfield Scott held a formal peace treaty with the Sauks and Meskwakis. President Andrew Jackson had ordered Scott to obtain another land cession, and as a result the tribe relinquished the "Black Hawk Purchase" in eastern Iowa. However, the name of the purchase was deceptive, since Black Hawk remained incarcerated at Jefferson Barracks in St. Louis. Keokuk headed the Sauk and Meskwaki negotiators, and because Keokuk and Meskwaki chief Wapello had remained at peace, they were permitted to retain a strip of land—the Keokuk Reserve—along the Iowa River, in the midst of the ceded region. In addition, Scott instructed both the Sauks and Meskwakis "to look upon . . . obey and respect Keokuk . . . as a chief appointed by the President of the United States." Scott's pronouncement not only elevated Keokuk (at least in the government's estimation) to the office of civil chief—an office that his clan membership did not allow him to hold—but also declared him the principal leader of a confederated Sauk and Meskwaki tribe, despite the fact that the Meskwakis had their own chiefs and did not consider themselves to be fully integrated with the Sauks. The treaty also stipulated that Black Hawk and other hostile leaders in the recent war could not form separate villages but must reside in villages headed by pro-American chiefs.[19]

Although Black Hawk had been defeated, settlers remained afraid that the Sauks might renew the conflict, and during the autumn of 1832 rumors swept the Illinois-Iowa frontier that Keokuk had decided to rally his followers and take up Black Hawk's cause. To assuage American suspicions, Keokuk dictated a letter to Governor John Reynolds of Illinois, saying, "Myself and the greater part of the Sacs [Sauks] and Foxes [Meskwakis] have firmly held you by the hand; we followed your advice, and did as you told us. . . . We wish to live in friendship with the whites." Reynolds later commented that Keokuk was so concerned by the rumors that he purchased frontier newspapers to keep abreast of such allegations and to defuse them before bloodshed erupted.[20]

Since Black Hawk and several followers remained in custody in St. Louis, Keokuk and an entourage journeyed to Missouri in March 1833 to seek their freedom. Keokuk was unaware that the government already had decided to release most of the prisoners, except for Black Hawk and five of his closest comrades, who were to be sent to Fort Monroe in Virginia. When most of the imprisoned Indians were released, the Sauks believed that Keokuk had secured their freedom. Black Hawk was sent east where he met with President Andrew Jackson, who told him to "listen to the counsels of Keokuk and other friendly chiefs." In May 1833 Clark suggested that Black Hawk and his comrades be returned to the west where they would be placed under Keokuk's supervision—yet another of Clark's efforts to solidify and enhance Keokuk's power and leadership.[21]

While Black Hawk was imprisoned, Keokuk strengthened his control over the Sauks and Meskwakis. At a council in June 1833 Keokuk reminded federal officials that the president had "great confidence" in him, and he petitioned the Commissioner of Indian Affairs to distribute all Sauk annuities to a delegation of chiefs led by Keokuk, who first would pay off tribal debts, then distribute the remainder of the funds to heads of families. According to Keokuk, "the whole Nation is unanimous in this recommendation." Indian agent Marmaduke Davenport agreed, arguing that "lump-sum" payments to Keokuk and the chiefs would enhance their power and influence, "make them more respected and render their people much more tractable, obedient, and respectful."[22]

The government acceded to the request, and Keokuk was given primary control over all annuity funds distributed to the Sauks and Meskwakis. The control of these funds cemented Keokuk's position as principal chief. Indeed, in 1833 his authority and influence among the Sauks and Meskwakis was unparalleled. He had kept his followers from participating in the disastrous Black Hawk War, the government recognized him as primary chief over the Sauk and Meskwaki tribes, and federal officials handed him the purse strings for all tribal annuities.

Keokuk's position of prominence was demonstrated in the circumstances surrounding Black Hawk's release. In the summer of 1833, when Black Hawk was formally released amidst much ceremony at Rock Island, Illinois, officials publicly placed the old war chief under Keokuk's supervision. However, when Major John Garland, who was in charge of Black Hawk, reminded the old chief of his orders to submit to Keokuk's authority, Black Hawk exploded, "I will act for myself; no one shall govern me!" Keokuk quickly rebuked him,

"Why do you speak so before the white men? I will speak for you." Keokuk then apologized for Black Hawk's remarks, and Black Hawk also expressed regret over his outburst. To American observers, it appeared that Keokuk exercised paramount influence over the Sauks and Meskwakis.[23]

Regardless of American accolades, Keokuk soon found that his leadership was threatened. By 1834 American settlement had crossed the Mississippi, surrounding the Keokuk Reserve; game had declined, and the Sauks and Meskwakis had become increasingly indebted to traders. In response, Keokuk complained to Indian agents that too many whites were trespassing on tribal lands in eastern Iowa, selling large quantities of whiskey from which too much "mischief could result." As a remedy, Keokuk proposed the sale of additional Sauk and Meskwaki land to the United States. He asked for a "liberal" payment to provide for his people so they could live in peace and to minimize the necessity for them to travel across the Missouri to hunt buffalo on the plains, where they often were forced to fight with other Indians. He also requested three new blacksmith shops, a trading post, and an agency headquarters on the remaining Sauk territory along the Des Moines River.[24]

Keokuk's proposal to sell additional lands angered the Meskwakis, who complained to President Andrew Jackson about Keokuk's leadership. In August 1834 they charged that Keokuk was using tribal funds owed to the Meskwakis to arbitrarily reimburse favored traders from the American Fur Company. They additionally complained that under Keokuk's administration Sauks received the lion's share of annuities while Meskwakis got less than they deserved. The Meskwakis asked the government to distribute the money to the heads of families instead of making lump-sum annuity payments to Keokuk and the chiefs.[25]

In turn, William Clark, attempting to bolster Keokuk's leadership, suggested that if funds were paid to family heads, the money would be squandered. He pointed out that payments to Keokuk and the principal chiefs allowed these individuals to buy articles necessary for the general welfare of the tribe, or to provide assistance to indigent tribal members. He also noted that having the chiefs control tribal funds helped dissuade younger warriors from organizing war parties, for they could be bribed to desist.[26]

Despite Clark's support, Keokuk faced growing opposition from his people. In May 1836, a tribal council declared that after all tribal debts were paid, Hardfish, an outspoken critic of Keokuk and a member of the Sturgeon clan (the clan who had traditionally supplied civil chiefs), should replace Keokuk as principal chief. Indian agent Joseph Street, who considered Keokuk to be "a very extraordinary man of a high order of talent," rejected the decision. Street believed that such an action would violate the Treaty of 1832 and that

Keokuk "through the prudent management of his followers . . . was mainly instrumental in restoring peace and security for the Sacs [Sauks] and Foxes [Meskwakis]." In Street's eyes, Keokuk merited the undisputed support of the government.[27]

Keokuk's Sauk and Meskwaki detractors in Iowa were also joined by Sauk and Meskwaki critics in Missouri. Early in the nineteenth century, the Sauks and Meskwakis of the Missouri had separated from their kinsmen in Iowa and Illinois, relocating in north-central Missouri. They also believed that Keokuk had failed to share tribal annuities equitably with them. Complaining to federal authorities, their spokesman declared, "[Keokuk] is now the friend of the American people. He may well be so; he ought to be so, for who would not love a nation who built him a fine house to live in and gave him a silver saddle to ride on," saying also that the "artful traders who have made themselves rich out of the spoils of your treaties and who have helped Keokuk to cheat you, ought to love you as much as he does." Nevertheless, federal Indian agents continued to strongly support Keokuk, envisioning him as a source of stability amidst the Sauk and Meskwaki tribe and ascribing much of the dissent to disgruntled followers of Black Hawk, whom they believed were jealous of Keokuk's position.[28]

Bolstered by government support, in 1836 Keokuk again approached federal officials about ceding the Keokuk Reserve and moving the agency headquarters from Rock Island. Since hunting had declined, the tribe needed money to pay off debts and to purchase more goods from white traders. Moreover, when tribal members traveled to Rock Island, they were forced to enter areas that had a growing white population, and altercations often occurred. In September, Keokuk and other tribal leaders met with federal officials and sold their land along the Iowa River. Henry Dodge, who negotiated the treaty for the United States, attempted to purchase all the remaining Sauk and Meskwaki land in Iowa and to remove the tribe beyond the Missouri, but Keokuk refused to sell additional tribal land.[29]

Facing continued intratribal pressure, Keokuk returned to St. Louis in June 1837 and protested to Clark that the government had not fulfilled its treaty obligations. He complained that he had heard that the government planned to alter the 1836 treaty and substitute trade goods for the promised cash. He also pointed out that the government had failed to provide the tobacco, salt, and horses that the treaty had promised. The horses were particularly needed for an upcoming buffalo hunt on the plains. These protests may have been launched through Keokuk's determination to retain control of tribal funds, but they also provided an opportunity for the chief to step forward as the champion of his people, an effort to convince many of his tribal critics that he continued to represent the interests of the Sauks and Meskwakis against the federal government.[30]

In 1837, warfare against the Sioux again erupted, and in an effort to negotiate a permanent peace, Commissioner of Indian Affairs C. A. Harris invited Sauk and Meskwaki chiefs (led by Keokuk), Sioux chiefs, and some Ioway Indians to Washington. In this council Keokuk verbally sparred with the Sioux chiefs and declared that all the disputed Indian land in Iowa belonged to the Sauks and Meskwakis through their conquest of the region; he would accept no compromises! While no peace settlement developed, Keokuk received praise from the Sauks and Meskwakis for his militancy. At the same time, he did attempt to placate the United States, for after some negotiation, Keokuk and the other members of the Sauk and Meskwaki delegation agreed to sell an additional one million acres to the government. Following the land cession agreement, Keokuk and his delegation toured eastern cities, where he was wined, dined, and praised as "one of the most sagacious Indians on our frontier."[31] He even received a silver headed sword-cane from Henry Clay and a brace of pistols from Governor Edward Everett of Massachusetts.[32]

But when Keokuk returned to Iowa, his problems increased. Trade goods valued at $5,000 promised to the Sauks and Meskwakis in the recent treaty signed in Washington failed to materialize, and in June 1839, when Keokuk inquired about them, Street replied that the government had changed the treaty. Instead of the trade goods, Street informed him that federal officials had decided to substitute $10,000 in funds that would be used to pay for the plowing of Indian land. Keokuk replied that it was strange that one party to a treaty could alter the document after it had been signed. He informed Street that the tribe already had sufficient funds set aside for breaking land and building fences. He and his people wanted the trade goods! Meanwhile, Iowa Territorial Governor Robert Lucas clamored for the purchase of all remaining Sauk and Meskwaki land in Iowa and the removal of the tribes across the Missouri River. In response, Keokuk asked to return to Washington to discuss the missing trade goods and perhaps to sell another small section of the tribes' Iowa lands, but Lucas used his influence with federal officials to prevent such a journey. Lucas argued that the government should buy all the Sauk and Meskwaki land, or none at all. He feared that the Indians would expect a high price for every small parcel of land that they might surrender, and that if they sold their remaining lands on a piecemeal basis, it would "keep them constantly hovering upon the frontier."[33]

While Keokuk sought peace, pursued tribal economic solvency through small land cessions, and attempted to keep the Sauks and Meskwakis in Iowa, his power continued to be challenged. Aware that Governor Lucas did not favor Keokuk's leadership, Hardfish contacted Lucas hoping to enlist his support for the distribution of annuity funds to the heads of families. Eager to undercut Keokuk, Lucas endorsed Hardfish's request and sent it on to Commissioner of Indian Affairs Hartley Crawford. Keokuk learned of the request and sent Crawford his own petition, urging that payments be made as in the past. Crawford rather reluctantly agreed with Keokuk and ordered that the annuities should be paid to Keokuk and three other "money chiefs" per usual. However, when the money arrived in Iowa, tempers flared, and Hardfish and his supporters threatened to seize the funds. Agent John Beach, who had earlier opined to Crawford that "justice, propriety, [and] policy earnestly demand that Keokuk, so long at least, as his customary friendly reliance upon our Gov't. continued, should be sustained," decided with Keokuk to return the money to St. Louis, claiming that they were going to exchange the paper money for specie.[34]

While the funds remained in St. Louis, political power struggles raged in Iowa. Lucas, who considered the delayed payment as a threat to his authority, wrote to Crawford and blamed the delay on the "malign influence of the traders on Keokuk." Crawford ordered Beach to let the Indians decide the matter. An angry Hardfish initially would not alter his stance. Keokuk stated that he would wait until May 1841, when the funds could be distributed with the 1841 annuities. In March 1841, John Chambers replaced Lucas as territorial governor, and Chambers wanted a resolution to the conflict. Finally, a compromise was reached. All sides agreed that the 1840 annuities would be given to Keokuk and the "money chiefs"; the 1841 payments would be divided—$16,000 to Hardfish for heads of families, and $24,000 to Keokuk and the chiefs to spend as necessary; and in 1842 all the annuities would go to heads of families.[35]

In 1841 when the Sauks and Meskwakis gathered to receive both the 1840 and 1841 annuities, they found that government officials had additional plans. Crawford requested that they sell more land. He informed them, "There is no safety for you unless you are removed beyond the reaches of white men, where they have nothing to do with your funds, or anything that concerns you." Both Crawford and Chambers then attempted to persuade the Sauks and Meskwakis to move to new homes in Minnesota, where they would build farms, schools, and mills. Ironically, this unanticipated suggestion by the government to relocate to Minnesota engendered so much opposition among the Sauks and Meskwakis that Keokuk and Hardfish joined in opposition to it. Both chiefs and their followers had no desire to live closer to the Sioux, or to embrace either schools or farming. With Hardfish's support, Keokuk assumed the role of primary spokesman, declaring, "We have never heard so hard proposals." The land in Minnesota, he asserted, was "the poorest in every respect." As for schools, he said, "We have always opposed them and will never consent to have them introduced into our nation." The Sauks and Meskwakis, now united against the government's "Minnesota plan," accepted their annuities and went back to their villages.[36]

But time was on the government's side; the tribes' economic status continued to deteriorate. By 1842 they had become so indebted to traders that their accumulated debts threatened to surpass their annuity payments. Meanwhile, as white settlement spread across Iowa, game decreased. The Sauks and Meskwakis found themselves without the resources to meet their families' needs. In 1842 Keokuk, Hardfish, and other leaders met in council and finally decided that they would sell their remaining land in Iowa, withdraw from the Sioux, and remove to Kansas. In October they met with Chambers and signed a treaty of removal, exchanging their remaining land in Iowa for about one million dollars (a fourth of which went to traders for accumulated debts), and for land south of the Missouri River. The Sauks and Meskwakis also agreed to withdraw to western Iowa by May 1843 and to be settled in Kansas by October 1847. They still refused any provisions for schools or agricultural training, and Keokuk, no doubt still bitter over federal changes to the Treaty of 1837, demanded that nothing in the treaty be altered without the consent of the Indians.[37]

Keokuk served as the principal negotiator for the Sauks and Meskwakis in this treaty, and although he had the support of Hardfish and other chiefs, he struggled to get many of his tribespeople to accept it. The Meskwakis particularly opposed removal. Although gifts were distributed to placate the malcontented, many refused to remove. For his part, Keokuk took his followers to western Iowa, where game remained scarce, and in September 1845, he led them out of Iowa toward their new home in Kansas. They arrived in southeastern Kansas in early 1846, where they planted corn, then hunted buffalo. Agent Beach reported that over 700 Sauks and about 250 Meskwakis arrived with Keokuk at the Kansas agency.[38]

Federal officials credited Keokuk's leadership for the relatively successful removal process; in gratitude, Beach presented Keokuk with a "suitable . . . but not too expensive" sword. Beach reported to his superiors that Keokuk's "aptness to understand motives and arguments, and to appreciate the conditions of his people" and "his readiness to cooperate, and forward every measure suggested by me, merits the approbation of the department." Beach further added, "It is his [Keokuk's] constant endeavor to cause no trouble to the government. He used all his influence and exertions to bring about the last treaty. . . . He has throughout fulfilled with utmost promptitude all his engagements." Governor Chambers of Iowa concurred in Beach's appraisal, although he remained dismayed by Keokuk's fondness for alcohol, noting, "What a noble Indian that would be, but for his intemperate habits."[39]

Although some Sauks and Meskwakis continued to complain about his self-indulgent habits and his distribution of funds, Keokuk remained as the principal chief of the Sauks and Meskwakis. Even though now living far from his Mississippi Valley homeland, nearly seventy years old, and perhaps reflecting on the events that had shaped both his people and his lifetime, he did not change his ways. Although he steadfastly had opposed Christian missionaries, in 1847, after Beach convinced him that mission schools would cost his people no annuity funds and actually would bring additional money onto the reservation, he agreed to "advocate the measure" among the other chiefs. As in the past, Keokuk would endorse actions that might enhance tribal funds as well as please government authorities. Yet Keokuk never lived to see any missionaries arrive. He died in 1848, succumbing to "dysentery brought on by a drunken frolic."[40]

Any assessment of Keokuk's leadership among the Sauks and Meskwakis and his relationship with the federal government must balance his role in promoting peace against his desire for personal aggrandizement and his seeming acquiescence to the demands of federal Indian policy. Americans traditionally have focused their attention on Native American leaders who opposed federal officials through armed resistance, glamorizing "war chiefs" who led brave but futile military actions against the United States. Indeed, these war chiefs (Tecumseh, Crazy Horse, Geronimo, and Osceola) have been immortalized in history and folklore and described by twentieth-century historians as "Patriot Chiefs": leaders whose patriotic devotion to their people epitomized Native American resistance. Black Hawk, of course, fits admirably into this stereotype.[41]

Yet Keokuk and other Native American leaders who attempted to walk the tightrope between providing for their people and assuring their tribe's continued existence through an accommodation with the demands of federal Indian policy were also patriots, although their role was more complex and more difficult to analyze. As a young warrior, Keokuk realized that the United States was emerging as the dominant power in the upper Mississippi Valley, and he attempted to placate American officials while at the same time protecting his people from both the Sioux and unruly white settlers. He wisely kept his followers out of the Black Hawk War, but he was unable to keep them from falling further into debt to white traders. During his tenure as chief, Keokuk and many of his followers fell victim to white whiskey peddlers, and the tribe's population decreased. Like other Native American leaders of his era, Keokuk was eventually forced to sell his homeland piecemeal in order to acquire sufficient funds to feed and supply his people. His leadership engendered opposition, but with the exception of Black Hawk, his opponents focused more on the distribution of the government's largesse rather than offering any meaningful alternatives to Keokuk's policies.[42]

Unquestionably, the political power and military capability of the Sauks and Meskwakis deteriorated during the first half of the nineteenth century, but such deterioration probably would have occurred regardless of who served as chief during this period. By utilizing bravado, threats, compromise, cooperation, accommodation, and diplomatic statesmanship, Keokuk labored diligently to maximize his people's leverage with the federal government and to protect them from the Sioux and other tribal enemies. He sought alliances with American officials and utilized his position to reward his supporters and friends, but he also negotiated higher payments per acre for tribal lands— when these lands had to be sold—than did many other Native American leaders of his time. Keokuk was a proud man, given to self-indulgence and sometimes swayed by flattery; moreover, he engendered opposition from factions within his tribe—but the same can be said for most other successful politicians and statesmen of the Jacksonian Era.

In retrospect, Keokuk's leadership is indicative of the genre of Native American leadership that would later emerge in the twentieth century: Indian leaders who attempted to "work within the system" to protect their people's sovereignty and well-being. The struggle continues.

Notes

1. Emma Hunt Blair, ed., *The Indian Tribes of the Upper Mississippi Valley and the Region of the Great Lakes*, 2 vols. (Cleveland: Clark, 1912), 2:190n70.

2. George Catlin, *Letters and Notes on the North American Indians*, ed. Michael MacDonald Mooney (New York: Gramercy, 1975), 338.

3. The various remarks and comments offered over the years by historians and others about Keokuk are too numerous to cite in this context. For a general discussion of this controversy, see Thomas Burnell Colbert, "Sycophant or Sage: Views and Appraisals of Sauk Chief Keokuk," unpublished paper delivered at the Northern Great Plains History Conference, Minneapolis, 1994.

4. Frederick J. Dockstader, *Great North American Indians: Profiles in Life and Leadership* (New York: Van Norst, 1977), 127; Cyrenius Cole, *Iowa through the Years* (Iowa City: State Historical Society of Iowa, 1940), 65; Catlin, *Letters and Notes*, 337. Also see P. Richard Metcalf, "Who Shall Rule at Home? Native American Politics and White-Indian Relations," *Journal of American History* 61 (December 1974): 659, 661; Perry Armstrong, *The Sauks and the Black Hawk War* (Springfield, Ill.: Rokker, 1887), 231–32; Thomas McKen-

ney and James Hall, *The Indians Tribes of North America with Biographical Sketches and Anecdotes of the Principal Chiefs,* 2 vols. (Edinburgh, Scotland: Grant, 1934), 2:131. Also see Benjamin Drake, *The Life and Adventures of Black Hawk* (Cincinnati: Concklin, 1838), 119; A. R. Fulton, *The Red Men of Iowa* (Des Moines: Mills, 1882), 231–32; Anthony F. C. Wallace, "Prelude to Disaster: The Course of Indian-White Relations which Led to the Black Hawk War, 1832," in Ellen M. Whitney, ed., *The Black Hawk War Papers, Illinois Historical Library Collections, 35–39,* 4 vols. (Springfield: Illinois State Historical Library, 1970–1978), 1:35; G. I. Groves, *Famous American Indians* (Chicago: Groves, 1944), 142.

5. Donald Jackson, ed., *Black Hawk: An Autobiography* (Urbana: University of Illinois Press, 1964), 73; Metcalf, "Who Should Rule at Home?" 659; Drake, *Life and Adventures,* 121–25; Fulton, *Red Men of Iowa,* 232.

6. Alvin M. Joseph Jr., *The Patriot Chiefs: A Chronicle of American Indian Resistance* (New York: Penguin, 1958), 230; Roger L. Nichols, *Black Hawk and the Warrior's Path* (Arlington Heights, Ill.: Davidson, 1992), 62–63.

7. William T. Hagan, *The Sac and Fox Indians* (Norman: University of Oklahoma Press, 1958), 88–89.

8. Wallace, "Prelude to Disaster," 23; Josephy, *The Patriot Chiefs,* 232–33; Nichols, *Black Hawk,* 71–72; Dockstader, *Great North American Indians,* 135; Hagan, *The Sac and Fox Indians,* 94–96. Also see Martha Royce Blaine, *The Ioway Indians* (Norman: University of Oklahoma Press, 1979), 135; William Salter, *The First Free State in the Louisiana Purchase* (Chicago: McLery, 1905), 128–29; William E. Wilkie, *Dubuque on the Mississippi, 1788–1980* (Dubuque, Iowa: Loras College, 1987), 124; and David M. Voss, "Indian Land Cessions in Iowa: A Case Study of Removal" (master's thesis, Marquette University, 1965), 3.

9. Charles A. Abele, "The Grand Indian Council and Treaty at Prairie du Chien" (PhD diss., Loyola University of Chicago, 1969), 134–35; Bruce E. Mahan, *Old Fort Crawford and the Frontier* (Iowa City: State Historical Society of Iowa, 1926), 89–98; Nichols, *Black Hawk,* 72–74; Hagan, *Sac and Fox Indians,* 96–98; Salter, *Iowa,* 131.

10. Hagan, *Sac and Fox Indians,* 99, 101; Nichols, *Black Hawk,* 77–78.

11. Jacob Van der Zee, "The Black Hawk War and the Treaty of 1832," *Iowa Journal of History and Politics* 13 (July 1915): 418; John Hamburg, "The Black Hawk War, 1831–1832," *Illinois State Historical Society Transactions for the Year 1932* (Springfield: Illinois State Historical Society, 1933), 97–98; Miriam Gurko, *American Indian: The Black Hawk War* (New York: Crowell, 1970), 95.

12. Council at Prairie du Chien, August 4, 1829, folder 56, box 3, Sac and Fox Materials, State Historical Society of Iowa, Des Moines; William J. Peterson, *Steamboating on the Upper Mississippi* (Iowa City: State Historical Society of Iowa, 1968), 115. Also see Mahan, *Old Fort Crawford,* 151; and Hagan, *Sac and Fox Indians,* 113.

13. Council with the Sac and Fox, March 27, 1830, folder 88, box 3, Sac and Fox Materials, State Historical Society of Iowa; Council at St. Louis, March 23, 1830, Letters Received by the Office of Indian Affairs, (M234) record group 75, National Archives, Washington, D.C. Hereinafter, materials from this archive group will be cited as "M234."

14. Council with Clark, June 16, 1830, folder 107, box 4, Sac and Fox Materials, State Historical Society of Iowa; Nichols, *Black Hawk,* 94.

15. Extracts from Minutes of the Council at Prairie du Chien, July 7–13, 1830, folder

108, box 4, Sac and Fox Materials, State Historical Society of Iowa; Roger Nichols, ed., "The Black Hawk War: Another View," *Annals of Iowa,* 3rd series, 36 (Winter 1963): 529; Nichols, *Black Hawk,* 94–95.

16. Clark to Gaines, May 28, 1831, folder 138, box 5, Sac and Fox Materials, State Historical Society of Iowa; Mahan, *Old Fort Crawford,* 158; Hagan, *Sac and Fox Indians,* 123–33; Salter, *Iowa,* 193; Nichols, *Black Hawk,* 99.

17. 22nd Cong., 1st sess., *Senate Executive Document 2,* vol. 1 (Serial 216), 203–4; Fulton Scrapbook, vol. 4 (State Historical Society of Iowa), 88.

18. George Davenport to William Clark, May 27, 1832, folder 188, box 6, Sac and Fox Materials, State Historical Society of Iowa. For accounts of the Black Hawk War see appropriate chapters of Hagan, *Sac and Fox Indians;* Nichols, *Black Hawk;* Jackson, *Black Hawk;* Wallace, "Prelude to Disaster"; and Frank E. Stevens, *The Black Hawk War, Including a Review of Black Hawk's Life* (Chicago: Frank E. Stevens, 1903).

19. Michael D. Green, "'We Dance in Opposite Directions': Mesquakie (Fox) Separatism from the Sac and Fox Tribe," *Ethnohistory* 30 (1983): 132; Salter, *Iowa,* 196–97; Hagan, *Sac and Fox Indians,* 196–97; Jackson, "Prelude to Disaster," 72n52.

20. *Niles Register,* February 9, 1833; John Reynolds, *The Pioneer History of Illinois* (Chicago: Fergus, 1887), 293.

21. Hagan, *Sac and Fox Indians,* 197–99.

22. Minutes of a Council at Rock Island, June 1, 1833, M234, roll 729; M. S. Davenport to the Commissioner of Indian Affairs, June 20, 1833, ibid.; Hagan, *Sac and Fox Indians,* 209.

23. Nichols, *Black Hawk,* 152–54; Hagan, *Sac and Fox Indians,* 200–201.

24. Statement by Keokuk, August 19, 1834, M234, roll 729.

25. Mesquakies to the President of the United States, August 26, 1834, M234, roll 729.

26. William Clark to the Commissioner of Indian Affairs, folder 245, Sac and Fox Materials, State Historical Society of Iowa.

27. Council Meeting, May 28, 1836, M234, roll 729; Hagan, *Sac and Fox Indians,* 210.

28. John Dougherty to M. Duncan, June 10, 1836, M234, roll 729; Joseph Street to Henry Dodge, August 3, 1836, in John Porter Blum, ed., *The Territorial Papers of the United States* (Washington: National Archives and Record Service, 1969), 27:632–33.

29. *Gate City* (Keokuk, Iowa), November 7, 1869, newspaper microfilm, State Historical Society of Iowa; Royce Delbert Kurtz, "Economic and Political History of the Sauk and Mesquakie: 1780s–1845" (PhD diss., University of Iowa, 1986), 275; Ronald A. Raymon, "Joseph Montfort Street: Establishing the Sac and Fox Agency, 1838–40," *Annals of Iowa,* 3rd series, no. 43 (1976): 261; William J. Peterson, *The Story of Iowa: The Progress of an American State* (New York: Lewis, 1952), 1:154; Royce Delbert Kurtz, "Timber and Treaties: The Sauk and Mesquakie Decision to Sell Iowa Territory," *Forest and Conservation History* 35 (April 1991): 61; Lawrence Eugene Christ, "Indian Land Cessions in Iowa, 1830–1851," (master's thesis, Illinois State University, 1971), 63. Also see Hagan, *Sac and Fox Indians,* 211–13; and Fulton, *Red Men of Iowa,* 241–42.

30. Minutes of a Council at St. Louis, June 26, 1837, M234, roll 729.

31. *Niles Register,* October 7, 1837.

32. J. M. Reed, *Sketches and Anecdotes of the Old Settlers and New Comers, the Mormon Bandits, and Danite Band* (Keokuk, Iowa: Ogden, 1876), 23; Fulton, *Red Men of Iowa,*

237–38; Blaine, *Ioway Indians,* 169; Hagan, *Sac and Fox Indians,* 215–17; and Raymon, "Joseph Montfort Street," 236.

33. Joseph Street to Robert Lucas, June 11, 1839, M234, roll 730; Robert Lucas to Hartley Crawford, October 10, 1839, ibid.

34. Ruth A. Gallagher, "Indian Agents in Iowa: Agents among the Sac and Fox," *Iowa Journal of History and Politics* 14 (July 1916): 364–65; Jacob Van der Zee, "The Opening of the Des Moines Valley to Settlement," *Iowa Journal of History and Politics* 14 (October 1916): 505; Michael D. Green, "The Sac-Fox Annuity Crisis of 1840 in Iowa Territory," *Arizona and the West* 16 (Summer 1974): 141–50; Donald J. Berthrong, "John Beach and the Removal of the Sauk and Fox from Iowa," *Iowa Journal of History and Politics* 54 (October 1956): 318–20. Also see Green, "'We Dance in Opposite Directions,'"133–34; Raymon, "Joseph Montfort Street," 270.

35. Green, "Annuity Crisis," 150–55; Fulton, *The Red Men of Iowa,* 243–46.

36. 27th cong., 2nd sess., Senate Executive Document, Report of the Commissioner of Indian Affairs, 270–73; *Niles Register,* November 6, 1841; Berthrong, "John Beach," 323; Green, "Annuity Crisis," 155–56.

37. "Articles of a Treaty with the Sac and Fox Indians, October 10, 1842," in Charles J. Kappler, comp. and ed., *Indian Treaties, 1778–1883* (Mattituck, N.J.: Amereon, 1972), 546–49; "Sac and Fox Council of 1842," *Annals of Iowa,* 3rd. series, 12 (July 1920): 341; Thomas Peter Christensen, *The Iowa Indians: A Brief History* (Iowa City: Athens Press, 1954), 57. Also see Hagan, *Sac and Fox Indians,* 221–22; Berthrong, "John Beach," 327–29; and Kurtz, "Timber and Treaties," 63.

38. Grant Foreman, *The Last Trek of the Indians* (Chicago: University of Chicago Press, 1946), 145–46; Michael D. Green, "Indian Affairs in Iowa Territory, 1838–1846: The Removal of the Sacs and Foxes" (master's thesis, University of Iowa, 1965), 109; Berthrong, "John Beach," 333n89.

39. Report of John Chambers, September 6, 1845, *Annual Report of the Commissioner of Indian Affairs, 1845–1846* (Washington: Federal Printing Office, 1846), 34; Charles R. Green, *Early Days in Kansas in Keokuk's Time on the Kansas Reservation* (Olathe, Kan.: Green, 1912), 7–8; John Beach to T. H. Harvey, May 1, 1846, Sac and Fox Agency, vol. 1, Letter Book, roll SFSA4, Indian Archives, Oklahoma Historical Society, Oklahoma City; Foreman, *Last Trek of the Indians,* 145–47.

40. John Beach to T. H. Harvey, July 15, 1847, Sac and Fox Agency Records, vol. 1, Letter Book, roll SFSA4, Oklahoma Historical Society; Louise Berry, comp., "Kansas Before 1854: A Revised Annals," *Kansas Historical Quarterly* 30 (Winter 1864): 498; Louise Berry, ed., *The Beginning of the West: Annals of the Kansas Gateway to the American West, 1540–1854* (Topeka: Kansas State Historical Society, 1972), 752.

41. See Josephy, *Patriot Chiefs.*

42. Maria Peck, "Fort Armstrong," *Annals of Iowa,* 3rd series (January 1985): 607; Hagan, *Sac and Fox Indians,* 205–6.

4. The Ohio Shawnees'
Struggle against Removal, 1814–30
STEPHEN WARREN

During the War of 1812, American artillery officer Ensign William Schillinger was stationed at Fort Amanda in modern Auglaize County, Ohio. By July 1813, the war had shifted safely to more northern theatres, and Schillinger spent most of his days supervising the manufacture of ammunition and defending the fort from would-be attackers who never materialized. In an apparent fit of boredom, on July 13, 1813, Schillinger mounted his horse and rode several miles to the neighboring Shawnee village of Wapakoneta. Relations between the soldiers and the people of Wapakoneta were friendly, driven in part by the important role played by Shawnee scouts in the success of the American war effort. In his diary, Schillinger recorded that he "took a survey of the Indians gardens or farms (for they know no difference between their farm or Garden)." What he saw inspired both envy and revulsion in the young officer, for he had eaten very little beyond salted pork and the occasional deer or turkey brought in by the hunters in his regiment. Schillinger witnessed a profusion of "vines, such as Pumpkins, Water & Musk mellons, cucumbers, beens of various kinds, growing among their corn which was planted without any kind of order." But the Shawnees' worst offense, according to Schillinger, was that "the work is principally all done by the squaws."[1]

Both the perceived disorder of the Shawnee gardens and real differences over gender roles drove the soldier's critique. The Shawnees did not raise cash crops, such as wheat, that were typical of the Ohio frontier. Also absent is any mention of fruit trees and livestock, particularly pigs and cattle. Simply put, Schillinger was struck by the distance between American and Algonquian agricultural practices. But he was especially disturbed by the dominance of Shawnee women in the agricultural sphere. Both Indian and

American women on the frontier raised "kitchen gardens," complete with vegetables meant for home consumption. But American women did not tend the fields of corn or wheat, typical of most Ohio farms. Moreover, the vegetables Americans raised, including onions, potatoes, turnips, lettuce, and cabbage, distinguished their gardens—and the food they consumed—from their Indian neighbors. Schillinger confirmed his belief in the primitiveness of Shawnee culture by focusing his attention on the differences between American farms worked by men and Indian gardens cultivated by women.[2]

Americans who visited and lived among the Shawnees echoed this soldier's confusion over the important role played by Indian women in agriculture, trade, erecting camps, preparing skins, cutting and hauling firewood, and cooking. At the same time, Americans voiced their disdain for Shawnee men who seemed to be interested in little more than "the chase and war pursuits," and who seemed to casually ignore the agrarian values that most American men valued. Americans linked these gender differences to the oppression of Indian women. John Johnston, the Indian agent at Piqua, Ohio, admitted that Native American women "look upon such things as their appropriate duties" but commented that "nothing can be more degrading, servile or menial than the condition of their females in the married state."[3]

Shawnee men were equally troubled by the gender roles imposed with increasing force by American missionaries and government officials. Agricultural practices—and the gender differences associated with them—became one of the primary means by which both Shawnees and Americans defined themselves personally and collectively as they attempted to live among each other between 1814 and 1833.

When Schillinger returned to Fort Amanda later that evening, messengers informed him of the combined British and Indian siege of Fort Meigs, an American post on the Maumee River, approximately eighty miles to the north. Soldiers commanded by Green Clay lifted the siege, but the Americans continued to battle against hostile warriors. These skirmishes between militants and American troops occurred regularly to the north of Wapakoneta, complicating attempts by the Ohio Shawnees to remain neutral. By February 1814, John Johnston compelled the peaceful Shawnees and their neighbors to move from neutrality to armed support for the American war effort. Johnston told the Shawnees, Wyandots, Senecas, Miamis, Potawatomis, Ottawas, and Kickapoos that for the Americans, "war is our trade and you cannot live quiet and take no part in it." He went on to explain that if the Shawnees and their neighbors refused to fight, they would be considered enemies of the United States.[4]

In response, additional Shawnees volunteered for the Americans. Some of the men, including François Duchoquet, were the children of French fathers and Shawnee mothers. They worked as hired hunters, providing meat for the soldiers' larders. Other Shawnees served as scouts and interpreters. Many of these young men were the children of hereditary leaders. They believed their support of the Americans would enhance their leadership roles in the future. Moreover, combat-tested friendships with American soldiers would facilitate their role as mediators across cultures, an important element of chiefly authority in the postwar Midwest.[5]

Relationships between Shawnee hunters and scouts and American soldiers and settlers raise important questions about the limits of cultural pluralism on the American frontier. As border combatants, many Shawnees and set-tlers had been sworn enemies between the mid-1770s and 1794. Following the Treaty of Greenville (1795), however, growing ties between American officials and Shawnees residing at Wapakoneta had encouraged some fron-tiersmen to envision the Shawnees as friends. Yet the American victory over the British in the War of 1812 bolstered the confidence of American settlers who emphasized the cultural differences between Indians and Americans. In the war's aftermath, some of these frontiersmen clamored for the Shawnees to be removed from Ohio. Echoing such sentiments, in September 1815, the editors of the *Niles Weekly Register* urged that formerly hostile tribes "must be brought to a sense of justice . . . they must be *Jacksonized,* as the saying goes in the west."[6]

Yet some Americans remained friendly to the tribespeople, and the Shaw-nees sought American allies in an attempt to remain in their homeland. Re-gardless of American opinions, the Ohio Shawnees firmly opposed relocation west of the Mississippi. In August 1816, former Shawnee scouts who had served with the American army, including Black Hoof and John and William Perry, left their villages near modern Lima, Ohio, and rode to Lexington and Bour-bon County, Kentucky, to visit with old friends from the army and to see the country. Black Hoof and the Perry brothers hoped to build on their friendships with American soldiers and foster a new era of openness and cooperation.[7]

The tour through his former hunting grounds must have been bittersweet for the aged chief Black Hoof, who as a young man had opposed American settlement in Kentucky and Ohio. Although he had served the Americans as a scout during the recent war, he had paid a heavy price. In January 1813, while visiting an American military camp, he had been shot in the face by an American soldier who doubted his loyalty. Yet Black Hoof had remained faithful to the American cause, and in 1816 he had decided to make the journey to Lexington at the request of a Kentuckian whose life he once saved in the decades of conflict between the settlers and Shawnees. Black Hoof believed the trip to be successful. He was treated like an "honored guest" in the Bluegrass region of central Kentucky, and the Shawnee chief hoped to enlist support and goodwill for his people.[8]

Younger Wapakoneta Shawnee leaders such as John and William Perry generally shared Black Hoof's perspective. Born at the dawn of American dominance in the Old Northwest, these sons of the Shawnee war chief Logan both chose to follow Black Hoof's path of accommodation with the Americans. During the War of 1812 they had enlisted as scouts at Fort Laramie, Ohio, and assisted an American company of Rangers "to know the friendly Indians from those who are not so." In fact, their father, who also had assisted the Americans, was killed in a skirmish with pro-British Potawatomis. The *Niles Weekly Register* later reported that the Perry brothers had "always conducted themselves with faithfulness and gallantry." But personal ambitions also had spurred the Perry brothers' enlistment. Serving the Americans as scouts had strengthened Shawnee-American ties. It also had enabled them, and other younger Shawnee men, to achieve status in their villages at a time when traditional outlets for prestige through warfare and hunting were rapidly declining. Grateful Americans initially had fueled both their egos and their optimism with the thought that a long-overdue era of peace and stability was about to begin in the Ohio country.[9]

Such optimism initially convinced the Ohio Shawnees and their Indian neighbors that they might enjoy a continued residence in Ohio. Following the War of 1812, the Shawnees, along with about sixteen hundred Senecas, Delawares, Ottawas, and Wyandots, remained in the northwest corner of the state. The land they occupied was sparsely settled by whites, in part because of the challenges associated with draining the swampy and wooded lands south of Lake Erie along the Maumee River and its tributaries. Meanwhile, Methodist, Baptist, Moravian, and Quaker missionaries worked with the tribes after the war. The Wyandots, located near Sandusky, initially attracted much of the public's attention, since the African-American preacher John Stewart and a circuit-rider named James Finley helped to publicize this tribe's "progress" toward American notions of "civilization." The Wyandots' command of English and their participation in the grain and cattle trade also contributed to the tribe's popularity among philanthropists.[10]

Other frontier Americans, particularly Andrew Jackson, Lewis Cass, and Thomas Hart Benton, considered those Indians who remained in the eastern states to be sad hangers-on, vanquished relics of another era. In a speech before the United States Senate in 1824, Benton complained that the Indians "must know that . . . the power of the state is against them; and that, sooner or later, they must go." Population imbalances encouraged Benton and his colleagues to promote Indian removal. At the time Benton made his remarks, there were an estimated 2,350 American Indians in Ohio, with another 11,579 in Indiana and Illinois. Indian people lived among solid American majorities in all three states. In 1815, nearly 69,000 settlers lived in Indiana, while more than 300,000 had settled in Ohio.[11]

But the tribespeople struggled to remain despite overwhelming differences in population and resources. From the Indians' perspective, removal beyond the Mississippi was not an option. Many Indian allies of the Americans, including Logan and several other Shawnees, had died in hand-to-hand combat with their enemies during the recent war. They had shed their own blood for the Americans, and many Indians believed their sacrifices had earned a place for their kinsmen within their old homelands. Coexistence with whites was the only means of survival, and in consequence, the Shawnees rejected the binary racial and ethnic division between Indians and whites advocated by Benton, Cass, and their supporters. Black Hoof had witnessed the advancing American settlements for decades. He reminded Indian agent John Johnston that his people "were arrived at the point, beyond which they could not go, that when they looked over the Mississippi they saw the White people moving there as fast as in former times they spread themselves over Kentucky and Ohio." The Shawnees tied their survival to their ability to live as useful neighbors amid their former enemies.[12]

American Indian agents demanded drastic changes in tribal leadership in exchange for a place in Ohio. They were eager to terminate the multi-tribal, "Ohio Indian" identities of the eighteenth century. Johnston and Benjamin Stickney, the Fort Wayne Indian agent, dedicated themselves to the establishment of separate tribal governments in the Midwest. Both men used treaties to consolidate authority around leaders who had remained loyal to the Americans. According to Stickney, tribes allied with the British in the late war "should not hereafter be permitted to exercise any separate government . . . to kindle a council fire" within the boundaries of the United States. Government officials found willing partners in Black Hoof and similar leaders among the Wyandots, Delawares, Ottawas, and Senecas: allies who hoped to increase their own power and influence. These Ohio village chiefs competed with tribal rivals scattered across what is now Arkansas, Missouri, Indiana, and Ohio for control of American treaty annuities. They sought the acknowledgment by both their kinspeople and by American officials that they indeed were the "national leaders" of their respective tribes. In exchange for his past support of the Americans, Black Hoof expected officials to envision him as the primary chief of the Shawnees: he should negotiate with officials on behalf of his entire tribe.[13]

When the war had ended, however, the Shawnees were in dire economic straits. The postwar ceremonial affection showered on Black Hoof and the Perry brothers in Kentucky belied the depredations suffered by the Shawnees during the conflict. Between 1812 and 1815, neighboring whites repeatedly had destroyed Shawnee property and stolen or killed Shawnee livestock, significantly weakening the ability of the 840 Shawnees living at Wapakoneta to maintain a self-sufficient economy. Black Hoof frankly admitted that "the war took everything from us." Government annuity payments had arrived sporadically, if at all, during the war, while farming declined as Shawnee women no longer felt safe working in the fields outside of their villages. In consequence, some Wapakoneta Shawnees had bartered with British traders, or went on long winter hunts, far beyond their recognized lands, to feed and clothe their children.[14]

Refugees from other tribes contributed to the Shawnees' problems. Small numbers of straggling tribespeople arrived in Ohio from the Southeast and New England, causing Black Hoof to complain to the Secretary of War that "many other Indians . . . come here . . . they are poor and we have to divide with all." A coalition of leaders, including Black Hoof, Walker of the Wyandots on the Sandusky River, and Civil John, a Seneca from Lewistown, reminded the Secretary of War that he had promised to "do every thing that would be of assistance to us," including "having our land divided from the other tribes." In turn, American policymakers used the tribally controlled annuity payments and the harsh reality of postwar poverty to isolate Indians into tribal categories. Under the American regime, recognized tribes were compelled to exclude refugees from village membership and to establish specific boundaries over village-owned lands.[15]

The Shawnees, Wyandots, Delawares, and other pro-American tribes in the region pressed on in spite of these setbacks. They attempted to retain their homelands through transforming their economies and relying on Black Hoof and other hereditary leaders whose diplomatic skills enabled them to negotiate with the Americans. Some Shawnee men took advantage of new opportunities created by American schools, raised livestock, and sought employment as interpreters and hunters.[16] Moreover, they were eager to convince Indian agents that they could "walk the white man's road." Under Black Hoof's leadership, during the spring of 1816 the Shawnees at Wapakoneta planted large acreages of grain and vegetables. In August, just prior to the chief's departure for Kentucky, they harvested a large portion of these crops. A delegation of Quakers who visited Wapakoneta in August 1816 were amazed at the Shawnees agricultural success, especially since the tribespeople had cultivated their crops without horse-drawn plows. The Quakers reported that Shawnee women had worked the village-owned fields using hoes to dig irrigation canals and had rid the cornrows of weeds. The Quakers also indicated that the Shawnees had harvested over 250 acres of corn and other vegetables.[17]

Encouraged by the Shawnees' "progress," Quakers from Mount Pleasant, Ohio, constructed a grist mill at Wapakoneta, and Quaker representatives reported that "the chiefs furnish promptly from day to day, any number of young men that may be wanted to aid in such work." Since Shawnee women traditionally had converted corn into bread or hominy by grinding it with a pestle in a wooden mortar called a *botaga,* the completion of the mill seemed to indicate that Shawnee men would become more involved in agriculture and in the production and sale of corn meal and flour to newly arriving settlers.[18] Indeed, the Quakers believed that the Shawnee mill workers signaled the tribe's commitment to a new way of life. In 1816 Quaker James Ellicott happily reported that "the Indians have been at all times disposed to furnish every assistance in their power" to the missionaries.[19]

But Quaker missionaries, like their Methodist and Baptist competitors, used gendered work roles as their template for the cultural transformation of Indian societies. During the summer of 1817 a new Quaker missionary, Joseph Rhodes, arrived at Wapakoneta and implored the Shawnees to break their communal fields into family-run plots worked primarily by men rather than their women and children. Unknown (or ignored) by Rhodes, this emphasis on male labor and the nuclear family posed a direct challenge to the unity of Shawnee families and villages. The Shawnees had traditionally lived in communal villages and their fields had been tended by women. Some Shawnee men were willing to work at the mill, but if they embraced the Quakers' plans, they would be forced to shift from their time-honored role as "life-sustaining killers" to the female world of food production associated with the vagaries of the plant world.[20] These changes threatened to transform Shawnee identity. Missionaries and Indian agents wanted to turn male and female tasks upside down, contradicting the dominant status enjoyed by Shawnee hunters since the fur trade had increased the importance of hunting three centuries earlier.

The American civilization program also threatened Shawnee women, who were asked to adopt what they viewed as alien and demeaning tasks. Quaker missionaries attempted to move Shawnee women out of the fields and into the home, where they would learn "domestic arts" common among many white women in the nineteenth century. The Quakers intended to restrict and redefine the cultural geography of the Shawnee people. According to the Quaker plan, men would be brought in from the forests to the fields, while women would be moved from the fields to the home. There they would milk the cattle; spin and weave cloth; fashion, repair, and clean clothing; make soap; and cook and preserve food.[21]

Rhodes argued that the conversion of Shawnee men from hunters to small yeoman farmers could be facilitated through education, and he hoped to illustrate agricultural techniques by recruiting Shawnee laborers to work on his model farm. In turn, Black Hoof and other Shawnee leaders believed that if Shawnee warriors volunteered to assist Rhodes, both the missionary and federal agents would interpret their cooperation as evidence that the Shawnees were committed to the Americans' "civilization" program. More-over, laborers on the model farm would be well fed, since Rhodes promised to provide meals for those Shawnees who accepted his offer. Consequently, in the summer of 1817 Shawnee laborers nearly overwhelmed Rhodes's wife, Martha, who had to feed thirty-six Shawnees after her husband requested some assistance in constructing a head-gate for the sluice at the grist mill. Rhodes reported that he had "never had so large a company" over for dinner. Shawnee laborers also helped Rhodes to clear additional farmland. They were less willing, however, to work in the fields.[22]

Rhodes's diary also reveals that he assisted the Shawnees. In July 1817 Rho-des received news that Black Hoof intended to slaughter a cow and harvest the wheat crop the Shawnees had planted. The Quaker missionary hurried to the chief's residence and witnessed more than twenty Shawnees, both men and women, harvesting a half-acre of wheat on the chief's lands. Always eager to please, Rhodes "showed them how to reap which they were anxious to know . . . likewise how to put up a shock, which there was great room for amendment." In return, "the good old Chief gave me (Rhodes) a good piece of meat (and) I returned to my cabin well satisfied." During his tenure at Wapakoneta, Rhodes often exchanged information, material goods, and labor with the Shawnees.[23]

The Shawnees reciprocated when the missionary's wife, Martha, became ill in August 1817. Isolated from Euro-Americans, including other Quakers, Rhodes lamented that throughout her sickness, he and his wife had received "not so much as the scratch of a pen" from members of the Ohio Yearly Meet-ing of Friends, but they had relied instead on medicine he obtained from a Shawnee healer at Wapakoneta. Moreover, Shawnee runners traveled many miles to notify members of Rhodes's family of his wife's illness. Unfortunately, Rhodes's wife died, but the missionary did not blame the Shawnee herbalist and recorded that "all the chiefs of that nation" visited him shortly after his wife's passing. Clearly grateful for their support, Rhodes acknowledged, "We are wonderfully supported in our lonesome abode."[24]

Other Ohio Shawnees sought to protect their community through building closer ties with American Indian agents. John Wolf, a subchief at Wapakoneta and a scout for the Americans in the War of 1812, accompanied Indian Agent John Johnston on his seasonal visits to the Indian villages of northwestern Ohio. Wolf assisted Johnston in establishing temporary camps and sometimes prepared food for Johnston and other officials. Wolf's support for Johnston secured his own status as an important leader at Wapakoneta and provided food and clothing for his family while many of his kinsmen went hungry. Yet some of his Indian neighbors ridiculed Wolf and referred to him as "Johnston's negro" during their travels together. Wolf was clearly bothered by the name-calling, and Johnston recalled that, after drinking, Wolf sometimes became belligerent toward him, telling Johnston that he "must get another negro for he would be my negro no longer." Johnston dismissed Wolf's protests as the result of his inebriation, and Wolf continued to assist the agent, even though some Shawnees remained critical of the friendship. Wolf eventually named his son after Johnston, and the two remained lifelong friends. Years later, in 1846, after the Shawnees had been removed, Wolf wrote to Johnston from Kansas seeking the agent's help for his son, who was then fighting his own battle with alcoholism. Wolf hoped that his son would "hearken to you and leave off whiskey."[25]

Like Rhodes, Johnston also attempted to transform Shawnee gender roles. He hired white laborers for the Shawnees, and he placed great importance that these frontier male laborers would provide role models and "instruct them [the Shawnees] in farming" now that "the wild game is gone."[26] Johnston also reported that some Shawnees believed "that they have no alternative, but [to] abandon their habits, and apply themselves to agriculture,"[27] and he assured officials in the War Department that "many families are moving out from the towns and settling on their lands; to such I hold out inducements of ploughs, hoes, etc."[28]

In contrast, many Shawnee men attempted to ease the transition from hunting to yeoman agriculture by raising livestock. Herding seemed a viable compromise between the pursuit of game in the forests and the backbreaking labor necessary for frontier farming. Moreover, the tribe's proximity to Cincinnati, then one of the country's largest cattle and hog markets, gave the Shawnees confidence that they could make a good profit from animals raised near their villages. Between 1818 and the late 1820s, Black Hoof and other chiefs at Wapakoneta spent more than a third of their annuities on cattle. Neighboring whites closely monitored these purchases. Most applauded the endeavor, believing that livestock would "contribute to the comforts of these children of the forest." Indeed, in this regard, the Shawnees' animal husbandry mimicked similar patterns practiced by white frontiersmen. The typical midwestern farmer raised pigs, and many tended small herds (usually five to fifteen animals) of cattle.[29]

While the Shawnees sought ways to assure the Americans that they could fit into American life, pressure mounted on the tribe to relinquish much of their remaining land base in Ohio. The Shawnees, Wyandots, Delawares, and other Ohio tribes still held title to much of northwestern Ohio (above the old Greenville Treaty line), and federal officials were eager to purchase the region and assign the Shawnees and their neighbors smaller reservation tracts in the region. But the government much preferred to negotiate with individual tribes rather than the coalition of tribes that had signed the Treaty of Greenville. Moreover, Lewis Cass and other federal officials believed that if political power was concentrated in the hands of paramount "tribal chiefs," then these individuals could be more easily coerced into ceding tribal lands and moving their people to the west. According to Cass, "once admit an Indian confederacy founded on an acknowledged community of interest, and we need be troubled with no more Indian negotiations. We should never procure another acre of land." Better to cultivate individual tribal chiefs, and purchase the remaining Indian lands in Ohio on a piecemeal basis.[30]

Black Hoof initially appeared to cooperate with Cass and Johnston in their efforts to purchase additional Indian lands. In the summer of 1817 he met with other Shawnee leaders, and with chiefs of neighboring tribes to lay the groundwork for a treaty to be held at Fort Meigs, in northwestern Ohio, in the following fall. Yet Black Hoof reminded Johnston that the lands had been assigned to a coalition of tribes at the Treaty of Fort Greenville; chiefs from all the neighboring tribes should participate in the negotiations."[31]

Concluded in September 1817, the Treaty of Fort Meigs ceded northwestern Ohio to the United States and established reservations for the remaining Shawnee, Wyandot, Seneca, and Ottawa tribes. More important, the treaty made explicit the American strategy of using treaty annuities to reinforce the power of pro-American chiefs and the villagers they represented. "The chiefs and their successors" in each of the remaining tribes were awarded the legal right to distribute reservation lands to tribal members listed on the treaty schedule. Treaty stipulations granted fee-simple land patents to chiefs. Black Hoof, Wolf, John Perry, and other subchiefs gained a tract of ten square miles surrounding Wapakoneta, while Captain Lewis, Civil John, the Turtle, and other Shawnee and Seneca chiefs gained a tract of forty-eight square miles at Lewistown. Piachtha, Onowaskemo, and other subchiefs of the Hog Creek Shawnees received a twenty-five-square-mile tract adjoining the Wapakoneta reservation. Chiefs now controlled tribal resources and distributed them to their supporters. This change provided coercive power to chiefs and improved their ability to speak on their peoples' behalf. The Treaty of Fort Meigs allowed American Indian leaders to become mediators between American officials and rank-and-file members of their tribes.[32]

The treaty also awarded "tribal" chiefs control over yearly annuity payments. Among the Shawnees, Black Hoof now received the $2,000 (later $3,000) annually provided to the tribe at Wapakoneta. The disbursement of these annuity funds only to Black Hoof and the Shawnees in Ohio angered the Shawnees residing west of the Mississippi, who by 1817 were the majority of the tribe. Black Hoof and his followers (the "Maykujay" division of the tribe) now controlled the majority of the tribe's annuity payments—a critical factor since Shawnee dependency upon the United States continued to deepen. The Wapakoneta Shawnees' longstanding commitment to a new American order in the Midwest began to have serious consequences for those Shawnees who wished to remain free from their authority.[33]

In the fall of 1817, following the Treaty of Fort Meigs, Black Hoof probably reached the apex of his power as the "Grand Chief" of the Shawnee people. In reality, the position of "Grand Chief" was a fiction foisted on the Shawnees by the federal government. Many other Shawnees—particularly those west of the Mississippi—refused to acknowledge his hegemony, but Black Hoof worked diligently to protect his influence. Aware that federal officials would question the legitimacy of any descent-based leaders who might challenge their policies, Black Hoof and his fellow Shawnee chiefs attempted to reinforce their hereditary claims to power by educating their children in American schools, securing property for their families, and conducting activities designed to perpetuate the esteemed position of their descendants. Black Hoof sent his son, along with two other children from prominent families, to an American school, despite the fact that it was nearly thirty miles from Wapakoneta. These children later became influential leaders after the Shawnees were removed to Indian Territory. Land grants to the children of prominent Shawnee leaders, including 640 acres to Nancy Stewart, daughter of the late Shawnee chief Blue Jacket, also reinforced their power. Land grants, education, and federal employment all bolstered the status of a small number of leading families among the Ohio Shawnees and among other Great Lakes tribes. Indeed, by 1830, fifteen hundred Indian students, most from tribes still living east of the Mississippi, were attending fifty-two schools funded by the federal government.[34]

Black Hoof and other Shawnee "treaty chiefs" used their position to benefit their families. Those Shawnees with access to the agents or missionaries enjoyed access to influence and materials goods, while the less fortunate had to rely on the patronage of their kinsmen. Quaker missionary Henry

Harvey noted that 40 percent of the money earmarked for improvements to reservation lands went to a handful of Shawnee chiefs. Fewer than five Shawnee leaders at Wapakoneta and Hog Creek controlled nearly half of all Shawnee assets between 1815 and 1832.[35] Treaty commissioners furthered their influence by paying chiefs who attended treaty negotiations.

These tactics contributed to the increasing dissonance between tribal chiefs and the rank-and-file members of the tribe they claimed to represent. Federal officials also undermined Black Hoof's influence. Although Wapakoneta continued to be the dominant Shawnee village in Ohio, the Treaty of Fort Meigs had recognized two other Ohio Shawnee villages, Hog Creek and Lewistown, as autonomous or separate political units. Village leaders at each locale controlled their own village's resources, but they were jealous of each other's influence, and American policymakers increasingly pitted them against each other in a contest for control of the tribe as a whole. In 1818, at the Treaty of St. Mary's, negotiators purchased a small section of eastern Ohio from the Miamis, but they assigned additional acreages from the tract to the Wapakoneta and Lewistown reservations. The Shawnees at Hog Creek received nothing. Moreover, federal agents took pains to differentiate between the mixed population of Shawnees and Senecas at Lewistown, assigning one section of lands to the Shawnees and another to the Senecas.[36]

Regardless of the cooperation between Black Hoof, the missionaries, and well-meaning Indian agents, tension between the Shawnees and other Americans increased. The Shawnees caused part of the problems. Although they had ceded lands in Ohio during the Fort Meigs (1817) and St. Mary's (1818) treaties, and had agreed to occupy smaller reservation tracts, during the winter months they regularly left their reservations to hunt, trap, or even to make maple sugar. They often strayed into Hamilton and Madison counties, in Indiana, and even ranged as far southwest as Vincennes, to barter pelts for trade goods. Morris Birkbeck, an English Quaker who later published a diary of his travels in the Midwest, reported that "considerable numbers" of Indians traveled to Vincennes "to trade fur for skins." Birkbeck was clearly surprised by the "motley assemblage of inhabitants and visitors" who traded at the post, including a Shawnee hunter who was "well remembered . . . for the trouble he gave during the late war."[37]

Encounters between "roving Indians" and settlers sometimes led to violence. In May 1824, a small party of frontier "neer-do-wells" massacred nine Seneca and Shawnee Indians near modern Markleville, Indiana, as they rested in their hunting camp. Surprisingly, three of the murderers were hanged for their crimes, the first time that Americans were found guilty of murdering Indians in Indiana.[38] But the Indians' victory in court was fleeting. Most frontier Americans were eager to acquire the remaining Indian lands and staunchly supported the removal of all tribes to the west. In Ohio, the Shawnees, Wyandots, and other tribes who continued to occupy small reservations came under increased attack by white frontiersmen who trespassed upon Indian lands and destroyed tribal property. Wyandots residing along the Sandusky River regularly complained about illegal hunters who killed game and raided their beehives. The Shawnees repeatedly discovered "hogs shot down . . . and in other cases a half, or quarter of the animal taken off and the rest left to the great loss and vexation of the Indians." Settlers regularly wreaked havoc on Indian homes and property while tribespeople were away on their winter hunts. Some of this intimidation was obviously designed to break the Shawnees' morale and force them to leave the state, but the Shawnees persisted. The Wapakoneta Shawnees still held title to over 19,000 acres, while the Wyandots owned another 85,680 acres. Well ensconced, they were embattled, but they refused to be intimidated.[39]

Aware of the harassment, the Quakers rallied to the Shawnees' defense. Isaac Harvey and William Hadley, two Quaker missionaries working among the Shawnees at Wapakoneta, attempted to buttress the Shawnees' reserve by purchasing land surrounding their reservation. In addition, the Baltimore, Ohio, and Indiana Yearly Meeting of Friends set aside money to purchase additional acreages, so that Shawnee fields located near the reservation boundaries, and therefore vulnerable to American depredations, might be protected. Yet the Quakers' benevolence angered settlers (many of whom were from Virginia and Kentucky) who reviled the Quakers as "meddlers," or even worse, "abolitionists."[40]

John Johnston also attempted to help the Shawnees, but he ran afoul of politicians in Washington. An ardent expansionist, Secretary of War John C. Calhoun served as Johnston's superior and he favored removing the Indians to the west. He encouraged Johnston to champion Indian removal and grew suspicious when Johnston pleaded for "the privilege of dealing with the Indians in my own way." Accused of being "unfriendly to the removal of the Indians," Johnston was also plagued by charges of nepotism and fraud from local and state politicians who attempted to secure his removal from office. He was forced to respond to accusations that enmeshed him in reams of paperwork but prevented him from adequately addressing the Shawnees' problems.[41]

Like many tribal chiefs, the Shawnee leaders believed that if they could meet with the president or some of his close advisors in the capital, they could convince them to allow their people to remain in Ohio. Johnston at first opposed the trip but eventually acquiesced, claiming, "I will have no peace until a delegation from my Indians is permitted to go to Washington." The Shawnees wanted to change the land tenure provided for their Ohio reservations by the Treaty of St. Mary's. In the treaty the government had increased the size of the reservations but had terminated previous Shawnee patents to these tracts. Instead, the treaty had "reserved [the reservation] for the use of the Indians . . . unless ceded to the United States." But as pressure for Shawnees' removal mounted, Black Hoof and other chiefs became alarmed that the government might arbitrarily terminate their reservations. They wanted President James Monroe to personally guarantee they could remain in their homelands.[42]

In the spring of 1821, federal officials reluctantly permitted a delegation of Shawnee and Seneca chiefs (Black Hoof, Wolf, John Perry, and Colonel Lewis) to travel to the capital. En route, the Shawnees again sought help from the Quakers. On April 11, 1821, the chiefs met with P. E. Thomas, an influential member of the Baltimore Yearly Meeting of Friends, who first arranged a meeting with Secretary of War John C. Calhoun, then accompanied the delegation on to Washington. The meeting did not go well. In addition to their attempts to secure land patents, the Shawnees also sought small reservations for the descendants of pro-American Shawnee warriors killed during the War of 1812. Similar small individual tracts had provided neighboring Miamis and Potawatomis with de facto reservations after their communal reservation lands were sold. Calhoun met with the Shawnees, but he refused most of their requests. Disappointed, the Shawnees first authorized Thomas to use most of their 1821 annuity funds to purchase livestock and other goods for the tribe; then they returned to their homes.[43]

In Ohio, political pressure for Shawnee removal increased. Governor Ethan Allen Brown and other state officials complained that although the Shawnees were "morally depraved," they still occupied "the most prominent situations" in Ohio. According to the governor and his political allies, the continued Shawnee presence at Wapakoneta "retard(ed) the improvements of the country." They flooded both Johnston and federal officials in Washington with accusations that the Shawnees were drinking to excess and committing depredations against white homesteaders. In February 1824, Will Oliver, a removal advocate and close friend of the governor, met with Johnston at Johnston's home and lodged a series of formal complaints. In response, Johnston admitted, "The cases are not rare where I have to give them money to pay their Tavern bills," and he assured Oliver that he believed the Shawnees eventually would sell their reservations and move west of the Mississippi."[44]

Johnston's growing support for removal resulted from several factors. Unquestionably, he was susceptible to political pressure from both his superiors, and from state and local officials, but he also was concerned about the Shawnees increased dependence on alcohol. By the mid-1820s, frontier grog shops abounded in the region, and growing numbers of tribespeople, including some influential chiefs, frequented them. Capt. John Perry, one of Black Hoof's secondary chiefs, became so addicted to whiskey that he clashed repeatedly with local settlers, eventually stabbing several white patrons, including the editor of a local newspaper, while drinking at a tavern in Piqua, Ohio. Other Shawnees interceded in his behalf, and charges against Perry were eventually dismissed, but the incident seemed to epitomize the continued difficulties between the Shawnees and their white neighbors.[45] Although Johnston had once advocated the integration of Native American and white farmers, by 1824 he believed that both Indians and whites would be better off living in separate worlds. He conceded that "effects on the Indians of the increase of the whites on the continent" had been "dreadful" and "contaminating." His official reports to Washington reflected a growing pessimism about the Shawnees commitment to the government's "civilization" program and their ability to manage their own annuity funds. Yet unlike neighboring whites, Johnston claimed his support of removal was motivated not by greed but by altruism. In a letter to Governor Brown, Johnston explained, "I am as anxious as any man to move the Indians from a sincere regard for them."[46]

The Shawnees' attempt to remain in Ohio was further undermined when federal officials allowed Tenskwatawa, Tecumseh's brother and an old rival of Black Hoof's, to return to the United States from his forced exile in Canada. Following the War of 1812, Tenskwatawa had lost most of his influence, but he remained a persuasive orator, and in return for federal permission to return to the United States, he promised Lewis Cass, the Governor of Michigan Territory, that he would prevail upon the Shawnees in Ohio to remove to the West. Cass agreed, and in May 1825 Cass and Tenskwatawa met in council with the Shawnees at Wapakoneta and championed their removal to the West. Most of Black Hoof's followers rejected their pleas, but some were alarmed by the steady migration of white settlers into the region and by the depredation of Shawnee crops and livestock. Cass returned to Detroit, but Tenskwatawa remained at Wapakoneta, and by the following summer he had persuaded 250 Shawnees to voluntarily emigrate from Ohio. In September 1826, to the consternation of Black Hoof, these Shawnees, ostensibly now led by Tenskwatawa, abandoned their villages and removed west of the Mississippi.[47]

The Shawnees who remained in Ohio were saddened by their kinsmen's departure, but they were determined to stay in their homeland. Afraid that the recent exodus might spur state and local politicians to demand that they follow in their kinsmen's wake, Black Hoof and other chiefs sought to buttress their ties with the Quakers, whom they believed also opposed removal and who were their most dependable allies. When Methodist missionaries attempted to proselytize the tribe, they rejected them as untrustworthy and declared that the Quakers were "the only real peaceable people that we can find . . . they do not change."[48] Moreover, they emphasized that they had embraced the government's "civilization" program and were endeavoring to become small farmers. According to Wewellipu, a spokesman from Wapakoneta, the Shawnees "know we cannot remain here without changing our habits and customs," but the tribespeople were willing to do so. In addition, the villagers remaining at Wapakoneta even tried to put a positive "spin" on the recent removal of Tenskwatawa and some of their kinsmen. They assured local officials that they were ready to join frontier society, for their "bad people have all gone to the West and left us."[49]

Ironically, Shawnee success at adapting to American ways sparked a backlash among some white Ohioans. Indeed, as the tribespeople produced growing harvests of corn and wheat or sold increased numbers of livestock at local or regional markets, some Ohioans worried that they were "fitting in" too well. Residents near the Shawnee/Seneca reservation at Lewistown became alarmed that the Indians might leave their reservation communities entirely and integrate themselves into American settlements. They were particularly outraged that other white Ohioans (particularly the Quakers) might encourage such integration. In 1829, residents of Bellafontaine complained to Governor Allen Trimble that "a number of the inhabitants [who] are but little better than the Red Brethren around us" had informed the Shawnees "that they are entitled to all the privileges of the white male inhabitants of our country . . . which is no small grievance to the honorable part of this community." Obviously, the "honorable part" of Bellefontaine's citizenry wanted such integration to stop.[50]

Yet other Ohioans, although a minority, rallied to the Shawnees' defense. In eastern Ohio, the "Ladies of Steubenville" advocated a more pluralistic racial and political society. In a memorial to Congress, they attempted to shame white, male voters, declaring that "*there are times* when duty and affection call on us to *advise* and *persuade* . . . our husbands and brothers" to treat Indian people more equitably. Determined to fight the Indian removal, the ladies of Steubenville argued that the Shawnees and others possessed an "*undoubted natural right*" to their lands in Ohio.[51]

Andrew Jackson disagreed. In 1828 Jackson was elected president of the United States, and two years later his supporters pushed the Indian Removal Bill through Congress. Pressure for removal increased, and during the late spring of 1831, the Shawnees lost their staunchest opponent of removal to the west. Nearing age ninety, the elderly Black Hoof died at Wapakoneta in May or June 1831. Quaker missionary Henry Harvey aptly memorialized the old chief, writing that "he was always an advocate for his own nation" and that "he was of such an age that recollections carried him back" to Shawnee dealings with William Penn in eighteenth-century Pennsylvania. The Shawnees honored the old chief with an elaborate funeral. Shawnee hunters scoured the forests for two days, killing several deer and turkeys, and after a large funeral feast was held in his honor, Black Hoof's body, covered in a blanket and wrapped in calico, belts, and ribbons, was laid to rest in the soil of his beloved homeland. John Perry, the middle-aged warrior who had accompanied Black Hoof on his victory tour through Kentucky in 1816, led the funeral procession. Though much younger and inexperienced than Black Hoof, John Perry now became the head chief of the Shawnees remaining in Ohio.[52]

The transition in leadership from Black Hoof to Perry marked the beginning of a new era in Shawnee life. Shawnee leaders such as Tecumseh, Blue Jacket, Tenskwatawa, and Black Hoof all initially had opposed the American occupation of Ohio. Blue Jacket died in 1808, and Tecumseh had been killed fighting the Americans. Black Hoof and Tenskwatawa eventually came to terms with the Americans; however, Black Hoof had chosen to cooperate only because he believed that accommodation offered the singular hope of remaining in Ohio. He regarded most Americans as a "necessary evil," not as friends. In contrast, John Perry and other younger Shawnee leaders had learned of the old struggles against the Americans through stories rather than hard experience. As a young man, he had fought alongside American soldiers in the War of 1812. Perry and others like him had gained prestige and positions of leadership through alliances with Americans, first in war and later through missionaries and their schools.[53]

During the summer of 1831, less than two months after Black Hoof's death, American officials met with Perry and other Shawnee leaders at Wapakoneta and Lewistown. James Gardiner, the principal American spokesman, pressed the Shawnees for a removal treaty and outlined their fate if they continued to remain in Ohio. According to Gardiner, the Shawnees would have to pay taxes exclusively "for the benefit of the white people" and would be required to work on public roads. Moreover, the government no longer would intercede on the Shawnees' behalf in cases of violence between Indians and whites. Gardiner warned the Shawnees that "they might be beaten or killed by white men" and that "no matter how many Indians [were] present—unless they could prove it by a white man, they had, or would have, no remedy." Denied legal protection, most Shawnees understood Gardiner's words to mean that the increasing pattern of intimidation and depredations they had endured during the past decade now would escalate. Bereft of Black Hoof's leadership and threatened with continued discrimination, the Wapakoneta Shawnees signed a removal treaty in August 1831.[54]

In the aftermath of the treaty, the Shawnees felt abandoned. They believed that they had endeavored to make the changes that the government had requested, but that Jacksonian Democrats in Washington had succumbed to local political pressure from Ohio and forced a removal treaty upon them. Unlike the Cherokees, they did not struggle against removal through a series of highly publicized court cases, but they had attempted to meet quietly with both missionaries and local officials in an attempt to fit into frontier society in Ohio. Ironically, their success at accommodation only kindled white Ohioans' fears that they never would leave. After signing the removal treaty, an embittered Wewellipu charged that the Shawnees had been cheated by the same men who once had promised the tribe a permanent home. Turning to Gardiner, Wewellipu reminded him that the Shawnees already "have good homes here" and that it had taken "an abundance of labor and pains to make them." The government, according to Wewellipu, had ignored the Shawnees' "progress" and capitulated to the demands of the American settlers who now surrounded them. The Shawnees had honored their promises; the federal government had betrayed them.[55]

During the fall of 1832, most of the Shawnees residing at Wapakoneta, Hog Creek, or Lewistown left Ohio for the West. They eventually were united with their kinsmen on reservations in Indian Territory. Their departure from Ohio closed a chapter in their long struggle to retain tribal lands in the state. Ironically, however, their unsuccessful efforts to remain in Ohio eventually served them well in the West. Tactics and negotiating skills honed in the defense of their Ohio reservations enabled them to negotiate successfully with missionaries and Indian agents in the West. After joining with other Shawnee bands that earlier had emigrated across the Mississippi, many of these recent emigrants rapidly rose to positions of leadership. They would use the political experiences they had gained in their struggle to remain in Ohio to forge a new Shawnee nation in the West.[56]

Notes

1. "Journal of the Ensign William Schillinger: A Soldier of the War of 1812," *Ohio Archaeological and Historical Quarterly* 41 (January 1932): 80, 82.

2. John Mack Faragher, *Women and Men on the Overland Trail* (New Haven, Conn.: Yale University Press, 1979), 50.

3. John Johnston to Benjamin Drake, 30 March 1833, *The Papers of John Johnston, Indian Agent,* from the Draper Collection, vol. 11YY, in the State Historical Society of Wiscon-

sin. Transcribed and edited by Richard C. Knopf (Columbus: Ohio Historical Society), 39–41.

4. Johnston quoted in R. Douglas Hurt, *The Ohio Frontier: Crucible of the Old Northwest, 1720–1830* (Bloomington: Indiana University Press, 1996), 342.

5. "Journal of Ensign William Schillinger," 83.

6. For more on the differences between frontier inhabitants after the Treaty of Ghent, see Andrew Cayton, *Frontier Indiana* (Bloomington: Indiana University Press, 1996), 262. *Niles Weekly Register,* 23 September 1815, 64. For the "perceived racial differences between native and newcomer," see Elizabeth A. Perkins, "Distinctions and Partitions among Us: Identity and Interaction in the Revolutionary Ohio Valley," in *Contact Points: American Frontiers from the Mohawk Valley to the Mississippi, 1750–1830,* ed. Andrew R. L. Cayton and Fredrika J. Teute (Chapel Hill: University of North Carolina Press, 1998), 234.

7. "John and William Perry," *Niles Weekly Register,* 7 September 1816, 32.

8. Lucien Beckner, "Eskippakithiki: The Last Indian Town in Kentucky," *Filson Club Historical Quarterly* 6 (October 1932): 379. R. David Edmunds, "'A Watchful Safeguard to Our Habitations': Black Hoof and the Loyal Shawnees," in *Native Americans and the Early Republic,* ed. Frederick E. Hoxie, Ronald Hoffman, and Peter J. Albert (Charlottesville: University Press of Virginia, 1999), 186–87.

9. "John and William Perry," *Niles Weekly Register,* 7 September 1816, 32.

10. George W. Knepper, *Ohio and Its People* (Kent, Ohio: Kent State University Press, 1997), 115–16.

11. "Report of Mr. Benton, Committee on Indian Affairs," 18th Cong. 1st sess., 14 May 1824, 79. Hurt, *Ohio Frontier,* 375. Cayton, *Frontier Indiana,* 264. Samuel R. Brown, "From *The Western Gazetteer;* or, Emigrant's Directory," in *Indiana as Seen by Early Travelers, Indiana Historical Collections, Vol. III,* ed. Harlow Lindley (Indianapolis: Indiana Historical Collections, 1916), 148.

12. Timothy D. Willig, "Prophetstown on the Wabash: The Native Spiritual Defense of the Old Northwest," *Michigan Historical Review* 23 (Fall 1997): 115–58; Ronald Miriani, "Against the Wind: The Shawnee at Wapakoneta," *Queen City Heritage* 48 (Spring 1990). Black Hoof quoted in letter from John Johnston to J. C. Calhoun, 20 January 1819, Shawnee File, Great Lakes–Ohio Valley Indian Archives, Glenn A. Black Laboratory of Archaeology, Indiana University, Bloomington (hereinafter cited as GBLA).

13. Benjamin Stickney to William H. Crawford, 12 November 1815, Shawnee File, GBLA. Michael McConnell, *A Country Between: The Upper Ohio Valley and Its Peoples, 1724–1774* (Lincoln: University of Nebraska Press, 1992).

14. John Johnston to the Secretary of War, 26 November 1816, Shawnee File, GBLA; Shawnee Chiefs to the Secretary of War, 29 December 1815, Shawnee File, GBLA.

15. Shawnee Chiefs to the Secretary of War, 29 December 1815, Shawnee file, GBLA. For more on government policies and the creation of modern tribal identities, see Alexandra Harmon, *Indians in the Making: Ethnic Relations and Indian Identities around Puget Sound* (Berkeley: University of California Press, 1998), esp. 103.

16. "Treaty with the Shawnee, 1831," in *Indian Affairs: Laws and Treaties,* ed. Charles J. Kappler, 2 vols. (Washington: Government Printing Office, 1904), 2:238.

17. James Ellicott and Philip E. Thomas, "Report on the Feasability of Introducing Farming and Other Activities among the Indians at Waupaghkonnetta and Lewis Town

by the Society of Friends," 1 August 1816, Shawnee File, GBLA; Leonard U. Hill, *John Johnston and the Indians in the Land of the Three Miamis* (Columbus, Ohio: Stoneman Press, 1957), 95.

18. Knepper, *Ohio and Its People,* 130. James H. Howard, *Shawnee! The Ceremonialism of a Native American Tribe and Its Cultural Background* (Athens: Ohio University Press, 1981), 49–52.

19. Henry Harvey, *History of the Shawnee Indians, from the Year 1681 to 1854, Inclusive* (Cincinnati: E. Morgan, 1855), 131; Shawnee Chiefs to the Secretary of War, 29 December 1815, Shawnee File, GBLA. Ellicott and Thomas, "Report on the Feasibility of Farming."

20. John Mack Faragher, *Daniel Boone: The Life and Legend of an American Pioneer* (New York: Holt, 1992); Gregory C. Dowd, *A Spirited Resistance: The North American Indian Struggle for Unity, 1745–1815* (Baltimore: Johns Hopkins University Press, 1992), 6.

21. For more on the Quaker model, see A. F. C. Wallace, *The Death and Rebirth of the Seneca* (New York: Vintage Books, 1972), 272–77. The best single source on the Quaker missions to the Shawnees is Harvey, *History of the Shawnee Indians.*

22. Benjamin Hallowell, "Memorial of the Religious Society of Friends, in the States of Ohio, Indiana, and Illinois, Praying for the Adoption of Measures for the Civilization and Improvement of the Indians," 23 December 1818 (Columbus: Ohio Historical Society); Benjamin Hallowell, "Memorial of the Society of Friends in Regard to the Indians," n.d. (Columbus: Ohio Historical Society). For information on the Society of Friends and the effect of their missions, see Joy Bilharz, "First among Equals: The Changing Status of Seneca Women," in *Women and Power in Native North America* (Norman: University of Oklahoma Press, 1995); see also Thomas D. Hamm, *The Transformation of American Quakerism, Orthodox Friends, 1800–1907* (Bloomington: Indiana University Press, 1988), 22.

23. Joseph Rhodes, "Diary of Joseph and Martha Rhodes' Mission to the Shawnee Indians, 1817: Part of the Story" (Columbus: Ohio Historical Society).

24. Ibid.

25. John Johnston to Charles Cist, 14 May 1846, *The Papers of John Johnston,* Ohio Historical Society, 71–72; John Wolf to John Johnston, 20 July 1846, mss. 42, roll 3a, (Cincinnati Historical Society, Cincinnati).

26. Ellicott and Thomas, "Report on the Feasibility of Introducing Farming"; John Johnston to William H. Crawford, 22 October 1816, Shawnee File, GBLA; The Chiefs and Headmen of the Shawanoes Tribe of Indians to the President of the United States, 20 April 1809, in *Letter Book of the Indian Agency at Fort Wayne, 1809–1815,* ed. Gayle Thornbrough (Indianapolis: Indiana Historical Collections, 1961), 22: 45.

27. Johnston to Drake, 30 March 1833, in *Papers of John Johnston,* 39–41.

28. Hill, *John Johnston and the Indians,* 97.

29. R. Douglas Hurt, *Ohio Frontier,* 175; John Mack Faragher, *Sugar Creek: Life on the Illinois Prairie* (New Haven, Conn.: Yale University Press, 1986), 71.

30. Lewis Cass to Duncan McArthur, 24 May 1818, RG 75, M1, roll 3, Michigan Superintendency, National Archives; McArthur to Johnston, 26 July 1818, Johnston Papers, mss. 42, roll 3a, Cincinnati Historical Society. Also see Cass to William Crawford, 24 April 1816, Shawnee File, GBLA.

31. John Johnston to Lewis Cass, 13 June 1817, Shawnee File, GBLA.

32. Harvey, *History of the Shawnee Indians*, 164–66. "Treaty with the Wyandots, etc., 1817" in Kappler, *Indian Treaties*, 2:235.

33. Treaty annuity payments were annual disbursements of either cash or goods for a specific period or in perpetuity.

34. John Johnston to George Graham, 6 January 1817, Shawnee file, GBLA; "Treaty with the Wyandots, etc., 1817," in Kappler, *Indian Treaties*, 2:235. Francis P. Prucha, *The Great Father: The United States Government and the American Indians*, 2 vols. (Lincoln: University of Nebraska Press, 1984), 1:154.

35. Harvey, *History of the Shawnee Indians*, 226.

36. Duncan McArthur to John Johnston, 26 July 1818, Johnston Papers, mss. 42, roll 3a (Cincinnati: Cincinnati Historical Society); "Treaty with the Wyandots, etc., 1818," in Kappler, *Indian Treaties*, 2:255–56.

37. Lewis Cass to Duncan McArthur, 18 September 1818, *American State Papers: Indian Affairs*, 2 vols. (Washington: Gales and Seaton, 1832–1834), 2:177; C. Vandeventer to Lewis Cass, 29 June 1818, ibid., 175–76. Morris Birkbeck, *Notes on a Journey in America from the Coast of Virginia to the Territory of Illinois* in Lindley, *Indiana as Seen by Early Travelers*, 181.

38. For more on the massacre, see Brian M. Doerr, "The Massacre at Deer Lick Creek, Madison County, Indiana, 1824," *Indiana Magazine of History* 43 (March 1997): 19–47; R. David Edmunds, "Justice on a Changing Frontier: Deer Lick Creek, 1824–1825," ibid., 48–52. Also see Ronald N. Satz, *American Indian Policy in the Jacksonian Era* (Lincoln: University of Nebraska Press, 1975), 45.

39. "Mount-Pleasant," *Niles Weekly Register*, December 12, 1818, 268. Faragher, *Sugar Creek*, 66, 71. John Shaw to Lewis Cass, 11 November 1820, Shawnee File, GBLA. For more on white homesteads in the Midwest, see Knepper, *Ohio and Its Peoples*, 117; Cayton, *Frontier Indiana*, 179.

40. Indiana Yearly Meeting of Friends, *Minutes of the Indiana Yearly Meeting of Friends Held at Richmond, Indiana* (Richmond: Ballinger Press, 1821–1822), 8. For racial prejudice on the Ohio frontier, see Hurt, *Ohio Frontier*, 386–88.

41. John Johnston to J. C. Calhoun, 20 January 1819, Shawnee File, GBLA. John Johnston to Lewis Cass, 9 May 1820, RG75, M1, roll 7.

42. R. David Edmunds, *The Shawnee Prophet* (Lincoln: University of Nebraska Press, 1983) 166–67; "Treaty with the Wyandots, etc., 1818," in Kappler, *Indian Treaties*, 2:255–56. Also see Leonard U. Hill, *John Johnston and the Indians*, 106; and John Johnston to Lewis Cass, 9 May 1820, Shawnee File, GBLA.

43. Philip E. Thomas to J. C. Calhoun, 11 April 1820, Shawnee File, GBLA. John Calhoun to John Johnston, 21 April 1821, RG75, M1, roll 8. Charles F. Wilkinson, "Indian Tribes and the American Constitution," in *Indians in American History*, ed. Frederick E. Hoxie and Peter Iverson (Wheeling: Harlan Davidson, 1998), 109–10.

44. Will Oliver to Ethan Allen Brown, 3 February 1824, folder 4, box 3, roll 4, Ethan Allen Brown Papers (Columbus: Ohio Historical Society). Oliver to Brown, 23 February 1824, ibid.

45. "Indians," *Niles Weekly Register*, July 28, 1827, 559–60.

46. John Johnston to Ethan A. Brown, 31 July 1821, folder 9, box 2, roll 3, Ethan Allen Brown Papers (Columbus: Ohio Historical Society); John Johnston to E. A. Brown, 27

January 1824, folder 4, box 3, roll 4, ibid.; John C. Calhoun to John Johnston, 10 April 1821, RG75, M1, roll 8 (National Archives).

47. Edmunds, *Shawnee Prophet,* 173–74.

48. "Wapaghkonetta," *Piqua Gazette,* July 9, 1825, 14.

49. Ibid. Also see Donald L. Huber, "White, Red, and Black: The Wyandot Mission at Upper Sandusky," *Timeline* (May/June 1996): 14, 17.

50. Citizens of Bellafontaine to Allen Trimble, 3 April 1829, folder 10, box 1, roll 1, Allen Trimble Papers (Columbus: Ohio Historical Society).

51. "Memorial of the Ladies of Steubenville, Ohio: Against the Forcible Removal of the Indians without the Limits of the United States," 15 February 1830 [rep. no. 209], 21st Cong., 1st sess. (Columbus: Ohio Historical Society).

52. Harvey, *History of the Shawnee Indians,* 185–89.

53. Blue Jacket died in 1808 near Detroit, still opposed to American expansion. Tecumseh was killed in October 1813, at the Battle of the Thames. Tenskwatawa died in Kansas in 1836. See John Sugden, *Blue Jacket: Warrior of the Shawnees* (Lincoln: University of Nebraska Press, 2000), 254, 311–12n1; R. David Edmunds, *Tecumseh and the Quest for Indian Leadership* (Boston: Little, 1985), 208–12; Edmunds, *Shawnee Prophet,* 187.

54. Harvey, *History of the Shawnee Indians,* 193–94.

55. Ibid., 197–98. For examples of scholars who place the blame for removal on American Indians, see Reginald Horsman, *Expansion and American Indian Policy, 1783–1812* (East Lansing: Michigan State University Press, 1967), 170. See also Hurt, *Ohio Frontier,* 4. Robert V. Remini, *Andrew Jackson and His Indian Wars* (New York: Viking, 2001).

56. Grant Foreman, *The Last Trek of the Indians* (Chicago: University of Chicago Press), 71–85.

5. Jean Baptiste Richardville

Miami Métis

BRADLEY J. BIRZER

In the two decades that followed the War of 1812, Anglo-Americans flocked into the territories north of the Ohio and east of the Mississippi rivers. Indeed, as the region's population increased, three new states, Indiana (1816), Illinois (1818), and Michigan (1837) entered the union. Yet new Anglo-American immigrants were not the only residents of the region. All three states, plus the future states of Wisconsin and Minnesota, boasted large numbers of Native American people. Many of these people were métis: a people of mixed Indian-Creole French, or even Indian-Celtic lineage, but since they often functioned as part of larger Native American communities, they generally were described as "half-breed Indians" by their new Anglo-American neighbors.

Population figures for métis people in this region are hard to ascertain, but by all accounts they were numerous: as many as fifteen thousand. Although the percentage of the métis population differed considerably from tribe to tribe, among the Miami Indians of Indiana they were particularly prominent. The Miamis had long intermarried with the Creole-French, and American officials complained that the Miami tribe was replete with "French traders, boatmen, half bloods, and those who had, or thought it probable that they might have had children by Indian women." Both Indian agents and missionaries had difficulty ascertaining the lineage of members of the Miami villages, and in 1826 Governor James Ray of Indiana reported that he believed the Miamis had become so intermarried with Europeans that the entire tribe consisted of people of mixed lineage. According to Ray, there were "not twenty genuine (full-blood) Miamis in that nation."[1]

The genetic and cultural amalgamation that produced the métis endured. In the late seventeenth century, French traders who had journeyed among the Great Lakes tribes had been welcomed by the Miamis, and many had married Miami women and fathered growing families. During the 1700s this biological blending had increased, augmented by an interchange of Miami and European cultures, so that "the boundaries" of the Miami and Creole French worlds "melted at the edges and merged." According to historian Richard White, "Although identifiable Frenchmen and identifiable Indians obviously continued to exist, whether a particular practice or way of doing things was French or Indian was, after a time, not so clear." The Miami métis were part of the tribal communities, but they had adopted many tenets of Creole French culture.[2]

This acculturation manifested itself in the métis' economic activities. Unlike the agriculturally oriented Anglo-American settlers, many of the early French inhabitants had been traders, not farmers, and the métis followed in their fathers' footsteps. Traders were men of wealth and influence but were free from the monotonous labor associated with agriculture. Moreover, the traders' close ties with the Indian communities enabled the merchants to pass freely among the tribal villages. Most traders (and métis) were fluent in the tribal languages, but they also possessed the rudiments of a frontier education. They kept sophisticated ledger books and dealt successfully with wholesalers in Canada and on the East Coast.[3]

The Miami métis were particularly influential in tribal affairs. When the fur trade deteriorated following the War of 1812, métis leaders shared their personal wealth with less fortunate tribespeople. This benevolence originally had been based on widespread kinship obligations, but the politically astute métis realized that generosity engendered political allegiance, and by the 1820s métis leaders had consolidated their power and served as middlemen in the tribe's negotiations with the government.

Federal agents might have cultivated métis leaders as cultural brokers between the tribes and the onrushing Americans, but the métis' political influence aroused the Indian agents' suspicions. Federal officials preferred to negotiate with less acculturated, more traditional Indian leaders. Moreover, the métis chiefs and their followers rarely used land for agricultural purposes, but they knew tribal lands in Indiana were valuable and they were reluctant to relinquish them. In response, Indian agents condemned the métis as "connivers" and claimed that their adherence to Roman Catholicism made them the agents of "foreign papists." In addition, some métis traders retained ties to British merchants in Canada, business relationships that also rankled Americans who still suspected British intrigue behind Indian resistance to any facet of American Indian policy. American descriptions of the métis reflected the Indian agents' acrimony. According to William Keating, in 1820 the Miami métis at Fort Wayne, Indiana, were a "mixed and apparently very worthless population, the inhabitants are chiefly of Canadian origin, all more or less imbued with Indian blood." Obviously, both American officials and American frontiersmen envisioned métis people as "obstacles to progress."[4]

The leading citizen of that "mixed and apparently very worthless population" at Fort Wayne was Miami métis Jean Baptiste Richardville. Richardville epitomized the successful métis traders who were active in Miami and other tribal politics in the early nineteenth century. Born near Fort Wayne around 1761, Richardville (also known as "Peshawa" of "the Wildcat") was the son of Joseph Drouet de Richardsville, a French trader, and Taucumwah, a sister of the prominent Miami civil and war chief Pacanne. Richardville's father returned to Canada, and Richardville evidently spent some time with him, for he attended school at Three Rivers in Ontario. Taucumwah remarried another trader, Charles Beaubien, and Richardville soon returned to Indiana, where he lived with his mother and stepfather in Kekionga, the Miami village near Fort Wayne. Richardville learned the "Indian trade" from his stepfather and mother, and during the American Revolution he seems to have favored the British, although his role in the conflict is uncertain.[5]

Following the war, Richardville remained at Kekionga and became associated with the Miami chief Little Turtle. Although he maintained commercial ties with British traders at Detroit, he did not participate in the border warfare of the 1790s; like Little Turtle, he favored negotiating with Anthony Wayne prior to the Battle of Fallen Timbers. He already had emerged as a spokesperson for the Miamis, for in 1795 he signed the Treaty of Greenville as a chief of the "Miamis and Eel Rivers." Meanwhile, he erected trading houses at the forks of the Maumee and the forks of the Wabash, dominating the portage between the two rivers and charging traders and other travelers to transport goods between the two watersheds. During the first decade of the nineteenth century he opposed the rise of Tecumseh and the Shawnee Prophet, journeying to Washington to meet with Thomas Jefferson and other officials. In 1802 and 1803 he signed treaties relinquishing Miami claims to lands in southern Indiana, but he initially opposed the Treaty of Fort Wayne (1809). He signed the document after federal officials agreed to recognize Miami claims to lands south of the Wabash. Richardville sought sanctuary in Canada during the War of 1812, but he did not support the British efforts, and American officials believed he had fled only for his personal safety.[6]

Although Richardville's lineage was half Miami, he appeared, according to one of his contemporaries, "more like a Frenchman than an Indian, . . . very tall . . . with blue eyes and features like the picture of Louis XIV." By all accounts, Richardville was a robust, handsome man with broad shoulders, a Roman nose, and dark hair, which grayed somewhat as he aged. Still, he maintained a youthful appearance, even in his later years. In 1834 a reporter who attended the Miami annuity payment mistakenly estimated the seventy-two-year-old métis to be no more than fifty.[7]

Richardville's contemporaries all agreed that he dressed well. Although he occasionally wore only European clothing ("a grey frock coat, blue cloth pantaloons, black vest, boots and spurs, and wore a black hat"), he more commonly dressed like other métis on the Indiana frontier; he combined European garments with traditional Miami attire. Richardville often wore a coat of blue cloth, gilt buttons, and a buff waistcoat, but he added broadcloth leggings, buckskin moccasins, a brightly colored sash, and large gold earrings. He may have emphasized his Indian clothing when he solicited political support within the Miami villages, but his garments reflected his status as a métis, an identity he valued. He rarely, if ever, dressed entirely in Miami clothing.[8]

Richardville was fluent in Miami, French, and English. He spoke Miami when meeting with tribal people, but he conversed in English with American officials. He also was literate in both English and French, and the Miamis relied on Richardville and other métis leaders such as Francis Godfroy to carefully examine and translate treaties, annuity receipts, and other important documents.

A shrewd businessman, Richardville's monopoly over the portage between the Maumee and Wabash rivers proved very profitable, and travelers on the Indian frontier described his home near Fort Wayne as "sumptuous, . . . handsome and genteel." Hugh McCulloch, who later served as the Secretary of the Treasury under Lincoln, described Richardville as "a man of great natural shrewdness and sagacity, of whom no one ever got the better in a trade." Wary of paper money, Richardville only accepted payment in specie, from either the government or private individuals. In 1816, when Indiana entered the union, he was reputed to be the richest man in the state.[9]

Prior to the War of 1812 Richardville had amassed a fortune in the fur trade, but in the postwar period, as the fur trade gradually declined, he refocused his commercial interests toward the "Indian business": the process of providing the Miamis and other tribes with food and supplies paid for by the federal government through the tribe's yearly annuity payments. Between 1818 and 1840 the Miamis ceded most of their lands in northern Indiana and southern Michigan, and in each case the federal government agreed to pay the accumulated debts of the tribe and provide them with increased annuities. Richardville either participated in or signed most of these agreements, and the funds resulting from these treaties and annuity payments often were dispersed at or near his trading posts.[10]

Obviously, Richardville's participation in these treaties worked to his personal advantage. The Miamis used their annuity funds to purchase supplies from Richardville's stores; moreover, he readily sold goods on credit to tribe members in between annuity payments and then collected the debts from federal paymasters before the remaining funds were dispersed to the tribe. Yet Richardville also extended both charity and goods on credit to impoverished tribespeople, assuming the role of a benevolent and caring village chief or *patron*. He supported indigent kinsmen and was known for his generosity throughout the Miami villages. In turn, as grateful tribespeople followed his advice, and acquiesced in his leadership, both his personal fortune and political influence increased.

Richardville's growing political power aroused the suspicions of federal Indian agents. Benjamin Stickney had been appointed Indian Agent at Fort Wayne in 1811, and he served in that position during the War of 1812. Following the war, however, Stickney believed that the British in Canada still exercised too much influence among the Indians in Indiana, and since Richardville had fled to Canada during the war, Stickney accused him of being a British agent. Richardville denied the charge, but Stickney asserted that the métis leader was a threat to the United States and even suggested that he be assassinated. Federal officials wisely refused, but Stickney continued his campaign to undermine Richardville's influence, even burning one of Richardville's trading posts after claiming that the métis had illegally sold liquor at the store. Both Richardville and other Miami leaders protested, and after federal officials investigated the charges, they reimbursed Richardville for the property he had lost. Stickney eventually lost his job, and Richardville's influence increased.[11]

Richardville also clashed with John Hays, one of Stickney's successors. Hays, who served as Indian agent at Fort Wayne from 1820 to 1823, also objected to Richardville's influence and described the chief as a "half breed" and a "trifling fellow [who] will say anything today, and deny it tomorrow to suit his own interest." Hays labored assiduously to minimize Richardville's control over the distribution of annuities. He complained that Miamis from the Wabash-Maumee portage and the mouth of the Mississinewa—tribespeople under Richardville's influence—continued to receive the lion's share of annuity payments, while other Miamis on the Eel River were underpaid. Hays personally distributed part of the Miami annuities on the Eel River, but Richardville wrote to Hays's superiors, alleging that the agent was incompetent, remained ignorant of most Miamis' band affiliations, and was financially irresponsible. Richardville ultimately prevailed, and in 1823 Hays resigned and moved to Illinois.[12]

Yet Richardville's dominance in the Miami trade engendered opposition from other traders. Charging that Richardville's dual role as head chief and primary merchant to the tribe created a conflict of interest, traders such as Alexis Coquillard, a merchant at South Bend, and Benjamin Kercheval, a former Indian agent and speculator at Fort Wayne, complained that Richardville used his influence among the Miamis in an attempt to monopolize their trade. Coquillard and Kercheval were joined by the Ewing brothers (William G. and George W.), who maintained trading posts at Fort Wayne, Logansport, and other locations in the Wabash and Maumee valleys. The Ewing brothers were notorious for luring Indians into debt, then "padding" or inflating Indian accounts with false entries until the amount of the original debt almost doubled. The Ewings (and other traders, including Richardville) then presented these debts to the government just prior to the annuity payments, demanding that the agents first pay the tribespeople's debts before distributing the annuities.[13]

Richardville feared the influence of non-Indian traders among the Miamis because he knew that increased debt made the tribe more vulnerable to federal influence. Though a trader himself, Richardville counseled the Miamis against excessive debt and warned them that the government would use such indebtedness as a pretext for taking their homelands and removing them to Kansas. In 1825, to minimize Miami indebtedness to outsiders (and to increase his own dominance over the Miami trade) Richardville erected additional trading posts on the Wabash and Mississinewa rivers. He then persuaded Le Gros, another Miami chief, to write to federal officials and request that he (Richardville) be allowed to distribute all annuity payments to the tribe. At Richardville's bidding, Le Gros also asked that Richardville be granted a trading monopoly among the Miamis "in order to prevent as much as possible the impositions practiced on the Indians by (other) traders."[14]

Although officials reluctantly approved of Richardville's new trading posts, they refused to allow him to oversee the distribution of all Miami annuities or to exercise a monopoly over the tribe's trade. In 1826 the Miamis met with federal officials and relinquished a large tract of land at the Treaty of the Mississinewa, but Indian agents were wary of Richardville's influence in the treaty proceedings and feared strengthening his hand. Local officials warned that with regard to the Miamis, Richardville "carries the key and nothing can be done without his assent," while the Logansport *Miami Times* reported that "no man ever had a people more completely under his control than Richardville has (over) the Miamis." In response, in 1829 John Tipton, the Miami Indian agent, moved the Miami annuity payments away from Richardville's trading posts.[15]

Tipton's action angered Richardville, who protested to Washington. Richardville's protest was supported by other Miami leaders, including his ally, Francis Godfroy, who sent a petition to Lewis Cass, complaining that Tipton had illegally and immorally "usurped a power which we do not believe properly belongs to his office." Moreover, the Miami chiefs complained that since the white settlers had either killed or frightened away all the game and fur-bearing animals, the tribe had been forced to sell much of its land and had become dependent on the federal government. The least the government could do, the Miami chiefs claimed, was to grant them the dignity of choosing the place for the annuity payment.[16]

The Ewing brothers, trading rivals of Richardville, were eager to exacerbate the dispute. After spreading rumors among the tribe that Tipton had boasted he "did not give a damn for Chief Richardville," William Ewing then wrote to Tipton, describing Richardville as a "false faced, former hypocritical friend, who hope(s) to throw obstacles in your road." According to Ewing, Richardville was determined to have Tipton removed as the Miami Indian agent.[17] Initially, the Ewings were successful. Both Richardville and Tipton were angered by the rumors, and relations between the two men deteriorated. Yet both men needed the other if they wished to continue in their current roles. Richardville envisioned himself as a buffer between the Miamis and the government, but he needed the support of both the tribe and Indian agents. To serve as the Miami spokesperson, he needed the support of the tribe, but his position as chief was enhanced by his role in disbursing annuities. When Tipton had moved the annuity payment, Richardville had asked the Miamis not to accept the annuities, but they desperately needed the money and supplies, and many had attended the payments in defiance of his requests. Richardville feared that if he removed himself completely from the annuity proceedings, his influence among the Miamis would decline.[18]

Tipton also needed Richardville. An ambitious man, Tipton realized that his political career was based on an image of success. He was familiar with frontier politics, and he knew that a prolonged struggle with Richardville and the Miami leadership, replete with numerous petitions to Washington, publicity in local newspapers, and charges and countercharges, would play into the hands of his enemies. He also knew that both the state of Indiana and the federal government were eager to acquire the remaining Indian lands in Indiana, and any government purchase of Miami lands would be much easier with Richardville's cooperation. Tipton could not afford to remain alienated from the Miami leader.[19]

Fortunately, Governor James Noble of Indiana interceded and the two men solved their differences. Like Tipton, Noble believed that Richardville had grown too powerful, but he also realized that federal officials would need Richardville's support to purchase remaining Miami lands in the state. Tipton backed down and agreed to distribute the annuities at a place of Richardville's choosing, and Richardville "apologized" to the agent. Tipton attempted to save face, insisting that he "would have paid the Miamis where Richerville wanted them paid" if the chief had only told him what the Miamis wanted, but privately Tipton boasted that he had "recd. the surrender of the Grate [*sic*] Chief Richerville." Yet from Richardville's perspective, the Miamis continued to receive their annuities adjacent to his or Francois Godfroy's trading posts, and Richardville's influence was not diminished.[20]

Some of Richardville's opponents may have been motivated by jealousy. He lived rather well: profits amassed from his trading posts and land speculation, coupled with federal payments for his role in negotiating treaties, enabled the métis to maintain two amply furnished residences, one at Fort Wayne and the other near his store on the Mississinewa. Frontier travelers described Richardville's home at Fort Wayne as "handsome" and "genteel," but in 1833 he moved from the city to the forks of the Wabash, just north of modern Huntington, where he erected a large frame house and several outbuildings. The house, built in the Greek Revival style, remained a showplace in the region for the rest of Richardville's life, and after his death it continued to be occupied by his descendants.[21]

Richardville was famous for his hospitality. He regularly entertained large numbers of friends, providing banquets of salt pork, hams, wild game and fowl, and seasonal fruits and vegetables. During the warm months, guests often were served "out-of-doors" and the meals were accompanied by bottles of wine, bourbon, and even French brandy. Indian Agent Abel C. Pepper claimed to have eaten the "best meal of his life" at Richardville's table, while Susan Man McCulloch, a Fort Wayne matron, reported that she dined upon dishes such as "broiled chicken and currant jelly."[22]

Dancing, serenades, card games, and other festivities often accompanied the feasts. Many of the métis were skilled musicians, particularly violinists or "fiddlers," and they provided merriment well into the night. On other occasions Richardville hosted horse races at his estate, inviting riders, both Indians and whites, from throughout the region. The races were occasions for betting and other gambling, but Richardville maintained a sense of decorum and order, and when arguments erupted, they quickly were defused. The "recollections" of many early Fort Wayne residents contain fond memories of their attendance at Richardville's estate. As Abel C. Pepper later recounted, "We do not live as well here (in Ft. Wayne), as we did there (at Richardville's estate near Huntington).[23]

Richardville also was blessed with a large family. In about 1800 Richardville had married Natoequah, a Miami woman, and the union produced at least two sons, Jean B. Jr. and Joseph, and three daughters, Maria Louisa ("LaBlonde"), Catherine ("Catees"), and Susan. The children also were prominent members of the greater Miami community. Both sons followed in their father's footsteps, serving as merchants and land speculators, while all of the daughters "married well." Susan married the trader Ossem; Maria Louisa married James Godfroy, the son of Francis Godfroy, the elder Richardville's business associate and political ally; Catherine married Francis Lafontaine, another wealthy métis who succeeded Richardville as "principal chief of the Miamis."[24]

Richardville's children were relatively well educated, but the chief seemed to have some misgivings about sending them to American schools. An ardent Catholic, Richardville was described by a contemporary as "somewhat bigoted in the principles of that sect (Roman Catholicism) and no person can convince him otherwise." He initially sent his children to Catholic boarding schools, and when the government set aside funds to educate Miami children, he requested that the money be used to finance parochial schools rather than public or Protestant institutions.[25]

Reflecting the anti-Catholic bias of the Jacksonian period, federal officials refused Richardville's request. They pressured Richardville and other métis leaders to enroll their sons at the Choctaw Boarding School, a multi-tribal boarding school maintained by government funds at Great Crossings, Kentucky. Richardville was hesitant to send Miami children to the institution because he disliked the school's emphasis on manual training. In 1836, however, Richardville finally agreed that his grandson, Lewis Cass Richardville, and several other Miami boys would "conditionally" enroll at the academy. If the boy's experiences proved successful, the Miamis would regularly send some of their children (and part of their educational annuities) to the institution.[26]

The trial enrollment proved disastrous. Richardville envisioned his grandson as eventually becoming a trader and wanted him to be educated "as his clerk, in the merchantile business." Instead, administrators at the school enrolled the boy in "the tailor trade," and Richardville was incensed. Moreover, he received reports that all the Miami students at the academy had been stripped of their fine clothing and were forced to wear "such coarse apparel as to make their parents ashamed of them." Richardville demanded that the students be returned to Indiana, and Indian agent Abel C. Pepper was dispatched to bring the boys home. Richardville later complained that he had little use for American schools, and that he believed neither his sons nor grandsons had ever learned anything useful in them.[27]

By the 1830s Richardville's influence among the Miamis was uncontested. Both the tribe and federal officials looked to him as a "middle-man" in negotiations between the two sides, and Richardville had utilized his office in these events to enhance both his personal fortune and his status in the Miami community. His enemies (and some historians) argued that Richardville used his role as a "go-between" to acquire large tracts of land for himself and his family, and upon first glance the charges seem to have merit. In 1818, at the Treaty of St. Mary's, he received seven sections of land near Fort Wayne and two more at the forks of the Wabash. Several other Miami chiefs also were awarded land at this treaty, but only Richardville was given permission to sell his lands without federal approval. He received an additional three and one-half sections at the 1826 Treaty of the Mississinewa; three and one-quarter sections at a treaty in 1834; twelve and one-half sections at a treaty in 1838; and seven sections at the final Miami removal treaty of 1840. Article IV of the 1834 treaty also transferred to Richardville "in fee simple" ten sections of land at the forks of the Wabash that previously had been set side "for the use of said [the Miami] tribe" in the 1826 Mississinewa Treaty. In summary, the total acreage awarded to Richardville between 1818 and 1840 amounted to forty-five square miles of Indiana farmland, or almost twenty-nine thousand acres. In addition, the treaties awarded other sections of land to his sons and friends and also provided funds for the construction of houses and the purchase of farm implements and animals for Richardville and his allies.[28]

Richardville used some of these lands for personal profits. He speculated in farmland and city lots in the Fort Wayne region and attempted unsuccessfully to plat a village near the forks of the Wabash. But much of the land he held in fee simple was shared with the Miami people. During the late 1820s and 1830s, as the government continued to purchase Miami lands in central Indiana, many Miami people moved onto Richardville's privately held land where he gave them sanctuary. Indeed, by the late 1830s most Miamis in Ohio resided on lands belonging to Richardville, Francis Godfroy, members of their families, or on the "Big Miami Reserve," a tribally held tract in modern Miami, Howard, and Tipton counties, just south of the Wabash in central Indiana. Some of these Miamis were traders, trappers, small farmers, or worked at odd jobs for surrounding settlers, but others eked out an existence through annuity payments and the largesse of Richardville and other prosperous merchants.[29]

Their days were numbered. By 1840 white settlement had advanced north of the Wabash and was spreading across the prairies toward Lake Michigan. Both state and local politicians clamored for the Miamis and other Indians to be removed from the state, and even Richardville admitted that many traditional Miamis seemed adrift in a world increasingly foreign to them. Federal agents reported that alcoholism and violence plagued the Miami villages, and growing numbers of tribespeople, both men and women, rarely left their homes without weapons. Now convinced that many Miamis would be happier in the west, in 1840 Richardville and his secretary, Allen Hamilton, drew up a treaty in which the Miamis agreed to cede the "residue of the Big Miami Reserve" to the government and to go west within five years. Yet removal was not universal. Although the Miami government would remove to Kansas, and all future tribal annuities would be paid in the west, many Miamis were exempt from the removal process. Members of the Richardville, Godfroy, and several other métis families were allowed to remain on their private lands in Indiana, and Meshingomesia was given a patent for the lands previously set aside for his band two years earlier. This small reservation would continue to be occupied by Meshingomesia's followers, but the chief would hold title to the lands. The government also agreed to pay the tribe's debts to local traders, to provide additional payments to members of Richardville's and Godfroy's families, to pay "every expense attending such removal, and to furnish rations to said tribe for twelve months after their arrival" in Kansas.[30]

Richardville and other Miami leaders signed the treaty on November 28, 1840, but Richardville, past age eighty, died less than a year later on August 13, 1841. Leadership of the Miami tribe passed to his son-in-law, Francis Lafontaine, but the younger man proved far less adept at walking the tightrope of leadership between the Miamis and the government, and in 1846, 323 Miamis, about two-thirds of the tribe, were removed to Kansas. Yet over 150 others, descendants of Richardville, Godfroy, or other métis, in addition to Meshingomesia's followers, remained behind on private lands in Indiana.[31]

Richardville epitomized the status of many métis people in the Great Lakes region. Truly a man "in between," he combined many cultural values from both of his parents' families, sometimes playing the role of Creole entrepreneur and land speculator, at other times functioning as the wise and munificent village chief. Unquestionably, Richardville profited personally from his position as negotiator for the tribe. Miami treaties signed between 1818 and 1840 contain numerous articles in which Richardville and his family and friends received sections of land, money, and other benefits. Obviously, much of this wealth became part of Richardville's personal estate, and he used it for his own purposes.

Yet Richardville labored diligently to protect the interests of the Miami tribe. Unfortunately, he was forced to fight a series of rear-guard actions. Defending Indian lands from American settlers in the Jacksonian era was a losing struggle, and although Richardville's tactics may have postponed Miami removal, they could not prevent it from taking place. Still, Richardville's strategy of obtaining lands in fee simple, both for himself and for other Miamis, had a profound effect on the future of the Miami people. The sections set aside for members of the Richardville and Godfroy families, and the small reservation held in fee simple by Meshingomesia, became islands of refuge, not only for Miamis opposed to removal, but also for Miamis who originally moved to Kansas and then returned to Indiana. By 1850 the Indiana Miami population had increased to 250; by 1870 it had grown to about 350. In 1895 it reached 440. Meanwhile, the Miami population in the west declined. By 1847, so many western Miami emigrants had already returned to Indiana that their population had declined to about 250; ten years later they numbered 205. In 1873, when the western Miamis were removed to a new reservation in Oklahoma, consolidated and attached to the Quapaw Agency, they numbered only seventy-two people.[32]

At the beginning of the twenty-first century the Miamis in Oklahoma number about fifteen hundred and continue to be recognized by the federal government as the "official" Miami tribe. In contrast, about twenty-eight hundred "unrecognized" Miamis still live in their old homelands. They, too, strongly identify as "Miami Indians" and maintain tribal offices in modern-day Peru, Indiana. These Indiana Miamis are the descendants of the Richardvilles, Godfroys, and other métis families; of Meshingomesia's followers; and of Miami refugees who returned to Kansas. They owe a debt of gratitude to Jean B. Richardville, who wisely secured the private title to sufficient lands to provide for a continued Miami presence in the state.[33]

Notes

1. Jacqueline Peterson, "Many Roads to Red River: Métis Genesis in the Great Lakes Region, 1680–1815," in Jacqueline Peterson and Jennifer S. H. Brown, eds., *The New Peoples: Being and Becoming Métis in North America* (Lincoln: University of Nebraska Press, 1985), 63; Benjamin Parke to John C. Calhoun, December 7, 1818, Benjamin Parke Papers, Indiana Historical Society, Indianapolis, Indiana; James Ray, Message to the General Assembly, December 8, 1826, in Dorothy Riker and Gayle Thornbrough, eds., *Messages and Papers Relating to the Administration of James Brown Ray, Governor of Indiana, 1825–1831*, 3 vols. (Indianapolis: Indiana Historical Bureau, 1954), 1:177.

2. Richard White, *The Middle Ground: Indians, Empires, and Republics in the Great Lakes Region, 1650–1815* (Cambridge: Cambridge University Press, 1991), 50. White's volume contains the most complete discussion of this acculturation process.

3. R. David Edmunds, "'Unacquainted with the Laws of the Civilized World': American Attitudes toward the Métis Communities in the Old Northwest," in Peterson and Brown, *New Peoples*, 188.

4. John Tipton to John Eaton, April 5, 1831, Robertson and Riker, eds., *Tipton Papers*, 2:400; William H. Keating, *Narrative of an Expedition to the Source of the St. Peter River*, 2 vols. (London: George P. Whitaker, 1825), 1:79. Also see Edmunds, "Unacquainted with the Laws," for a general discussion of American attitudes toward métis people.

5. For a brief biographical sketch of Richardville, see R. David Edmunds, "Richardville, John Baptiste (Peshewa)," in Frederick E. Hoxie, ed., *Encyclopedia of North American Indians* (Boston: Houghton, 1996), 549–50.

6. Ibid.

7. Wilhelmina Richards and Clifford Richards, eds., "The Recollections of Susan Man McCulloch," *Old Fort News* 44 (1981): 10; "An Indian Payment," Logansport *Telegraph*, November 1, 1834.

8. Richards, "Recollections of Susan Man McCulloch," 10; "An Indian Payment," Logansport *Telegraph*, November 1, 1834; Gerrard Hopkins, *A Mission to the Indians from the Committee of the Baltimore Meeting to Fort Wayne in 1804* (Philadelphia: T. Elwood Zell, 1862), 189; Keating, *Narrative*, 1:107. For excellent illustrations of Miami and Potawatomi métis and their clothing, see Sarah E. Cooke and Rachel B. Ramadhyani, eds., *Indians and a Changing Frontier: The Art of George Winter* (Indianapolis: Indiana Historical Society, 1993).

9. Thomas Scattergood Teas, "Journal of a Tour of Fort Wayne and the Adjacent Country, in the Year 1821," in Harlow Lindley, ed., *Indiana as Seen by Early Travelers* (Indianapolis: Indiana Historical Commission, 1916), 250; Hugh McCulloch, *Men and Measures of Half a Century* (New York: Scribner's, 1888), 109; Allen Hamilton to Louis B. Barthelet, December 28, 1839, folder Q, box 5, Godfroy Papers, Indiana State Library.

10. Bert Griswold, *Pictorial History of Fort Wayne* (Chicago: Robert O. Law, 1917), 237; Logansport *Telegraph*, January 18, 1840; "The American Fur Trade," *Hunt's Merchant Magazine* (September 1840): 185–204. The Miami land cession treaties can be found in Charles J. Kappler, comp. and ed., *Indian Treaties, 1778–1883* (Mattituck, N.Y.: Amereon House, 1972), 171–534.

11. Stickney to Lewis Cass, June 23, 1816, Miami File, Great Lakes Indian Archives, Glenn A. Black Laboratory of Archeology, Indiana University, Bloomington, Indiana; Stickney to Cass, May 6, 1818, ibid.; Benjamin Parke to Jean B. Brouillette, January 19, 1816, Benjamin Parke Papers, Indiana Historical Society, Indianapolis. Also see Griswold, *Pictorial History of Fort Wayne*, 252–53.

12. John Hays to John C. Calhoun, August 14, 1820, Miami File, Great Lakes Indian Archives, Glenn A. Black Laboratory of Archeology, Indiana University, Bloomington, Indiana; Hays to Cass, November 1, 1820, ibid.; Hays to Calhoun, February 24, 1823, in Riker and Robertson, *Tipton Papers*, 1:296–300. Also see Nellie A. Roberston, "John Hays and the Fort Wayne Indian Agency," *Indiana Magazine of History* 39 (1943): 221–36.

13. For an excellent account of the falsification and inflation of Indian debts and their impact upon tribes in Indiana, see R. David Edmunds, "'Designing Men Seeking a Fortune': Indian Traders and the Potawatomi Claims Payment of 1836," *Indiana Magazine of History* 77 (June 1981): 109–22. Also see Paul C. Phillips, "The Fur Trade in the Maumee-

Wabash Country," *Studies in American History* (1926): 91–118; and Robert Trennert, *Indian Traders on the Middle Border: The House of Ewing, 1827–1854* (Lincoln: University of Nebraska Press, 1981).

14. Tipton to John C. Calhoun, September 4, 1825, in Robertson and Riker, *Tipton Papers,* 1:391–92; LeGros to Thomas McKenney, January 27, 1826, National Archives, record group 75, Letters Received by the Office of Indian Affairs (M234), Miami Agency, roll 416.

15. Cass to Tipton, October 14, 1824, in Robertson and Riker, *Tipton Papers,* 1:398; Treaty Negotiations and Treaty Commissioners' Report, 1826, ibid., 1:577–606; Hugh McKeen to Tipton, June 28, 1826, ibid., 1:546–47; Tipton to Eaton, February 15, 1830, ibid., 2:250–51; "Conditions, Manners, and Customs of the Indians," Logansport *Miami Times,* January 9, 1830.

16. Richardville to James Noble, January 30, 1830, National Archives, M234, roll 416; Miami Chiefs to Cass, 1830, ibid.; Nicholas Grover to Tipton, August 14, 1829, in Roberston and Riker, *Tipton Papers,* 2:185.

17. Ewing to Tipton, December 24, 1829, in Robertson and Riker, *Tipton Papers,* 2:231–32; Ewing to Tipton, February 8, 1830, ibid., 2:244–47.

18. Tipton to Richardville, November 18, 1830, in Riker and Robertson, *Tipton Papers,* 2:371–72; William Ewing to Tipton, December 24, 1829, ibid., 2:231–39.

19. Ewing to Tipton, December 24, 1829, in Riker and Robertson, *Tipton Papers,* 2:231–39; Tipton to John Eaton, April 5, 1831, ibid., 2:399–401.

20. James Noble to John Eaton, February 15, 1830, National Archives, M234, roll 416; Tipton to Cass, October 6, 1829, in Riker and Robertson, *Tipton Papers,* 2:209–10; Tipton to Calvin Fletcher, November 30, 1830, ibid., 376–77.

21. Teas, "Journal of a Tour of Fort Wayne," 250; Robert M. Taylor Jr., Errol W. Stevens, Mary Ann Ponder, and Paul Brockman, *Indiana: A New Historical Guide* (Indianapolis: Indiana Historical Society, 1989).

22. Richards, "Recollections of Susan Man McCulloch," 10; Abel C. Pepper to Allen Hamilton, January 8, 1837, Allen Hamilton Collection, Indiana Historical Society, Indianapolis.

23. For an excellent account of social life on the early Indiana frontier, see Milo M. Quaife, ed., "A Narrative of Life on the Old Frontier: Henry Hay's Journal from Detroit to the Miami River," *Proceedings of the State Historical Society of Wisconsin* 63 (1915): 208–61. Also see Cooke and Ramadhyani, *Indians and a Changing Frontier,* 53; Bessie K. Roberts, *Richardville: Chief of the Miamis* (Fort Wayne: Fort Wayne Public Library, n.d.), 11; Pepper to Allen Hamilton, January 8, 1837, Hamilton Collection, Indiana Historical Society.

24. Donald Chaput, "The Family of Drouet de Richerville: Merchants, Soldiers, and Chiefs of Indiana," *Indiana Magazine of History* 74 (June 1978): 114; Craig Leonard, "Chief Jean Baptiste Richardville," in Dwight Ericsson and Ann Ericsson, eds., *The Forks of the Wabash* (Huntington, Ind.: Historic Forks of the Wabash, 1991), 79, 88.

25. John Forsyth to Tipton, January 26, 1829, in Riker and Robertson, *Tipton Papers,* 2:134; George Mather Ross, *Frontier Faith: The Story of the Pioneer Congregations of Fort Wayne Indiana* (Fort Wayne: Allen County-Fort Wayne Historical Society, 1992), 14; Samuel Milroy to Allen Hamilton, December 18, 1839, Hamilton Collection, Indiana State Historical Society; J. B. Duret to Allen Hamilton, December 4, 1839, in Allen Hamilton Collection, Indiana Division, Indiana State Library.

26. John T. Douglass to Tipton, May 6, 1838, in Riker and Robertson, *Tipton Papers*, 3:621.

27. Samuel Milroy to Richard M. Johnson, August 14, 1839, in 26th Congress, 2nd. Session, House Document 109, 132; Pepper to Carey Harris, September 10, 1836, ibid., 100–101; Pepper to Harris, March 28, 1837, ibid., 106. Also see S. W. Widney, "Pioneer Sketches of DeKalb County, *Indiana Magazine of History* 25 (June 1929): 108; and Leonard, "Chief Jean Baptiste Richardville," 86.

28. These treaties can be found in Kappler, *Indian Treaties*, 171–74, 278–81, 425–28, 519–24, and 531–34.

29. Leonard, "Chief Jean Baptiste Richardville," 84–85; Stewart Rafert, *The Miami Indians of Indiana: A Persistent People* (Indianapolis: Indiana Historical Society, 1996), 100–101.

30. Rafert, *Miami Indians of Indiana*, 102–3. The 1840 treaty can be found in Kappler, *Indian Treaties*, 531–34.

31. The most complete account of Miami removal can be found in Bert Anson, *The Miami Indians* (Norman: University of Oklahoma Press, 1970), 213–33. Anson argues that Lafontaine was an effective leader during the removal period. Also see Rafert, *Miami Indians of Indiana*, 108–13; and R. David Edmunds, "'Paint Me as Who I Am': Woodland People at the Beginning of the Twenty-First Century," in Rita Kohn and Lynwood Montell, eds., *Always a People: Oral Histories of Contemporary Woodland Indians* (Bloomington: Indiana University Press, 1997), 4–6.

32. Rafert, *Miami Indians of Indiana*, 122–25, 141, 168; Anson, *The Miami Indians*, 238–39, 241–42; Muriel H. Wright, *A Guide to the Indian Tribes of Oklahoma* (Norman: University of Oklahoma Press, 1951), 183.

33. Edmunds, "'Paint Me as Who I Am,'" 5–6.

6. Resistance to Removal

The "White Indian," Frances Slocum

SUSAN SLEEPER-SMITH

Nineteenth-century Indian communities in the Old Northwest that success-fully resisted forced removal often paid a tragic price. Many villages became enmeshed in the construction of white facades, which masked their Indian identity and thwarted removal, thereby consigning successive generations to hide in plain view. Invisibility led to persistence but ultimately denied the Miamis of Indiana federal recognition as a tribal community.

In examining the covert but successful resistance strategies devised by Deaf Man's Village in Indiana's Mississinewa River valley, this chapter focuses on Frances Slocum and examines why her presence encouraged this commu-nity to consciously construct itself as white and to mask its Indian identity. Frances's presence, coupled with skillful political maneuvering, successfully garnered the necessary public support to thwart forced removal. The develop-ment of this unusual Miami resistance strategy occurred as a response to the emotionally charged national debate about whether removal was or was not necessary for the civilization of Indians. In racist antebellum America, few people considered Indians civilized; thus, despite the presence of sedentary agricultural communities, new exclusionary standards emerged that forced agricultural villages of Miamis westward.[1]

Scholars traditionally have focused on nineteenth-century removal in the Southeast, while the equally egregious behavior of people in the Old Northwest has generally escaped historical notice. However, forced removal in this region was often as brutal as the more infamous Cherokee Trail of Tears. Midwestern frontiersmen behaved as shamefully as Andrew Jackson's plantation brethren when they brutally forced Indians west and greedily ap-propriated their lands.[2] In 1838, for instance, when Potawatomis from chief

Menominee's Indiana village were forcibly removed, over one-third of the nine hundred Potawatomis contracted typhoid fever. Rations supplied to the emigrating Indians were so spoiled that militia accompanying the removal refused to eat them, and Native women were forced to prostitute themselves to obtain food for their families. Before the Potawatomis reached Kansas, forty-two people died and many more people succumbed after their arrival. Even Father Benjamin Marie Petit, the young Catholic missionary priest who had followed them west, did not survive this "Trail of Death."[3]

In response to such suffering, many Great Lakes people redoubled their resistance to removal. They devised strategies that drew on their prior interaction with Euro-Americans. Thus, the nineteenth-century Miamis constructed themselves as white because of their seventeenth- and eighteenth-century involvement in the fur trade.

The western Great Lakes trade had prospered because Indian villages evolved flexible boundaries of identity that allowed them to incorporate and coexist with a diverse range of people. In this region, furs were numerous and easily accessible, and people had migrated to the area from a variety of geographical locations. The network of interconnected riverways facilitated travel. Thus, as early as the seventeenth century, refugees from the Fur Trade Wars arrived from the Huron, Neutral, and Erie nations; these refugees were adopted into Great Lakes communities, as were Abenakis, Mahicans, and other New England Indians who were dispossessed of their lands.[4] There was also a Panis, or Indian slave, presence that was occasioned by conflicts with such western nations as the Pawnees and Sioux.[5] Panis were exchanged in the Caribbean and New Orleans for African slaves. However, free men of color also had settled in these villages. Jean Baptiste Pointe Du Sable, for instance, married among the Potawatomis and was an established fur trader before relocating to Chicago, where he is credited with being the African American founder of that community.[6] French traders married to Native women resided in these villages, as did later arriving eighteenth-century Anglo traders. Consequently, mixed-ancestry offspring became a prominent part of the fur trade's social landscape.

The fur trade created not only a diverse society but also broadened the range of economic activity in many Indian communities. Those villages adjacent to river portages or located near French trading posts not only supplied peltry but also became agricultural suppliers to the trade. Traders were dependent on the indigenous food supply. Montreal trade permits allowed each recipient only two canoes for the Upper Country, and men with Native wives devoted the limited space of their transport canoes almost entirely to trade goods. Native people produced a marketable surplus and many communities became skilled providers of products manufactured for the trade, such as canoes, snowshoes, and clothing.[7]

Fur trade interaction dramatically changed Native communities. The increased level of indigenous agricultural activity and the diverse social landscape of indigenous communities fostered the belief that Indians could live side by side with American emigrants. Consequently, Miamis of mixed ancestry assumed an increasingly prominent role in the fight against removal. During the colonial period, Indian women who married fur traders often became cultural mediators, and their children frequently served as headmen and treaty negotiators. These people often spoke a number of languages, lived in Euro-American settlements, and appeared physically to be Caucasian.[8]

Three mixed-ancestry Miami headmen, Jean Baptiste Richardville, Francis La Fontaine, and Francis Godfroy (also known as Pa-Lonz-Wa by his people), became particularly prominent as skilled treaty negotiators, and they occupied positions that insured the persistence of their communities. The Miamis were politically well organized. In 1831, Indian Agent John Tipton wrote to Secretary of War John Eaton that "the Miamies are reduced to a small number but well organized in their kind of government, with one of the most shrewd men in North America at their head."[9] Thus, in 1840, when the Miami National Reserve was dissolved, Godfroy obtained the lands surrounding Nan-Matches-Sin-A-Wa, his village, as a personal reservation. These former communal lands were titled in his Christian name to ensure his village effective legal protection. Godfroy was aware that individual property claims were defensible in court and lawyers could be hired to prevent encroachment and trespass. One of Godfroy's sons, for instance, trained with a well-known Indiana lawyer. Consequently, Godfroy ensured the persistence of his village, and as a headman he used his land to resettle displaced kin or forcibly removed Miami who had returned to Indiana. For example, during the 1840s cabins were built to accommodate sixty Miamis who returned from Kansas.[10] In contrast, those Miamis who held villages or lands communally had no access to the courts for protection; their appeals against trespass were dependent on the vigilance of Indian agents.

Godfroy's village had the appearance of a non-Indian community. Godfroy's family lived in a large two-story house; adjacent to it were five or six two-story houses that housed other village families.[11] The village was built in the style of a New England village, but it was surrounded by a square enclosure, with visitors admitted through a gate.[12]

George Winter, a British-born, Indian frontier artist, sketched Godfroy's house in 1839. Winter depicted Godfroy's dwelling as a spacious, two-story, timber-framed house accompanied by outbuildings. Written records from the 1830s describe the house's fine furnishings and the sophisticated entertainment provided by Godfroy and his neighbors to guests and visitors. They also indicate that the Miamis operated a mill at this location and stored perishable food in a "springhouse" close to the nearby Mississinewa River.

Francis Godfroy was accorded the positive attributes associated with European lineage. Instead of being depicted as a "slovenly, lazy Indian," he was shown as an intelligent man who possessed "wealth, and influence, besides a shrewd head on his shoulders." Most writers failed to mention that Francis Godfroy did not speak English, weighed close to 350 pounds, and was far from being the hard-working farmer most Easterners equated with upward mobility on the frontier. He had, however, the requisite facade of "whiteness." He lived in a two-story timber-framed building, kept livestock, raised horses, and, most important, was referred to by his Christian name.

The resistance strategy of the Miamis in the Nan-Matches-Sin-A-Wa village is not difficult to discern, but in other villages resistance was more clandestine and coded. Communities that resisted were not eager to draw attention to themselves, and it is apparent that many of these communities constructed a white facade that purposefully obscured their Indian identity. In Deaf Man's Village, which was near Nan-Matches-Sin-A-Wa, the presence

Figure 6.1. *Nan-Matches-Sin-A-Wa, 1839, Chief Godfroy's Home*, by George Winter. Tippecanoe County Historical Association, Lafayette, Indiana. Gift of Mrs. Cable G. Ball.

of Frances Slocum shaped this community's resistance strategy. She was an elderly white captive, the widow of Deaf Man, a Miami chief, and had lived for over sixty years as an Indian. Despite repeated opportunities, she never revealed her white identity until the 1830s, when her village was threatened with forced removal to the West.

The Transformation of Mo-con-no-qua into Frances Slocum

Frances Slocum was a "White Indian," a term applied to Anglo-Americans kidnapped and adopted into tribal communities who later did not return to white society.[13] During the American Revolution Slocum was taken from Pennsylvania's Wyoming River valley at age five. She was raised by the Delawares, where she married and later divorced a Delaware man. She subsequently married among the Miamis and raised four children.[14] Both her sons had died, and she lived in a double log cabin with her daughters when forced removal began. At age sixty-five, Slocum, or Mo-con-no-qua ("Little Bear Woman") proclaimed herself a white captive. Her claims to being white were dismissed for two years until her identity was confirmed by an elderly sister and younger brother who were contacted by officials in Indiana, traveled west, and met with her. As soon as Mo-con-no-qua's white identity was substantiated and she had public creditability as a captive, the reconstruction of Deaf Man's Village as white began. Mo-con-no-qua was reinvented as "the Lost Sister," Frances Slocum. Public opinion on the frontier and further east rallied to her support, illustrating the success of the Miamis' strategy. Mo-con-no-qua did not speak English, could not remember her Christian name, was a dark-skinned woman with dark hair, and continued to dress in the Indian fashion.

Numerous captivity narratives have been written by and about people who were ransomed and returned, but little information exists about those who chose to remain among their adopted people. Mo-con-no-qua was one of the few "white Indians" whose story has been told through a series of published narratives. Most writers depicted her as a civilizing force that transformed Miami society. They referred to her by her English name, Frances Slocum, or by her nickname, "the Lost Sister." Writers described the settled appearance and prosperity of her Indian village and attributed its houses, barns, and cultivated fields to the "civilizing" presence of this white woman. Frances Slocum was depicted as a white woman who survived the "imagined" horrors of captivity and had brought civilization to the Indians.

Using her English name, Frances Slocum petitioned Congress for redress, played on the sympathies engendered by her captivity, and relied on stereo-typical Indian references to convince readers that her captivity was not only involuntary but that she was a helpless victim. Her petition related how she had been sold as a bride but did not mention that she had married twice and had divorced her first husband. The petition even emphasized her attachment to her white Slocum family to garner political support on her behalf, despite two formal and rather uncomfortable visits by a sister and brother.

> She was taken, as she states, I think, by the Shawnee Indians, at the age of about six years, somewhere near Wyoming. Her friends made fruitless search for her for a great number of years, and she likewise for many years made every endeavor to return to them, without effect. In the progress of time, she was sold and became the wife of one of the head men of the Miamis, known as the deaf man, with whom she moved to the Mississinewa, where she has continued to reside at or near the place where she was captured, and are among the most respectable families in that part of the country . . . I have no doubt she would willingly meet death, than either to be obliged to remove west of the Mississippi, beyond the reach of her white relatives. . . .[15]

Mo-con-no-qua reinvented herself as Frances Slocum, white woman and mother, who could not be separated from her children. Her petition cast her in a familiar role: a frail flower among the Indians who required the protection of male figures, particularly the men of Congress.[16] "She says she has lived a life of hardships, and is now quite old, and wishes to spend the remainder of her days among her children, on their lands here; and she does not see why her great white father should not grant them the . . . privilege to remain here upon their lands, and receive their annuities here."

The bill was introduced in the House by Benjamin Bidlack, the Pennsylvania congressman from the Wyoming River valley where Frances had been kidnapped. He informed his fellow representatives that as a white woman Slocum should not be "compelled to move west of the Mississippi" and live among the Indians. When the bill was discussed in the Senate, vociferous objections came from the Indian agents in Indiana who were in charge of removal, and who feared that "the adoption of the joint resolution might disincline other Miamis to remove to their new homes." These men lost the contest and Frances Slocum's lawyer secured her financial independence by having her annuities paid to her at Fort Wayne. In addition, to insure her Indiana future, Frances was given an entire section of land, 640 acres. Most important, she and her family were accorded legal immunity from the removal militia. Frances's petition carried the names of her immediate family, so that they could not be removed; and this list, phonetically spelled out in

Miami, was appended to her petition. When translated, the list revealed the names of her entire village: her daughters, their present and former husbands, the sister of her dead husband, all their children, husbands, and even a miscellany of other names that included children of Godfroy and a young Mahican boy adopted by Slocum. From the Miami perspective, the claim of family included kin relations and, in this instance, all of Deaf Man's Village.

Mo-con-no-qua's transformation into a subservient white woman was then further reinforced by the work of the Indiana artist George Winter. He was commissioned to paint Slocum's portrait by her white family. This work became Winter's most widely circulated painting and was reprinted in newspapers, magazines, and in published captivity narratives. Winter kept careful notes during his visit to Deaf Man's Village because the Miami gave him permission to sketch the white captive but denied him permission to sketch anything or anyone else in the community. Once he returned to his studio his notes and sketches allowed him to accurately transfer what he had observed onto canvas.

George Winter's work provides a surprisingly objective view of the Indians who lived in Deaf Man's village. Winter was a recent English immigrant who, new to both the country and the territory, did not possess more commonly held American notions of Indians as being uncivilized. Winter, in fact, dismissed the standard antebellum portrayal of Indians in "aboriginal dress" and observed that among the Miamis these fictional representations of "the more 'poetic Indian,' that is represented always in nudity, with a fine Roman nose, shaven head—with the scalp lock decorated with tufts of feathers . . . never [came] within my observations."

Although Winter was intent on capturing the details of Indian life, he was also aware that in a commissioned portrait the patron often expected an idealized version of reality. The portrait of Slocum was commissioned by Frances's younger brother, who disliked being visually reminded that his sister was an Indian. Therefore, Winter created two distinctively different portraits of Frances Slocum. The first was recorded in his sketchbook and was accompanied by written notes about her physical appearance. She emerges from this evidence as Mo-con-no-qua, a gaily clad, elderly Indian woman. However, in the final portrait sent to the Slocum family she was portrayed as the white woman, Frances Slocum.

> Her toute ensemble was unique. She was dressed in a red calico skirt, figured with large showy yellow and green flowers, folded within the upper part of a metta coshee, or petticoat of black cloth of excellent quality. Her nether limbs were clothed in red leggings, winged with green ribbons and her feet were moccasinless.

Kick-ke-se-quah, her daughter, seemed not to be without some pride in her mother's appearing to the best advantage, placed a black silk shawl over her shoulders—pinning it in front.

In two hours operation, I had transferred a successful likeness . . . Frances looked upon her likeness with complacency. Kick-ke-se-quah eyed it approvingly, yet suspiciously. . . . The widowed daughter, O-Shaw-se-Quah would not look at it . . . but turned away from it abruptly. I could feel as by intuition that my absence would be hailed as a joyous relief to the family.[17]

The somber Frances Slocum of the commissioned portrait bore faint resemblance to her more colorful everyday appearance. In Winter's sketchbook, we see a bare-footed elderly woman in a colorful but rather ostentatious flowered skirt, paired with a pink calico blouse and red leggings trimmed with multicolored silk ribbons. George Winter sketched her with both her Indian daughters (see figure 6.2), but they, like the colorful clothing, are also absent from the final portrait. Winter's final work, an upper body portrait, made it unnecessary to include either Frances' colorful leggings or her bare feet (see figure 6.3).

Figure 6.2. *Frances Slocum*, by George Winter. Tippecanoe County Historical Association, Lafayette, Indiana. Gift of Mrs. Cable G. Ball.

Figure 6.3. *Frances Slocum,* by George Winter.
Tippecanoe County Historical Association, Lafayette,
Indiana. Gift of Mrs. Cable G. Ball.

The Removal Debate

Frances Slocum reinvented herself as a white woman because being white
became the most effective defense against removal. Many southern Great
Lakes Indian villages exhibited the agrarian behaviors expected of civilized
white people, but by the 1830s new behavioral standards had evolved that
excluded even these communities. Many nineteenth-century Americans who
arrived in the Northwest Territory were at first surprised, and also angered, to
find sedentary Indian villages. Many settlers discovered that some of the best
agricultural lands were already occupied and farmed by Indians. Faced with

an unexpected but persistent Indian presence, many recently arrived eastern immigrants became removal advocates rather than supportive neighbors.

By 1830, most eastern immigrants on the Old Northwest frontier actively supported President Andrew Jackson's Removal Bill. Jackson, like his midwestern supporters, not only ignored indigenous agricultural behavior but also argued that Indians had made little progress toward becoming civilized. Jackson asserted that Native populations faced inevitable demise unless they could be removed west to Indian Territory to undergo a "civilizing" process, isolated from corrupting influences.

Opponents of Jackson's removal policies, who supposedly spoke on behalf of the Indians, proved equally problematic because they equated "being civilized" with "being Christian." The most vociferous congressional opponent of removal was Jeremiah Everts, who led the fight against the removal bill. Everts believed that Protestant missionaries and Christian education were central to the "civilization" process. Everts emphasized Christianity and was suspicious of pagan Indian communities, even if they had adopted white agricultural practices. Yet the Miamis in Deaf Man's Village attempted to utilize the reinvention of Mo-con-no-qua as Frances Slocum as an effective way to avoid removal; regardless of her religious persuasion, Mo-con-no-qua and her family should not be removed because they were "white."

By the early 1840s, the emotionally charged national debate about removal generated competing captivity narratives in which Frances Slocum was described as either a "white civilizer" who had transformed Indian society or as a white woman who had descended from a civilized to an uncivilized state. The debate focused on whether it was better to civilize Indians in situ or through removal. Both sides denied the reality that Indians were already civilized. This debate facilitated Frances Slocum's direct appeal to Congress for protection against removal. Her petition appealed to congressmen because it played on stereotypes about Indians as "uncivilized" and worked to the Miamis' advantage in thwarting removal.

Yet her petition against removal touched off a new debate in which removal advocates attempted to dismiss the "transformative powers of whiteness." Eastern ministers, as well as missionaries sent to the Old Northwest by the American Home Missionary Society, described the inhabitants of even the most affluent agricultural villages as "savages" whose resistance to Christianity made them unworthy neighbors for white families. Indians were increasingly identified as the racialized, non-Christian other.

One of the most inflammatory captivity narratives was written in 1842 by the Reverend John Todd, an advocate of removal who believed Indians to be impervious to the biblical teachings of Protestant missionaries. For

Todd, Frances personified what happened to white people when "heathen" Indians were not removed. Todd transformed the discovery of Frances by her relatives into a profound shock rather than a joyful reunion. "On pursuing the investigations, there remained no doubt on the minds of any of the party, that she was the lost sister—the Frances Slocum of sixty years ago! But what a change, from the fair-haired, pale-faced little girl, to the old, jealous, ignorant, suspicious savage! The contrast was so great, that the brother and sister were almost overwhelmed."[18]

In Todd's scenario the family was reunited with their sister, but their discovery that she was not a Protestant Christian produced such anxiety that "they did not sleep that night." Instead, according to Todd, Slocum's two siblings engaged in mutual commiseration and then dismissed her as a heathen, even though she was their sister. "'Was she so very ignorant' said I to the brother who gave me the narration, 'Sir, she did not know when Sunday came!'—what a consummation of ignorance for one actually born in New England! She was rich, and much respected and beloved;—but she was a poor, darkened savage."[19]

Todd also argued that prolonged Indian resistance to evangelical Christianity had stripped them of all claims to "civilized" status.[20] "How striking the difference between the heart that has been educated and trained under heathenism, and the same heart trained under the light of the Gospel. The sweet sympathies of the heart are not there, and no chords in the bosom respond to the touch of affection and love. . . . The intellectual, immortal part is put into dark subjection to the animal part of man."[21]

For those frontiersmen who coveted Indian land, evidence that tribal communities had embraced agriculture was ignored. They were eager to muster any excuse as a rationale for taking Indian land, and they continued to adhere to the stereotype of "lazy" Indians because it served their purpose. Moreover, if Indians could achieve economic prosperity without laboring as small yeoman farmers, much of the agrarian myth of nineteenth century American was threatened. Antebellum Americans intent on upward mobility believed that hard work and yeoman agriculture were the keys to success. If Indians could achieve prosperity without following such a formula, frontier whites might also be lured into such a lifestyle. Todd reported that Frances Slocum lived in a village of indolent Indians scattered "among the long blue grass which without cultivation covers the luxuriant soil." In addition, Todd complained, "The Indians were here found, some lounging about their huts or wigwams, and some few at work in the corn-fields with their ponies tied near,—for all savages are so indolent, that they never work if they can help it, and never walk if they can ride."[22]

Todd's captivity narrative invoked Indians as a direct threat to fledgling frontier communities. Separated from neighbors and distant from church, even white Americans might descend into savagery. Todd magnified those fears and drew attention to the flexible boundaries of Indian identity and the integration of white captives. His shrill condemnation of Frances Slocum increased fears about the dangers that such integrative behaviors posed for immigrants as they streamed into the Old Northwest; the malleability of the border between Indian and white societies raised alarm.

These malleable boundaries of Indian identity were quite apparent in a practical joke played on artist George Winter. When Winter sketched "Yo-ca-top-kone," a supposed Potawatomi "chief," the man posed in a silk turban topped with feather plumes, a pastel shirtwaist, an elaborately tasseled belt, and leggings with streamers of differently colored ribbons. He seemed to be one of the most resplendent Indians in Winter's portfolio. But the contemplative Indian of this sketch was in reality Henry Taylor, a white man. His Indian mother-in-law, Mas-sa, provided Henry with his elaborate outfit, and only after Winter's portrait was complete did they reveal their joke to George Winter.[23] To many Americans, Taylor's ruse was indicative of how easily frontier whites might be lured into a "savage" lifestyle, but it also illustrated how readily many mixed-lineage people might also "pass for white." Indeed, the malleability of these racial boundaries provided a window of opportunity through which many Miamis "vanished" into frontier society and escaped removal.

This transformation was ingenious, but it also held unforeseen consequences. When Indian communities in the Old Northwest "hid in plain view," they often doomed subsequent generations to invisibility. In the case of the Mississinewa Valley Miamis, who had learned to negotiate the flexible boundaries of identity, they thwarted removal, but by the end of the nineteenth century they paid a high price for their camouflage: the loss of their tribal status. In 1897, the federal government administratively terminated its recognition of the Indiana Miamis. They declared that the Indiana Miamis no longer were "Indians." In response, the state of Indiana revoked the Miamis' tax-exempt status. Gabriel Godfroy, the leader of the Miami community, appealed the state's actions to the Indiana appellate court, but his appeal resulted in a ruling that proved even more devastating. The court ruled that it was the Miamis' "degree of 'whiteness' or acculturation" that had determined tribal status and, therefore, tax status. The court judged Gabriel Godfroy no longer an Indian because he sent his children to public schools and dressed like a white person. His behavior "had voluntarily placed [him] within the legal definition of citizen."[24] In the years before the Civil War, the

Miamis' "construction of whiteness" ensured their persistence in their Indiana homeland, but by the end of the nineteenth century, the Indiana court had decided that Indians who behaved like white people were no longer Indians.

In consequence, the modern Miami Nation of Indiana remain federally unrecognized as a tribal community. Repeated Miami attempts to regain recognition have failed. In 1990, the federal government issued a four-hundred-page report stating that although the 1897 decision illegally removed federal recognition from the Miamis of Indiana, the consequent breakup of the Miami land base had irreparably damaged Miami culture. The Miamis no longer were Indians.

Yet despite sustained government efforts and errors, the Miamis of Indiana have persisted. Tragically, however, they have paid a high price. The "construction of whiteness" masked their identity and thwarted removal, but these same behaviors were used by the Indiana appellate court to declare the Miamis to be non-Indians. The Miamis have, in the twentieth century, endured social and psychological trauma more profound than forced removal when they became strangers in their own land.[25]

Notes

1. Information about Frances Slocum can be obtained from the captivity narratives written about her. The three that figure most prominently in this research include George Winter, "Journal of a Visit to Deaf Man's Village," in *The Journals and Indian Paintings of George Winter, 1837–1839* (Indianapolis: Indiana Historical Society, 1948), 151–96; John Todd, *The Lost Sister of the Miami, an Authentic Narrative by Rev. John Todd* (Northampton, Mass.: J. H. Butler, 1842); John F. Meginness, *Biography of Frances Slocum, the Lost Sister of Wyoming* in the series entitled *Women in America from Colonial Times to the Present*, reprint ed. (New York: Arno Press, 1974).

2. The terms "emigrants" and "immigrants" are used throughout this chapter as opposed to the terms "settlers" or "pioneers." Terms such as "pioneer" and "settler" are the language of conquest and imply that this was an empty landscape. Gazetteers or guides to the Old Northwest generally used the terms "emigrant" or "immigrant" rather than "settler."

3. "Journal of an Emigrating Party of Pottawatomie Indians, 1838," *Indiana Magazine of History* 21 (December 1925): 315–36; "A Continuation of the Journal of an Emigrating Party of Potawatomi Indians, 1838, and Ten William Polk Manuscripts," *Indiana Magazine of History* 44 (December 1948): 396–404; Irving McKee, ed., *The Trail of Death: Letters of Benjamin Marie Petit* (Indianapolis: Indiana Historical Society, 1941); Irving McKee, "The Centennial of the Trail of Death," *Indiana Magazine of History* 35 (March 1939): 27–41; Daniel McDonald, *Removal of the Pottawatomie Indians from Northern Indiana* (Plymouth, Ind.: McDonald, 1989).

4. This dispersion of people and their clustering in refugee centers in the western Great

Lakes is described by Richard White in *The Middle Ground* (Cambridge: Cambridge University Press, 1991); see esp. 10–23.

5. For a description of African American slavery in the Illinois Country, see Carl J. Ekberg, "Black Slavery in Illinois, 1720–1765," *Western Illinois Regional Studies* 12 (1989): 5–9. For Native American slavery in the Great Lakes, see Russell M. Magnaghi, "Red Slavery in the Great Lakes Country During the French and British Regimes," *Old Northwest* 12 (Summer 1986): 201–17.

6. On June 30, 1788, Congress authorized a bill that granted four hundred acres to the head of every Illinois family who enrolled in the militia. DuSable claimed that in 1780 he built a house and cultivated lands in Peoria. American State Papers, Class III, Public Lands, III:3; also see Thomas A. Meehan, "Jean Baptiste Point du Sable, the First Chicagoan," *Journal of the Illinois State Historical Society* 56 (Autumn 1963): 439–53.

7. James M. McClurken, "Augustin Hamlin, Jr.: Ottawa Identity and the Politics of Persistence," in *Being and Becoming Indian*, ed. James A. Clifton (Prospect Heights, Ill.: Waveland, 1989), 85.

8. People who served as cultural brokers are described by Jacqueline Peterson in "Many Roads to Red River: Métis Genesis in the Great Lakes Region, 1680–1815," in *The New Peoples: Being and Becoming Métis in North America*, ed. Jacqueline Peterson and Jennifer S. H. Brown (Manitoba: University of Manitoba Press, 1985), 37–73; Daniel K. Richter, "Cultural Brokers and Intercultural Politics: New York–Iroquois Relations, 1664–1701," *Journal of American History* 75 (June 1988): 40–67; Nancy L. Hagedorn, "'Faithful, Knowing, and Prudent': Andrew Montour as Interpreter and Cultural Broker, 1740–1772," in *Between Indian and White Worlds: The Cultural Broker*, ed. Margaret Connell Szasz (Norman: University of Oklahoma Press, 1994), 44–60; James H. Merrell, "'The Cast of His Countenance': Reading Andrew Montour," in *Through a Glass Darkly*, ed. Ronald Hoffman, Mechal Sobel, and Fredrika J. Teute (Chapel Hill: University of North Carolina Press, 1997), 13–39.

9. John Tipton to John Eaton, April 5, 1831, in *The John Tipton Papers*, ed. Nellie Armstrong Robertson and Dorothy Riker (3 vols; Indianapolis: Indiana Historical Bureau, 1942), 2:399–401; Robert A. Trennert Jr., *Indian Traders on the Middle Border: The House of Ewing, 1827–54* (Lincoln: University of Nebraska Press, 1981), 40.

10. Stewart Rafert, *The Miami Indians of Indiana: A Persistent People, 1654–1994* (Indianapolis: Indiana Historical Society, 1996), 134.

11. Godfroy's father James or Jacques traded at Eeltown. He married and lived among the Miamis. For a description of Jacques Godfroy's trading activities, see Lasell, "The Old Indian Traders," II (1905), 5; *Combination Atlas Map of Miami County, Indiana* (Indianapolis, 1877), 13; Bert Anson, *The Fur Traders in Northern Indian, 1796–1850* (PhD diss., Indiana University, 1953), 22.

12. Winter, "Visit to Deaf Man's Village," in *Journals and Indian Paintings*, 162–63. The original of George Winter's journal is in the archives of the Tippecanoe County Historical Museum, West Lafayette, Indiana. The most recent edition of George Winter's book contains selections from Winter's journal, but only the 1948 volume contains the entire journal. Also see *Indians and a Changing Frontier: The Art of George Winter* (Indianapolis: Indiana Historical Society in cooperation with the Tippecanoe Historical Association, 1993).

13. James Axtell, "The White Indians of Colonial America," in *The European and the Indian*, ed. James Axtell (New York: Oxford, 1981), 168–206.

14. June Namias cites research by Daniel K. Richter and Alden Vaughan that confirms that a high percentage of white women captured by Indians survived and that during the colonial period, between 30 and 37 percent remained with the French and Indians; 44 percent returned to New England. June Namias, *White Captives* (Chapel Hill: University of North Carolina Press, 1995), 25.

15. Meginness, *Biography of Frances Slocum*, 127–28.

16. June Namias contends that during the 1830s women were increasingly depicted in captivity narratives as frail flowers. Namias associates such depictions with the "rise of True Womanhood and the mass marketing of sentimental fiction." In these depictions the captive or heroine "turns frailty, motherhood, cleanliness, and disgusting Indians into highly salable works. . . . She is the poor, hapless woman who is taken unawares." *White Captives*, 36–37.

17. *Art of George Winter*, 113–17; George Winter, "Journal of a Visit to Deaf Man's Village, 1839," George Winter Manuscript, Tippecanoe County Historical, Lafayette, Indiana, 2–23 [13].

18. Todd, *Lost Sister*, 126.

19. Ibid.

20. Many Natives communities in the Great Lakes were nominally Catholic, but following the successful conclusion to the War of 1812, evangelical Protestant missionaries streamed into the Old Northwest. According to R. David Edmunds, most rebuffed or ignored the Protestant assault; the Potawatomis, for instance, would have preferred a Catholic priest. R. David Edmunds, *The Potawatomis* (Norman: University of Oklahoma Press, 1939), 222–23. For a description of the frontier Catholicism and Catholic kin networks that linked Native and French peoples involved in the fur trade, see Susan Sleeper-Smith, "Women, Kin, and Catholicism: New Perspectives on the Fur Trade," *Ethnohistory* (2000): 423–52. Following her death, Francis Slocum's inventoried possessions included a Jesuit cross. She, like many of the Miami, may have professed an interest in Catholicism, or she may have acquired the cross through trade. Silver crosses, both large and small, were part of trade good inventories.

21. Todd, *Lost Sister*, 156–57.

22. Ibid., 120.

23. *Art of George Winter*, 62, 72, Plate 26.

24. Rafert, *Miami Indians*.

25. In 1900 the Miamis still owned almost one thousand acres in Indiana, but by 1920 they had lost over half that acreage, and by 1921 the Aetna Insurance Company foreclosed on the last lands left from the Ozahsinquah Reserve (lands originally held by Frances Slocum's youngest daughter). Rafert, *Miami Indians*, 201–4.

7. Michigan Murder Mysteries

Death and Rumor in the
Age of Indian Removal

GREGORY EVANS DOWD

Contrary Obituary, 1846

Henry Rowe Schoolcraft, very much alive and breathing, read his own obituary on July 13, 1846. A resident of Washington, D.C., Schoolcraft read the report of his death in a clipping from the *Albany Argus,* a leading newspaper in upstate New York. Amazed, Schoolcraft wondered at *his own* reported assassination in remote Sault Ste. Marie, Michigan, a place he knew well but had not seen in years. The report stated that Schoolcraft had been shot by a hidden gunman, "a half breed, named Tanner," who had escaped, but was being pursued by "the entire population" of the Sault.[1] Shaken, Schoolcraft knew that that the "rumor of [his] murder" was false, but he nevertheless suspected that the story held, somewhere within its flawed husk, more than a germ of truth.[2]

This chapter investigates several rumors held by Ottawas, Ojibwes (Chippewas), and American citizens that circulated in or about Michigan during the era of Indian removal. Michigan's Indians were not without resources as they struggled to remain in the state. Although many suffered enormous losses in land and political autonomy, most persisted and thwarted federal attempts to remove them west of the Mississippi. As Susan Gray and James McClurken have separately demonstrated, a combination of circumstances created relatively good conditions for Native American persistence in Michigan. Ottawas (also known as Odawas) and Ojibwes (also known as Ojibwas or Chippewas) lived for the most part on lands that were of marginal interest to U.S. farmers, or in fertile microclimates unattached to the broadening band of U.S. settlement. The largest of the state's land cessions came on the eve of the Depression of 1837, which halted a powerful land rush south of the Grand River, providing many of the state's Indians with a few extra— and critical—years, during which federal removal policy lost its force. The proximity of the still potentially dangerous Canadian border combined with the currency of the Seminole war and the Cherokee removals to restrain American officials from deploying increasingly scarce bayonets in the far north.[3] Out of a population of perhaps eight thousand Indians who inhabited lands that became Michigan in 1837, only 651 were removed to the West; by 1853, a third of federally counted Indians still living east of the Mississippi resided in Michigan.[4]

Indian resistance to removal did not make Michigan a multicultural haven in the 1830s and 1840s. Native Americans and settlers both failed to fully articulate, much less to share, a vision of cohabitation in the state. Real violence was limited (in comparison to many other areas of the country), but imagined violence periodically resulted in rumors and alarms. This essay focuses on Michigan in the era of Indian removal and examines a series of such alarming reports about mass murders, massacres, and assassinations.[5]

Alarming rumors and intercultural horror stories emerged from many ethnic groups. The authors of these alarms included New England editors, midwestern governors, and leading Ottawa and Ojibwe spokesmen. Less prominent settlers and natives also contributed rumors of each other's violent intentions or deeds. American expansion and Jacksonian Indian policy created considerable insecurity among Native Americans throughout the United States. In Michigan, both American citizens and Indians were aware of the Seminole Wars in Florida and the forced removal of the Cherokee Nation from Georgia. Closer to home, they were familiar with the removal and subsequent suffering of Potawatomi tribespeople from Indiana. Moreover, the continued presence and proximity of the British in Canada also caused alarm among the Americans. Meanwhile suspicious tribespeople and even some settlers fostered rumors about germ warfare, ethnic cleansing, and genocide (although not with those terms). Both Indians and federal officials alike stood accused of crimes they certainly had not committed.

Yet many rumors contained "half-truths" that buttressed their credibility.[6] Thick with misinformation, the reports of Henry Schoolcraft's early demise, for example, were nonetheless correct in some details. For example, the false report of his death correctly referred to him as a former Indian agent. Indeed, between 1820 and 1841, Schoolcraft had served as an Indian agent and had participated in a dozen treaties. He had also once resided at Sault Ste. Marie. Most reports called him a scholar or a writer, and some pointed out that he had married a woman of Indian descent. All true: he published widely, sometimes jointly with his wife, Jane Schoolcraft (d. 1842), the well-educated eldest daughter of the Anglo-Irish trader John Johnston and the prominent Ojibwe Oshaguacodaywaygua (Susan Johnston). He had been mentored by Lewis Cass, had served under President Jackson, and by 1830 he had embraced Democratic policies, including Indian removal. Studious, prolific, intellectually ambitious, in the 1820s he became a nationally recognized authority on North American Indians. By the 1830s he increasingly voiced the lofty and high-handed Anglo-Saxonism that had become a strong intellectual current of his day.[7]

Schoolcraft had good reason to be alarmed by the false news of his death. He immediately feared that reports had confused him with his younger brother, James, or one of his "several nephews," all of whom had continued to reside at Sault Ste. Marie or elsewhere in Michigan. Schoolcraft knew that both he and James had angered a man named Tanner, the alleged killer. And indeed, as Schoolcraft soon learned, the victim was James, his younger brother. The papers, in turn, soon corrected themselves: the *Argus* responsibly admitted that public "rumor" had "confounded" the two Schoolcrafts. James was the victim; Henry, still alive, "is now in the city of Washington."[8]

False, inaccurate news is no stranger to our own time, or any time. That Henry Schoolcraft, far better known than his brother, had been taken by Eastern editors for the Schoolcraft killed at the Sault is an understandable error. But there is more here than a simple error in transmission. While rumors are often thought to originate in "faulty perception," in a "distortion in serial transmission," or in an "inaccurate reproduction" of information, rumor itself is a kind of medium, one that constitutes and reveals states and frames of mind. Rumor "is not an individual creation that spreads, but a collective formation that arises in the collaboration of many." Rumor, in this tradition, is the product of a collective effort to understand unexplained events or conditions. Whatever its origin, rumor cannot thrive without the support of groups of people. As the sociologist Tamotsu Shibutani states, rumor results from "the social interaction of people caught in inadequately defined situations. To act intelligently such persons seek news, and rumor is essentially a type of news." Or, as Jean Noël Kapferer has more recently written: "Rumors do not *take off* from the truth but rather *seek out* the truth."[9] Thus, the misinformation in the rumor of Henry Schoolcraft's death went far beyond the victim's identity. The story of Schoolcraft's death not only revealed much about Schoolcraft, but it also said a lot about Indians and American citizens in Michigan.

James Schoolcraft and the Removal Expedition of 1838

James Schoolcraft, the real victim of 1846, never approached his older brother in reputation or achievement. He did serve as an Indian agent, however. In 1836 the government signed a treaty with "the Ottawa and Chippewa Nation of Indians," in which the Indians agreed to seriously consider plans for their removal from Michigan. The agreement stipulated that the Indians would go west only if an exploratory party from the tribes visited the plains and found a suitable location for their new home.[10] Two years later, in 1838, James Schoolcraft served as the federal "conductor" of an "exploratory party" of Ottawas and Ojibwes that journeyed to Kansas to examine a tract of western lands to which the government hoped they would remove.[11]

As the brothers Schoolcraft knew, the Ottawas and Ojibwes who had signed the treaty actually were opposed to removing west of the Missouri River. In 1838, when the exploring party assembled, Ojibwes from Michigan's upper peninsula refused even to accompany the expedition. Their spokesman, Szhegud, emphatically stated: "We all say, our chiefs and our young men, that we will not go with the officer sent by our great father, to visit the country west of the Mississippi; we do not wish to go there; we object to it entirely, this is all we have to say." That decision reflected badly on James Schoolcraft, who lived at the Sault and had yet failed to persuade the local bands to cooperate.[12] Henry Schoolcraft was not too concerned with that result; he was more interested in persuading the Ottawas in the Lower Peninsula, especially those who belonged to the Grand River bands, to depart from the state. But there he too met with strong opposition. The Grand River Ottawas, closely affiliated with certain Potawatomi bands whose relatives already had been removed, had heard "unfavorable stories"—many all too true—that refugees from deportation "told of the west." The Ottawas also were reluctant to leave Michigan.[13]

To advance the Ottawa removal and at least a limited Ojibwe removal, the brothers improvised an exploring party to conduct to the West, where they intended to obtain the expedition members' collective approval of western removal "*before their return*" (emphasis in the original) to Michigan. The Indians in the exploring party had little influence in their bands, but the Schoolcraft brothers portrayed them as a diplomatic embassy empowered to make momentous decisions regarding their people's removal.[14] As the expedition returned from the West, they paused at Green Bay, Wisconsin, where James Schoolcraft secured the Indians' agreement "to remove" to the lands on the Plains, "in the event of our [the Indians'] emigrating from our present country, sold by us, to the United States." But the document meant little. The "event" of the Indians' emigration to lands southwest of the Missouri had not occurred. The Indians still had not agreed to remove. Upon his return to the Sault, he noted that "they will attempt to avoid emigrating."[15] Henry Schoolcraft briefly waved the document at leading Ottawas and Ojibwes, but they presented him with "fixed opposition," denying "the power" of the explorers "to bind them to the location on the Osage," and expressing "their determination not to remove to it."[16]

James Schoolcraft's efforts at removal only reduced the Indians' already low estimation of federal agents. The tribespeople now envisioned Schoolcraft and other officials as "*mere Disbursers of Annuities and Emigrating Officers.*"[17] But given the Ottawas' and Ojibwes' successful denigration of the bogus removal agreement and their evident opposition to removal, one might wonder what led any individuals to join the expedition in the first place.

Henry Schoolcraft and the Maple River Alarm of 1838

From the beginning of March through September 1838, as the exploring party assembled and toured the west, other Ottawas and Ojibwes of the Lower Peninsula faced increased pressure to remove from the state. Knowledge that the Potawatomis already had been removed, that the Cherokees faced removal, and that a catastrophic war raged in Florida all alarmed the Ottawas and Ojibwes, but local events added to their sense of crisis. While Schoolcraft's exploring party was assembling to leave for the west, the Indian bands in the Lower Peninsula found themselves accused of murder and massacre.[18]

In 1837 a New Hampshire Yankee, Ansel Glass, had moved with his family to a new home in the Maple River valley in south-central Michigan. The Maple River, a tributary of the Grand River, flows westward through historic Ottawa country into Lake Michigan; its headwaters rise on lands that also drain into the Shiawassee River, which flows northward through historic Ojibwe country into Saginaw Bay on Lake Huron. No one doubted that the Maple Valley had been formally ceded in treaty to the United States, and Ansel Glass had settled on U.S. lands in a time of peace. By American custom, Indian treaty, and recent history, he should not have expected any violence. Still, his cabin was remote; the closest settlement of American citizens was four miles away.

Hiram Brown, one of Glass's "nearest settlers," ascended the Maple in late March 1838 and discovered the charred wreckage of the Glass cabin and three fire-blackened corpses. Investigation proved the remains to be those of Glass's wife and children, unnamed in the surviving Indian Office records. Ansel Glass's corpse was not found among them, but newspapers soon reported the "strong presumption" that he had perished with his family, the victim of an Indian massacre. The house, after all, had been deliberately set aflame, a fact that resonated with legendary Indian violence.[19] What's more, according to a letter that first appeared in the March 30 edition of the *Detroit Free Press*, then printed elsewhere, "Several locks of the woman's hair" lay "near the door of the house, with the skin and flesh attached." Across the North, Americans read of a citizen family murdered, burned, and scalped on the Michigan frontier.[20]

Federal Indian agent Henry Schoolcraft, then at Detroit, promised settlers "the most energetic measures pursued to punish the outrage." He vowed to hold Grand River Ottawa bands collectively responsible for the guilty party's "apprehension, and surrendering to justice."[21] By April 10 he expanded his investigation to include the Saginaw Ojibwes. The Ottawas had strenuously denied any involvement, and several skilled Ottawa hunters had found a trail, partially concealed, leading from the Maple River toward the Shiawassee and the Ojibwes.[22] Citing such "intelligence from Maple River," Schoolcraft ordered his subagent at Saginaw to look into it, although he still believed the Ottawas might be guilty. He gave both the Ottawas and Ojibwes forty days to deliver the guilty party. He noted, without reflection, that Glass's remains had yet to be found.[23]

Several influential U.S. citizens entertained doubts about the Indians' guilt. At Detroit, Brigadier General Hugh Brady, Commander of the Northwestern Department of the U.S. Army, refused to act "until the outrage is proved to have been committed by the Indians."[24] Other Michiganders speculated about the absence of Glass's body and wondered if the murders were an example of domestic homicide rather than acts of violence by domestic dependent nations. Rev. Leonard Slater, a Baptist missionary who knew the Grand River Ottawas well, noted the increasing suspicion "that the man who could [not] be found murdered his own family."

But Slater's quiet challenge was overshadowed by growing alarm. On April 19, 1838, 196 citizens of the Grand River valley petitioned President Martin Van Buren for protection from "hostile" Ottawas and Ojibwes. They even raised the specter of "another *Florida War*."[25] Moreover, they levied serious charges against the federal Indian Office and its agents, including, indirectly, Henry Schoolcraft. The killings, the petitioners stated, stemmed from a federal act of "injustice visited upon the Ottawa and Chippewa Nations." The United States had failed in 1837 to adequately deliver annuity payments owed to the Grand River Ottawas under the 1836 Treaty of Washington. The treaty stipulated that the Indians were to be paid in "hard money," but because of the Panic of 1837, the Indian Office was short of specie and had attempted to partially pay the 1837 annuities in goods that few Indians desired. Ironically, many tribal leaders sought payments in hard money so that they could purchase Michigan lands in fee simple. To add insult to injury, the government in 1837 had sought to dispense the goods at Mackinac Island, a great and dangerous distance from the Grand River.[26] The petitioners alleged, then, that local Grand River Ottawas, infuriated by a genuine injustice—a failure to honor promised annuity payments—had slaughtered a family of citizens in revenge, creating so great an alarm that "many of the settlers have left their farms." Calling for troops, the petitioners also requested—as they saw it—for "justice" to the Indians, or "the Inhabitants on this frontier will be compelled to leave or to be sacrificed to Indian vengeance."[27]

Even before the Glass affair, Grand River citizens had sounded sharp alarms about the treaty violation. The editor of a Grand Rapids paper protested the faulty payment in gory terms: "The exasperated feelings of those Indians . . . render the situation of the northern settlements of that State extremely exposed, not only to depredations upon property, but to massacre and Savage butchery!"[28] Yet mixed with the citizens' fear was also a loss of economic opportunity, for the annuity money, in silver coin, meant a great deal to Grand Valley citizens. Cash was short in the best of times; in these years of financial depression, the shortage was acute. Enterprising Grand River settlers saw economic salvation in the Indians' treaty moneys. The tribespeople would spend the cash to purchase goods and services from local merchants. If they received trade goods from the government, they would purchase relatively little.[29]

As the rumored connection between faulty annuities and Indian violence spread to the east, it became politically inflected. Whig Party papers as far away as New Hampshire stated that the massacre of the Glass family, described as a certain Indian attack, had been "occasioned by non-fulfillment of the treaties by the United States." Indeed, many Whigs interpreted the killings in Michigan within a broader political perspective that also included events such as the flimsy Treaty of New Echota (1835) and the removal of the Cherokees. All these events had been triggered by Jacksonian Indian policy. Whigs complained, "It is not disgrace enough, that the authorities at Washington avow their determination to carry into effect treaties which are clearly proved to have been fraudulently made, in pursuance of the 'Indian policy,' but we have to record the pitiful spectacle of the violation of those made in good faith by both parties, on the part of the stronger."[30]

Whigs alleged not only that annuity payments had failed to reach the Grand River Ottawas, but that a major New York government contractor had received a huge payment in hard currency to ship goods to Mackinac in 1837: "But the darkest feature of this faithless transaction is the fact that Suydam, Jackson & Co. last summer obtained a draft for forty thousand dollars in *specie*."[31] Yet if the Whigs circulated rumors that the Democrats were responsible for federal corruption and the misadministration of Indian removals, like Democrats, they assumed that the Indians in Michigan were responsible for the bloody vengeance. These rumors, like those studied by scholars elsewhere, passed "judgments," they "expressed opinions on society and political affairs," and they "took established forms and were based on motifs which gave them force and logic."[32] Ironically the Whigs, alleging Indian Office corruption, drew upon ideological impulses shared with Democrats: impulses that evoked images of Indian corruption and degeneration. Against these, the voice of missionary Leonard Slater, who insisted that Glass had killed his own family, was only dimly heard. Slater saw treaty violations, but not Indian violence. In fact, he asserted "The white people have made more noise about the [missing annuity] money than the Indians have ever done."[33]

As an Indian agent, Democrat Henry Schoolcraft first investigated, then stoked and fanned the allegations against the Ottawas and Ojibwes. While Grand River citizens deployed imagined Indian murder to secure Indian annuities, and while Whigs grabbed the allegations to cudgel the Democrats, Schoolcraft found the massacre resonant with Jacksonian goals. It was amid this uproar over the horrid deaths that the Schoolcraft brothers attempted to recruit Indian participants for the exploring party to the Plains. The Maple Valley massacre strengthened their hand. Meeting with the local Ottawas at Grand Haven in early June, Henry Schoolcraft reached a "compact" with them: the government would honor its obligations and conveniently make future payments in the Grand Valley as long as the President deemed it proper. For their part, the Ottawas agreed in a gesture of good will to contribute members to the exploratory party. The agreement reached, Schoolcraft announced in a letter to the *Detroit Free Press* that the Ottawas were both innocent of the killings and satisfied with all government dealings.[34]

Schoolcraft, however, continued to nourish his own suspicions of Indian guilt in the Maple River massacre. At his request, Saginaw subagent Henry Connor had arrested and confined two Saginaw Ojibwe men. Schoolcraft asked that counsel be found for the prisoners, then alerted federal authorities in mid-June that "No doubt exists in my mind . . . that the Saginaws are alone guilty."[35] It is noteworthy that the Saginaw Ojibwes had no part in the 1836 treaty, the violation of which Grand River settlers had locally alleged to be the cause of Indian hostilities. Yet Schoolcraft could not have designed a better outcome. The initial pressure on the Ottawas induced them to join the exploring party, while later assertions of Saginaw Ojibwe guilt provided continued ideological evidence that Indian communities and U.S. settlements were best kept apart.

The evidence was rumor, and to the credit of subagent Connor, the two falsely accused Saginaw men were quickly released, against Schoolcraft's objections, for lack of evidence. Schoolcraft insisted that Cobmoosa, a Grand River Ottawa leader, had convinced him that the Saginaws were guilty and that their guilt had been concealed by the Saginaw leader, Keegido. But by mid-June, both Rev. Slater near the Grand River and subagent Connor at Saginaw had concluded that no Indians had any part in the killings.[36]

Schoolcraft did not mention the Maple River massacre in his *Annual Report* of September 1838. But two years later, he referred to it in the most pessimistic, brooding, and racist *Annual Report* he ever penned. Promoting removal by once again deploying the massacre of the Glass family, he enshrined the event in an official, published government document: "The murder of Glass and his family on the head waters of Grand River in 1838, which yet remains unexpiated, indicates that it is impossible to shield the settlers, at all points, from occasional outbreaks of personal vindiction. The earlier the local separation is therefore effected between masses of population so wholly dissimilar as the white and the red, the more auspicious will it be for the peace and prosperity of both."[37]

Schoolcraft wrote definitively in 1840 of the "murder of Glass," whose trail had gone cold but whose unlocated body may still have been warm. Suspicions that Glass had slain his own wife and children had been addressed to the agent, who might have considered them as militating against Indian guilt. Instead, Schoolcraft fed rumor in the service of removal.

The Grand Valley alarm of 1838 placed two Ojibwe men in brief confinement, labeled Indians as killers, and induced the Ottawas to join the exploration party that James Schoolcraft led to Missouri and Kansas. It is also noteworthy for what did *not* happen. The Grand River Ottawas remained in Michigan—they were not forced west. The jailed Saginaws were not charged, not lynched; they were released. Grand River citizens rumored war, but they did not mobilize against Indians or unite in calls for Indian removal. Henry Schoolcraft continued into late 1840 to draw lines between the triangular dots of the killings, the Indians, and removal, but few paid attention to his picture. That year's election would lead to his own removal from office.

A decade later, Schoolcraft included an account of the Maple River killings in his *Personal Memoirs,* a published and highly edited version of his journals.[38] Under the date March 30, 1838, Schoolcraft discussed the Glass affair, including much detail that could only have been added after that date.

Suspicion first fell on the Grand River Ottawas. I investigated the subject, and found this unjust. They are a peaceable, orderly, agricultural people, friendly to the settlers, and having no cause of dislike to them. Suspicion next fell on the Saginaws, who hunt in that quarter, and whose character has not recovered from the imputation of murder and plunder committed during the war of 1812. . . . But on an investigation made by Mr. Connor, at Saginaw, this imputation was also found improbable, . . . leaving the horrible mystery unexplained.

In a footnote, Schoolcraft added (in the inconclusive, passive language of rumor): "*Mr Glass was subsequently, in 1841, found alive in Wisconsin.*"[39]

The killings of an unnamed woman and her two unnamed children went unsolved, but not without unveiling the Michigan frontier as a complicated zone in which settlers feared Indian vengeance while they, at the same time, utilized a continued Indian presence, if only instrumentally. It was also a place where a probable act of domestic homicide could be manipulated to implicate or advance federal Indian policy. It was, finally, Indian country, where the effects of such rumors left Ottawas and Ojibwes to speculate about their highly uncertain futures.

Ottawa and Ojibwe Rumors of Removal, and Worse, 1834–41

James Schoolcraft's expedition to the Plains, taking place amid the rumors of Indian violence, intensified the Ottawas' and Ojibwes' sense of impending calamity. As the winter of 1838–39 drew to a close, their apprehension mounted. Potawatomis from southern Michigan and Indiana, tribespeople to whom the Ottawas were related, had been forcibly, and even violently, removed. While typhoid, malnourishment, exhaustion, and exposure had killed many members of the emigrant bands, there were others who escaped from the dying columns and returned to the Great Lakes country with accounts of their personal experiences and with hearsay.[40]

Saginaw Ojibwes felt removal pressures most strongly, having signed treaties surrendering their remaining lands. By treaty, they theoretically had agreed to leave the state for western lands in 1842. The *Ogema,* or leader, Keegido, whom Schoolcraft described as "a man of strong passions and ungoverned will," had marked a removal treaty in 1837. On June 26, 1839, Schoolcraft learned of Keegido's death from a migrating party of his people. They had come to Mackinac Island to visit the agent as they emigrated from their homeland. But they were not headed to the Plains; they were instead fleeing what they feared might be an impending federally sponsored removal from the Great Lakes by crossing Lake Huron—to Canada.[41]

Nor were they alone. Schoolcraft observed that other Indians from the region adjoining Lakes Michigan and Huron were joining them. He commented that a "considerable number of the Lake Indians have transferred their residence from the U. S. territories to the Manatouline Islands, during this season." Amid fears of forced removal, Potawatomis, Ojibwes, Ottawas, and others were choosing Canada over the Great Plains. According to Schoolcraft, "Something like a panic was created among the bands along Lake Huron and Michigan, by a report . . . that the United States intended, this season, to send steamboats, and take them off, by force, to the west of the Mississippi."[42] He blamed the flight upon both British "inducements" and the Great Lakes Indians' reluctance to leave their wider homeland: "They fear going west: they cling to the north."[43] The agent believed the majority of the Indians remaining in Michigan, even those who had not yet signed any agreements, eventually would be forced from the state: he did remarkably little to ease their fears.

The rumors of forced removal were, by 1839, highly informed and familiar. In 1834, the Roman Catholic priest Father Frederick Baraga had noted that Ottawas at Grand Rapids were "very much depressed as they hear that perhaps they will have to leave this place and move far from here." Government assurances that all lands would be justly purchased did little to dissuade the Ottawas that they would be cheated of their lands and forced west, Baraga noted, because the United States found ways to "deceive the Indians and deprive them of nice lands, as has been the case, until now, in all treaties of this kind." The Ottawas believed and passed on rumors, Baraga continued, that the governor already had assigned a federal commission to treat with them for their remaining Michigan lands.[44]

The rumor was (in 1834, at least) false; the territorial governor held no such commission. But by 1836, after the Treaty of Washington, removal fears intensified. In the initial treaty, signed on March 28 by Ottawa and Ojibwe leaders in Washington, the attending bands ceded to the United States almost all of their remaining lands in the Lower Peninsula and much of the eastern Upper Peninsula, retaining fourteen permanent reservations, among the treaty's many provisions. The treaty paved the way for the tribes' westward withdrawal to either Minnesota or Kansas, but only (as we have seen) when the Indians agreed to remove. Henry Schoolcraft served as the treaty's federal commissioner.[45]

Before ratifying the treaty in May, the Senate drastically revised it, creating conditions that helped to propagate rumors. The Senate imposed a five-year tenure on the hitherto permanent reservations and promised a compensation for the change (in a manner not relevant to this chapter). It also eliminated

Minnesota as a potential future home in favor of the Central Plains. However, despite these two drastic changes (and there were others), the Senate did not alter any of the wording that left the final decision to emigrate from Michigan in the hands of the Indians themselves. The amendments increased the pressure to remove by terminating reservations after five years, but removal remained a matter for the Indians to decide. A cautious authority on treaty making has concluded of this treaty that "no wholesale removal was involved."[46]

The changes nonetheless alarmed Indians living from Sault Ste. Marie to the Grand River. From the Sault, James Schoolcraft wrote to his brother that John Holiday, a recently blinded fur trader who had served as the official interpreter at the treaty, was now spreading "much 'bad dog' talk [about the revised treaty] amongst the Indians." At Grand River, veteran fur trader Rix Robinson also heard "vague reports" about the Senate's changes that had "circulated amongst the Indians which has caused some uneasiness amongst them." Robinson claimed that he had persuaded local Ottawas not to believe "such unfounded kind of reports." Neither James Schoolcraft nor Rix Robinson stated exactly what the rumors were, but both connected them to the Senate's alterations, and both claimed to have persuaded the Indians that the rumors were false.[47]

The Senate's revisions added to the widespread Indian conviction that the United States was untrustworthy. While Schoolcraft assembled new delegations to agree to the Senate amendments in July, rumors continued to circulate, and they impelled Indians to action. Ottawas in the Little Traverse Bay region openly discussed emigration to Canada, and many actually left the United States. In 1887 the Ottawa historian Andrew Blackbird, a boy in 1836, recalled that his people "thought when signing the treaty that they were securing reservations of lands in different localities as permanent homes for themselves and their children in the future; but before six months had elapsed from the time of signing the treaty . . . they were told by their white neighbors that their reservations of land would expire in five years, instead of being perpetual, as they believed."

Having accurately described a major difference between the document signed in Washington and that ratified by the Senate, Blackbird proceeded to describe a panic-laden rumor, which held that the government meant to forcibly remove the Indians. After five years, "they would be compelled to leave their homes, and if they should refuse they would be driven at point of bayonet into a strange land, where, as it is almost always the case, more than one-half would die before they could be acclimated. At this most startling intelligence more than half of my people fled into Canada."[48]

This last figure was probably an exaggeration, but parties of Indians did head north. These flights to Canada, and talk of such flights, precipitated by rumors of forced removal, paradoxically restrained American policy. Difficulties remained between the United States and the British Empire following the War of 1812. The boundary between British territories and the United States would not be settled in the Lake Superior region until 1842, and not in Oregon until 1846. In the several years following the treaty, a minor Canadian rebellion known as the "Patriot Movement" threatened peace along the border from Michigan to New York.[49] As Indians from Michigan paddled massive trade canoes to Manitoulin Island, American authorities worried about the British meddling in Indian affairs in Michigan; the Indian Office had no wish to see Ottawas and Ojibwes emigrating en masse to the Crown.

In his *Annual Report* of 1838, the U.S. Commissioner of Indian Affairs quoted Schoolcraft's concerns about British efforts "to colonize the Ottawas and Chippewas [Ojibwes] in Upper Canada." If the British sought such colonies, the Commissioner believed, the United States should try to prevent them.[50] The Indians' removal alarms of 1834–1839 thus helped deflect removal itself. Encouraging actions undesired by the United States, the rumors constituted a "counter-power" against any immediate removal plans by the government.[51]

The Senate's surprising amendments of 1836 were resubmitted to the Ottawas and Ojibwas for approval in July 1836. Enough Indians agreed to the changes that officials in Jackson's administration believed that these tribes had accepted the new terms. But rumors still persisted and were fed by the government's failure to provide adequate annuities. In 1837, when the Ottawas and Ojibwes assembled for their annuities at Mackinac Island, Major Jonathan Garland and agent Henry Schoolcraft again endeavored to persuade the Ottawas and Ojibwes to accept goods in lieu of cash. They encountered stiff opposition. Antigovernment rumors abounded. According to Garland, "Among other fabrications to prevent the Indians from taking the goods, they were made to believe that their great Father [President Van Buren] had caused them to be infected with some fatal malady; and as evidence of it, instanced the alterations made by the Senate and now the offer of goods in lieu of specie."[52]

That European Americans had deliberately infected or poisoned goods in acts of wanton mass murder was an established motif by the nineteenth century, and it lives on in the Great Lakes today. The line between rumor, legend, and history can blur, and it is not "by chance" that old rumors are often recycled, retaining certain elements from earlier forms and employing these in a new "context."[53] Evidence suggests that unscrupulous traders sometimes adulterated hard liquor, although such allegations are difficult to document. That alcohol itself was a killer in Native North America is more demonstrable, though again, the precise causes of death varied greatly from person to person. There is no doubt, however, that even in the late eighteenth century, many Native Americans equated alcohol with Euro-Americans and with death. Ottawas in the Little Traverse Bay region had already experienced an indigenous temperance movement deriding liquor as a deadly European evil.[54]

A well-documented instance of deliberate British-colonial germ warfare against Native Americans took place in the Upper Ohio region during Pontiac's War.[55] The documented instance resembles that told in legend by Little Traverse Bay Ottawas, according to Andrew Blackbird. He tells of a gift received by Ottawas from the British during the Seven Years' War. It was a tin box, which they only opened upon returning to their villages. Inside, they found another box, and inside that, another. On it went, until "they found nothing but moldy particles inside the last little box!" Soon, there "burst out a terrible sickness among them. . . . Lodge after lodge was totally vacated . . . entire families being swept off with the ravages of this terrible disease."[56]

Rumors and legends that Euro-Americans possessed control over disease were invigorated in this period by federal efforts to inoculate Indians *against* smallpox. The inoculations made good sense, both as indicative of American concern about Indians and as a hedge against the disease spreading from the tribespeople to the larger American population. Curiously, the two federal treaties that mention "vaccine matter" are the Treaty of Washington (1836) and the Treaty of Detroit (1837), treaties that included most of the Ottawa and Ojibwe bands in the Lower Peninsula and several in the Upper Peninsula. Henry Schoolcraft served as commissioner at each treaty.[57]

The suspicion that the United States might intend Indian extermination resonated, too, with American citizens' expectations that Euro-American expansion foreordained Indian death and disappearance. Ben Franklin opined in the 1790s that if it were the "design of Providence to extirpate these savages in order to make room for the cultivators of the earth," hard liquor would be "the appointed means."[58] The concept that Indian peoples would somehow fade away before the advance of settlers was already enshrined in literature and widely assumed—even desired—in the republic's dominant culture; American citizens were but a few critical steps away from imagining the worst of the Indians' own fears.[59]

Indians in Michigan were well aware that many Americans believed they were doomed to extinction. In 1841 Presbyterian missionary Peter Doughtery informed local traders that Ahgosa, a leader of the Grand Traverse Ottawas and Ojibwes, had complained to him that George Johnston, Schoolcraft's brother-in-law, had informed them they "had better prepare for removing." According to Dougherty, Ahgosa and his people refused to do so and would "hold on to this place as a bird clings to a branch of a tree waiving and ready to fall." But they also distrusted the Schoolcrafts, and they wanted the trading company to "tell them the truth." Henry Schoolcraft's 1840 report, the frightening contents of which they were well aware, aggravated their fears.[60] Schoolcraft had not only urged removal by citing the Glass murders; he also warned of the destruction of Indians who failed to remove: Schoolcraft ominously had predicted, "There are no lateral causes to be evolved, it is believed, which will arrest the spread of the Saxon race over the whole continent, and it is not probable that any provision can be made for the preservation of the Aboriginal race, which promises to be so effectual as their colonization or transference to a separate territory."[61]

Dougherty tried to persuade Ahgosa that the cosmic report was but the opinion of one man. He suggested that President-Elect William Henry Harrison might well have different views. But Dougherty could not be sure of the immediate future, and Ahgosa's Ottawas and Ojibwes needed more information. They could not afford to be as complacent or patient as Dougherty. They requested that Dougherty seek out other sources. Uncertain about their future, they revealed their "unwillingness" to passively accept "formally approved" reports.[62]

Like their neighbors at Grand Traverse, the Grand River Ottawas also heard rumors of "a general removal from the state." And much farther to the north, at Sault Ste. Marie, Ojibwes told one another that "they were immediately to be removed, by the Department, to the West of the Mississippi river." Indeed, "so great was the alarm, that many of them would have gone over to the Canadian side," had not James Ord, the local agent, intervened to contradict the false news. Ord did not let his superiors forget that in his part of the world, war with Great Britain might lead to "atrocities of the worst kind." In his last months in office, Henry Schoolcraft did little to counter these false reports, stating only, "There will be a change in the head of the Indian office at Washington on or after the 4th March [inauguration day]."[63]

In 1841, when Robert Stuart, the new Whig Indian agent, assumed office in Michigan, he was inundated by alarms from Indians that they soon would be forcibly removed from the state. Stuart immediately sought confirmation from both the Indian Office and the War Department that such reports were groundless. According to Stuart, the Ottawas and Ojibwes were "alarmed through malicious reports, that they should be forced (at the point of the bayonet) to go west of the Mississippi." Because of such news, he reported, many had fled to Canada. Stuart predicted that he could induce recent Indian emigrants to return to the United States if the government dropped its plans to resettle tribespeople on the Plains in favor of Minnesota. He also sought permission to assure Indians in his agency "that they will not be suddenly disturbed, without my consulting with and giving them notice?"[64]

While citizen-settlers rumored outbreaks of Indian violence, Indians rumored germ warfare and mass deportation. Panicked by the prospect of a long and arduous removal to the Plains, Indian families fled in canoes to Canada. The shifting and unfulfilled treaty promises of the United States, combined with the devious but bungled 1838 effort by the Schoolcraft brothers to secure a removal agreement, fed Indian rumors of federal malevolence. The rumors also revealed the inability of the United States to defend and rationalize its Indian policies; they demonstrate that Indians contested Jacksonian ideologies. At times, Ottawa and Ojibwe rumors even configured federal policy, restraining it by promoting federal fears of an Indian presence in the British territories.

John Tanner, Rumored Murderer of 1846

In July 1846, when a gunshot killed one of the two Schoolcraft brothers, newspapers initially confused the living Henry for the dead James. In contrast, they left little doubt as to who pulled the trigger. Official pronouncements took the same tack. Governor Alpheus Felch of Michigan announced a $500 reward for the apprehension, not of the "suspected" or "alleged" murder, but of *the* "murderer of James Schoolcraft": John Tanner.[65] This was an assumption, a surmise based upon the evidence of Tanner's character and his probable motives. Reported as fact, it was instead rumor. In 1846 Henry Schoolcraft firmly believed Tanner to be the killer, and he said so four years later in his published memoirs. Modern historians have generally been more careful, some leaning toward Tanner's guilt, others away, but all admitting to uncertainties.[66]

It is easy enough to imagine that Tanner killed James Schoolcraft. Tanner had suffered many injuries—physical, psychological, and social. Having been torn, at about age nine, from his Kentucky family, he had spent two miserable years among his captors before being sold to Net-no-kwa, an Ottawa woman who became his stepmother and lovingly cared for him. Tanner spent two relatively happy years with his stepfamily in Michigan before his adopted Ojibwe father was killed in a brawl. Net-no-kwa then took Tanner and her children and accompanied other members of their band west of Lake Superior, where they lived between Rainy Lake, the Assiniboine River, and the upper Red River. Tanner forgot the English language but remembered his family of origin. He suffered a permanent, partial hearing loss following an illness in his youth, and he also broke several ribs when he fell from a tree. An assault by a jealous hunter left him with a fractured skull, and his right arm was shattered by a gunshot fired by a friend of his wife's, who strongly opposed Tanner's decision to have their children educated in mission schools.[67]

His *Narrative of the Captivity and Adventures of John Tanner* discusses these travails. Written in 1827 with Army surgeon Edwin James (Tanner could sign his name but was not literate), the book reveals a man who fought often with others. He loved and trusted Net-no-kwa, and he struggled for the care and control of his children, but he had few other friends. According to Tanner, he endured "persecutions" from both Indians and Euro-Americans. His marriages failed. He spent long periods with his children, isolated from Ottawa-Ojibwe band members.[68]

Much battered and in his forties, in 1824 Tanner finally made his way to Mackinac Island; by 1828 he had settled at Sault Ste. Marie. Some of his children joined him, and he once more engaged in a struggle over their care. In 1830, the Michigan Territorial Legislative Council authorized the sheriff at Sault Ste. Marie to take away Martha, Tanner's daughter. Henry Schoolcraft, a council member, secured the passage of this extraordinary legislative order. What abuse prompted the act is unrecorded; what is clear is that several of the Sault's leading citizens supported it.[69] With two Ojibwe marriages behind him, Tanner married a Euro-American woman—unnamed in the accounts of his life. The marriage was brief; in 1832 she left him. Tanner believed that leading members of the Sault, including Henry Schoolcraft and Baptist minister Abel Bingham, arranged her departure.[70]

As early as 1828, Indian Agent George Boyd, writing from Mackinac, asserted that Tanner had "repeatedly threatened the lives and property of individuals on the Island, as well as Indians," the last distinction odd, prejudicial, and suggestive. In the 1830s, following their interference in his household at the Sault, Tanner included the Schoolcrafts and Bingham among those whom he might injure.[71] John Fierst, the leading Tanner scholar, plausibly suggests that the Schoolcraft brothers not only exploited the impoverished, injured man for his knowledge of the Ojibwe language, but that they also defrauded him of the little income he earned. Tanner, Fierst reveals, had cause to act on his threats.[72]

In addition to the evidence of his arguably violent character, his threats, and his cause for anger, his contemporaries alleged two circumstances as evidence of his guilt. There was forensic evidence from the shooting itself. A wad of paper, torn from a Baptist hymnal, had been used to load the musket. The scorched piece of paper was found at the crime scene. According to Rev. Bingham, Tanner formerly had been part of his congregation and had assisted in the translation of the hymnal into Ojibwe.[73] The gun itself confuses matters, for judging from the "buck [shot] and ball cartridge," it was U.S. Army issue.[74] Henry Schoolcraft explained Tanner's possession of such a gun as a loan from a soldier, whom he did not name.[75]

More compelling, somehow, was the knowledge that Tanner's neat, white cottage had exploded into intense flames on Independence Day, two days before the shooting. William Cullen Bryant, poet and editor of the *New York Evening Post,* passed through the Sault that fatal summer, and he noted the Sault rumor that Tanner had "himself set fire to his house . . . before murdering Mr. Schoolcraft." Rev. Bingham later stated that Tanner had deliberately set the fire, using gunpowder "to give the impression that he himself was burned within it." Bingham also claimed that Tanner, armed with a gun and "a bundle at his side"—and here we must note the passive voice so common to rumor—"was seen in a thicket" the day between the fire and the shooting. Residents of the Sault carefully picked over the smouldering ruins of the house, but found "no part" of Tanner's remains.[76]

Rumors of Tanner's hovering around the Sault region after the shooting spread fear throughout the summer of 1846. Sixty years later, Angie Gilbert, Bingham's daughter, remembered the summer of 1846 as "Tanner Summer," in which residents reported sightings of Tanner, and the old man's name was invoked to explain all manner of minor events. He became that year a "bogie man" to the town's children, who "shivered and shuddered throughout the entire summer."[77] Writing in 1846, John Hulbert commented: "We have frequent reports that Tanner has been seen in this vicinity, but little reliance is to be placed upon them, yet it is my opinion that he still lingers about the place." Hulbert added to the speculation: "I believe there are those who know his place of concealment."[78] George Johnston, a year later, used the language of rumor when he said that the local customs inspector, one Richardson, "was seen," shortly after the murder, passing "under pretense of hunting pigeons," carrying a bundle into the woods, only to emerge "without such articles he had in his bundle, it was surmised by many that he took provisions to Tanner." Richardson, Johnston disclosed, had made himself unpopular among the "worthy part of our citizens." Johnston also observed, "There has been several reports of his having been seen, sometimes on this side of the [St. Mary's] river, and at other times on the other side, but these were idle reports." Johnston added that a "coat belonging to Tanner" had been found in the woods, and it was identified by its mender. Ojibwes on the American side, Johnston stated, believed that Tanner had fled to the Red River region of Canada.[79] James Schoolcraft's new widow, Anne Maria Schoolcraft, reported rumors that Tanner had been seen on the Canadian side "and talked to an old woman who saw him."[80] As time passed, a rumor placed him west of Lake Superior, though at least one reported source for this report soon retracted it, denying in a letter to Henry Schoolcraft that Tanner was anywhere in the Red River district, calling it a case of mistaken identity, since one of Tanner's Ojibwe sons still lived, hunted, and traded in the region. In a recent introduction to an edition of his narrative, Louise Erdrich reminds us that we simply do not know Tanner's fate, but she also reports, in an intriguing echo of Gilbert's "bogie man" story, told among Sault citizens, that "there are still Ojibwa who were frightened into good behavior, as children, by threats of Tanner's ghostly appearance. He is said to haunt certain rivers."[81]

No one at the time questioned Tanner's ability to commit murder and get away with it. Lanman, in a "letter" from the Sault that summer, stated, "A party of white men and Indians is now on Tanner's trail, but the prospect of capturing him is, alas, uncertain, and the white savage will probably seek a home in the Hudson's Bay Territory." Another report indicated that fear of Tanner's prowess inhibited his pursuers.[82] To be sure, if his narrative is reliable, Tanner had been an expert hunter in his youth. He knew guns; he knew how to kill. Yet his personal narrative reports no instance, not one, in which he killed anyone. He never described himself as out to kill a human being.[83]

That he could, at sixty-six years of age, shoot James Schoolcraft in broad daylight at a time when others heard the shot and saw the smoke, and then flee unaided and without capture into the boreal forest pursued by young soldiers and skilled Indian hunters was, startlingly, not identified as a problem. But it is worth pondering. Seeking government assistance in 1837, Tanner had stated, "I can't do any kind of heavy work because I am cripple by Ojibwe Indians."[84] With a bad right arm, the aging, much-injured man could not have been of much help in a canoe.

It is hard to explain his clean getaway. Some individuals were so convinced of the fury of the mob that they predicted Tanner's lynching.[85] But others called into question the vigor of the manhunt. In 1847, Henry Schoolcraft wondered: "Are all efforts of the civil powers to bring him to justice, at an end?"[86] In 1846, John Hulbert at the Sault saw something "very mysterious" in Tanner's apparent escape. Despite a considerable county and state reward totaling $600, Hulbert noted, "Little effort is put forth; in fact but little interest is taken in the matter." Anne Maria Schoolcraft complained within three weeks of the murder that "with regard to the search for the murderer, nothing has been done—It is true that some of the people went out the very day the deed was done, but since that, no one troubles themselves about it." These last two letter writers, each related by marriage to Henry Schoolcraft, also separately alleged that Sault Indian agent James Ord and customs collector Richardson had dissuaded local Ojibwes from tracking down Tanner—apparently fearing the consequences should these Indians kill Tanner, a white man, while trying to capture him.[87]

The story has another side. James Schoolcraft drank heavily, gambled excessively, and womanized, or so it was rumored. In 1830 he had stabbed a man, was jailed, and had escaped. There is some evidence that he had spent the morning of his last day sleeping off a night, so to speak, on the town. Perhaps his death aroused more relief than fury.[88] Perhaps, too, the international border with British Canada, to which Tanner was imagined to have fled, placed a significant barrier before any U.S. posse. Henry Schoolcraft was early urged to "demand," through the Governor of Michigan, that the Governor of Upper Canada permit "bold Chippewas" to flush Tanner out of the northern "fastnesses."[89] Schoolcraft pursued the suggestion, but while Michigan's governor Alpheus Felch issued a large reward for Tanner's apprehension, he balked at demanding anything of Canadians until he had good evidence that Tanner had fled into their territory.[90]

The manhunt, then, may have been drained by feelings against James Schoolcraft or obstructed by concerns about relations with British Canada. But another likelihood demands attention: that Sault residents only sluggishly pursued Tanner because they suspected others of the crime. Their suspicions grew with time. George Johnston, visiting the Sault in 1848, learned from the local doctor that most residents "now" believed that Lieutenant Bryant Tilden killed James Schoolcraft. The weapon was said to be army issue, something understood very early on. Legend later had it that an empty musket—and therefore a fired one—had been returned to the Sault's garrison at Fort Brady only minutes after the shooting. Tilden and James Schoolcraft were said to have quarreled, and two men of the garrison, Samuel Peck and Captain Clark, were rumored to have overheard Tilden uttering threats to kill the man.[91] Tanner's daughter Martha, the very daughter removed from his care by legislative action, was later said to have received from Lt. Tilden's wife a letter revealing that Tilden had confessed on his deathbed to the Schoolcraft murder. Martha Tanner, a devout Catholic, was further said to have shown the letter to a bishop, who, with the stereotyped secrecy of confessors, set it aflame. This is all legend, since it is unverified, and as legend, it experiments with popular notions of Catholic conspiracy. We know Martha Tanner was Catholic and that she outlived Tilden (he died in 1859), but not much more. Providential intervention even enters the Tilden legend, in tales that he had acted in collaboration with two soldiers, both of whom were later struck dead, simultaneously, by a single bolt of avenging lightening.[92]

Legends aside, Tilden had, within weeks of the shooting, been ordered to Mexico for war. While there, as public prints soon reported, an American court martial found him guilty of a different murder. Opinion against him at Sault Ste. Marie soared; George Johnston became convinced, at least for a time, that Tilden was James Schoolcraft's killer.[93] Henry Schoolcraft remained publicly unshaken in his belief in Tanner's guilt, despite his direct knowledge of Tilden's conviction by the U.S. Army commission. Why Tilden was released after the judgment and allowed to remain in Mexico (he did not stay long) remains an open question.[94]

The rumor that Tanner killed Schoolcraft spread fast and nationwide; that the news could quickly reach metropolitan America from the distant north was news itself. A steamer had sailed from Chicago to Buffalo in a mere three days, picking up the news along the way. From Buffalo, telegraphs carried the story to Albany, and from there it dotted and dashed instantaneously across the nation. Speed did not make for accuracy, however, and the reports carried not only the false news that Henry Schoolcraft was the victim, not only the unverified report that John Tanner was the killer, but also the intriguing misrepresentation of Tanner as a "half-breed."[95] Tanner's false "half-breed" status led the Democratic press to opine that Indians had poorly repaid American generosity. Lavishing praise upon the (mistakenly) late Henry Schoolcraft, the *Albany Argus* found it lamentable that "one who has contributed so much to meliorate the condition of the aborigines, and to portray their character and history, should have met his death by violence from one of them—if indeed the half-breed can be strictly classed as such."[96]

Tanner had no known Native American ancestry. His narrative makes it clear that he was no "half breed" in the conventional sense of the abusive term. In the Upper Great Lakes of his day, "mixed blood" or "métis" might still in some quarters better describe how, and among whom, one lived than it did one's descent. But Schoolcraft, a hard racist by the late 1840s, alerted several papers that Tanner was no "half breed," as the term clearly would have been understood in the East. Why did the papers err, in their own terms at least, in the first place, and why did the error carry so widely?[97] Marc Bloch long ago recognized that "interpretive work" goes into the making and sustaining of rumor, work that is "inseparable from" the initial, flawed "perception itself." A rumor, for instance, that Tanner was a "half breed" must resonate with the beliefs of those misinterpreting the information and those passing the rumor along. It is not a single error, an individual's slip.[98]

The notion that passionate savagery came with native "blood," a notion consonant with Jacksonian removal, permeates literature during this period. The great mid-Atlantic Democrat Walt Whitman first published a novella, "Arrow-Tip," in a party-line magazine in 1845; and he republished it in his Brooklyn newspaper in serial form (the month before James Schoolcraft was killed) under the title "The Half Breed." Its moral—that fatal disaster follows contact between rough if deliberating frontiersmen and noble if impulsive Indians—was pure Democratic Party rationalization. The novella's epilogue, in which an Indian chief leads a remnant of his tribe "still farther into the West, to grounds where they never would be annoyed, in their generation at least, by the presence of white intruders"—was fictive removal itself. Its conclusion, with a malignant, deformed, guilty "half breed" disappearing, perhaps into "the wilds"—weirdly anticipates stories of the "half breed" Tanner's escape.[99]

Eastern editors soon realized what those who knew Tanner already understood: that a bad mixing of racial "blood" could not explain Tanner; still, Tanner's moral corruption by a life among Indians became a compelling object lesson in the need for racial separation, a late argument for Indian removal. Tanner, rumored to be a killer, was a white man degenerated, according to several American officials in the region. This view of Tanner surfaced long before 1846. In 1828, Indian agent George Boyd stated that Tanner "is an Indian—and I am sorry to say, about as bad a one as belongs to the agency." The view was echoed in the later part of the century by an anonymous "back-woods philosopher, who knew Tanner personally." At the Sault, he told antiquarian Judge Joseph Steere that Tanner "was a regular Injun; more of an Injun than any of the Injuns, and a d——d mean Injun too."[100] In 1846, Schoolcraft described Tanner as a "kind of outlaw" and a former captive "brought up among the Indians, whom he exceeds, in ferocity, ignorance, and evil passions."[101] Schoolcraft's wording appeared, barely revised, two days later, in the Washington, D.C., *Union*.[102] Schoolcraft's Tanner was "so inveterately savage that he cannot tolerate civilization."[103] Tanner's decades of wallowing "in the depths of Indian prejudices and superstitions" left him irretrievable: a "very savage in his feelings, reasonings, and philosophy," a true "realization of Shakespear's idea of Caliban." Tanner, the older Schoolcraft reasoned, having returned to his nation of origin, nonetheless demanded to be "supported in his idleness," and since civilization would not allow that, he became bitter and revengeful.[104]

Tanner's connections with and alleged contamination by Indians powered both suspicions that he might have killed and rumors that he *did kill* James Schoolcraft. His moodiness, his bad temper, his abusive character, and his inability to shed Indian lessons for the lessons of gentle civility drove the con-

viction that, like an Indian, he had killed out of revenge. Some stories circulated that Tanner had recently threatened to kill James Schoolcraft, Rev. Abel
Bingham, and others in response to "some difficulty."[105] Others implied that
he shot the younger Schoolcraft to avenge himself against the out-of-reach
older brother.[106] Henry Schoolcraft, the *New York Evening Mirror* alleged, had
written "something" that aroused Tanner's fury.[107] Dr. Charles Lee, claiming
in New York City that he had recently himself been held a virtual prisoner
for hours in Tanner's Sault Ste. Marie house, published a dramatic account
of his conversation with the troubled old man. According to Lee, Tanner—
former captive turned captor, white man become savage—erupted into rage
when Lee mentioned Henry Schoolcraft by name. Schoolcraft, Tanner madly
charged, brought on "all his trouble and misery," having "been the cause of
his wife and daughters leaving him." Lee, writing under the power of the
early rumor that Henry Schoolcraft was the victim, concluded that Tanner's
"state of mind, . . . feelings of revenge toward" and intention "to kill" Henry
Schoolcraft were common knowledge at the Sault. Tanner—"savage, vindic-
tive, suspicious, and . . . demoniac"—had passionate motives for murder.[108]

Such an Indianized John Tanner formed a most plausible killer. Unredeem-
able, having spent too many years among Native Americans, he exemplified
the dangerous plunge into lawless violence that advocates of removal expected from Indian-white contact. "Half breed" or not, he had absorbed the
worst characteristics of Native America, and rumor had it that he killed.

Rumoring with Vengeance

Throughout the eastern United States, Indian removal, as an official policy of
the federal government, resulted in the death of thousands of Indians and the
forcible deportation of many others. It did far less direct harm to Michigan's
Native Americans than it did to those in states from Ohio and Indiana to the
Gulf of Mexico, but still it was powerfully felt. Although Indians persisted in
the state, they lost vast acreages during the 1830s, and they did so in treaties
that did not reduce Indian fears about American intentions. In 1838, Henry
and James Schoolcraft exacerbated those fears as they urged the exploration
of western lands and as they toyed with a fraudulent Michigan Indian removal
agreement. Rumors that the federal government would imminently concentrate Ottawas and Ojibwes and march them to the central plains induced
individuals and families to leave Michigan for Canada. Removal, in short,
screamed through the false reports that raced among Indians and citizens
during the 1830s and 1840s, even when those reports—as in the murders on
the Maple and at the Sault—had nothing to do with removal itself.

John Tanner's name became entangled in the struggle over removal, perhaps through no intention of his own. His *Narrative* was published in the very month of the passage of the Removal Act. Its introduction, by Tanner's collaborator Edwin James, vigorously condemned Jacksonian policy, which, James said, was "more pregnant with injustice and cruelty to those people than any other." James described United States treaties with the Indians as a "vain mockery," for the "*negotiation,* and the *reciprocity,* is all on one side." Of the civilizing mission, James saw it as "feeble and misdirected": showing *no* evidence that American citizens and their governing officials have "either a regard for [Native American] rights, where they happen to come into contact with our interests, or a sincere desire to promote the cause of moral instruction among them." The "best" policy toward Indians, James argued, was "*to let them alone.*"[109]

Edwin James's condemnations of the federal Indian office troubled his Sault Ste. Marie neighbor, Henry Schoolcraft, then Indian agent, advocate of removal, frequenter of treaties, and coordinator of federal "civilizing" efforts. Schoolcraft slammed the *Narrative* as inaccurate, accusing James of shoddy work and Tanner of being "more suspicious, revengeful, and bad tempered than any Indian I ever knew."[110] In doing so, Schoolcraft revealed his affinities with James, who, for all his opposition to removal, for all his advocacy of the Indians' right to direct their own destinies, was as much taken by certain elements of contemporary American ideology as any citizen. His bold criticisms accompanied conventional Anglo-American thought.[111] On the first page of his introduction, James describes Tanner as filled with the "indomitable and untiring spirit of revenge, so prominent in the Indian character." Edwin James's Tanner shared with Indians—indeed drew from Indians—that very trait that would years later make the missing Tanner the leading suspect in the shooting of James Schoolcraft: vengeance. Imagined vengeance also prompted citizens to allege Ottawa (or was it Ojibwe?) guilt in the massacre of Ansel Glass and his family in 1838. On the wings of rumor flew vengeful Indians, seeking passionate satisfaction from the innocent citizens of a not-so-innocent nation.

Native Americans and some citizens contested the particulars, arguing, for instance, that Ansel Glass had massacred his own household. That argument gained strength, but Ansel Glass was never formally indicted for the murder of his wife and children, who are not even named in the Indian Office records. By contrast, Tanner's indictment for James Schoolcraft's murder was accompanied by a governor's proclamation and reward money from the county and the state. What's more, when the "white Indian" Tanner had earlier been accused of domestic abuse, the legislature sprang into action to rescue Martha Tanner from her too-Indian father, John.

Although it was difficult for citizens in Jacksonian America to publicly consider the possibility that Glass had murdered his family, lawless Native American violence against women and children was a matter of American ideology. It is embedded in the *Declaration of Independence,* where frontier inhabitants suffer attacks by "Indian Savages, whose known rule of warfare is an undistinguished destruction of all ages, sexes, and conditions." The understanding ran strongly in 1838, as Grand River citizens claimed to anticipate an Indian war of revenge. Such expectations were also later projected onto the Tanner story, which had little to do, directly, with Indian warfare against settlers.

Among Indian assaults on American farmsteads in the Tanner *Narrative,* there are no killings. Tanner himself is kidnapped without a shot; his family goes physically unscathed. But when Angie Bingham Gilbert described the capture in 1906, it was all gore (whether Gilbert was inventing inaccuracies or reporting Sault legend is unclear). Gilbert's Indians killed almost everyone; they even swung "small children by the feet," dashing "their brains out."[112] That similar instances of swinging infanticide appear in the writings of such notables as Cotton Mather and James Fenimore Cooper suggests that it is a rhetorical convention warranting some scrutiny. The rhetoric about the dashing of infants' heads goes deeper than real violence, which, to be sure, children on all sides did suffer in the wars of colonialism. Swinging infanticide enters the realm of scripture.[113]

Baby-head dashing recalls a promise, in the Psalms (138:9), of providential destruction to God's enemies: "Happy shall he be, that taketh and dasheth thy little ones against the stones." In Hosea (13:16), the dashing of heads is providentially threatened upon Israel as a severe punishment for apostasy: "Their infants shall be dashed in pieces." If there is anything to this, if Gilbert, Mather, and Cooper scripturally configured an act of imagined Indian atrocity, then the biblical texts raise another issue, for the divine anger of scripture is allied more with the killers than with the parents of the children to be dashed. In Gilbert, Mather, and Cooper, the parents, the mothers who witness the horror, are British-colonial or U.S. settlers. What sins had brought retribution upon their houses? As American citizens rumored Indian vengeance, they knew that vengeance implied grievance, that grievance implied wrong, and some made it clear that those wronged were those whom Gilbert herself called "the dark men whose homes we have taken."[114]

A rumor, observed historian Marc Bloch, does not "spread, it does not take on life, unless it harmonizes with the prejudices of public opinion. It then becomes a mirror in which the collective consciousness surveys its own features."[115] As Sociologist Tamotsu Shibutani noted forty years ago, "The concept of the enemy is often constructed by projecting onto it all the attributes most hated or despised in one's own group; the enemy thus becomes the exact opposite of oneself."[116] Rumors that blamed vengeful Indians, phony "half breeds," and unredeemed "white Indians" for frightening, unsolved murders in an era of rapid Indian dispossession did more than denigrate Indian or "mixed blood" character; they raised even on an essentially peaceful borderland the concern among U.S. citizens that American misdeeds called for satisfaction. Rumor, in that sense, acknowledged and accommodated American injustice. As American citizens, in far-flung rumor, falsely condemned Indians (and Indian character) for real crimes—as citizens spoke into Marc Bloch's mirror—they did not find much comfort in the opposing image. Michigan's Native Americans and newer settlers alike who created and spread rumors of forced deportations, mass poisonings, massacre, and murder in an atmosphere of relative peace commented knowingly upon the violence inherent in American expansion.

Notes

I wish to thank Phil Deloria, Tiya Miles, and Michael Witgen for their help with this chapter.

1. Richard Bremer, *Indian Agent and Wilderness Scholar: The Life of Henry Rowe Schoolcraft* (Mount Pleasant, Mich.: Clarke Historical Library, 1987), 290–91; For articles reporting Henry Schoolcraft's murder see, for example, clippings from the *New York Express,* the *New York Evening Mirror,* the *New York Herald,* the *New York Evening Post,* the *Albany Argus,* and the *New York Commercial Advertiser* of July 11, 1846, in *The Papers of Henry Rowe Schoolcraft, 1782–1878* (hereinafter HRSP), microfilm edition, Manuscript Division, United States Library of Congress (Washington, D.C., 1962), copy in Archives and Regional History Library at Western Michigan University, Kalamazoo, cont. 86: 41226–41234. (Note: these papers are organized in "containers" [or "boxes"], and they are published in microfilm reels. Institutions holding the microfilm collections number the reels variously. For consistency's sake, this report uses the container numbers.) For Schoolcraft's initial reaction, see his letter to Edwin Croswell, July 13, 1846, in HRSP, cont. 48: 443. For the spread of the story beyond New York, see, for example, [New London, Connecticut] *Morning News,* July 13, 1846, vol. II, iss. 208, 3; [Keene] *New Hampshire Sentinel,* July 15, 1846, vol. XLVII, iss. 28, 3; [Amherst, New Hampshire] *Farmer's Cabinet,* July 16, 1846, vol. 44; iss. 48, 3; *Argus* quoted in [Barre, Massachusetts] *Barre Patriot,* July 17, 1846, vol. 2, iss. 52, 2, Early American Newspapers, Series I, Infoweb.newsbank, American Antiquarian Society, online, through University of Michigan Library (hereinafter, EAN AAS Infoweb).

2. Henry Rowe Schoolcraft (hereinafter HRS) to Croswell, Washington, D.C., July 13, 1846, HRSP 48: 443.

3. Susan E. Gray, "Limits and Possibilities: White-Indian Relations in Western Michigan

in the Era of Removal," *Michigan Historical Review* 20 (1994): 71–91; James McClurken, "Ottawa Adaptive Strategies to Indian Removal," *Michigan Historical Review* 12 (1986): 29–55. A general introduction to Michigan's Indians in the period is Charles Cleland, *Rites of Conquest: The History and Culture of Michigan's Native Americans* (Ann Arbor: University of Michigan Press, 1992), 198–233.

4. Elizabeth Neumeyer, "Michigan Indians Battle against Removal," *Michigan History* 55 (1971): 276–77.

5. Murder underpins much social and cultural history, for it often produces a compelling and informative written record. See, for example, the most influential chapter, "The Middle Ground," in Richard White, *The Middle Ground: Indians, Empires, and Republics in the Great Lakes Region, 1650–1815* (Cambridge: Cambridge University Press, 1991), 50–93. Studying marriage, sex, and murder (or, better, the resolution of murder), White elaborates a social world.

6. Rumor is a powerful current story, circulating broadly, that is defined not by a lack of truth but by a lack of verification. As Han-Joachim Neubauer puts it, whether rumors "are true or false counts for little. What is important is that they are up to date and that they do not hide their status as rumors." *The Rumour: A Cultural History*, trans. Christian Braun (London: Free Association Books, 1999 [1998]), 1.

7. Robert E. Bieder, *Science Encounters the Indian, 1820–1880: The Early Years of American Ethnology* (Norman: University of Oklahoma Press, 1986), 146–93, provides an overview of Schoolcraft's intellectual career. Bremer, *Indian Agent and Wilderness Scholar,* provides a fine overall biography, including discussions of his scholarship in the broader antebellum intellectual climate.

8. Bremer, *Indian Agent and Wilderness Scholar,* 291. For the Schoolcrafts' worries, see HRS to Edwin Croswell, Washington, July 13, 1846, in HRSP 48: 443. *Albany Argus* quoted in *Pittsfield Sun,* July 16, 1846, vol. XLVI, iss. 2391, 2; *Morning News,* July 15, 1846, vol. II, iss. 210, 3; EAN AAS Infoweb. The papers added new misinformation to the old: James was Henry's "uncle"; or: the murder took place in the "neighborhood of Detroit." For the family and Jane, see Bremer, *Indian Agent and Wilderness Scholar,* and Jeremy Mumford, "Mixed-Race Identity in a Nineteenth-Century Family: The Schoolcrafts of Sault Ste. Marie, 1824–27," *Michigan Historical Review* 25 (1999): 1–23.

9. Neubauer, *Rumour,* 8; Tamotsu Shibutani, *Improvised News: A Sociological Study of Rumor* (Indianapolis: Bobbs-Merrill, 1966), 3, 5, 7, 14, 17; Jean Noël Kapferer, *Rumors: Uses, Interpretations, and Images,* Bruce Fink, trans. (New Brunswick, N.J.: Transaction Publishers, 1990; Paris: Du Seuil, 1987), 3.

10. HRS to C. A. Harris, Detroit, March 1, 1838, National Archives Microfilm ser. 234, roll (or reel) 423 (hereinafter NAM234R423) fr. 119–21, also in National Archives microfilm series 1, roll (or reel) 37 (hereinafter NAM1R37) 422; HRS to James Ord, Michilimackinac, May 14, 1838, NAM1R37 fr. 484; C. A. Harris to HRS, Washington, D. C., May 11, 1838, NAM1R44 (this abbreviation follows the previous form for National Archives Microfilm, and so on through this chapter), 225. The literature on Jacksonian removal is large. For a general introduction see Ronald Satz, *American Indian Policy in the Jacksonian Era* (Norman: University of Oklahoma Press, 1975), 39–44, 51–56.

11. Charles J. Kappler, ed., *Indian Affairs: Laws and Treaties* [vol. 2, *Treaties]* (Washington, D.C.: Government Printing Office, 1904), 453.

12. Reply of the Sault Ste. Marie, Carp River, Tequimenon [*sic*] River and Grand Island Indians. . . . [Sault Ste. Marie, June 5, 1838] NAM234R415 fr. 615, 617. James Schoolcraft attributed the resistance to the rumors of traders (a perennial favorite, and he was himself a trader), who supposedly controlled Indians by "circulating erroneous reports, and inventing absurd lies, connected with the objects of this expedition." The older brother, meanwhile, accused the Sault's Baptist missionary and minister, Rev. Abel Bingham, of speaking falsely against the government's efforts. Bingham denied it; if the Sault leaders refused to participate, it was their own sound decision to resist removal to a place where "warmth and sickliness" prevailed. The Ojibwes, he added in a point that rang true across much of the state, mistrusted a government that had already violated treaty obligations through improper 1837 annuity payments. See James Schoolcraft to C. A. Harris, Sault Ste. Marie, May 28, 1838, NAM234R415 fr. 609; same to same, Mackinac, June 9, 1838, NAM234R415 fr. 612; Abel Bingham to HRS, Sault Ste. Marie, June 22, 1838, NAM1R44 fr. 420–22. For Ottawa responses to the expedition see James McClurken, "Ottawa Adaptive Strategies," 39–40. For Bingham's relations with the Schoolcrafts, see John T. Fierst, "Return to 'Civilization': John Tanner's Troubled Years at Sault Ste. Marie," *Minnesota History* 50 (1986): 23–36, and Bremer, *Indian Agent and Wilderness Scholar*, 128–29.

13. On HRS and the Grand Valley: HRS to C. A. Harris, Detroit, March 1, 1838, NAM234R423 fr. 119–21, also in NAM1R37 fr. 422. On Potawatomi rumor: Mr. Patrick to HRS, Grand Rapids, June 9, 1838, NAM1R44 fr. 379. Removal forced many Indiana and a sizeable minority of Michigan Potatwatomi bands westward. See R. David Edmunds, *The Potawatomis: Keepers of the Fire* (Norman: University of Oklahoma Press, 1978), 258–72; Susan E. Gray, "Limits and Possibilities: White-Indian Relations in Western Michigan in the Era of Removal," *Michigan Historical Review* 20 (1994): 75.

14. Quotation: HRS to Isaac McCoy, Mackinac, June 23, 1838, NAM1R37 fr. 515. For Seminole War, see, for example, Francis Paul Prucha, *The Great Father: The United States Government and the American Indians* (Lincoln: University of Nebraska, 1984), 231–32. Of the twenty-four Ottawas and Ojibwes who did join the expedition, there were few of rank. They were, at best, explorers for bands at Beaver Island, Manistique on Upper Peninsula, and the western Lower Peninsula bands from Grand River northward. McClurken, "Ottawa Adaptive Strategies," 40, accurately points out that only five appear in the text of the Treaty of Washington, 1836, as worthy of annuities, and only two of these had been listed as "chiefs of the first class." James Schoolcraft described them differently, as "fully" representative. He identified three as "principle chiefs": Maxadawazha of Grand River, Kemene jaw gan of the Northern Ottawas, and Keway quo skum of North Manistee [or Mainistique]; the last, however, appears only as a third-class chief from Chenos on the Treaty of 1836. See JS to C. A Harris, June 26, 1838, Mackinac, NAM234R415 fr. 623–26; James Ord to HRS, Sault Ste. Marie, June 5, 1838, NAM1R44 fr. 363.

15. The "Agreement" contains the usual inconsistencies. It bears three Native American names (Shagnonano, Peentonwan, and Ishkewabick) absent from the original exploring party, while four names on that original list (Kesiswabay, Naw a ge qua bay, Saw saw ge to, and Chingo no quom) are absent from the agreement. "Memorandum of an Agreement," August 23, 1838, NAM234R415 fr. 459; James Schoolcraft to C. A. Harris, Sault Ste. Marie, August 29, 1838, NAM234R415 fr. 641. See also McClurken, "Ottawa Adaptive Strategies," 40.

16. HRS to Harris, Michilimackinac, September 29, 1838, NAM1R37 fr. 546.

17. J. S. Schoolcraft to R. Stuart, Michilimackinac, December 31, 1841, NAM1R51 fr. 743.

18. A brief discussion is in James McClurken, "We Wish To Be Civilized: Ottawa-American Political Contests on the Michigan Frontier" (PhD diss., Michigan State University, 1988), 202–3.

19. For houses as metaphors in the writing of Indian conflict with English colonists, see Jill Lepore, *The Name of War: King Philip's War and the Origins of American Identity* (New York: Knopf, 1998), 71–96.

20. Quotations appear, word for word, in both "Extract of a letter," Lyons, Ionia County, Michigan, March 30, 1838, NAM234R423 fr. 140, and *New Hampshire Patriot and State Gazette,* April 30, 1838, vol. IV, iss. 187, 2, EAN AAS.

21. HRS to W. Lyon, Detroit, April 6, 1838, NAM1R37 fr. 452.

22. HRS to Henry Connor, Detroit, April 10, 1836, NAM1R37 fr. 458.

23. HRS to Henry Connor, Detroit, April 10, 1838, NAM1R37 fr. 458; HRS to "the Chippewas of Saginaw and to the Ottawas of Grand River," April 10, 1838, NAM1R37 fr. 460.

24. Lieut. F. Sibley [writing for Brady], to HRS, Detroit, April 7, 1838, NAM1R44 fr. 195; For Hugh Brady, see "The Brady Guards" at http://www.michigan.gov/dmva.

25. Leonard Slater to HRS, Ottawa Colony, Richland P. O., April 20, 1838, NAM1R44 fr. 237; Adam L. Root, Philo Bates, and 194 others to the President of the United States, April 19, 1838, NAM234R402 fr. 705–8.

26. It should be noted that this explanation could not apply to the Saginaw Ojibwes, who were not party to the 1836 treaty in question.

27. Adam L. Root, Philo Bates, and 194 others to the President of the United States, April 19, 1838, NAM234R402 fr. 705–8.

28. N. H. Finney to C. A. Harris, March 1, 1838, NAM1R44 fr. 127–29.

29. Gray "Limits and Possibilities, 71–91, leaves little doubt about new settler intolerance toward Ottawas but establishes that cash from annuities limited settler pressure for removal in a society strapped for specie after the onset of the serious economic depression that followed the panic of 1837. See also McClurken, "Ottawa Adaptive Strategies," 45–46.

30. *New Hampshire Sentinel,* May 31, 1838 (citing *Detroit Daily Advertiser,* May 3), vol. XL, iss. 22, 3, EAN AAS.

31. Ibid. HRS later accused such stories, which he called rumors, circulating in Whig newspapers as leading to his removal from office by Whig Secretary of War John Bell in 1841. See Schoolcraft, "Memorandum for the President," August 1846, in HRSP 48, n.p.

32. Arlette Farge, *Subversive Words: Public Opionion in Eighteenth-Century France,* Rosemary Morris, trans. (Cambridge, Eng.: Polity Press, 1994 [1992]), 57–58.

33. Slater to HRS, Ottawa Colony, Richland P. O., April 20, 1838; NAM1R44 fr. 237.

34. HRS to John Garland, Grand Haven (district agent at Detroit), June 7, 1838, HRS to Harris, Mackinac, June 12, 1838, and HRS to J. Bragg, Mackinac, June 16, 1838, NAM1R37 fr. 493, 494, 505. McClurken, "We Wish To Be Civilized," 202–3, identifies the Maple River accusations as important to the Grand River Ottawa's decision to participate in the exploratory party.

35. HRS to Harris, Mackinac, June 15, 1838, NAM1R37 fr. 501.

36. McClurken, "We Wish To Be Civilized," 202–3. I follow McClurken's spelling of the Ottawa name. HRS to Henry Connor, Mackinac, June 15, 1838, NAM1R37 fr. 504.

37. HRS to T. Hartley Crawford, Annual Report, September 24, 1840, NAM1R38 fr. 366–90.

38. As Schoolcraft biographer Richard Bremer points out, it is very unclear exactly where, in this work, journal ends and memoir begins; much of the material was obviously written in 1850, and its "credibility . . . varies greatly from one paragraph to the next." Bremer, *Indian Agent and Wilderness Scholar,* 303–4, 418n18.

39. Henry Rowe Schoolcraft [HRS], *Personal Memoirs of a Residence of Thirty Years with the Indian Tribes of the American Frontiers* (Philadelphia: Lippincot, 1851 [AMS reprint, NY, 1978]), 591. To my knowledge, the report that Glass was alive and in Wisconsin has not been verified.

40. Edmunds, *Potawatomis,* 264–68.

41. HRS, *Personal Memoirs,* 658.

42. HRS to T. Hartley Crawford, Mackinac, June 26, 1839, in NAM234R423 fr. 374–77. Entries in HRS *Personal Memoirs* for June 26, 28, and 29 reveal similar concerns.

43. HRS *Personal Memoirs,* 648; entry for May 16, 1839.

44. Rev. Fred. Baraga to the Leopoldine Foundation, June 26, 1834, Mission of St. Mary on Grand River [translated typescript], ALF. XIV. VI. #35. BBC. Mf. 66–2; 29–32, type-script, translating the original German, courtesy Clarke Historical Library, Mount Pleasant, Michigan, and the Notre Dame Archives, University of Notre Dame, South Bend, Indiana.

45. The treaty is discussed widely in works on Michigan Indian history. See, for example, Bremer, *Indian Agent and Wilderness Scholar,* 158–74.

46. Quotation: Francis Paul Prucha, *American Indian Treaties,* 197; Kappler, *Treaties,* 2:451–52; "In the Senate of the United States," May 20, 1836, NAM1R72 fr. 478; Bremer, *Indian Agent and Wilderness Scholar,* 171; McClurken, "Ottawa Adaptive Strategies," 35–36.

47. HRS, *Personal Memoirs,* 538–39; James Schoolcraft to HRS, Sault Ste. Marie, June 29, 1836, and Rix Robinson to HRS, Grand River, June 27, 1836, both in HRSP cont. 41, prt. 2, fr. 14323–24, 14318–19.

48. Andrew J. Blackbird, *History of the Ottawa and Chippewa Indians of Michigan* (Ypsilanti, Mich.: Ypsilanti Job Printing House, 1887), 98.

49. On the patriot movement, see Samuel Eliot Morrison, *The Oxford History of the American People,* 3 vols. (New York: Oxford University Press, 1972), 209–13, and "The Brady Guards," HRS to T. Hartley Crawford, New York, February 26, 1839, NAM1R37 fr. 624–26.

50. Quotation: Extract of a report by Henry Rowe Schoolcraft in T. Hartley Crawford, "Report of the Commissioner of Indian Affairs," Nov. 25, 1838, in Thomas C. Cochran, gen. ed., *The New American State Papers: Indian Affairs,* vols. 1–4 (Wilmington, Del.: Scholarly Resources, 1972), 1:532. For U.S. concerns about British relations with Michigan's Indians, see, for example, William Clark and Lewis Cass to the Senate, "Proposed Revision of Laws on Indian Affairs," December 27, 1828, in ibid., 1:188–89; HRS to C. A.

Harris, August 29, 1837, and September 15, 1837, NAM1R37 fr. 299, 318; McClurken, "We Wish To Be Civilized," 205; Janet Chute, *Legacy of Shingwaukonse: A Century of Native Leadership* (Toronto: University of Toronto Press, 1998), 80.

51. Kapferer, *Rumors*, 215, observes, that the "very essence of rumors . . . is that they involve speech that takes place outside the field of official speech. They constitute a counterpower. First and foremost, they allow one to avoid exposing oneself directly: others speak in one's stead, becoming the willing or unknowing bearers of rumors."

52. Major Jonathan Garland to C. A. Harris, Detroit, September 24, 1837, NAM234R402 frs. 315–19.

53. Farge, *Subversive Words*, 71.

54. For Ottawa temperance, see John Askin Jr. to John Askin Sr., St. Josephs, September 1, 1807, in *The John Askin Papers*, ed. Milo Milton Quaife (Detroit, Mich.: Detroit Library Commission, 1931), 568–69; for alcohol generally, see Peter C. Mancall, *Deadly Medicine: Indians and Alcohol in Early America* (Ithaca, N.Y.: Cornell University Press, 1995), 4–6, 86, 91–100.

55. In 2005, Ojibwe elders in the neighborhood of Manitoulin Island similarly reported their history. The episode from Pontiac's War is widely known: see, for example, Elizabeth A. Fenn, *Pox Americana: The Great Smallpox Epidemic of 1775–1782* (New York: Hill, 2001), 88–89.

56. Blackbird, *History*, 9–10.

57. Kappler, *Treaties*, 2:452, 483.

58. Quoted in Richard Slotkin, *The Fatal Environment: The Myth of the Frontier in the Age of Industrialization, 1800–1890* (Norman: University of Oklahoma Press, 1998 [1985]), 79.

59. For the importance of this view in the removal era, see Brian W. Dippie, *The Vanishing American: White Attitudes and U.S. Policy* (Middletown, Conn.: Wesleyan University Press, 1982), 56–78; see also Slotkin, *Fatal Environment*, 62, 222, 408–9, 426, 492–93.

60. P. Dougherty to Biddle and Drew, Grand Traverse, February 15, 1841, NAM1R50 75.

61. HRS to T. Hartley Crawford, Annual Report, September 24, 1840, NAM1R38 fr. 366–90.

62. Quotations: Shibutani, *Improvised News,* 213; P. Dougherty to Biddle and Drew, Grand Traverse, February 15, 1841, NAM1R50 fr. 75.

63. James Ord to Robert Stuart, Sault Ste. Marie, September 8, 1841, NAM1R51 fr. 271–74; HRS to Messrs. L. Campau and Dr. Charles Shepard, Detroit, March 2, 1841, NAM1R38 478.

64. Robert Stuart to T. Hartley Crawford, Detroit, June 25, 1841, NAM1R38 fr. 511. Replies to Stuart were not too comforting. Both Indian Commissioner T. Hartley Crawford and Secretary of War John Bell predicted removal, though they promised fair notice. They did suggest that they would attempt to find a future home for the Ottawas and Ojibwes in Minnesota. While no removal would take place immediately, it might happen in a year or two hence, according to Bell. As Crawford put it, "When the project of a northern settlement is fixed they will have to go." Crawford to Stuart, July 19, 1841, NAM1R51 fr. 43–49; Bell to Stuart, July 30, 1841, NAM1R51 fr. 125. That the Indian rumors of forced removal prompted Stuart's inquiries recalls Kapferer's observation, "*A rumor constitutes*

a relation to authority: divulging secrets, suggesting hypotheses, it constrains authorities to talk while contesting their status as the sole source authorized to speak. A rumor is a spontaneous vie for the right to speak, no previous invitation having been made." Kapferer, *Rumors*, 14.

65. Reprinted in New London, Connecticut, *Morning News*, September 9, 1846, vol. II, iss. 259, 2, EAN AAS Infoweb.

66. HRS, *Personal Memoirs*, 316–17. Bremer points out that the *Memoirs* reflect the former agent's "personal bitterness" toward both Tanner and a later agent, Robert Stuart (*Indian Agent and Wilderness Scholar*, 304). John T. Fierst, "Return to 'Civilization': John Tanner's Troubled Years at Sault Ste. Marie," *Minnesota History* 50 (1986): 23–36, allowing that the murder is unresolved, makes the best case that Tanner had reason to hate the Schoolcrafts. HRS failed to pay Tanner adequately for his services as an interpreter (he transferred that position to a brother-in-law), and he assisted his brother, James School-craft, in recovering debts of dubious merit from Tanner by docking them from the agency payroll. Fierst finds that the Schoolcrafts mercilessly exploited Tanner. What's more, HRS had the territorial legislature remove Tanner's daughter from his household and sent her away. These events took place in the early 1830s. The brothers also cooperated, at least so Tanner believed, with other leading members of the Sault in removing Tanner's third wife from his reach and securing a divorce. For similar views, see Joseph H. Steere, "Sketch of John Tanner, Known as the 'White Indian'" *Michigan Pioneer and Historical Collections* 22 (1899): 246–54.

67. John Tanner and Edwin James, *A Narrative of the Captivity and Adventures of John Tanner (U.S. Interpreter at the Saut de Ste. Marie) during Thirty Years Residence among the Indians in the Interior of North America* (Minneapolis: Ross, 1956 [New York, 1830]), 1–14, 21–40, 95–98, 204, 231–32, 266–76.

68. Ibid., 209, 228.

69. Fierst, "Return," 30; John T. Fierst, "Strange Eloquence: Another Look at *The Captivity and Adventures of John Tanner*," in *Reading beyond Words: Contexts for Native History*, ed. Jennifer S. H. Brown and Elizabeth Vibert (Peterborough, Ont.: Broadview Press, 1996), 225; Steere, "Sketch of John Tanner," 246–47. Gordon M. Sayer, "Abridging between Two Worlds: John Tanner as American Indian Autobiographer," *American Literary History* 11 (1999): 480–99, sees Tanner's family identity as far stronger than any national or racial identity. At least one son still lived with Tanner in 1836, the ten-year-old John Tanner. He is listed in John W. Edmonds to C. A. Harris, Hudson, February 9, 1837 in Larry M. Wyckoff, transcriber, 1836 Mixed Blood Census Register, http://www.grboi .com/pdf/1836mb.pdf.

70. Fierst, "Return," 25, 32–36. As Fierst points out (27n12), Tanner's marriages are difficult to sort out. He reportedly married a fourth time in 1843 to a Lake Superior Ojibwa, Betsy Ge-zhe-go-qua. See John H. Pitezel, *Lights and Shades of Missionary Life* (Cincinnati, Ohio: Western Book Concern, 1861), 44.

71. George Boyd to McKenney, Mackinac, July 27, 1828, NAM234R402, 8–15; Angie Bingham Gilbert, "The Story of John Tanner," *Michigan Pioneer and Historical Collections* 38 (1912): 200; Steere, "Sketch of John Tanner," 246–47, 253; Ralph D. Williams, *The Honorable Peter White: A Biographical Sketch of the Lake Superior Iron Country* (Cleveland, Ohio: Penton, 1907), 104–5; Abel Bingham, "Reminiscences of Rev. Abel Bingham," in

Anon., *History of the Upper Peninsula of Michigan* (Chicago: Western Historical, 1883), 224; the editor of this volume states that it was later "proven conclusively that Tanner was not the assassin of Schoolcraft" (222).

72. John T. Fierst, "Return to 'Civilization,'" 23–36.

73. Fierst, "Return to 'Civilization,'" 36; HRS, *Personal Memoirs*, 316; Williams, *Peter White*, 105; Gilbert, "Tanner," 199.

74. Steere, "Sketch of John Tanner," 249. Writing to her father, Jane A. Schoolcraft reported hearsay from Canada that the gunshot consisted of a "ball and two buck shot," to HRS, Dundas, July 16, 1846, in HRSP 48: 549.

75. HRS, *Personal Memoirs*, 317, n.

76. Bingham, "Reminiscences," 224; Gilbert, "Tanner," 200; Steere, "Sketch of John Tanner," 249; William Cullen Bryant to the *Evening Post*, Sault Ste. Marie, August 13, 1846, Thomas G. Voss, *The Letters of William Cullen Bryant*, 2 vols. (New York: Fordham, 1977), 2:454.

77. Gilbert, "Tanner," 200; Williams, *Peter White*, 103–6 (Gilbert claims to have drafted the pages relating to Tanner in this book).

78. John Hulbert to HRS, Sault, September 14, 1846, HRSP 48: 591

79. George Johnston to HRS, November 8, 1849, HRSP 49, pt. 2: np. Rev. Bingham later wrote of hearing that Tanner had fled to the Red River, only to die within a few months. Bingham, "Reminiscences," 224.

80. A. M. Schoolcraft to HRS, Sault Ste. Marie, July 27, 1846, HRSP 48: 499–500.

81. George Johnston to HRS, Sault Ste. Marie, July 26, 1849, HRSP 51: 485; John Ballenden to George Johnston, Fort Gary, Red River, July 27, 1849, HRSP 51: 489; Louise Erdrich, "Introduction," *The Falcon: A Narrative of the Captivity and Adventures of John Tanner* (New York: Penguin, 1994), xv.

82. Lanman, *Adventures in the Wilds*, 124; John Hulbert to HRS, Sault Ste. Marie, September 14, 1846, HRSP 48: 591.

83. For his war experience, see Tanner and James, *Narrative of the Captivity*, 108–14, 141–44, 209–10, 214–16. Walter O'Meara, *The Last Portage* (Boston: Houghton Mifflin, 1962), 256, states that Tanner was never himself convicted of any violence, and Noel M. Loomis maintains that "no major act of violence has ever been proved against him," ("Introduction," ix–x).

84. Tanner to President Martin Van Buren, November 10, 1837, reproduced in Fierst, "Return to 'Civilization,'" 25. One of Tanner's daughters recorded this letter for him.

85. Tanner "fled Sault Sainte Marie just ahead of bloodhounds and a lynch mob," according to P. Richard Metcalf, "Tanner, John, 1780?–1847?" in *Handbook of North American Indians*, William C. Sturtevant, gen. ed., 15 vols. *History of Indian-White Relations*, ed. Wilcomb E. Washburn, vol. 4 (Washington, D.C.: Smithsonian Institution, 1990), 689; for the "entire population," see this chapter, opening paragraph; for authorities, see John R. Livingston to HRS, Sault Ste. Marie, July 9, 1846, HRSP 48: 465; Governor Alpheus Felch to HRS, Detroit, September 9, 1836, HRSP 48: 581; for lynching see Charles Lee to HRS, NYC, July 14, 1846, HRSP 48: 449; George Johnston to HRS, Sault Ste. Marie, November 8, 1847, HRSP 49, pt. 2, n.p.

86. Henry Schoolcraft to George Johnston, Washington, D.C., August 23, 1847, in Chase S. Osborn and Stellanova Osborn, *Schoolcraft, Longfellow, Hiawatha* (Lancaster, Pa.: Jacques Catell, 1942), 593.

87. John Hulbert to HRS, Sault Ste. Marie, September 14 and November 12, 1846, HRSP 48: 591, 706; A. M. Schoolcraft to HRS, July 27, 1846, HRSP 48: 498–99; George Johnston to HRS, Sault Ste. Marie, Nov. 8, 1847, HRSP 49, pt. 2: n.p.;

88. Osborn and Osborn, *Schoolcraft, Longfellow, Hiawatha,* 510; Bremer, *Indian Agent and Wilderness Scholar,* 112. It is tempting to imagine Sault residents allowing Tanner to escape justice in the fashion of the middle ground: see White, *The Middle Ground,* 89. But it is too uncertain that Tanner was even the killer.

89. Ramsay Crooks to HRS, July 18 and July 23, 1846, HRSP 38: 463, 483.

90. Alpheus Felch to HRS, September 9, 1846, HRSP 48: 581.

91. George Johnston to HRS, Sault Ste. Marie, June 29, 1848, HRSP 50: 482.

92. Gilbert, "Tanner," 201; Williams, *Peter White,* 106–7. Maxine Benson, "Schoolcraft, James, and the 'White Indian,'" *Michigan History* 54 (1970): 327, following Osborn and Osborn, *Schoolcraft, Longfellow, Hiawatha,* 511–12, calls the rumored confession a "local tradition," favored by the Johnston family. See the Osborns for Tilden's biography. Metcalf, "Tanner, John," treats the confession as a fact, as does Walter O'Meara in *The Last Portage,* 269. Martha, perhaps following the example of her Ojibwa mother, converted to Catholicism on Mackinac Island and became a teacher in a Catholic school for métis children. See Keith R. Widder, *Battle for the Soul: Métis Children Encounter Evangelical Protestants at Mackinaw Mission, 1823–1837* (East Lansing: Michigan State University Press, 1999), 97, 123.

93. George Johnston to HRS, Sault Ste. Marie, June 29, 1848, HRSP 50: 482. Maxine Benson, "Schoolcraft, James, and the 'White Indian'," 311–28, makes the strongest case for the guilt of Lieutenant Bryant Tilden of Fort Brady. For similar views, see Osborne and Osborne, *Schoolcraft, Longfellow, Hiawatha,* 510–12; Noel M. Loomis, "Introduction," in Tanner and James, *Narrative of the Captivity,* ix–xi.

94. A. R. Jones to Henry R. Schoolcraft, Adjutant General's Office, July 13, 1848, HRSP 50: n.p., and copy, sent to George Johnston, in Osborn and Osborn, "Schoolcraft, James, and the 'White Indian,'" *Schoolcraft, Longfellow, Hiawatha,* 596. For the case against Tilden and his subsequent career, see ibid., 511–12, and Benson, "Schoolcraft, James, and the 'White Indian,'" 326–27.

95. The *Charleston Patriot* (July 20, 1846) called the killer, simply, "a drunken savage" (Henry Schoolcraft, "Notices of the Murder of James Lawrence Schoolcraft, supposed, at first, to have been Henry R. Schoolcraft," in HRSP 86: fr. 41226–34). The killer is identified as a "half breed" in the *New York Express,* July 11, 1846; the New *York Evening Mirror,* July 11, 1846; the *New York Herald,* July 11, 1846; the *New York Evening Post,* July 11, 1846; the *Albany Argus,* July 11, 1846; the *Philadelphia Ledger,* July 13, 1846; the *New York Sun,* July 13, 1846, the *Albany Atlas,* July 11, 1846 (all in HRSP 86: frames 41226–34); the *Albany Morning News* (quoting the *Albany Evening Journal*), July 13, 1846; *Albany Evening Journal,* July 13, 1846; *New Hampshire Sentinel,* July 15, 1846, July 22, 1846; *Farmer's Cabinet,* July 16, 1846; *Barre Patriot* (quoting the *Albany Argus*), July 17, 1846. Tanner was named but not racially identified in the *Pittsfield Sun* (quoting the *Albany Argus*), July 16, 1846; *Farmer's Cabinet* (quoting the *Detroit Advertiser*), July 23, 1846 (all in EAN AAS Infoweb), the *Albany Evening Journal,* n.d., and the *New York Sun,* July 15, 1846, in HRSP 86, frames 41226–34. Tanner was not a "half breed Indian," said the *New York Evening Mirror* of July 11, but a former captive. Tanner is identified as "of white parents," raised by Indians, a man who bore a "savage malignant expression," in the *New York Commercial*

Advertiser of July 11 (but must be after July 13, for it contains a letter of that date), 1846, quoted also in the *New York Journal of Commerce,* July 14, 1846. He is called "a captive brought up among the Indians, and more than an Indian in the ferocity of his character," a "sort of out-law" in the *Washington [D.C.] Union,* July 15, 1846. He is described as "of white parents," captured by Indians, and a man who had tired "of civilized society," in the *Albany Evening Journal,* July 14, 1846, and as a "desperado, . . . who had been raised by the Indians, and had sworn vengeance against the Rev. Mr. Bingham" in the *Detroit Free Press,* July 10, 1846, quoted also in the *Albany Argus,* July 14, 1846. He is a "captive taken by Indians . . . who returned to civilized life, but would not conform to its customs and requirements," in the *Philadelphia Ledger and Transcript,* July 14, 1846. He is a "partially deranged" former captive who had "resided with the Indians nearly all his life," in the *New York Globe,* July 14, 1846, all in HRSP 86: frames 41226–34.

96. *Albany Argus,* July 11, 1846, in HRSP 86: frames 41226–34; reprinted also in the *Barre Patriot,* July 17, 1846, EAN AAS Infoweb.

97. "Original Notes to Mr. Croswell respecting the report of my murder," Washington, July 13, 1846, HRSP 48: 443. For the term "half breed," see, for example, Thomas N. Ingersoll, *To Intermix with Our White Brothers: Indian Mixed Bloods in the United States from Earliest Times to the Indian Removals* (Albuquerque: University of New Mexico Press, 2005), xxi. I thank Michael Witgen for these observations on the fluidity of social categories.

98. Marc Bloch, "Réflexions d'un Historien sur les Fausses Nouvelles de la Guerre," accessed at http://www.vho.org/F/j/Akribeia/1/Bloch5–28.html. Neubauer, *Rumour,* 85–94, provides an examination of Bloch's essay.

99. Walt Whitman, "The Half Breed: A Tale of the Western Frontier," in *The Half Breed and Other Stories by Walt Whitman,* Thomas Ollive Mabbott, ed. (New York: Columbia, 1927) quotation, 76; see also editor's introduction, 11–12, 14. For attitudes of Whitman and other writers of the period, see Ingersoll, *To Intermix with Our White Brothers,* 195. Ingersoll points out that Jacksonian policy was particularly hostile to "mixed blood" Indians, 221–36.

100. Boyd was in a dispute over Tanner's pay, in the course of which Tanner apparently accused Boyd's son of the murder of an Indian girl. George Boyd to McKenney, Mackinac, July 27, 1828, NAM234R402 fr. 8–15; Steere, "Sketch of John Tanner," 254.

101. "Original Notes to Mr. Croswell respecting the report of my murder," Washington, July 13, 1846, HRSP 48: 443.

102. HRSP 86: frs. 41226–34.

103. Tanner, Schoolcraft explains, "had so long looked on the dark side of human nature that he seldom or never smiled." HRS, *Personal Memoirs,* 316.

104. For Schoolcraft's worries about racial corruption, and for most of the passages quoted in this paragraph, see Joshua David Bellin, *The Demon of the Continent: Indians and the Shaping of American Literature* (Philadelphia: University of Pennsylvania Press, 2001), 142, 144–45, 245n27, 28. Bellin also evaluates Edwin James's introduction to the Tanner narrative, which James and Tanner published in 1830. James, opposing removal, did argue for a federal policy advancing the "civilization" of Indians. He expressly opposed any notion that Indians were "forever stationary, or retrogrant." Schoolcraft saw in Tanner a man who had been defeated by "Indian notions." For "idleness" see Schoolcraft,

quoted in Orin Edwin Wood, *Historic Mackinac: The Historical, Picturesque and Legendary Features of the Mackinac Country* (New York: MacMillan, 1918), 234. Sayen suggests that Schoolcraft saw in Tanner a rival with a superior grasp of Ojibwe culture, "Abridging between Two Worlds," 493.

105. Extract from John R. Livingston, Sault Ste. Marie, July 9, 1846, HRSP 48: 465; George Johnston to HRS, Sault Ste. Marie, July 26, 1849, HRSP 51: 485.

106. Anne Maria Schoolcraft to HRS, Sault Ste. Marie, July 27, 1846, HRSP 48: 498.

107. *New York Evening Mirror,* July 11, 1846, in HRSP 86: fr. 41226–34.

108. Charles Lee in the *New York Commercial Advertiser,* July 11, 1846, reprinted in the *Albany Evening Journal,* July 14, 1846, *New York Journal of Commerce,* July 14, 1846, in HRSP 86: fr. 41226–34. Once Lee learned that James Schoolcraft was the victim, he described Tanner in a letter to Henry Schoolcraft as, again, "devilish," "malicious," and "revengeful." Charles Lee to HRS, New York, July 14, 1846, in HRSP 48: 449. HRS *Personal Memoirs,* 316: Tanner was "his own judge and avenger in every question." Angie Bingham Gilbert states that "like an Indian," Tanner "nourished his feeling of revenge and hatred." Gilbert, "Tanner," 199.

109. Edwin James, "Introductory Chapter," in John Tanner, *Narrative of the Captivity,* xxvii–xxviii. See also Fierst, "Strange Eloquence," 230–36, and Sayen, "Abridging between Two Worlds," 480–99.

110. Schoolcraft, from 1838, quoted in Wood, *Historic Mackinac,* 234–35.

111. For a concise discussion of ideology and discourse, see Philip J. Deloria, *Indians in Unexpected Places* (Lawrence, Kan.: University Press of Kansas, 2004), 7–11.

112. Gilbert, "Tanner," 197.

113. [attrib. to Cotton Mather] *Humiliations follow'd with Deliverances* (Boston: B. Green and J. Allen, 1697), 43, online at NewsBank, Archive of America, accessed through the University of Michigan Library; this volume contains Mather's narrative of the captivity of Hannah Duston; James Fenimore Cooper, *The Last of the Mohicans: A Narrative of 1757* (New York: Stringer and Townsend, 1854), 255–56.

114. Gilbert, "Tanner," 196.

115. Marc Bloch, *The Historian's Craft,* trans. Peter Putnam (New York: Knopf, 1953), 106, 107.

116. Shibutani, *Improvised News,* 190.

8. Reworking Ethnicity

Gender, Work Roles, and Contending Redefinitions of the Great Lakes Métis, 1820–42

REBECCA KUGEL

In June 1831, the prestigious and well-financed American Board of Commissioners for Foreign Missions (ABCFM) commenced proselytizing operations among the Native peoples, primarily Ojibwes and Odawas, of the western Great Lakes, an expanse of land Americans still vaguely defined in the early 1830s as the Michigan Territory. The small initial cohort of six individuals (two married men, their wives, and two single men) considered themselves poised on the brink of a momentous historical undertaking. Self-consciously, they viewed themselves as "pioneers," "planting a tender shoot" of Christianity and civilization in "the unbroken wilderness." The men did most of the writing to ABCFM headquarters in Boston, indicating from the start the primacy the missionaries accorded the public and professional (and largely male) work of missionization and the lesser significance both men and women attached to private and domestic (and largely female) work. Yet the two worlds of men and women, and the gender roles that undergirded these socially constructed spaces, were always interconnected. The missionaries captured that interconnection in the lists of historic "firsts" they recorded. At the same time that the men solemnly reported the first sermon preached, they noted that their party included the first white women in the territory, and that they had constructed the region's first schoolhouse.[1]

Even as they wrote, however, the missionaries encountered a reality vastly different from the one they described. Far from venturing "beyond the limits of civilization" to a wilderness isolated from all things of European origin, they traveled from one fur trade town to another, from Mackinac to Sault Ste. Marie to LaPointe (Wisconsin), in the company of more than seventy persons who were part of the big fur trade brigades on their annual supply runs. They penned their romantically inaccurate missives home to Boston sitting in the libraries of the "comfortable" frame houses of chief factors (head fur traders) of British or Anglo-American origin. The missionaries' destination for their first year was the town of LaPointe, nearly 130 years old in 1832, and supporting a population of several hundred people remarkable for their ethnic, linguistic, and cultural diversity. LaPointe was no homogenous New England town, and the six missionaries, all born and raised in New England, enumerated with surprise the "several houses, stores, barns and out buildings" that made up the community.[2]

While the missionaries conceded that LaPointe was, in fact, a "village," and "much more pleasant than we had anticipated," they remained unshaken in another, more significant conceptualization of "the frontier." However pleasant, the frontier was peopled by two distinct, exclusive, and easily identifiable racial groups—"Indians" on the one hand and "whites" on the other. The permeable multiethnic reality of what Richard White has called the "middle ground" was readily in evidence at LaPointe. Yet the ethnic diversity of the Upper Great Lakes largely escaped missionary notice. They collapsed the distinct ethnic and political identities of the region's dozens of Native nations into the convenient but inaccurate racial label "Indians." Likewise, the several European-descended ethnic groups who ranged from French Canadians to Scotsmen and New England "Yankees" were reduced to the equally inaccurate racial catch-all term, "whites." When confronted with people who could not be easily understood within these culturally constructed parameters of race, the missionaries were deeply perplexed. The sizeable population of ethnically and racially heterogeneous persons, whom current-day scholars call the Métis, proved particularly troubling to identify, precisely because they did not fit the missionaries' preconceived ideas about "race."[3]

Convinced of the correctness of their own conceptions of "race," the missionaries were equally committed to particular understandings of gender and the work roles appropriate to those genders. Indeed, gender and work were highly significant, mutually reinforcing concepts in missionary thought. Reflecting the pseudoscientific opinion of their day that ranked human societies on a scale from most primitive to most advanced, the missionaries described Native life, regardless of tribal affiliation, as "savagery," the lowest form of human social organization. The central and defining features of this "rudest state" of human society—features that marked its utter degradation and contrasted it perfectly to its antithesis, "civilization"—were its gender roles. Specifically, women, and not men, performed agricultural labor.[4]

The missionaries deplored the Native division of labor, which they described uncritically in accordance with stereotypes that were already old in Anglo-American culture by the 1830s. They viewed Native women's work as farmers, gatherers, and processors of raw materials as "drudgery," and they believed Native men shared this perception. Native men, they stated, "regard[ed] work as degrading and fit employment only for women." According to the missionaries, this well-known Native male contempt of women, which the missionaries eagerly documented, stemmed from the Native male contempt of physical labor, and by extension, the laborers. The missionaries' characterization of the supposed Native male view is significant. In seeking to convey the depth of Native male mistreatment of Native women, the missionaries drew analogies to a relationship of profound inequality in their own society. Native men, they asserted, treated Native women as "the most menial servant[s]."[5]

The missionaries' inability to look beyond their preconceived ideas of Native gender roles had another significant ramification. The missionaries were never able to acknowledge the work of Native men—as hunters, trappers, and fishermen—as real labor. In keeping with their view that Native men disdained physical labor, the missionaries claimed that the little work Native men performed was wrung from them only by direst need. Native men "seldom engage[d] in any kind of labour except when driven to it by necessity." It was clear to the missionaries that they needed to persuade these "extremely indolent" and "prodigal" Native men to accept their proper gender role as sedentary agriculturalists. Once Native men were "induced to settle down & cultivate the ground," the missionaries confidently believed, Native women would be "freed" to assume their supposedly natural roles as housekeepers and caregivers for children.[6]

Paradoxically, while the missionaries inveighed against Native gendered work roles, they believed these gender roles offered important clues to racial and ethnic identity. The missionaries viewed Native gender roles in simplistic, stereotypic ways, but in missionary thought, there was symmetry between Native male and female work. Métis gender roles, like much else about them, confused the missionaries because they did not perceive a comparable symmetry. Thus Métis gendered work roles added to the missionaries' uncertainty about the correct racial categorization of the Métis.[7]

Efforts to redefine race and gender roles became further complicated by the missionaries' implicit assumptions about social class. Race defined class for the missionaries, who expected that persons of color would occupy social and economic positions subordinate to those of "white" people. In a classic Lockean articulation of socioeconomic dependence, the missionaries assumed persons of color would work for wages. Métis men, who by and large did perform wage work as employees of the fur trade companies, conformed to these expectations. Métis women, on the other hand, were far more difficult to categorize. Their work roles and personal attributes impressed the missionaries favorably but only muddied the issue of assigning them proper racial and class identity.

In their efforts to redefine race and gender relations, the missionaries of the 1830s and 1840s foreshadowed the mass of Anglo-Americans who would colonize the Great Lakes region. Their new definitions of race and gender presented enormous challenges to all the peoples of the "middle ground," and to none more so than to the multiethnic and multiracial Métis. Indeed, previous scholarly interpretations of the Great Lakes Métis reveal that a distinct Métis ethnic identity did not survive American colonization of the region. The disappearance of a unique Métis ethnicity, in addition to individual Métis towns such as LaPointe and Mackinac in those territories that fell under American dominion, is all the more striking because it stands in stark contrast to the Métis experience in Canada, where Métis communities and ethnic identities both persist to the present. Previous scholarship on the American Métis communities is limited and has generally accepted the argument of one of the field's pioneering scholars, Jacqueline Peterson, with respect to the disappearance of American Métis communities. Arguing that Métis identity was "occupationally defined," Peterson concluded that Great Lakes Métis communities "collapsed" following the start of serious American colonization of the region in the 1820s. Because Métis social identity, as well as their economic mainstay, was inextricably bound up with the fur trade, Métis individuals were presented with compelling reasons to migrate west with the fur trade. Another pioneering scholar, R. David Edmunds, has emphasized a different facet of Métis existence that led to their leaving the region. Emphasizing the Métis' ongoing kinship and cultural ties to Native communities, Edmunds has found that Anglo-Americans tended to view the Métis as "uncivilized" and "too Indian." Thus, Métis families were pressured to remove from lands ceded by Native nations, just as tribal members were expected to remove.[8]

Yet other factors also contributed to conditions that caused the Métis to seemingly disappear from a region where their population had once numbered in the tens of thousands. In addition to radically different ideas on proper land use and a new legal code, Anglo-Americans also brought to the upper Great Lakes bipolar conceptualizations of race that did not allow for the existence of intermediate racial groups. The Métis, as a social and ethnic group, simply had no place in the American categorization of the races they expected to find on the "frontier." As the early missionaries demonstrate,

Anglo-American conceptions of the upper Great Lakes were at odds with its actual history. Anglo-Americans would reinterpret that history to fit their paradigm of westward expansion across a virgin wilderness. In that process, they would reinterpret the ethnicity and redefine the race of many of the region's Native and Native-descended inhabitants.[9]

The Anglo-American assertion of "proper" racial and ethnic definitions did not go unchallenged. This chapter underscores the way in which gender, especially, but also class status were central, if often unacknowledged, elements in debates over "race." Moreover, the chapter will examine the particular critiques of Anglo-American concepts of race that were mounted by a select group of Métis—literate, well-educated young women. As Jennifer S. H. Brown has pointed out, women were both the "centre and symbol" in Métis culture and society. This chapter will illustrate that the critiques brought forward by these young women indicate that the Métis, for several decades at least, contested Anglo-American definitions of race and sought to advance their own understandings of who they were, creating or reformulating definitions of identity not based on "race" itself.[10]

It is ironic that elite Métis women were the group challenged first and most forcefully by missionary efforts to reorganize Native cultures and societies. On the surface, these women would appear as potentially the missionaries' best allies. Nearly all Métis women considered themselves Christians (albeit Catholics, the Protestant missionaries ruefully noted) and welcomed the presence of clergymen. Many had obtained their educations from the region's only institution of formal, Western-style education, the Mackinaw Mission boarding school, located at present-day Mackinac Island, Michigan. While few of the students wished to transform themselves culturally into Anglo-Americans, they did value specific knowledge and skills that the school offered them. Literacy was important to both boys and girls. Girls, in addition, sought knowledge of Anglo-American standards of household maintenance, food preparation, and clothing construction, in anticipation of marriages to European-descended fur traders, who would value such skills in a mate. The small group of ABCFM missionaries was initially viewed favorably as additional sources of these valued skills. When the ABCFM missionaries began schools at their various mission stations, Métis children always made up the bulk of the pupils.[11]

For a minority of the Mackinaw students, the ABCFM missionaries' presence portended even greater things. As its name suggests, the Mackinaw Mission school included among its goals Christian conversion, specifically to an evangelical Calvinist Protestantism associated with Congregationalism and Presbyterianism. The school's teachers placed great emphasis on training pious, bilingual Native youth, with the expectation that these "first fruits" of the Gospel would be sent forth "to read the Scriptures to [their] Brethren." Self-consciously aware of their unique place in Christian history, this small cohort of pious young men and women looked forward to lives as "useful servant[s] in the Church," bringing the evangelical Protestantism that was meaningful to them to their Native kinfolk. Two of these devout young women blended new expectations to old traditions in a particularly striking way. In 1834 and 1835, respectively, Hester Crooks and Catharine Goulais married the two bachelor missionaries, William T. Boutwell and Edmund F. Ely. Although as committed Christian converts Crooks and Goulais doubtless viewed their marriages to missionaries as serendipitous acts of God, their subsequent actions make it apparent that they were also pursuing the long-standing incorporative strategy of the Great Lakes Métis. From their beginnings, Great Lakes Métis families had sought to integrate outsiders, especially the influential and powerful, via intermarriage, thereby creating networks of kin ties and obligations in place of potential social disruption.[12]

Marriages to missionaries made Catharine Goulais and Hester Crooks unique among the converted students at the Mackinaw Mission school. At the same time, the fact of those marriages should not obscure the ways in which Crooks and Goulais were representative of the larger community of devout students. Their commitment to proselytism was shared by a number of other pious young women, among them Josette Pyant, Susan Bennett, Isabella Greenough, and Elizabeth Beaulieu. As students, these devout young women created a network of friendship and support. Many later joined the ABCFM mission stations as they were built across northern Wisconsin and Minnesota, working as schoolteachers and interpreters. Even after marriage, they sought to remain active in the larger work of proselytism. Elizabeth Beaulieu was married by the time the ABCFM established a mission station at her husband's trading post at Yellow River, in modern-day eastern Minnesota. Nonetheless, she assisted ABCFM missionary Frederick Ayer by translating into Ojibwe "lessons for Sabbath & infant schools." As they left the Mackinaw Mission, these pious young women continued to maintain the ties they had forged. Goulais exchanged letters with Crooks and Susan Bennett once a month, for example, a feat made more impressive by the extreme irregularity of mail delivery in the western Great Lakes in the 1830s and 1840s.[13]

Young women such as Crooks, Goulais, and their friends confidently expected to take their place in the missionaries' ranks, doing their small part to bring the gospel to their "kinsmen according to the flesh." They assuredly did not expect to confront multiple and confusing challenges to so many significant aspects of their lives. Implicitly and explicitly, their class status, their gender roles, and their understandings of ethnicity and race all came under assault. Expecting to take part in crafting a new and Christian social order, these young women instead found themselves relegated to positions as social and racial inferiors. Even their moral worth was questioned. These several challenges were the more painful because they were mounted by the missionaries, the very people the Mackinaw students viewed as Christian allies, teachers, and friends.[14]

The missionaries' challenges to the several societies of the Great Lakes, Métis and Native alike, were not long in coming. As they established their first mission station at LaPointe, the missionaries were guided by a set of far-reaching assumptions about what Christian conversion entailed. These assumptions, both culturally and historically specific, did not explicitly address issues of gender, but conceptions of gender roles were deeply embedded within them. In addition to "regenerating" Native people's souls, the missionaries believed that conversion also should bring a radical cultural reorientation. The "Indians," whether Odawa, Potawatomi, Wyandot, or Ojibwe, would forsake their redistributive hunting and gathering economy. In its place, they would embrace the market-oriented agrarian economy based on private land ownership that the missionaries considered the only possible basis of "civilized" society. In the process, converts would eagerly assume all the cultural, social, and political aspects of Anglo-American life, including its undergirding gender roles. Catharine Goulais's husband, Edmund Ely, captured the American Board's confident expectations when he wrote, "[W]hen God converts them, they will flock to their homes and farms."[15]

To assist in this transformation, the mission stations were to provide concrete examples of "the advantages of civilized over savage life." The "proper" gender roles for men and women would be on prominent display. Each station was to support itself at least in part with a farm, which, of course, would be worked by the men. The mission houses were meant to demonstrate the proper domestic sphere for women and showcase desirable female attributes such as "cleanliness," "neatness," "order," and "domestic economy." The missionaries found Native women to be outspoken, verbally aggressive, and lacking in respect for male authority. The women of the mission households were also to present a "docile, tractable & contented" disposition.[16]

Needless to say, the missionaries found the work of constructing these paragons of home and farm extremely difficult. They quickly concluded that a mission "establishment cannot be formed and maintained without expense and labour." Much of the infrastructure they had taken for granted in New England was simply nonexistent on the Great Lakes frontier. There was an enormous amount of work involved in running a mission that had nothing to do with preaching the Gospel to the heathen. Buildings had to be constructed and maintained; obtaining adequate firewood was an ongoing concern. Actual farm work needed to be performed, and missionaries also were required to complete an enormous amount of paperwork, ranging from accounting for supplies (none of the missions was ever self-supporting) to corresponding with ABCFM headquarters, church aid societies, and families and friends.[17]

The missionaries soon learned that the missions needed "the aid of a labouring man" to do the farm work and fishing, to cut wood, and to maintain the mission's physical plant.[18] The two Anglo-American wives emphasized their need for domestic servants to help with the daunting workload of cooking, dishwashing, mopping, scrubbing, laundering, ironing, sewing, soapmaking, dairying, sickbed nursing, and childcare. Yet their husbands focused on the largely male-oriented priorities of mission work and hired only male laborers in their first year of operations.[19] While the missionaries simultaneously recognized that it would be "desirable that there be two females in the [mission] family," they sought to meet domestic labor needs by assigning the several single women who had joined the missions as school teachers, including Crooks, Goulais, Pyant, and other Métis, to different mission stations.[20] These women were expected to fill a variety of labor needs, including teaching, and interpreting, while still performing "domestic duties and . . . [taking] care of our children."[21]

Once the missionaries determined that they needed to hire male "secular labor for the Mission[s]," they were able to tap an existing pool of wage laborers. Métis men who ordinarily worked for the fur companies could be hired, usually on yearly contracts, terms that reflected established fur trade practice. The missionaries' first attempts to recognize and define Métis ethnicity arose in this arena of male wage labor. While they found fur trade society woefully lacking in nearly every respect—from religious piety to good work habits—the missionaries did detect in the hierarchy of the trade workforce a resemblance to their own ideas about race and class. This recognition was not entirely gratuitous; fur trade society was quite rigidly stratified and class lines were firmly drawn.[22] The prestigious and high-status positions of factor and clerk were largely filled by men of European descent, individuals the missionaries routinely characterized as "gentlemen," "respectable," "of good education," and "men of property and influence." Such status distinctions coincided with the missionaries' own assumptions.[23]

The labor force of the trade appeared, at first glance, to be congruent racially with the upper ranks. The working men, especially the unskilled manual laborers, were nonwhite. The missionaries were confounded, however, by the identification of these men of color as "Canadians" and "Frenchmen," terms reflective of their cultural orientation but not, as the missionaries viewed it, their "race." Such ethnic and cultural identifications did not reflect the primacy of "race" in assigning social identity, and within months of their arrival, the missionaries began to add "racial" identifiers to the ethnic labels used to describe the Métis. These included an interesting early effort at cultural specificity, "French half-breeds," as well as the more familiar "Half Breeds" and "half Indians." As the missionaries struggled to impose a bipolar racial order on the upper Great Lakes, Métis men were being defined as "Indians."[24]

The class position of Métis men reinforced the missionaries' racial conceptualization of them as "Indians." Their personal comportment and behavioral norms further persuaded the missionaries that they were "a lesser breed." Their preindustrial work habits combined with the overall fur trade work culture to antagonize the missionaries, who complained that they had to waste their time "superintending the work" because "awkward Canadians" were "incapable of carrying it forward without considerable direction."[25] Métis men's adherence to their folk Catholicism—even in the face of missionary efforts to "reclaim these poor blinded Catholics" by "proving" the superiority of Protestantism—was a further irritant.[26] Their sexual relationships with Native women scandalized the missionaries while confirming their low opinion of the men's social status. Even their foodways, their fondness for such delicacies as roast turtle, repulsed the missionaries, who concluded that the Métis were "as degraded, in intellect, and as disgusting with filth, as the Indians themselves."[27]

In striking contrast to Métis men, Métis women were more difficult to categorize and in fact offered highly contradictory images. At a basic but meaningful level, given the importance the missionaries attached to the externals of dress and demeanor, Métis women resembled Euro-American women in highly visible, culturally familiar, and thus culturally reassuring ways. Métis women dressed much the same as Native women, wearing moccasins, elaborately decorated leggings, and knee-length skirts (so short by the standards of the early nineteenth century that the disapproving missionaries often just called them "petticoats"). At the same time, there were significant differences. Métis women did not, evidently, use vermilion powder for facial or bodily decoration. Although Native women wore multiple earrings and a "profusion of silver ornaments & Bead work," Métis women wore fewer earrings, rarely pierced the cartilaginous upper portion of the ear, and contented themselves with necklaces of a religious nature, such as rosaries and crucifixes. In an act of personal comportment that appears humorous in retrospect, but in the early nineteenth century spoke tellingly of cultural difference—and cultural sameness—Métis women sat in chairs, rather than "seat[ing] themselves Indian fashion . . . on the floor."[28]

But in the final analysis, it was the Métis women's work roles that persuaded the missionaries that these seeming women of color were less "squalid in their habits" than their Native cousins, and in fact might merit a "racial" status above that of Indians.[29] From the missionaries' point of view, Métis women did not perform labor that should properly be performed by men. Métis women's work appeared to center on the household and thus conformed to the missionaries' gender ideals for women. And indeed, many Métis women did maintain Western-style households and did perform many of the same gendered tasks the missionaries considered appropriately female.[30] The fact that many Métis women lived in permanent houses, in distinction to the mere "temporary lodges" of Native families, was strong evidence of their being more civilized, in missionary eyes. So, too, were their standards of household maintenance and cleanliness. On numerous occasions the missionaries contrasted Métis women's "small, comfortable dwelling houses" to the "dirty," "smoky lodges" maintained by Native women.[31]

Similarities between Métis and Anglo-American female gender roles did not stop with dwelling in a "decent log house" as opposed to a "temporary" "encampment." Métis women also maintained household possessions such as bedsteads, tables, chairs, and crockery, all items Native women were unlikely to own. Métis women were familiar with the care and maintenance of clothing and bedding made from cloth; they washed, ironed, and mended clothing, while Native women, in the disparaging words of William Boutwell, needed "a competent femal [sic] teacher" to help "in learning them the use of the needle." Summarizing the complex welter of missionary perceptions that linked Métis female domesticity to proper gender roles, and proper gender roles with a higher racial status, Catharine Goulais's husband jotted notes about a Métis woman's household. All was "order & neatness," he observed approvingly; the house "bears the marks of Civilisation."[32]

The missionaries' favorable perception of Métis women's domestic work roles is all the more striking because there was much in Métis women's roles that was decidedly different from the roles of the Anglo-American women whom they were thought to resemble. As Lucy Murphy, Susan Sleeper-Smith, and other scholars have pointed out, Métis women often participated in the regional cash economy, utilizing traditional female-controlled resources, such as sugar bush, which could be turned to commercial production. It is also interesting to note that Métis women retained control over many of the same food resources that Native women controlled. This allowed them

to participate in a cash economy in much the same way their Native kins-
women did, but like their Native relations, they did so casually to supplement
a subsistence still largely obtained outside the wage economy. With such
economic resources at their control, Métis women had little reason to seek
domestic work for wages.[33]

The missionaries first confronted the contradictions in their developing
racial and class definitions of the Métis when they belatedly sought to obtain
female workers "to assist us in domestic labors." Envisioning Métis men as
dependent wage earners within the structured ranks of nineteenth-century
antebellum American society, the missionaries anticipated being able to draw
upon the women of this dependent colored class "for domestic help." They
envisioned hiring Métis women in a variety of domestic capacities to labor
under the supervision of a white mistress as laundresses, seamstresses, cooks,
nurses, and childcare givers. The missionaries were greatly perplexed when
ordinary Métis women, the daughters and wives of working men, evinced
little interest in undertaking wage work "suitable" to their race and class.[34]

When the missionaries found they could not persuade ordinary Métis
women to accept positions as domestic help, they turned to the one promising
source that remained, the young women of the Mackinaw Mission boarding
school. Ignoring the class connotations of domestic service for these daughters of the elite, the missionaries focused instead on the advantages, as they
saw them, that Mission school students possessed. Previously, the missionaries had complained that the limited "domestic help" they had managed to
hire was "of a poor quality." Mackinaw students, most of whom spent several
years at the school, comprised a major portion of the school's workforce,
where they washed and ironed clothes, knit socks, mopped and scrubbed
floors, and assisted with the cooking, the dairying, and the soapmaking.
They were thus intimately acquainted with the standards of housekeeping the
missionaries required. They also spoke English. Many were also "pious and
devoted," having converted to the evangelical Protestantism of their teachers.
This combination of shared cultural attributes and religious sensibility made
the Mackinaw Mission students an appealing workforce. Within three years
of the opening of the LaPointe mission station, such young women were
envisioned as valuable members of mission life. LaPointe's head missionary,
Sherman Hall, advised that each mission should include "one of the girls"
from the Mackinaw school who, in addition to mission work, "might be
useful also as a domestic."[35]

But Mackinaw-educated Métis women, however devoted and pious, were
as resistant to performing domestic labor as their uneducated peers. Those
young women who had embraced Protestant Christianity viewed themselves

as part of the larger missionary endeavor to convert their heathen relations. They hoped to be described, according to one of their number, as "a faithful missionary among her people." Certainly this was the expectation of Hester Crooks, Catherine Goulais, and their friends. Crooks and Goulais joined the mission staffs at different stations where they served as interpreters and "taught in the infant school." Neither considered herself a potential domestic servant. Both women recognized household labor as necessary work that was properly performed by women, but both resisted their fellow missionaries' tendency to view them exclusively as domestic "female help," while the work of Christianization was performed by their Caucasian "betters." Their complaints of "being treated ill" and "worked too hard" by their fellow missionaries should be understood within this context.[36]

The missionaries were surprised by the refusal of "our mission girls" to accept such respectable employment. They expected such young women to be grateful for the advantages the missionaries offered "to elevate [them] to civilized life by taking them into our families" as servants. In addition, they hoped these young people would encourage other Mackinaw students to work in the mission households. Instead, the former students actively discouraged other young women from accepting work at the missions. They "exert an influence against us," the missionaries complained. Having already labeled the work habits and work culture of both Ojibwe and Métis men as lazy and inefficient, the missionaries blamed Métis women's unwillingness to work as domestics on their "Indian blood." According to the missionaries, even a sound boarding-school education seemed unable to eradicate the "indolence [which] is a national trait" of all persons of Indian descent. Increasingly, the missionaries collapsed Métis and Indian identity into one. "[C]onnected by marriage with the Indians," the Métis had become "so nearly assimilated to them in habits, that they are almost identified with them." The implications of this merger of racial statuses were chilling: a distinct Métis ethnicity was being denied at the same time that the Métis were being subordinated within a new social order on the basis of their redefined "race."[37]

Hester Crooks, Catharine Goulais, and their friends were stung by such criticism. They were further troubled to learn that some of the male missionaries considered it beneath their social standing to marry a Native or Métis woman. One bachelor missionary was "persuaded" that "such a step" would "contribute little to [his] influence among the Indians" and "destroy it forever" among the Anglo-American population. The young women recognized the connections between such attitudes, the emerging racial order, and their new subordinate place within that order. These women were sincere Christians; their faith was enormously important to them. It is not surprising that when they sought to refute accusations of social and racial inferiority, they drew on the teachings and biblical interpretations of early nineteenth-century evangelical Protestant Christianity. With its powerful egalitarian emphasis, the evangelical tradition provided them with a potent weapon in their own defense. "C[hrist] came on earth to save all—Ind[ian]s & whites," they reminded their fellow missionaries. They argued that from an evangelical perspective, racially based characterizations of personal worth and assessments of racial progress were equally invalid. Although they conceded that they were "one color and [the Anglo-American missionaries] another," it was their conversion to evangelical Christianity and not their racial heritage that "made the difference in [their] condition." Familiar with the central metaphors of Christianity, they reiterated that each person was equal before God. Using the missionaries' own metaphors, they pointed out that all Christians "sat down together at the table as children of one common parent."[38]

Taking aim more directly at the developing race-based class hierarchy, they reminded their fellows that social class alone meant nothing. The most influential fur trade agent still needed "the influence of piety on his heart to make him a most accomplished gentleman." And a woman might combine "all the elegance and sound sense of Emily Dickinson" but without "the one thing needful," personal piety, could not consider herself "distinct in society." Class and race (in whatever ways they were being reformulated), the Mackinaw students suggested, were completely irrelevant in the estimation of a person's worth. In a final, carefully understated but significant gesture, they pointedly employed the classic evangelical terms indicative of social equality, calling all the men associated with the missions "brothers" and all the women "sisters."[39]

The Mackinaw students' assertion of social equality grounded in a Christianity that denied the importance of either race or class is highly significant. Ironically, these young women understood themselves to be the elite, and they recognized the newly emerging definitions of race and class as a direct threat to themselves and their families. Their complaints about "being treated ill" often stemmed from being expected to perform work that they considered beneath their class status. After all, some of their number, as wives of wealthy fur traders and mistresses of large households, could expect to command servants. They assuredly did not view their education as preparing them to *be* servants. But these Christian converts did not opt to reassert a class identity in their efforts to maintain equality with incoming Anglo-Americans. Bypassing race and class altogether, they shifted the terms of the debate. Racial identity and class status were impermanent and could be manipulated, as these young women had learned from personal experience. Rather than build their claims to social and racial respectability on such slippery foundations, the Mackinaw students chose to assert their continued equality on grounds that were unassailable. In Christianity's most significant egalitarian assertion that "[t]here is neither Jew nor Greek, there is neither bond nor free, there is neither male nor female: for ye are all one in Christ Jesus," they found an unimpeachable argument with which to combat assertions of an inferiority based on race. Armed with their understanding of evangelical theory, they could argue confidently that persons such as themselves, Métis and Native, "were not greater fools by nature than other men—they were capable of acquiring knowledge like others." And of course that knowledge of Christianity, once acquired, would eliminate all differences of race or class.[40]

The Mackinaw students did not have far to look for inspiration for their assertions that truly Christian communities were without racial or class divisions. Both their teachers at the Mackinaw Mission school and the ABCFM missionaries asserted the equality of all people (and their souls) in the eyes of God. Both teachers and missionaries sought to evangelize all members of all social and ethnic groups, whether Native, Métis, or European descended. Not surprisingly, given the patriarchal biases of their culture, they were androcentric and they focused on converting males, especially high-status males like Native political leaders and European-descended head fur traders, but they preached and ministered to everyone. An early prayer meeting held by Edmund Ely was typical in its inclusiveness. Elite status traders and clerks joined common fur trade laborers to listen to Ely's scripture reading; people of European, Métis, and Native descent sat side by side. When they organized churches, members of every social and cultural group in the Great Lakes were represented. At one communion Sunday in 1825 at the Mackinaw Mission church, for instance, seven new members were added to the congregation that was never confined simply to the boarding school students. The new communicants included one Anglo-American woman of elite status, the "wife of the Commanding Officer at the Garrison"; the Métis wife of a well-to-do fur trader; two Métis women of lower social standing, one apparently a widow; two Native women; and one man whose race was unrecorded. The two Native women were baptized, alongside a European-descended couple named Hegan. Native converts had many such opportunities to observe the principles of egalitarian Christianity in practice. Indeed, in these little churches organized by the ABCFM missionaries, the ideal of the community of Christians knowing no divisions of race or class was readily evident.[41]

The devout Métis women did not stop with verbal assertions, however trenchant, of the irrelevance of race and class. They sought to demonstrate in their personal lives the egalitarianism they believed characterized a truly

Christian community. Their commitment is exemplified in their treatment of those "sisters" who did perform domestic labor at the different mission stations. When Susan Bennett came to the Fond du Lac mission to assist Catharine Goulais, for instance, or when Josette Pyant was transferred to the Leech Lake station to assist Hester Crooks, the women emphasized that they were all mission co-workers and friends. Goulais described Bennett as her "confidential School Mate" from Mackinaw. Crooks always referred to Pyant as "Sister Josette."[42]

When they were co-resident at the same mission stations, Crooks and Goulais expanded upon this egalitarian emphasis. Both were married by this time, with growing families. Both highly valued their evangelical work and sought to continue it, despite the demands of marriage and motherhood. Rather than assigning domestic labor exclusively to one woman or the other, with the implications for inferior status such an arrangement suggested, they found another solution. Goulais and Crooks alternated the housework on a weekly basis. In this way, each was able to continue teaching and proselytizing, while also performing her fair share of the household labor. All the missionaries' wives confronted this dilemma of juggling private domestic work with public, professional missionary work. Crooks and Goulais's shared housework solution appears to have been unique to them—though, again, they may have drawn inspiration from their Mackinaw teachers. Regardless, they resolved the dilemma of combining mission work and housework more successfully than the women at other mission stations. Interestingly, two years after Crooks and Goulais had perfected their shared housework plan, the male missionaries from other stations had wearily concluded that nothing "would be of more service to us at present" than "a woman of pious character and contented disposition to come from the states to labor in our families."[43]

The devout Métis women could point to the irrelevance of race on yet another highly significant and personally meaningful level. They were able to form long-lasting, interracial friendships with their Anglo-American mission co-workers. Catharine Goulais and Delia Cooke, for instance, forged a firm friendship. They regularly exchanged letters, and it was Cooke who came to stay with the Elys after their first child was born. In recognition, the Elys named their second daughter Delia Cooke Ely. The friendship continued after Delia Cooke retired from mission work in 1837 and moved to St. Louis, Missouri. In the 1840s, the Elys sent their oldest daughter, Mary, to St. Louis to attend school; she boarded with Delia Cooke.[44]

The efforts of this small group of Métis women had some effect within the missionary community. Edmund Ely admitted that "the communion of

God[']s children" knew no divisions of race or class. All agreed with Hester Crooks's husband, William Boutwell, when he reminded them of the essential egalitarianism of their mission: "the gospel must be given to all men." Deeply troubled at the evident lack of Native interest in their message of Christianity and agriculture, the missionaries struggled to treat "our beloved brethren & sisters" without regard to race and found this enormously hard to do. After a decade or more in the upper Great Lakes, none of the missionaries ever grasped how much of their supposedly universal message was in fact specific to their own Anglo-American culture. Exposure to other cultural traditions, which might have made them more relativistic, instead hardened their commitment to their own culture. And race, defined in certain ways and always linked to class status, formed a fundamentally defining element of that culture. Race provided access to political power, to economic opportunity, to social respectability—or it denied all of those things. Members of their society's racial and economic elite, the missionaries themselves were too heavily invested in the "wages of whiteness" to think critically about such a central concept as "race."[45]

Racial definitions and the final racial categorization of the Métis did not occur in the twenty years the ABCFM missions were in operation. Métis racial identity and status continued to be debated for decades, with different people advancing different interpretations. The contribution to that debate by the young women of Mackinaw is highly significant. The basic position of these educated, elite, Protestant converts—that race was irrelevant and religion alone was the sole arbiter of status and worth—would have a long history in the upper Great Lakes region. In only slightly modified form, that basic contention would endure in Native intellectual circles, particularly among people who converted to Christianity, until the century's end. That one of the earliest articulations of this important and long-lived intellectual tradition arose among a group of people historically denied power, let alone personal agency—they were, after all, young, female, and nonwhite—offers an important caution to historians. Issues of power and agency can be as fluid and surprising as the multiple permutations of race with class and gender.

Notes

1. David Greene to Sherman Hall and William T. Boutwell, June 10, 1832 [1831], American Board of Commissioners for Foreign Missions Papers, box 1, Minnesota Historical Society [hereinafter ABCFM Papers]; "Journal of S. Hall," August 5, 1831, ABCFM Papers, box 1 [hereinafter Hall Journal]; Entry for August 17, 1833, Edmund F. Ely Diaries, Edmund F. Ely and Family Papers, box 1, Minnesota Historical Society [hereinafter Ely Diaries, Ely Papers].

2. Entry for August 11, 1831, Hall Journal, ABCFM Papers, box 1; Entry for June 23, 1832, in "Journal of the Rev. William T. Boutwell," William Thurston Boutwell Papers, box 1, MHS [hereinafter Boutwell Journal, Boutwell Papers]; Entry for August 30, 1831, Hall Journal, ABCFM Papers, box 1, MHS. See also Entry for August 8, 1831, Hall Journal, 1831; Hall to Greene, September 17, 1831, ABCFM Papers, box 1.

3. Entry for August 30, 1831, Hall Journal, ABCFM Papers, box 1, MHS; Richard White, *The Middle Ground: Indians, Empires, and Republics in the Great Lakes Region, 1650–1815* (Cambridge: Cambridge University Press, 1991). While Jacqueline Peterson, the pioneering scholar of the Great Lakes Métis, notes that the term "Métis" and its variant spelling, Metif, were known and used by some Anglo-Americans resident in the Upper Great Lakes in the 1830s and 1840s, none of the ABCFM missionaries ever mentioned or used the term. This is all the more curious because one of the Anglo-Americans who used the term was the knowledgeable Indian agent Henry Rowe Schoolcraft. ABCFM missionary William T. Boutwell accompanied Schoolcraft on the latter's exploratory voyage of 1832 in search of the source of the Mississippi. Boutwell obtained a great deal of information about the Ojibwe and Dakota peoples of Minnesota from Schoolcraft, but not, seemingly, familiarity with the ethnic designation "Métis." See Peterson, "The Many Roads to Red River: Métis Genesis in the Great Lakes Region, 1680–1815," in *The New Peoples: Being and Becoming Métis in North America,* Jacqueline Peterson and Jennifer S. H. Brown, eds., Manitoba Studies in Native History (Winnipeg: University of Manitoba Press, 1985), 35–71. On the village at LaPointe, see Peterson, 45, and *Atlas of Great Lakes Indian History,* Helen Hornbeck Tanner, ed. (Norman: University of Oklahoma Press, 1987), 32–33, 40–41, 57–58.

4. Hall and Boutwell to Prudential Committee, May, 1833, ABCFM Papers, box 1, MHS; and see this report also for an exhaustive summary that negatively evaluates every aspect of Native life, from work roles to standards of personal hygiene.

5. Joseph Town to David Greene, July 31, 1834, ABCFM Papers, box 1; Hall to Greene, October 24, 1838, ABCFM Papers, box 3; Entry for July 17, 1832, Boutwell Diary, Boutwell Papers, box 1; MHS.

6. Hall and Boutwell to Prudential Committee, May, 1833, ABCFM Papers, box 1; Boutwell to Abel Newton, February 11, 1833, Boutwell Papers, box 1; Ayer to Greene, December 1, 1833, ABCFM Papers, box 1, MHS.

7. For a perceived gender symmetry, see Town to Greene, July 31, 1834, ABCFM Papers, box 1; for a detailed description of Native gender roles that reiterated every stereotype, see Hall and Boutwell to Prudential Committee, May, 1833, ABCFM Papers, box 1.

8. Jacqueline Peterson, "Prelude to Red River: A Social Portrait of the Great Lakes Métis," *Ethnohistory* 25 (Winter 1978): 41–67; and Peterson, "The Many Roads to Red River: Métis Genesis in the Great Lakes Region, 1680–1815," in Peterson and Brown, *New Peoples,* 37–71; R. David Edmunds, "'Unacquainted with the Laws of the Civilized World': American Attitudes toward the Métis Communities in the Old Northwest," in Peterson and Brown, *New Peoples,* 185–93; see also John E. Foster, "Some Questions and Perspectives on the Problem of Métis Roots," in Peterson and Brown, *New Peoples,* 73–91. The quotations are from Peterson, "The Many Roads to Red River," 63, 64.

9. Both Peterson and Edmunds suggest that American racial attitudes were significant. See Peterson, "Prelude to Red River," and Edmunds, "'Unacquainted with the Laws of the

Civilized World.'" For American racial attitudes toward "mixed-race" Indians generally in the early nineteenth century, see Robert E. Bieder, "Scientific Attitudes toward Indian Mixed-Bloods in Early Nineteenth Century America," *Journal of Ethnic Studies* 8 (June 1980): 17–30. For an estimate of the Métis population of the upper Great Lakes in the early nineteenth century, see Peterson, "Prelude to Red River," 63.

10. Jennifer S. H. Brown, "Woman as Centre and Symbol of Métis Culture," *Canadian Journal of Native Studies* 3 (1983): 39–46.

11. For a detailed historical treatment of the Mackinaw Mission, see Keith R. Widder, *Battle for the Soul: Métis Children Encounter Evangelical Protestants at Mackinaw Mission, 1823–1837* (Lansing: Michigan State University Press, 1999). See also the letters of the Mackinaw missionary couple William M. and Amanda White Ferry, in "Frontier Mackinac Island, 1823–1834: The Letters of William Montague and Amanda White Ferry," Charles A. Anderson, ed., *Journal of the Presbyterian Historical Society* 25 (December 1947): 199–222; (June 1948): 101–27; and 26 (September 1948): 182–91 [hereinafter Ferry Letters, parts 1, 2, 3]. For the Métis predominance in mission schools, see Entry for August 22, 1832, and September 11, 1834, Boutwell Journal, Boutwell Papers, box 1, MHS; entry for October 2, 1834, Ely Diaries, Ely Papers, box 1, MHS; Sproat to Greene, August 3, 1838, ABCFM Papers, box 2, and Hall to Greene, August 3, 1852, ABCFM Papers, box 6, MHS.

12. Entries for February 1, 1836, and February 7, 1837, Ely Diaries, Ely Papers, box 1, MHS. For conversions of mission schoolgirls and their overall commitment to Christianity, see Amanda Ferry to her brother, October 29, 1827; Amanda Ferry to [?], August 30, 1828; Amanda Ferry to her parents, June 4, 29; and Amanda Ferry to [?], December 12, 1829, Ferry Letters, pt. 2, 108, 114–16, 120, and 125. For the marriages of Crooks and Goulais, see "Complete List of Dakota and Ojibwa Missionaries," n.d, ABCFM Papers, box 1, MHS; and Jacqueline Peterson, "Prelude to Red River," 23–64, for Métis social strategies.

13. Ayer to Greene, December 1, 1833, ABCFM Papers, box 1, MHS. See Ely Diaries, generally, for references to the network of pious Métis women. For Catharine Goulais's correspondence, see "Letters Sent," Catharine Ely Diary, Ely Papers, box 2; for Isabella Greenough's work as schoolteacher and interpreter at Fond du Lac mission, see entries for October 24 and October 28, 1834, Ely Diaries, Ely Papers, box 1, MHS; for Josette Pyant's activities, see September 14, 1835, and June 20, 1836, in Ely Diaries, Ely Papers, box 1, MHS.

14. Amanda Ferry to her brother, October 29, 1827, Ferry Letters, pt. 2, 107. For examples of the respectful treatment accorded elite Métis women, see entries for July 8 and July 10, 1833, Boutwell Journal, Boutwell Papers, box 1, MHS.

15. Ely to Greene, September 4, 1839, ABCFM Papers, box 2, MHS.

16. Hall and Boutwell to Prudential Committee, May, 1833, ABCFM Papers, box 1; Ayer to Greene, October 4, 1837, ABCFM Papers, box 2; Ayer to Greene, November 24, 1847, ABCFM Papers, box 4, MHS. For female speech and actions the missionaries found disrespectful of their male authority, see entries for June 24, 1836, Boutwell Journal, Boutwell Papers, box 1; and entry for October 25, 1837, Ely Diaries, Ely Papers, box 1, MHS. For other "unseemly female behavior," see entries for January 1, 1834, and February 25, 1834, Boutwell Journal, Boutwell Papers, box 1, MHS.

17. Hall and Boutwell to Prudential Committee, February 7, 1833, ABCFM Papers, box

1, MHS. For detailed discussions of the amount of work involved in running a mission, see Hall to Greene, October 17, 1834, ABCFM Papers, box 1; Hall to Greene, October 24, 1838, ABCFM Papers, box 2; Ayer to Greene, August 28, 1840, ABCFM Papers, box 3. See also Ayer to Greene, December 1, 1833, ABCFM Papers, box 1, on farm work, maintenance of buildings, and the constant need for firewood. With regard to accounting for supplies and overall paperwork, see entry for June 23, 1837, Ely Diaries, Ely Papers, box 1, MHS; Boutwell to Greene, December 21, 1836, ABCFM Papers, box 2, MHS; Hall to Greene, October 1, 1837, ABCFM Papers, box 2, MHS; Ayer to Greene, October 4, 1837, ABCFM Papers, box 2, MHS.

18. Hall and Boutwell to Prudential Committee, May 1833, ABCFM Papers, box 1, MHS. In reality, the missionaries quickly learned that *two* hired men were necessary for a mission to function smoothly, and they made strenuous efforts to hire them. See Ayer to Greene, October 4, 1837, ABCFM Papers, box 2, MHS.

19. Hall and Boutwell to Prudential Committee, May, 1833, ABCFM Papers, box 1, MHS; see also see Hall to Greene, February 2, 1842, ABCFM Papers, box 3, which indicates the LaPointe mission was never without a male laborer at any point in its existence after the second year. For the enormous but undervalued workload of the missionary women, see Catharine Ely Diary; and Amanda Ferry to [?], August 13, 1824, along with Amanda Ferry to Thomas White, November 3, 1825, Ferry Letters, pt. 1, 207–9, 219; and Amanda Ferry to [?], n.d., Ferry Letters, pt. 2, 126.

20. Hall and Boutwell to Prudential Committee, May, 1833, ABCFM Papers, box 1, MHS. For the movements of single women among the different missions, see Ayer to Greene, March 23, 1835, ABCFM Papers, box 1, (Sabrina Stevens as schoolteacher and domestic help at the Pokegama mission); Ely to Greene, October 19, 1835, and December 31, 1835, ABCFM Papers, box 1, (Delia Cooke as a domestic helper in the LaPointe mission family); Boutwell to Greene, December 21, 1838, ABCFM Papers, box 2, (Josette Pyant as domestic helper at the Leech Lake mission). For evidence that these women, who joined the missions to help convert Native peoples to Christianity, resented being asked to perform domestic labor instead of missionary work, see Delia Cooke to Greene, June 19, 1837, ABCFM Papers, box 2, MHS.

21. Hall to Greene, August 9, 1836, ABCFM Papers, box 2, MHS. For a general discussion by the male missionaries that single female missionaries would both teach school and perform household labor, as necessary, see Hall and Boutwell to Prudential Committee, May 1833, ABCFM Papers, box 1, MHS. There is no evidence the female mission staff members participated in this discussion allocating their labor.

22. Ayer to Greene, October 4, 1837, ABCFM Papers, box 2, MHS. For fur trade labor contracts, see entry for May 26, 1836, Boutwell Journal, Boutwell Papers, box 1, MHS; and entry for May 1, 1837, Ely Diaries, Ely Papers, box 1, MHS. Examples of class hierarchy in the fur trade are legion; see entries for September 23 and 28, 1833, Boutwell Journal, for explicit status distinctions based on performing manual labor; Amanda Ferry to "Sister H," December 1823, Ferry Letters, pt. 1, 199, sketches fur trade social distinctions at the town of Mackinac. For specific instances of high status persons being privileged above "common" trade workers, see entries for May 22, 1834 (high-status trade employees receive more food in lean times) and January 7, 1836 (high-status persons carried across a stream instead of fording on foot), Ely Diaries, Ely Papers, box 1, MHS.

23. Entry for June 23, 1832, and September 21, 1833, Boutwell Journal, Boutwell Papers, box 1, MHS; Hannah White to her parents [?], February 1, 1831, Ferry Letters, pt. 3, 188; and Amanda Ferry to her mother, July 10, 1825, Ferry Letters, pt. 1, 212.

24. Boutwell to Greene, June 25, 1832, ABCFM Papers, box 1; Journal of Sherman Hall, August 8, 1831, ABCFM Papers, box 1; Ayer to Greene, October 11, 1834, ABCFM Papers, box 1; Hall to Greene, August 16, 1838, ABCFM Papers, box 2, MHS.

25. Entry for June 24, 1832, Boutwell Journal, Boutwell Papers, box 1, MHS; Ayer to Greene, December 1, 1833, ABCFM Papers, box 1, MHS. See also entry for June 11, 1832, Boutwell Journal, Boutwell Papers, box 1, MHS, for additional complaints about Métis work culture.

26. Entry for August 14, 1836, Ely Diaries, Ely Papers, box 1, MHS. For the missionaries' hostility toward Catholicism, see entry for June 17, 1832, Boutwell Journal, Boutwell Papers, box 1, MHS; entries for February 14, 1834, November 22, 1835, and February 4, 1836, Ely Diaries, Ely Papers, box 1, MHS; and, for a very explicit statement, Hall to Greene, April 9, 1836, ABCFM Papers, box 1, MHS. For Ely's efforts to "prove" the superiority of Protestantism, see entries for December 24, 1833, February 23, 1834, and September 27, 1834, Ely Diaries, Ely Papers, box 1, MHS.

27. Entry for June 12, 1832, Boutwell Journal, Boutwell Papers, box 1, MHS. For alleged Métis sexual immorality, see entries for August 27, 1834, and March 3, 1835, Boutwell Journal, Boutwell Papers, box 1; Boutwell to Greene, December 18, 1833, ABCFM Papers, box 1, MHS, and Ayer to Greene, March 23, 1835, ABCFM Papers, box 1, MHS. For Métis foodways: entry for May 18, 1834, Ely Diaries, Ely Papers, box 1; entries for June 24, 1832, September 17, 1833, and April 23, 1834, Boutwell Journal, Boutwell Papers, box 1, MHS.

28. Entry for October 3, 1832, Boutwell Journal, Boutwell Papers, box 1, MHS; entry for May 4, 1834, Ely Diaries, Ely Papers, box 1; Amanda Ferry to her parents, May 17, 1829, Ferry Letters, pt. 2, 117. Clothing was extremely important to the missionaries as an indicator of a person's level of civilization, religious orientation, and social status. For representative remarks on clothing making a Native man or woman appear "civilized," see entries for October 17, 1833, and March 11, 1834, Boutwell Journal, Boutwell Papers, box 1; and entry for August 13, 1836, Ely Diaries, Ely Papers, box 1, MHS. Missionaries, both male and female, were also forcibly struck by how little clothing Native women wore. See entry for May 2, 1837, in "Journal of Granville T. Sproat," ABCFM Papers, box 1, and Amanda Ferry to Mary Arms White, March 9, 1824, Ferry Letters, pt. 1, 201, for descriptions of "scanty" female attire. For Ojibwe women using vermillion paint for facial and bodily decoration, see entry for August 27, 1833, Boutwell Journal, Boutwell Papers, box 1, MHS.

29. Entry for June 27, 1832, Boutwell Journal, Boutwell Papers, box 1, MHS.

30. There were some major departures from "proper" gender roles, however, which the missionaries noted with great disapproval. In particular, Métis women cut and hauled wood (as did Native women), a task the missionaries considered as rightly belonging to men. See entry for July 2, 1833, Boutwell Journal, Boutwell Papers, box 1, MHS.

31. Hall and Boutwell to Prudential Committee, May 1833, ABCFM Papers, box 1, MHS; entries for June 22, 1832, and June 23, 1832, Boutwell Journal, Boutwell Papers, box 1, MHS.

32. Boutwell to Greene, December 16, 1835, ABCFM Papers, box 1; Hall and Boutwell

to Prudential Committee, May 1833, ABCFM Papers, box 1; Entry for March 2, 1835, Ely Diaries, Ely Papers, box 1; Boutwell to Greene, December 18, 1833, ABCFM Papers, box 1; entry for June 8, 1834, Ely Diaries, Ely Papers, box 1, MHS.

33. Lucy Eldersveld Murphy, "To Live among Us: Accommodation, Gender, and Conflict in the Western Great Lakes Region, 1760–1832," in *Contact Points; American Frontiers from the Mohawk Valley to the Mississippi, 1750–1830,* Andrew R. L. Cayton and Fredrika Teute, eds. (Chapel Hill: University of North Carolina Press, 1998), 270–303; and Jeanne Kay, "The Land of La Baye: The Ecological Impact of the Green Bay Fur Trade, 1634–1836" (PhD diss., University of Wisconsin, Madison, 1977). Also see Lucy E. Murphy, *A Gathering of Rivers: Indian, Métis and Mining in the Western Great Lakes, 1737–1832* (Lincoln: University of Nebraska Press, 2004); and Susan Sleeper-Smith, *Indian Women and French Men: Rethinking Cultural Encounter in the Western Great Lakes* (Amherst: University of Massachusetts Press, 2001).

34. Hall to Greene, August 9, 1836, ABCFM Papers, box 2; Hall to Greene, October 17, 1834, ABCFM Papers, box 1, MHS.

35. Ayer to Greene, March 23, 1835, ABCFM Papers, box 1; Amanda Ferry to [?], n. d., Ferry Letters, pt. 2, 103; Hall to Greene, August 9, 1836, ABCFM Papers, box 2; Hall to Greene, October 17, 1834, ABCFM Papers, box 1, MHS. For evidence of the types and considerable amount of household labor performed by Mackinaw Mission schoolgirls, see Amanda Ferry to her mother, July 10, 1825; Amanda Ferry to Thomas White, November 3, 1825; Amanda Ferry to [?], August 13, 1824, Ferry Letters, pt. 1, 219, 215, and 207; Hannah White to [?], February 1, 1831, Ferry Letters, pt. 3, 187–88.

36. Amanda Ferry to [?], August 30, 1828, Ferry Letters, pt. 2, 114; Hall to Greene, October 17, 1834, ABCFM Papers, box 1, MHS; Ayer to Greene, April 3, 1835, ABCFM Papers, box 1, MHS; and Hall to Greene, October 19, 1834, ABCFM Papers, box 1, MHS.

37. Amanda Ferry to Thomas White, October 29, 1827, Ferry Letters, pt. 2, 108; Hall to Greene, October 19, 1839, ABCFM Papers, box 2; Amanda Ferry to her mother, July 10, 1825, Ferry Letters, pt. 1, 215; Hall to Greene, August 9, 1836, ABCFM Papers, box 1, MHS.

38. John Seymour to Greene, November 14, 1835, ABCFM Papers, box 1; entry for November 3, 1835, Ely Diaries, Ely Papers, box 1; entry for March 13, 1835, Boutwell Journal, Boutwell Papers, box 1; Ayer to Greene, April 1840, ABCFM Papers, box 3, MHS.

39. Amanda Ferry to "Sister H," December 1823, Ferry Letters, pt. 1, 199. Use of the evangelical "Brother/Sister" forms of address is found throughout the missionaries' correspondence. See entries for June 29, August 24, and September 14, 1835, and January 8, February 5, 15, and 19, 1836, Ely Diaries, Ely Papers, box 1. Also see entry for January 20, 1836, Catharine Ely Diary, Ely Papers, box 2, MHS. For an additional assertion that class status was insufficient without piety, see entry for July 23, 1833, Boutwell Journal, Boutwell Papers, box 1, MHS.

40. Entry for April 16, 1836, Ely Diaries, Ely Papers, box 1, MHS; Galatians 3:28.

41. Entry for June 15, 1834, Ely Diaries, Ely Papers, box 1, MHS; Amanda Ferry to Hannah White, October 2, 1825, Ferry Letters, pt. 1, 216.

42. Entry for October 11, 1835, September 14, 1835, and June 20, 1836, Ely Diaries, Ely Papers, box 1, MHS.

43. Hall to Greene, October 19, 1839, ABCFM Papers, box 2, MHS. For sharing the

housework, see entries for September 25 and October 2, 1837, Catharine Ely Diary, Ely Papers, box 2, MHS. Also see entries for October 20, 1837, and March 8, 1838, Ely Diaries, Ely Papers, box 1, MHS, which discuss Goulais's and Crooks's proselytism and the significance these women attached to such work. Keith Widder, through personal communication with the author, suggested the likely source of this solution in the housework arrangements at the Mackinaw Mission school, and grateful acknowledgment is made to him.

44. Information regarding Delia Cooke and Delia Cooke Ely can be found in entries for January 28, 1838, and September 2, 1841, Ely Diaries, Ely Papers, box 1, MHS. Additional information can be found in "Letters Sent," May 29 and July 18, 1836, Catharine Ely Diary, Ely Papers, box 2, MHS. Also see Cooke to Greene, June 19, 1837, ABCFM Papers, box 2, MHS.

45. Entry for May 25, 1836, Ely Diaries, Ely Papers, box 1; entry for October 15, 1834, Boutwell Journal, Boutwell Papers, box 1; entry for February 19, 1836, Ely Diaries, Ely Papers, box 1, MHS. Also see David Roediger, *The Wages of Whiteness: Race and the Making of the American Working Class* (New York: Verso, 1991).

9. A New Seasonal Round

Government Boarding Schools,
Federal Work Programs, and
Ojibwe Family Life during
the Great Depression

BRENDA J. CHILD

Historians writing about American Indians in the past century have not adequately addressed the problem of how the Great Depression proliferated in Indian Country, and perhaps with good reason. This new, random poverty landed on top of carefully maneuvered allotment policies that for decades had sanctioned rampant exploitation of tribal land holdings and resources. Oppressive strategies, such as the boarding school system, aimed at the cultural destruction of Indian families and communities and thrived in a climate hostile to tribal ways of life. In the 1930s the policies of a new administration shifted attention away from allotment and assimilation to ideas of self-government. The Indian "New Deal" also promised educational equality as a plan for public school integration organized in Congress.[1]

John Collier's reform agenda and the Indian Reorganization Act have overshadowed consideration of how the Depression uniquely troubled Indians. Ojibwe people in the Great Lakes region, already encumbered by a half-century of ruinous policies from state capitols and Washington, experienced additional hardship in the 1930s. Ojibwe communities responded to unemployment and dire economic circumstances in the most practical way, and completely in accordance with their own tribal values. Perhaps the best illustration of this adaptation to increased adversity is that during these years the controversial government boarding schools were given an enhanced role. Families, many facing conditions of near starvation, voluntarily sent their children away in unprecedented numbers. Their previous history of resistance to boarding schools was cast aside because of increased economic deprivation, making the 1930s the decade of highest enrollment in the history of the government boarding schools. A new seasonal round of residential schools, "New Deal" work programs, and the older, though vulnerable, Ojibwe economy combined in an indispensable triad that enabled families to patch together a livelihood in hard times.

* * *

Autumn once represented a season of plenty in the Great Lakes, a time for hard work and family harmony as Ojibwe communities cooperated in the wild rice harvest. Maude Kegg recalled her girlhood experiences with the Ojibwe seasonal economy as it was practiced near Portage Lake in central Minnesota. She was born around 1904 on the Mille Lacs Reservation, well before the Great Depression. Kegg's grandmother taught her to fish, make maple sugar, and harvest fruits and wild rice, all esteemed Ojibwe activities that evolved as Kegg's community made an uneasy adjustment to the changing population of central Minnesota. Her family incorporated some new activities, such as exchanging blueberries for supplies in Brainerd, a nearby non-Indian town, and selling fish to a wholesaler in Vineland. Yet the northern landscape showed the effects of timber companies. Kegg's grandmother could recall a time when "there were so many pines that it was dark" near shimmering Lake Mille Lacs, though Kegg herself remembered "a great big logging camp" that employed many Ojibwes.[2]

Mille Lacs was a place so beautiful that the state of Minnesota easily promoted tourism to the forests, sandy beaches, and bountiful walleye waters of Ojibwe Country. Yet the tourism did not bode well for the Ojibwes. Mille Lacs Ojibwes were burned out of their homes, arrested for infractions of state game laws in violation of treaty rights, and often returned to traditional ricing and sugaring spots to find new residents on their land. The pressure to remove and take allotments in other areas of Minnesota was relentless. When Kegg was a child, many Ojibwe people worked for wages in the tourist and lumber industries, while the beloved seasonal round remained a vital supplement to family incomes. Yet employment opportunities grew scarce for Indians once the Great Depression spread through the upper Midwest, a further challenge to family survival as Ojibwes struggled to take part in the seasonal round.[3]

Even before the Great Depression struck, boarding schools had infringed upon the Ojbwes' fall rituals. The opening of boarding schools in September presented problems for Ojibwe students and their families, whose lives had long revolved around seasonal rhythms. Harvesting rice was a family affair, and early mission and day schools in the Great Lakes were forced to cancel school during the fall harvest when parents collected their children for seasonal work and later as children joined their relatives in the spring sugar bush. Ojibwe family life was structured so that many of life's important lessons took place in the intimate surroundings of wild rice, maple sugar, and fish camps. It was an informal but precise and demanding education. Yet this tradition was threatened when Ojibwe students eventually left the western Great Lakes for schools in the east, such as Hampton Normal School in Virginia and the Indian Industrial School at Carlisle, Pennsylvania. By the turn of the century, Ojibwe students, along with thousands of other Indian children, were enrolled in a variety of mission schools and in federal boarding schools as well, including Haskell in Lawrence, Kansas, Flandreau in South Dakota, and Pipestone in southwestern Minnesota.

Ojibwe children, along with other tribes, still attended boarding schools throughout the Depression, despite the recent efforts of progressive reformers who increasingly viewed public school education as a logical alternative to the highly criticized residential school concept. A dozen boarding schools closed in the United States between 1928 and 1933. Yet remarkably, American Indians initiated much of the student enrollment at boarding schools during the 1930s. Concern for family survival transcended previous resistance to these controversial institutions, as these former weapons of assimilation began to resemble a form of poverty relief for Indian children. Boarding school enrollments continued to soar throughout the 1930s, leaving more Indian students in residential schools than ever before. Family distress was palpable in letters sent to boarding schools from Ojibwes in the Great Lakes.[4]

Families also found some relief from hardship through "New Deal" emergency government programs, such as the Works Progress Administration (WPA) and the Indian Division of the Civilian Conservation Corps (CCC-ID). American Indians in the western Great Lakes built roads to secluded areas, restored forests, and worked on housing projects. Flandreau graduate Alphonse Caswell watched for forest fires as a WPA employee on the Red Lake Reservation. The Indian Service anticipated a leadership role for returned students in emergency conservation work because of their training, particularly because a boarding school education had long yielded few tangible employment opportunities after graduation. Returned students entered emergency conservation work as carpenters, plumbers, truck drivers, machine operators, and cooks, and they became frequent candidates for the position of "foreman." The boarding school homily to graduates that "the world needs their leadership" was seldom realized apart from the humble employment offered by the WPA and the CCC-ID.[5] M. Inez Hilger, an anthropologist who worked at White Earth in 1938, pointed out the nearly universal reliance on poverty relief and pension programs in the community.[6] As with other Americans, Ojibwes weathered the worst miseries of the Depression through hard work and active participation in poverty-relief programs.

A barrage of letters and enrollment applications from reservations in Minnesota and Wisconsin indicate an increased reliance on Indian boarding schools during the 1930s. Boarding school letters laid bare intimate details of family life that bring to the foreground the separations, losses, and struggles of this era. Ojibwe people poured out their problems, and in the process they described with great candor how they survived hard times, unemployment, and a poverty without precedent in the Great Lakes region—one that intruded with dreadful repercussions as the older economy was being undone by decades of removals, land loss, and the outright criminalization of Indian participation in the seasonal round.[7] Government boarding schools, familiar but contested institutions, assumed a new role in American Indian family life throughout the Depression.

* * *

Facing hard times, a mother and father from rural Mahnomen, Minnesota, a small town on the White Earth Reservation, made an unhappy decision to send two sons to the Flandreau Indian boarding school in South Dakota and to enroll a daughter at Haskell Institute in Kansas in the 1930s, a period when the poor economy influenced the decisions of even some of the most intact reservation families. The parents were distressed by the enrollment of their sons and daughter in different institutions, and they were not convinced that they had "done the right thing." Still, their eighty-acre farm, with only a two-room house, had proved to be inadequate for an extended household of thirteen family members, and their children had been forced to miss long stretches of school because of the heavy snowfall during the north country's hard winters. Not long after parting with their children, the parents wrote this anguished letter to school administrators:

> I get so lonesome myself for them.
> —White Earth Ojibwe Woman

September 29, 1931

Dear Mr. Brophy,
Got your letter today I am sending the children's report cards. Its no wonder George is hav[ing] a hard time he is supposed to be in the seventh grade this year. I think he is home sick that why he can't make up his mind to study he has never been away from home before so sorry I sent him away he was our best

farmer and we sure miss his help. We had to hire a man we couldn't manage
alone. I do wish James could learn to play in the band he loves music.

   Did you get the check of $3.10 I sent you for our children[?] I sent it Sept 17.
I hope you get it and allow them each 25 cts a week. They help us so much so
now we have to give them spending money. I hope they will like it there. George
cried the nite before he left home he didn't like to leave but James was anxious
to go but he didn't like to go alone he coaxed George to go. I get so lonesome
myself for them.

   We have a little girl at White Earth Sisters school no sisters she is alone she
will be 8 years it must be lonesome for her. Hope this finds every one well.[8]

Ojibwe children were the first casualties of economic depression in the
Great Lakes. When family deprivation became extreme, every available space
in Indian boarding schools filled with students. As families experienced unemployment and food shortages in their own community, a multitude of
hungry children arrived from White Earth to be placed in Red Lake's on-
reservation boarding school. More than one young Ojibwe coped with an
entire childhood spent within the institution. Remarkably, personal resil-
ience and stable surroundings allowed some children to flourish. During the
summer of 1939, a White Earth teenager named Wallace transferred from a
boarding school in North Dakota to Flandreau in South Dakota. Since age
six, Wallace's only home had been a government boarding school. Wallace's
widowed mother lost her struggle with financial burden and corresponding
household instability, and she was ordered to the county workhouse. When
the state assumed guardianship of her children, Wallace and five siblings were
sent away to boarding school, separated between Flandreau and Wahpeton.
Wallace did not return to White Earth; instead, he lived his entire childhood
and adolescence in government boarding schools before entering the army
while still a teenager.

   When Wallace turned nineteen, he was sent to Fort Snelling in Saint Paul,
Minnesota. In a postcard addressed to Flandreau administrators and staff,
Wallace, a veteran of government institutions, cheerily wrote, "I'll be in uni-
form by the time you receive this card. Ft. Snelling is a nice place. Lots of
freedom, good food (best in U.S.) and two cities to visit." In his message,
Wallace fondly referred to his alma mater as "My Shangri-la." It is ironic that
boarding schools proved to be a haven for some children like Wallace—a
somber testimony to the poor quality of reservation life for Ojibwe families
during the 1930s.[9]

   Yet the fabric of Ojibwe community life persisted. For generations, Ojibwe
families and other tribal people had traditionally made room for parentless
children in their households. Orphans were treated with kindness, and little

distinction was made between "natural" children and those the families adopted. Often, adopted children were blood relatives who simply went to live with a grandparent or aunt and uncle after a parent died. But as family life suffered during the early reservation, post-allotment, and Great Depression years, traditional methods of absorbing orphaned children into the extended kinship group were not always possible. For a society that regarded caring for relatives as a virtue, with tender devotion to both the young and elderly, this was a troubling sign.

When Ojibwe families could no longer maintain traditional methods of adopting orphans, more children were sent away from Indian communities to live and be reared in government boarding schools. Reservations like White Earth, devastated by allotment and plundering timber companies greedy to gain title to Indian lands, were unable to provide homes for all their deserving children. When Clifford, a little White Earth boy, was sent to the Pipestone boarding school in Minnesota after the death of his father, a note on his application read, "The boy is absolutely homeless with no relatives to care for him." Described by a social worker as a "half starved undernourished child," Clifford was born in 1930, grew up in the community at Naytahwaush, and attended the Twin Lakes Day School from 1936 to 38. When his father died in January 1937, Clifford continued at Twin Lakes for a short time and attended the Summer Physical Health Camp at White Earth for two years before his fitness was restored to a point where he again could be considered "a normal healthy boy."[10]

Orphaned children often applied to government boarding schools as family networks failed. Ojibwe family life was complex and unstable. Children, left orphaned after the death of parents, were frequently shuttled from one home to another on the reservation as those families met with death, disease, or hardship. In 1937, Bernice, a young Ojibwe girl from Reserve, Wisconsin, who had just completed the eighth grade, applied to boarding school at Flandreau because her shattered family could find no alternative.

Bernice's mother had died in 1924 of tuberculosis. Her father had remarried, giving Bernice a stepmother and eventually two younger siblings. When her stepmother died in 1929 of pneumonia, Bernice and two half-brothers went to live with their maternal grandmother since their father was unemployed. The grandmother had also taken in the children of two of her recently widowed sons. At the time of Bernice's application to Flandreau, her younger brother, Antoine, a second-grader, was found to have an active case of pulmonary tuberculosis. Though Bernice had been a good student at the local school in Hayward, Wisconsin, achieving above average scores in science, history, arithmetic, English, and music, she stopped attending classes during the winter months because she lacked proper cold-weather clothing. In 1937, at the time she enrolled in the ninth grade at Flandreau, Bernice reportedly did not "have a place that she [could] actually call her home nor [had] her living conditions been satisfactory." By going to school in South Dakota, Bernice hoped to attend classes regularly and to study home economics.[11]

Mary Twobirds, a Bad River Ojibwe woman from the community at Odanah, Wisconsin, sent several of her grandchildren to Flandreau. Described as a "very intelligent old lady" by the local agent, Mrs. Twobirds had raised six of her grandchildren after the death of her daughter, the children's mother. She frequently counseled her grandchildren about the importance of an education and reminded them that she would not always be their caretaker. Mrs. Twobirds explained: "I am the guardian of these poor children since their mother died. I took care of them. I'm their grandmother and I've worked hard to raise these children on my own. Sent them to school here, our school here only goes as far as 8th grade."

A determined woman of fifty-eight, in 1932 Mrs. Twobirds regularly drove her "second-hand car" to retrieve her grandchildren during the summer vacation but was reluctant to leave behind the two youngest siblings in the local mission day school. While driving from northern Wisconsin to South Dakota, they even "tipped over once, on a certain curve." Mrs. Twobirds lived twelve miles from the nearest high school in Ashland, and daily transportation back and forth from school was problematic for the family, particularly during the northern Wisconsin winters. For the Twobirds grandchildren, Flandreau represented an opportunity for them to complete their schooling.[12]

Boarding schools increasingly became a solution to the problems of Ojibwe children regardless of age. In 1938, two Lac du Flambeau brothers, James and Carl, also enrolled at Flandreau. Their mother had died some years before, and they initially went to live with a grandmother, who subsequently passed away. James and Carl had been residing with two sisters, aged thirteen and twenty, when they left Wisconsin for Flandreau. Their older sister had attempted to protect and keep the family together in a neatly maintained house on the reservation but finally acknowledged that it would be best for the boys to "go on to school."[13]

A surprising number of homeless students, older and orphaned, were not being cared for by adults at all when they enrolled in boarding school. When David, a teenage Menominee, enrolled at Flandreau in 1936, the agent at Keshena, Wisconsin, reported that he was "without parents [and] has no home." The hard-working Menominee boy had been trying to support himself while he attended a local high school. The agent wrote that David had "used practically all of his money paying for board and lodging while attending a nearby high school, and we have decided that he can no longer afford to pay such expenses."[14]

Alphonse Caswell, one of many Flandreau students from Red Lake, decided to go away to school after his mother died. Alphonse planned to learn a trade and then return home to Red Lake to care for his younger brother and sister, Louis and Priscilla, who resided with relatives. As a young man, Alphonse felt completely responsible for his younger siblings and assumed the role of caretaker upon his father's death in 1935. By the time of his graduation, Alphonse was described as "an exacting workman, capable of thinking for himself," and with "a pleasing personality." As it turned out, Alphonse's time at Flandreau greatly influenced his later life. After graduation he married a young woman from White Earth, Ethelbert Branchaud, who attended Pipestone, just a few miles away in Minnesota. Later, Alphonse's younger sister Priscilla went to Flandreau. Flandreau was undergoing change in the 1930s, developing into a more sympathetic institution under Byron Brophy, a compassionate superintendent, and Alphonse successfully kept his family together with some help from the school. The Caswells remained a close and loving family.[15]

In 1933, an official in the Office of Indian Affairs sent a circular to the Wahpeton, Flandreau, and Pipestone boarding schools advising the superintendents there to accept only the neediest of children because of soaring enrollments. The commissioner understood that Indians in the upper Midwest were suffering, particularly during the winter months, and pointed to the poor economy as the reason families were asking to send children away to boarding school in unprecedented numbers. A girl named Florence dropped out of Red Lake High School in November 1937 "due to lack of clothing." Three months later, upon learning of her acceptance at Flandreau, Florence was "relieved at the idea of staying there." Boarding schools provided refuge during the Depression and were no longer viewed as institutions to be avoided at all costs.[16]

* * *

One quarter of all tribal members from the Lake Superior Ojibwe bands worked off the reservation at some form of wage labor in 1929, at the time of the economic collapse. When emergency work programs arrived in the Great Lakes in 1933, separation became a frequent resort of families who placed children in boarding schools while men joined WPA or CCC-ID crews. Ruth, a Saint Croix Ojibwe girl, was sent to Flandreau when her family had a difficult time making ends meet. Her father was a pulpwood cutter and earned forty dollars a month as a WPA laborer, still not enough to provide for all the needs of a family of seven. Ruth's father remembered a better time, when the seasonal round had nourished the Ojibwes, and he observed that it was difficult "for them to adjust to a 'white man's' way of living [and] when they were children an Indian family was never without meat or fruit as is now the case."[17]

The distinguished Ojibwe artist George Morrison, born in Chippewa City along the north shore of Lake Superior, remembered the protection that the Hayward boarding school in Wisconsin offered him and two brothers, as well as other Indian families, during the Great Depression. According to Morrison:

> The Hayward, Wisconsin, Indian school helped people with big families. It was available to a lot of poorer families during the Depression. Things got hard for us, especially during the Depression. I remember eating plain rice, or rice and potatoes together. Sometimes those old staples were the only things around. Now, my brother Mike and I kid about pork grease and potatoes.
>
> As I remember, I was nine when I started at Indian school. My older brother, Bernard, was already there. And Mike started a year or so after I left. There were maybe fifty to seventy-five boys and the same number of girls, on opposite sides of the campus. There was a central dining room; the meals were adequate. It gave us a good place to eat.
>
> When September came, the school provided transportation, either with a government car or by paying the bus fare for a group of young children. We stayed at the school during the whole nine-month period, and we never did see our parents.
>
> That's an awfully long time. I guess my parents were too poor to come—they didn't have a car and they couldn't pay to travel by bus. They never came to see us. As I recall, we accepted it, we kept busy with the activities, school, and playing. We were in it, so we weren't lonesome.
>
> Many of the kids probably spoke Indian. The school didn't repress it or stop it the way I've heard was done in some schools. . . . I've heard stories of the teachers in certain schools being very cruel to Indians. But as I recall, the teachers at Hayward were fairly decent. They all got along with the students and were liked by the students, too. It was all right.
>
> The teachers recognized talent. I was always chosen to do posters and things like that."[18]

Morrison and three siblings contracted tuberculosis during the Depression, though remarkably all four survived. Other boarding school students were not as fortunate. Communicable diseases flourished in Indian boarding schools, and many students contracted tuberculosis or the eye disease trachoma. During his second year at the Indian school, Morrison became ill and was eventually diagnosed with tuberculosis and arthritis of the hip. Morrison's sister and two brothers were sent to Ah Gwah Ching, the tuberculosis sanatorium in northern Minnesota, for tuberculosis of the lungs, while he was transferred to Gillette State Hospital for Crippled Children in St. Paul because of his orthopedic problems. Morrison spent a year in bed beginning at age eleven, but he was able to walk again after surgery and eventually returned home to Chippewa City.

The Depression continued, and Morrison mended books in the Grand Marais high school library under the WPA to earn pocket money. At seventeen he began to work in the CCC-ID camp in Grand Portage, where along with young Indians from across Minnesota he earned a monthly salary of thirty dollars. Morrison labored in both the kitchen and woods: "good healthy work" that encouraged community and friendship among the people from separate Ojibwe bands who assembled in the camps.[19] They lived in barracks, dined communally, and played baseball. In the forests they attacked the blight of blister rust, pulling diseased white pines out of the ground by their roots.

* * *

The first CCC-ID camp on the Red Lake Reservation in northern Minnesota was established November 15, 1933, a few months after the national program for American Indians started. Employees dispensed part of their wages to dependent relatives and received a modest salary of thirty dollars a month, contributing a small sum for food and shelter. Workers who lived at home, as did many from Red Lake, White Earth, and Lake Vermilion, could earn a monthly salary of forty-two dollars. Minneapolis served as the Great Lakes regional headquarters for the program, which provided relief work to Ojibwes and Dakotas in Minnesota, as well as Indians in Wisconsin and North Dakota.

The Red Lake projects varied in a region thick with brush and pine forests, a reservation where land remained unallotted and communally owned. Workers cleared fire hazards, cleaned off roadsides, "brushed" truck trails, cut new telephone poles and improved the stands of forest that stretched over several thousand acres of tribal land. By 1940 an impressive tree nursery project was in full operation, along with an important white pine blister rust control project. At the nearby Leech Lake Reservation, men dug wells, cut undergrowth, and cleared a wide fire line for some three miles around the village at Ball Club. Farther to the west, the camp at Nett Lake was a hub of activity: emergency conservation workers constructed trails, lookout towers, ranger stations, and telephone lines for a reliable system of fire detection and control.

Ojibwe men traveled considerable distances in northern Minnesota when work could not be found close to home. Families sometimes separated and young men bunked for weeks at a time in emergency work camps. Only a minority of workers at the Nett Lake camp were from that community. The Consolidated Chippewa Agency rotated men in and out of jobs to widen the pool of those participating in relief work. The Nett Lake Camp attracted workers from White Earth, Leech Lake, Mille Lacs, Fond du Lac, Lake Vermilion, and Grand Portage. In the winter of 1934, a group foreman described the winter camp of the Indian Emergency Conservation Work (IECW), painting a frigid but bustling scene of activity at Nett Lake[20]: "Far to the north, in the frontier country of Minnesota, close to the Canadian border, the Chippewas of the Nett Lake Indian Emergency Conservation Work Camp on the Bois Fort Reservation, continue their conservation work program, despite sub-zero weather, blinding blizzards and a welter of deep snow. It is a country where even thermometers freeze. At Christmas time, the thermometer that survived registered fifty-six degrees below. That night, watchmen were kept busy replenishing the fuel in red-hot stoves."[21]

By July of 1933, "a city in miniature" transformed the landscape around Nett Lake as "brown Army tents sprang up overnight—like symmetrically arranged toadstools." With autumn and cooler weather, "tents gave place to neat pine structures, built by Indians with lumber manufactured at the Red Lake Indian saw mill." As a chilly winter and an even colder Depression permeated the Great Lakes, the reservation-based work camp boasted "fourteen structures of freshly-cut yellow-colored pine nestled in the white snow, the blue smoke from their chimneys curling skyward against a dark background of spruce and balsam—three barracks, a mess hall, a commissary, a hospital, an office, a recreation building, a combined shop and warehouse, a bath house, a garage, a water tower and a heated latrine." The winter camp was orderly and bright, buildings were "labeled with a green and white sign over its main entrance" and the street had a red gasoline pump.[22]

Crews worked all day and part of the night to clear the roads of snow, while others spent long hours in the woods. At noon of each day "a truck loaded with a hot dinner was sent to men working" in the forest who then enjoyed an hour's rest by a Sibley stove. Camps workers reportedly appreciated the extra five to twenty pounds they gained through improved diet and plenty of outdoor exercise. Eight public schoolteachers were brought in to teach general education courses (and even "tap-dancing") at the Nett Lake camp. Recreational activities were encouraged, and the foreman recommended the

"wholesome pastimes" of reading books and magazines, listening to pho-
nographs and radios, and the occasional boxing match or basketball game.
The camp manager, a former Carlisle football player, was popular at Nett
Lake, and Indian men were promoted to "crew leaders" as a result of an
early "Indian preference" hiring policy. By the second year of the national
relief program, more than half of the salaried personnel and managers were
Indians.[23]

* * *

The fundamental goal of family preservation motivated many Ojibwe people
to temporarily abandon their reservation homelands during the Great Depression. Men departed for jobs in emergency conservation work camps as
children enrolled in boarding schools, in some cases hundreds of miles from
home. The close associations formed in boarding schools or relief camps may
have contributed to the growth of pan-Indianism, but many tribal people,
both students and their parents, missed the close relationships that char-
acterize Indian family life. Still, boarding schools, like the work provided
by the WPA and CCC, represented a significant form of poverty relief for
Indian families in the Great Lakes region. Indeed, for many Indian families,
boarding schools became a refuge of last resort. In an unlikely conclusion
to the history of federal boarding schools, Indian demand for these declining institutions went against the tide of educational and political reform in
the 1930s and encouraged the government to retain the schools for at least
another two decades.

Notes

1. A common interpretation in standard histories of American Indians in the twentieth
century is that because reservations were economically depressed before the 1930s, "economic woes affected Indians less than whites." For example, see Donald Parman, *Indians
and the American West in the Twentieth Century* (Bloomington: Indiana University Press,
1994).

2. Maude Kegg and John Nichols, *Portage Lake: Memories of an Ojibwe Childhood*
(Minneapolis: University of Minnesota Press, 1993).

3. A political climate hostile to Indian hunting, fishing, and gathering existed in Michigan, Wisconsin, and Minnesota. Arrests by state game wardens not only obstructed the
Ojibwe economy but also violated treaty rights throughout the Great Lakes.

4. The literature on the history of Indian education has grown substantially in recent
years. For example, see K. Tsianina Lomawaima, *They Called It Prairie Light: The Story
of Chilocco Indian School* (Lincoln: University of Nebraska Press, 1994); David Wallace
Adams, *Education for Extinction: American Indians and the Boarding School Experience,
1875–1928* (Lawrence: University of Kansas Press, 1995); and Brenda J. Child, *Boarding*

School Seasons: American Indian Families, 1900–1940 (Lincoln: University of Nebraska Press, 1998).

5. *Indians at Work*, September 15, 1933 (Washington, D.C.: Office of Indian Affairs), 15.

6. M. Inez Hilger, *Chippewa Families: A Social Study of White Earth Reservation*, reprint (St. Paul: Minnesota Historical Society Press, 1998), 131–34.

7. These issues are discussed in James M. McClurken, *Fish in the Lakes, Wild Rice, and Game in Abundance: Testimony on Behalf of Mille Lacs Ojibwe Hunting and Fishing Rights* (East Lansing: Michigan State University Press, 2000).

8. The boarding school letters featured in this chapter may be found in records of the National Archives, Bureau of Indian Affairs, RG 75, and in Child, *Boarding School Seasons*.

9. Child, *Boarding School Seasons*, 16–17.

10. Ibid., 17.

11. Ibid., 18.

12. Ibid., 18–19.

13. Ibid., 19.

14. Ibid., 19.

15. Ibid., 19.

16. Ibid., chap. 2, "From Reservation to Boarding School," which details the stories of many students from the Upper Midwest and how their families arrived at the decision to send them away for education.

17. Ibid., 22.

18. George Morrison as told to Margot Fortunato Galt, *Turning the Feather Around: My Life in Art* (St. Paul: Minnesota Historical Society Press, 1998), 37–38.

19. Ibid., 47.

20. IECW was the early name of the CCC-ID. News of Depression-era emergency conservation efforts was published from Washington in "Indians at Work," and regionally in Minnesota by the Consolidated Chippewa Agency as the "Chippewa Bulletin."

21. *Indians at Work*, February 15, 1934 (Washington, D.C.: Office of Indian Affairs), 19–22.

22. Ibid., February 15, 1934, 19.

23. Ibid., February 15, 1934, 23.

10. Indian Work and Indian Neighborhoods

Adjusting to Life in Chicago during the 1950s

JAMES B. LAGRAND

Beginning in the late nineteenth century, American Indian people seemed to become invisible to many Americans. Those who had been resisting the confines of the reservation had been subdued. Disease continued to take a tremendous toll on tribes, contributing to infant mortality rates that reached fifty percent on some reservations. Artists popularized the image of the "vanishing Indian" and suggested that Indians would slowly disappear from the national stage.[1]

Instead, the American Indian population increased steadily throughout the first half of the twentieth century, then swelled after 1950. Beyond this demographic explosion, another remarkable transformation occurred: large numbers of previously rural Indians became city dwellers. Starting in the 1940s and 1950s, a migration began that by 1980 would find over half of Indian people living in urban areas.[2]

Indians who migrated to urban areas were influenced by factors that affected many Americans, such as the effects of World War II and the economic expansion following the conflict. They also were affected by particular policies and programs sponsored by the Bureau of Indian Affairs (BIA). Since the late nineteenth century, the BIA had tried to assimilate Indians into mainstream American society. It first attempted to reach this goal by breaking up reservation land bases so that land would be owned by individual Indian men and women, and by establishing boarding schools for Indian children. During the 1950s, this assimilationist focus was accelerated by the relocation program, in which the BIA encouraged Indians living on reservations across the country to move to large cities, including the midwestern metropolis, Chicago.[3] Almost thirty thousand people participated in the program from 1952 to 1959. Chicago alone saw almost five thousand arrive, many of them from nearby Minnesota and Wisconsin. In addition to this large number of relocatees, countless other Indian people came to Chicago on their own.[4] By the 1990s, Chicago's Indian population was estimated to be between fifteen thousand and twenty-five thousand.

This mid-twentieth-century migration often went unnoticed. Indians continued to be invisible to many residents of Chicago. Non-Indian city dwellers seemed not to see Indian people at all, much less the institutions tribal people were building in the city. This is not completely surprising. From a large-scale, structural point of view, Indians in Chicago during the mid-twentieth century exercised little political or economic power. They could never approach the key role their forebears played in the fur trade during the eighteenth and nineteenth centuries, nor did they control any particular industry or sector of the economy in Chicago. In this regard they differed markedly from some of Chicago's European immigrants; no particular type of job was considered to be "Indian work" in the same way that certain jobs were widely associated with some of Chicago's other immigrant groups.

Yet Indians in mid-twentieth-century Chicago used their earnings and the connections they forged between work and community life to create a uniquely Indian adaptation to life in the city. Likewise, although no one Chicago neighborhood belonged to Indians alone, they made use of different neighborhoods for their own purposes. Under trying circumstances, Indians adjusted to urban life.

The Ojibwes, Ho-Chunks (Winnebagos), and other tribespeople who arrived in Chicago during the mid-twentieth century often brought with them limited and outmoded employment skills. Many were accustomed to patterns of seasonal economic activity, including subsistence agriculture, fishing, berry picking, and occasional wage labor.[5] At a time when high school diplomas were becoming much more common, even among the working class, only about one-third of the Indian migrants to Chicago had graduated from high school.[6] In many ways, they were poorly matched for Chicago's job market in the mid-twentieth century.

Furthermore, many who came to Chicago through the relocation program continually clashed with local BIA officials over the purposes of urban employment and urban life. Bureau workers hoped employment would lead to independence and individualism. As part of its assimilationist mandate, the BIA urged Indian people to acquire jobs in the same way as other Americans. Yet Indians were more comfortable acquiring jobs through familiar channels than in relying on impersonal job agencies. Those with minimal knowledge of English relied on family or friends who accompanied them when interviewing or signing papers. A 1956 study of Ojibwe and Sioux job-hunting practices in Minnesota showed that fewer than one in twenty-five had ever applied for a job directly in response to an advertisement. The study also claimed that many Ojibwes and Sioux had a "strong tendency to undersell themselves" when facing competition, the result of decades of isolation and harsh experiences with non-Indians. The BIA tried to discourage Indians from relying on others to find them work and believed that instilling individualism was part of its mandate in conducting the relocation program. One reservation newspaper told those who would soon be moving to cities, "Don't take anyone with you unless you are requested to do so—the employer wants to talk only to you." Such advice, though, was daunting and impractical for Indian newcomers to the city, and few Indians ever subscribed to the BIA's urban job-hunting suggestions.[7]

Once on the job, Indians quickly perceived the differences between rural and urban work. Like generations of urban migrants before them, they sometimes adjusted painfully to a world of time clocks and whistles dividing the workday into different parts with specified tasks. Little about Chicago's labor practices resembled those of traditional rural life with its seasonal and varying work schedule. The city's noise and congestion made many Indians homesick for wide-open prairies or still, deep forests. The demands of urban work, which struck many Indians as unreasonable, resulted in frequent job changes. Few stayed with the same company for long, moving either to another job in Chicago or back to the reservation.[8]

While in Chicago, some mixed old and new cultural patterns. Ann Lim deliberately chose seasonal work in order to be able to spend time back on the reservation every year. This Ho-Chunk (Winnebago) woman "couldn't leave Wisconsin during the summer" and so found work in a Chicago bakery that regularly would lay off workers during the summer months. Others managed to find jobs in Chicago similar to those they might have had back home. After serving in a number of dissatisfying industrial jobs, James Quiver, a Lakota from Pine Ridge, found employment to his liking at a stable on the outskirts of the city. Others worked outside in nurseries or gardens, where at least a few of the sights and smells of "outside work" might evoke pleasant memories of home.[9]

The majority of Indians in Chicago, however, took jobs similar to those of other Chicagoans during the 1950s, working for more than seven hundred different employers by the middle of the decade. Unskilled workers labored at B & B Enterprises and Paymaster, packed boxes at the Curtiss and Demets candy companies, and washed dishes and cleaned floors at Berghoff's and Stouffer's restaurants. Among the semi-skilled workers, some became factory operatives at Allis-Chalmers, Belmont Radio, Borg-Warner, Caterpillar, Dennison Manufacturing, Elkay Manufacturing, Farmrite Equipment, Hayden Manufacturing, Illinois Tool Works, International Harvester, Stewart-Warner, and Wells Manufacturing. Others clerked, filed, and typed at some of Chicago's largest service-sector employers—including Carson Pirie Scott, Montgomery Ward, Sears, and Spiegel. Publisher R. R. Donnelley offered Indians semi-skilled positions binding books and driving trucks. Others in this middling category included nurses' aides and cooks. A few of the best-trained and most fortunate individuals attained skilled positions. Some became finish laborers and rolling machine operators at U.S. Steel, Inland Steel, and Republic Steel. Other skilled workers were machinists, tool and die makers, welders, draftsmen, and mechanics.

Chicago boomed during the 1950s. An average of one hundred new industrial plants a year were erected in the decade following World War II. The city developed a diversified economy and emerged as one of the nation's leading manufacturers of machinery, primary metals, printing and publishing, and meat and confectionery products. One Chicago historian describes the 1950s as an "era of unparalleled prosperity," due in part to government money available for housing loans, veterans programs, and the G.I. Bill.[10]

Statistics confirm that Indian workers shared in this prosperity. During the 1950s the median income for Indian men in cities rose at 147 percent, almost twice as rapidly as that of those on reservations (79 percent). Indeed, no other ethnic group experienced a more marked increase in median income during the 1950s than urban Indian men. This was due in part to their economically deprived condition prior to migrating to cities, yet the figures remain startling. By 1969, urban Indian men boasted a median income slightly higher than African-American men, after having earned little more than half as much twenty years earlier. Indeed, Chicago's diversified economy provided some advantages over other cities into which Indians were also migrating during the mid-twentieth century.[11]

Like many other Americans during the 1950s, Indians in Chicago used some of their earnings to purchase radios, televisions, automobiles, and other consumer goods. The availability of both necessities and luxuries was far greater in Chicago than on reservations. Ojibwe Margaret Redcloud contrasted life back in Minnesota to Chicago, stating, "We were always scrounging and wearing second-hand clothes and hand-me-downs. . . . Nowadays, we can go to Sears or anyplace, and buy what we need." Letters or telephone calls from Indians in Chicago to their home reservations often carried news about such purchases. Ojibwes at the Turtle Mountain reservation in North Dakota, for example, were told in April 1954 that the Wilkie family, who had moved away two years earlier, already "had a television set for entertainment."[12]

Although the volume of Indian purchases in Chicago remains unknown, numerous references to this subject, together with studies from other cities, provide insights into the consumer goods that were selected. In Milwaukee, a survey showed that almost all Indians owned a radio, and one-quarter to one-third of all Indian families owned a television set. Likewise, more than half of all Navajos in Albuquerque owned televisions and automobiles in the late 1950s and 1960s. The BIA office in Los Angeles estimated that a majority of Indian families relocated there bought a television soon after their arrival.[13] The limited evidence available suggests that Indians in Chicago made similar purchases.

Some observers believed these trends foreshadowed Indians' rapid assimilation. One politician and writer who served as a tireless booster for the BIA's relocation program noted the urban Indians' purchases of consumer items and stated that it signaled a great cultural transformation. Yet these observers exaggerated the extent to which Indians were overwhelmed and stripped of their identity by mass consumer culture. Urban Indians often utilized increased opportunities in the city to enlarge and reinforce cultural patterns they had established on the reservations. Those who had listened to country-and-western music in bars and homes back on the reservation searched the dial for Chicago stations that played similar music. Moreover, they often listened to radio or watched television together as a group social activity. Indians in Chicago used automobiles not only to drive to the workplace and shopping center but also to return to reservations and visit family and friends during vacations. Community newsletters advertised a wide variety of items—necklaces, earrings, pins, and moccasins—that Indian readers could buy with earnings from their urban jobs. For some Chicago Indians, the money earned from urban employment and the ways in which it was spent aided in their adjustment to Chicago.[14]

Urban life brought a changing job market as well as available consumer goods. The year 1955 marked an important transformation in this process. Before 1955, blue-collar and industrial workers constituted a majority of the work force; after 1955 it was white-collar, professional, and service workers who gradually predominated. Among cities with large Indian populations, Chicago led the way during the 1950s in shifting from a strongly industrial economy to an increasingly service-oriented job market.[15] A few elite Indian workers in Chicago with extensive prior training and union membership worked their way into skilled jobs at Inland Steel, Republic Steel, and U.S.

Steel, jobs that paid as much as $3.57 an hour. Yet as the 1950s wore on, many of these jobs were eliminated through mechanization. Most Indians seeking work were unable to find jobs that paid wages approximating those of the steel mills. A wide gap separated the elite jobs from more attainable but less remunerative positions.

In response, many Indians in Chicago took service jobs, such as those offered by Spiegel, a mail order firm that employed hundreds of clerks, packers, billers, and warehouse workers at fairly low wages. Throughout the 1950s, wages at Spiegel hovered at about $1.00 an hour, rising very little over the course of the decade. As soon as the relocation program began, Spiegel asked the BIA for Indian employees. The firm even sent representatives to reservations in Wisconsin and Minnesota to look for workers and to administer the "Wonderlic Mental Alertness Test," which Spiegel used to screen applicants. These recruiting trips brought young women from Wisconsin to work at Spiegel, including the 1952 valedictorian of Flandreau High School. Although BIA employees acknowledged that the mail-order retailer offered "comparatively low wages," they welcomed the company's participation because of its ability to put large numbers of Indians to work and because of its on-site counselor, who helped Indian workers adjust to a new workplace and city.[16]

As Chicago's economy changed from an industrial base to a service economy, the earnings of Indian men in the city sometimes lagged behind those of their counterparts in other urban areas. For women, however, Chicago's growing service economy offered many advantages, and their wages were comparatively higher than female Indian workers in other cities.[17] Many Indian mothers as well as single women took advantage of these opportunities, and the number of Chicago Indian mothers working outside the home increased fourfold during the 1950s. BIA relocation offices provided advice about childcare, and some bureaucrats envisioned such "outside the home" employment as a useful step toward the integration and assimilation of both Indian mothers and children. One relocation officer directing Creeks and Seminoles to Chicago and other cities noted that his office encouraged those mothers who either had no children or who had secured childcare to look for full-time employment "as it is an accelerative step toward the rapid and complete integration of Indian people with the normal life of the nation."[18]

Indian women working in Chicago sometimes faced demands from their employers that seemed strange and unjust to recent reservation dwellers. Even firms that were eager to hire Native American women sometimes imposed strict physical requirements that eliminated Indian women whom they considered to be too short or too heavy. Aware of these restrictions, BIA workers on reservations attempted to screen female relocates and to warn them that their physical appearance might negatively affect their urban job prospects. One bureaucrat wrote approvingly of a nineteen-year-old single Ojibwe woman from Red Lake in Minnesota: "Reads some, listens to radio, goes to shows and dances. Physically OK. Wears lipstick, clean, well groomed, strong." Another bureau employee warned that any Indian women who wished to work in a restaurant or sales job in the city had to be "neat, well-groomed, and attentive to customers' wishes." They also had to be at least five feet seven inches in height "as they must be able to reach over the built-in fixtures in back of the counter" and "must be slender." Because of genetics, poor diet, and countless other factors, many Indian women failed these general screening tests.[19]

Others, however, found employment. Charlene Cooper, an Oneida woman, who with her husband was among the first to participate in the relocation program to Chicago in 1952, held several jobs over the next fifteen years. She started as a timekeeper at Container Corporation, then took a clerical job at Campbell Soup, and then worked nights at a Christmas card factory. After she separated from her husband, she attended real estate school and enrolled in beautician's school at night. Clara Packineau, an Arikara woman and single mother of two, took the opportunity to work nights in Chicago— which of all her new urban experiences she said she liked "most of all." She experienced considerable difficulty, however, in finding adequate childcare, especially after her sister returned to North Dakota. Yet, despite its problems, life in Chicago presented both of these women with more job opportunities than would have been found back home near their reservations.[20]

Although most Indians initially depended on the BIA office in Chicago to find jobs, after a period of adjustment many looked for work independently. Word spread quickly about which firms paid the best wages. Indians in Chicago readily exchanged information about their paychecks and frequently changed jobs when they learned of better pay scales. During a work break, a Ho-Chunk (Winnebago) woman who worked in the office of a gasket factory discovered that a sandwich company had moved in upstairs. The company needed workers and asked if she would be interested in working evenings on a part-time basis. She agreed because "you could make some good money by doing this, and they paid you by the sandwich." Eventually, she quit her job at the gasket factory and worked full-time making sandwiches.[21]

BIA employees at the Chicago relocation office hoped that Indians would work at firms where they would be surrounded by non-Indians so they could "learn good work habits," but Indian workers often gravitated toward firms who already employed other Indians. Publisher R. R. Donnelley employed more than ten Indians in 1957, while Union Station, the place where many Indians first stepped foot in Chicago after leaving their reservation homes, also employed many Indian workers. People from different tribal backgrounds sometimes met at these workplaces and helped each other adjust to their new lives. Marlene Strouse, a Tohono O'odham (Papago) woman, met her future husband when her father introduced her to the young Pima man who worked with him at Union Station.[22]

Some of Chicago's employment opportunities were less desirable. Some tribal people initially took poorly paying day labor jobs, in which workers were hired for only one day at a time and paid at the end of each day. Indeed, some Indians followed this pattern for years. Although eventually the BIA officially opposed daily pay labor for Indians, it initially supported these jobs out of a perceived necessity. In 1953, the Chicago BIA office placed fifteen unscheduled relocated Indians—all young, single men—in casual daily pay jobs. Some of these men were placed with Readymen, Inc., an employment firm which in the 1950s temporarily employed hundreds of Indian laborers at its office at 1 North LaSalle Street.[23]

For some, the day labor experience was harmful or destructive. In exchange for finding jobs for workers, Readymen and other daily pay offices took as much as twenty percent of workers' already slim paychecks. These day labor firms often perpetuated a cycle of desperation, leading a BIA employee to condemn them as "slave labor markets." More important, daily pay work often was tied to drinking problems and alcoholism for many Indian people (as well as non-Indians). A vicious cycle sometimes ensued in which a drinking problem prevented the acquisition of a better-paying job but could be fed by the small amount of money a daily pay job brought in. Also, most daily pay workers did not have bank accounts and often cashed their checks in local taverns and transient hotels, where their daily pay employer had made arrangements. Indian workers caught up in this cycle resembled workers in industrial-era company towns who were paid in scrip. Edward E. Goodvoice, a Sioux man from the Rosebud reservation, worked daily pay jobs and suffered from alcoholism for more than ten years in Chicago. Even after leaving to serve in the elite 101st Airborne Division, he still returned to his old habits after his discharge from the military service. Now a successfully recovering alcoholic and well-respected substance abuse counselor, Goodvoice remains critical of both the BIA and Readymen. "Some of us who were prone to drink too much would just sit there and drink up the eight-hour check. It wasn't a good idea," he says in hindsight.[24]

For others, though, daily pay labor was a satisfying way to combine old and new cultural patterns. It served as a step toward the white man's world without the shock and anxiety of a conventional, full-time industrial or office job. Some exchanged financial security for the freedom to socialize within the city or back home on the reservation. Although both "traditional" and "acculturated" workers were represented in semi-skilled employment positions in Chicago, daily pay work was primarily the domain of traditional people who lived in extended families. Some in this category accepted full-time employment after a while; for most, however, daily pay became part of their way of life. Similar to their ancestors, these people lived lives of constant mobility.[25]

Regardless of its employment practices, Readymen developed a reputation as an Indian employer. Ada Powers, a Sioux woman, remembered that Readymen was the place to be "with the Indians"; employment there enabled people to "follow the Indian life." Some tribesmen left regular jobs to join the group of Indians working out of Readymen, and others found they belonged there after going through a number of dissatisfying jobs. Either way, daily pay employment served as one of many ways in which some Indians adjusted to Chicago during the 1950s.[26]

Indians in Chicago also faced problems finding adequate housing. After World War II, Indians entering Chicago found neighborhoods that decades earlier had become segregated by race and ethnicity. They also found that housing was in very short supply. About one-fifth of all families were forced to double up in the first few years after the war ended. Some Chicagoans temporarily moved into streetcars, which the city had converted into homes.[27]

Since the BIA hoped to break up remaining Indian communities and force Indian people into the mainstream, it attempted to place Indian people in "apartments which are scattered about the entire city rather than having individuals and families clustered in a few congested buildings." This approach, the BIA official said, would "facilitate a more normal and happy integration of persons into the life of the community." To further the bureau's goals, the local Chicago office also used neighborhood councils and other civic and religious organizations to help Indians "take root in their local communities."[28] In 1956, a clergyman who worked with Indians in Chicago noted that there was "no large concentration of Indian population in any given spot in the city," while relocated individuals such as Phyllis Fastwolf, a Sioux woman, complained, "They placed us so that we never lived together. . . . They put us on the south side, others on the north side. That was their policy—to scatter us out over the city."[29]

Initially, the Chicago relocation office temporarily placed many relocated Indians in hotels and rooming houses near its location in the Loop. The BIA office also housed new arrivals at the Isham Memorial YMCA at 1508 North Larabee, on the Near North Side. At the "Y," Indians were provided with a bed for a couple of weeks while they adjusted to the city. They also had access to recreational facilities, including a basketball court and swimming pool. Within several months however, small Indian neighborhoods began to develop around 1500 North Larabee, a few blocks east of the cluster of industrial plants that hugged the Chicago River; and on the Near North Side, on North Clark Street, between Chicago and Grand. Much of the housing in these neighborhoods was poor, and it quickly soured some Indians on urban life. Despite working at upgrading its sources of temporary housing, the BIA achieved only limited success. After visiting the Dorset Hotel, where some Indians were staying in the late 1950s, a BIA official acknowledged with some embarrassment, "Our skirts are not neat and clean on temporary housing."[30]

Some less fortunate relocated Indians found residence west of the Loop in the infamous "skid row" of Madison Street. In this slum area, Indians could rent three-by-seven-foot cubicles for as little as seventy-five cents a night. Some Indians in this area also slept under bridges or in railroad yards. Although life here was hard and dangerous, one resident described it as no worse than conditions on his reservation, pointing out that even skid row housing had hot and cold running water and public bath houses. Further west, other Indians lived in the West Town neighborhood and near Garfield Park. These were mostly long-time Chicago residents who arrived before the relocation program began. These people enjoyed better housing than those along Madison Street, and some had achieved middle-class status.[31]

The initial Indian resettlement in Chicago ignored Native American kinship patterns. The hotels and YMCAs of the Near North Side were sufficient for young single people but not for large families. Although the average family participating in the relocation program during the 1950s had only four members, many were larger. One in five families relocating to Chicago had six or more members, and some had as many as ten. To acquire housing for these families, during the 1950s the Chicago relocation office turned to the south side and focused on the small community that already existed there. Some Indians had moved to Kenwood and Hyde Park near the University of Chicago campus during World War II. In the 1950s, these neighborhoods were in transition, with large numbers of African-Americans moving in, and the BIA took advantage of the resulting "white-flight" and subsequent low rental rates.

In this case, the BIA's strategy produced only limited results. Many Indians were reluctant to share the neighborhood with African-Americans, so Indians fled to the city's North Side. Many of these urban migrants moved to the Uptown and Lakeview neighborhoods, where they joined small pockets of Indian population that had emerged in the region in the late 1940s—around the intersections of Lawrence and Kenmore and of Wilson and Clarendon, just to the west of Lake Shore Drive. As the 1950s progressed, even more Indian people made the north side their home.[32]

Uptown had become part of Chicago in 1889 and had grown quickly during the early twentieth century as Swedes, Germans, and other immigrants moved there. By the 1920s, developers began tearing down single-family homes and building high-rise apartments and apartment hotels. Much of this new construction was east of Broadway, but after 1930 new residential construction almost came to a halt and existing buildings were divided into ever-smaller apartments. The neighborhood became a port of entry for poor migrants and a transient district, where people of many different ethnic groups frequently came and went. World War II saw even more single-family homes converted to rooming houses. A fairly typical type of structure found in Uptown during the early twentieth century—a three-story building containing six apartments of six or eight rooms—was usually converted to twenty or so two-room kitchenette apartments during the 1940s and 1950s.[33]

As a result of these conversions, Uptown became the second most densely populated neighborhood in Chicago by 1950, when two-thirds of all its apartment buildings had ten or more units. Other areas where Indians lived did not suffer from such crowded housing conditions, however. For example, only one-half of residences in Lakeview and one-tenth of West Town's structures had ten or more units in 1950. Moreover, these two neighborhoods—and Chicago at large—also had far more modest-sized apartment buildings of two, three, or four units. The neighborhood of Uptown and the city of Chicago as a whole continued on their opposite trajectories through 1960, when Uptown had even more high-density housing and Chicago more single-family housing than a decade earlier.[34]

Many of the large apartment buildings in Uptown and elsewhere in Chicago had as many as five or six stories. Indians often expressed unhappiness and fear about living on the highest floors of apartment buildings. A Sioux woman, for example, who moved from the Cheyenne River reservation in South Dakota into a small third-floor apartment without screens to cover the windows, feared the entire time she lived there that her children would fall through the window. Others felt trapped and disconnected from the world outside. Before Chicago officials began to publicly acknowledge the problems of large, multistory housing units in the 1960s, Indians living there understood intuitively how being separated from nature in imposing concrete boxes sapped the human spirit.[35]

Beyond being forced to live in intimidating high-rise buildings, many Indians in Uptown lived in apartments judged "substandard" or "dilapidated" by city housing officials. Although Uptown as a whole had roughly the same proportion of substandard dwelling units as did Chicago at large, Uptown's southeastern section, where most Indians lived, had far more housing in poor condition than did areas in the northern part of the neighborhood. The southeastern section faced many more problems, including clogged plumbing, broken furnaces, insect infestations, and general deterioration, than did the rest of Uptown or Chicago at large. Moreover, buildings in these tracts were even more divided than those elsewhere in Uptown. The average number of rooms in 1960 for dwelling units within a sixteen-square-block tract of high American Indian population was just 1.4, meaning that in the entire area there were few if any three-room apartments; almost all were either one or two room units.[36]

Although Indian housing in the Uptown region was substandard, it still remained superior to that available to Indian people living in many other places. For example, in the 1950s, while Indians in Chicago were cramped into dingy kitchenette apartments, a group of Ojibwes working on Minnesota's Mesabi Iron Range were living in tents. In other cities, too, housing conditions were as bad or worse than in Chicago. In Los Angeles, many families lived in trailer courts described as unsafe and "unsuitable for children," and low-rent housing for larger families was even more scarce there than in Chicago. In St. Louis, Oakland, and Dallas, Indians lived in large housing projects that were crowded, crime-ridden, and generally dangerous.[37]

Moreover, Indians in Chicago had limited options in finding housing. Because of excessive rents or ethnic and racial discrimination, many neighborhoods were closed to Indians. Throughout the 1950s, rents for apartments in Uptown remained relatively low and rose more slowly than rents for apartments in other parts of Chicago. In the city as a whole, both median income and median rent doubled during the 1950s. In those parts of Uptown where Indians most often lived, both figures rose only by an average of 50 percent during this time.

In addition, Indians in Chicago approached housing from a different perspective than did other urban dwellers. Because they frequently moved, they often tolerated what they envisioned as temporarily cramped quarters in Uptown and other parts of the north side. They believed that being with friends and family was more important than spacious quarters, and they made sacrifices to achieve this goal. Groups often moved together within the city, intent on staying together, even in the face of various challenges. Marlene Strouse, a Tohono O'odham (Papago) woman, remembers that a friend of her father led the way in moves around the city. "Wherever he moved, we moved with him."[38]

By the end of the 1950s, Uptown had become the primary area where Indians resided in Chicago. Various family members acquired apartments on the same floor, building, or block. Sometimes many members of a widely extended family—including grandparents, cousins, uncles, and aunts—all lived close by one another. Single young people also frequently moved in with each other after spending a short period in the city. A small, two-room apartment with six, seven, or eight tenants was not unusual. Although close quarters could lead to drinking and fights, this approach to urban living also allowed young people to save money on rent and provided social comforts. After a day filled with frustrating, frightening, or alienating experiences, newly urbanized Indians were reassured to know that there were others who understood their problems.[39]

By the end of the 1950s, Uptown had become an Indian neighborhood of sorts. It stood somewhere between the BIA's early idealized vision of tribal people evenly distributed across all parts of the city, and the ethnic neighborhoods formed in the nineteenth and early twentieth centuries. Indians were not as geographically concentrated in Chicago as they were in cities such as Minneapolis or in smaller towns near reservations. They continued to live on the south and west sides of Chicago, and also in different parts of the north side, including Lakeview and Lincoln Park. Moreover, many other groups—including Appalachian, Puerto Rican, and Asian migrants—shared Uptown with Indian people, making them a numerical minority there.[40]

Despite these limitations, Uptown achieved a special status in the minds of Indians in Chicago. It was the place to be with other Indians. Although some bureaucrats viewed the concentration of Indians in Uptown in negative terms, in retrospect the neighborhood should be envisioned as a venue for adjustment, just as immigrant neighborhoods in late nineteenth- and early twentieth-century Chicago helped Europeans adapt to a new environment. Although their numbers remained relatively small compared with those of other ethnic and racial groups, Chicago Indians living in Uptown were more likely to interact with other Native people from different parts of the country and from different tribal backgrounds than were those who lived elsewhere in Chicago. This interaction served as a first realistic step in urban adjustment, more so than living in isolation amidst a sea of non-Indians.[41]

While some scholars have complained that Indians were forced into "Indian ghettos" in Chicago and other cities, it seems that most Indian people simply wanted to live among other Native Americans.[42] A survey conducted by the Association on American Indian Affairs in 1957 claimed that observers repeatedly heard complaints from Indians that they were "lonesome because city Relocation Offices will not permit them to live in Indian neighborhoods."[43] The problem facing Indians, then, was not consolidation itself but the specific characteristics of the housing they had to accept in developing Indian areas. Urban renewal, the lack of new construction in parts of the north side, and the ongoing process of dividing buildings into ever-smaller units worked against Indians trying to find adequate housing in Chicago. Yet they persisted in order to be with each other and to enjoy the types of social benefits recognized by Ada Powers when she came to Uptown in the 1950s: "[For a long time] I never really got acquainted with the Indians. There were Indians on the south side. I met a few, and then we heard there were Indians on Clark Street. So we went down there and we met some. They were strangers to us. But we got acquainted with them and made friends. And then we decided to move on the north side because that's where the Indians were gathering."[44]

Because large numbers of Indians resided in Uptown by the late 1950s, various organizations and community centers moved there as well. The most significant was the American Indian Center, which in 1953 had been established in two floors of an office building in the Loop. In 1963, however, the center moved to a building in Uptown, where it became an important community institution and gathering place. The center fostered contact and solidarity among Indians of various tribes, provided for social and cultural activities, helped to develop Indian leaders, and served as a forum for the discussion (and often opposition to) BIA policy. For those who relied on the center for social and cultural benefits, it played a large role in making Uptown an Indian neighborhood.

Indeed, the development of Chicago's American Indian Center demonstrates the ways in which Indians used jobs and housing to adjust to life in mid-twentieth-century Chicago; they connected work, neighborhood, and community life. Although most Indians did not see a lucrative job or a spacious apartment as their primary goal, they were often able to use a job or apartment—in some small way—to help themselves and their fellow tribespeople "get by" in the increased pace of "city life." By the late twentieth century, Indians had emerged as a viable part of Chicago's multiethnic, urban society: an ethnic group well adapted to urban life.[45]

Notes

1. Brian W. Dippie, *The Vanishing Indian: White Attitudes and U.S. Indian Policy* (Middletown, Conn.: Wesleyan University Press, 1982); Frederick E. Hoxie, *A Final Promise: The Campaign to Assimilate the Indians, 1880–1920* (Lincoln: University of Nebraska Press, 1984).

2. Russell Thornton, "Patterns and Processes of American Indians in Cities and Towns: The National Scene," in *Urban Indians: Proceedings of the Third Annual Conference on Problems and Issues concerning American Indians Today* (Chicago: Newberry Library, 1981), 26; Nancy Shoemaker, *American Indian Population Recovery in the Twentieth Century* (Albuquerque: University of New Mexico Press, 1999), 77.

3. General accounts of the relocation program include Larry W. Burt, *Tribalism in Crisis: Federal Indian Policy, 1953–1961* (Albuquerque: University of New Mexico Press, 1982); Donald L. Fixico, *Termination and Relocation: Federal Indian Policy, 1945–1960* (Albuquerque: University of New Mexico Press, 1986).

4. Data drawn from "Report on Branch of Relocation Services," October 1957, box 8, Narrative Reports, Field Placement and Relocation Office Employment Assistance Records, record group 75, National Archives, Washington, D.C.; "BIA Voluntary Relocation Services Program," January 1962, box 14, Stanley D. Lyman Papers, Marriott Library, University of Utah, Salt Lake City, Utah.

5. Melissa L. Meyer, "'We Can Not Get a Living as We Used To': Dispossession and the White Earth Anishinaabeg, 1889–1920," *American Historical Review* 96 (April 1991): 368–94.

6. U.S. Bureau of the Census, *Census of Population: 1960, Nonwhite Population by Race.*

7. "Detail of Kent Fitzgerald to Minneapolis," 20 January 1956 to 30 March 1956, box 3, Financial Program, Field Placement and Relocation Office Employment Assistance Records, record group 75, National Archives, Washington, D.C.; E. M. McCauley to Dillon Myer, 20 October 1950, box 1, Placement and Statistical Reports, 1948–54, Field Placement and Relocation Office Employment Assistance Records, record group 75, National Archives, Washington, D.C.; *Fort Berthold Agency News Bulletin*, 2 June 1951, Robert Rietz Collection, Community Archives, Native American Educational Services (NAES) College, Chicago.

8. House Subcommittee on Indian Affairs, "Indian Relocation and Industrial Development Programs" (85th Cong., 2d sess., 1957), 14; William H. Kelly, "The Economic Basis of Indian Life," *Annals of the American Academy of Political and Social Sciences* 311 (May 1957): 75. On the responses of an earlier group of migrants to the regimented world of urban work, see Herbert G. Gutman, *Work, Culture, and Society in Industrializing America: Essays in American Working-Class and Social History* (New York: Knopf, 1976).

9. Interview with Ann Lim, Winnebago, 7 February 1984, Chicago American Indian Oral History Pilot Project, #019, Newberry Library, Chicago, and NAES College, Chicago; Chicago FRO report, July 1955, box 2, Reports on Employment Assistance, 1951–1958, Chicago Field Employment Assistance Office, record group 75, National Archives, Great Lakes Region, Chicago.

10. *A Survey of the Resources of the Chicago Industrial Area* (Chicago: Chicago Association of Commerce and Industry, 1950), n.p.; Roger Biles, *Richard J. Daley: Politics, Race, and the Governing of Chicago* (DeKalb: Northern Illinois Press, 1995), 4.

11. Alan L. Sorkin, "The Economic and Social Status of the American Indian, 1940–1970," *Journal of Negro Education* 45 (Fall 1976): 432–47.

12. Interview with Margaret Redcloud, Ojibwe, 12 February 1984, Chicago American Indian Oral History Pilot Project, #021, Newberry Library, Chicago, and NAES College,

Chicago; "Chit Chat from the Relocation Office," Turtle Mountain Consolidated Agency, 2 April 1954, Robert Rietz Collection, Community Archives, NAES College, Chicago.

13. Robert E. Ritzenthaler and Mary Sellers, "Indians in an Urban Situation," *Wisconsin Archeologist* 36 (December 1955): 159; William H. Hodge, *The Albuquerque Navajos,* Anthropological Papers of the University of Arizona, number 11 (Tucson: University of Arizona Press, 1969); "Indians & Industry," *Wall Street Journal* (28 December 1955): 1.

14. O. K. Armstrong and Marjorie Armstrong, "The Indians Are Going to Town," *Reader's Digest* 66 (January 1955): 42; Peter Z. Snyder, "The Social Environment of the Urban Indian," in Jack O. Waddell and O. Michael Watson, eds., *The American Indian in Urban Society* (Boston: Little, Brown, 1971), 222–27; Anadarko Area report, May 1953, box 2, Narrative Reports, Field Placement and Relocation Office Employment Assistance Records, record group 75, National Archives, Washington, D.C.; "A Little Newspaper about Indians," May 1953, Robert Rietz Collection, Community Archives, NAES College, Chicago. On the limited power and influence of mass culture among various urban dwellers, see also Joseph H. Stauss and Bruce A. Chadwick, "Urban Indian Adjustment," *American Indian Culture and Research Journal* 3, no. 2 (Spring 1979): 23–38; Lizabeth Cohen, "The Class Experience of Mass Consumption," in Richard W. Fox and Jackson Lears, eds., *The Power of Culture: Critical Essays in American History* (Chicago: University of Chicago Press, 1993), 135–60.

15. Raymond A. Mohl, "Shifting Patterns of American Urban Policy since 1900," in Arnold R. Hirsch and Raymond A. Mohl, eds., *Urban Policy in Twentieth-Century America* (New Brunswick, N.J.: Rutgers University Press, 1993), 13.

16. LaVerne Madigan, "The American Indian Relocation Program" (New York: Association on American Indian Affairs, 1956), 6, 13; Minneapolis Area reports, June and August 1952, box 2, Narrative Reports, Field Placement and Relocation Office Employment Assistance Records, record group 75, National Archives, Washington, D.C.; Consolidated Ojibwe Agency reports, August and September 1952, box 2, Narrative Reports, Field Placement and Relocation Office Employment Assistance Records, record group 75, National Archives, Washington, D.C.

17. U.S. Bureau of the Census, *Census of Population: 1960, Nonwhite Population by Race;* Chicago FRO reports, January 1953–November 1957, boxes 1–3, Reports on Employment Assistance, 1951–1958, Chicago Field Employment Assistance Office, record group 75, National Archives, Great Lakes Region, Chicago.

18. "Indian Relocation and Industrial Development Programs" (85th Cong., 2d sess., 1957), 5; Anadarko Area report, September 1952, box 2, Narrative Reports, Field Placement and Relocation Office Employment Assistance Records, record group 75, National Archives, Washington, D.C.

19. Case file CH-52–27, Employment Assistance Case Files, 1952–1960, Chicago Field Employment Assistance Office, record group 75, National Archives, Great Lakes Region, Chicago; Los Angeles FRO report, February 1952, box 1, Narrative Reports, Field Placement and Relocation Office Employment Assistance Records, record group 75, National Archives, Washington, D.C.

20. "Indians vs. the City," *Chicago Magazine* (April 1970), clip file: "Ethnic Groups-Chicago-Indians, American," Harold Washington Public Library; Packineau to Rietz, 6 August 1953, Robert Rietz Collection, Community Archives, NAES College, Chicago;

Report by Rietz, 1 September 1953, Robert Rietz Collection, Community Archives, NAES College, Chicago.

21. "Agenda: Placement and Relocation Field Meeting, Bismarck, North Dakota," 24–26 June 1953, Robert Rietz Collection, Community Archives, NAES College, Chicago; author's personal interview with Diane Maney, Winnebago, 20 June 1995.

22. "Indian Relocation and Industrial Development Programs" (85th Cong., 2d sess., 1957), 16; interview with Marlene Strouse, Tohono O'odham, 18 July 1983, Chicago American Indian Oral History Pilot Project, #011, Newberry Library, Chicago and NAES College, Chicago.

23. Charles Miller to John Cooper, 16 March 1953, box 1, Financial Program, Field Placement and Relocation Office Employment Assistance Records, record group 75, National Archives, Washington, D.C.; Chicago FRO report, February 1953, box 1, Reports on Employment Assistance, 1951–1958, Chicago Field Employment Assistance Office, record group 75, National Archives, Great Lakes Region, Chicago.

24. George D. Scott, John Kennardh White, and Estelle Fuchs, *Indians and Their Education in Chicago* (Washington, D.C.: Educational Resources Information Center, 1969), 8; Stanley Lyman to files, 7 January 1960, folder 20, box 14, Stanley D. Lyman Papers, Marriott Library, University of Utah, Salt Lake City, Utah; Virgil J. Vogel, "Chicago's Native Americans: Cheechakos, Old-Timers and Others in the City of the Wild Garlic," in Terry Straus, ed., *Indians of the Chicago Area* (Chicago, 1989), 183–87; author's personal interview with Edward E. Goodvoice, Sioux, 14 June 1995.

25. John Kennardh White, "The American Indian in Chicago: The Hidden People" (master's thesis, University of Chicago, 1970), 15, 33, 43; John W. Olson, "Epilogue: The Urban Indian as Viewed by an Indian Caseworker," in Jack O. Waddell and O. Michael Watson, eds., *The American Indian in Urban Society* (Boston: Little, Brown, 1971), 402–3.

26. Interview with Ada Powers, Sioux, 19 April 1984, Chicago American Indian Oral History Pilot Project, #012, Newberry Library, Chicago, and NAES College, Chicago; interview with Floria Forica, Ojibwe, 25 March 1983, Chicago American Indian Oral History Pilot Project, #004, Newberry Library, Chicago, and NAES College, Chicago; interview with Cornelia Penn, Sioux, 3 September 1983, Chicago American Indian Oral History Pilot Project, #017, Newberry Library, Chicago, and NAES College, Chicago; Edward E. Goodvoice, "Relocation: Indian Life on Skid Row," in Terry Straus and Grant P. Arndt, eds., *Native Chicago* (Chicago: McNaughton and Gunn, 1998), 131.

27. Karl B. Lohmann, *Cities and Towns of Illinois: A Handbook of Community Facts* (Urbana: University of Illinois Press, 1951), 37–38; William L. O'Neill, *American High: The Years of Confidence, 1945–1960* (New York: Free Press, 1986), 12.

28. Chicago FRO reports, February 1952 and January 1953, box 1, Reports on Employment Assistance, 1951–1958, Chicago Field Employment Assistance Office, record group 75, National Archives, Great Lakes Region, Chicago.

29. Report by Rev. E. Russell Carter, 23 May 1956, Church Federation of Greater Chicago Files, 28–4, Manuscript Collections, Chicago Historical Society; interview with Phyllis Fastwolf, Sioux-Oneida, 8 May 1983, Chicago American Indian Oral History Pilot Project, #006, Newberry Library, Chicago, and NAES College, Chicago.

30. "The Chicago Story," 9 April 1962, folder 23, box 14, Stanley D. Lyman Papers, Marriott Library, University of Utah, Salt Lake City, Utah; Stanley Lyman to files, 20 November

1959, folder 20, box 14, Stanley D. Lyman Papers, Marriott Library, University of Utah, Salt Lake City, Utah; "Transition Hard for Indians Here," *Chicago Sun-Times* (20 May 1957), clip file: "Ethnic Groups-Chicago-Indians, American," Harold Washington Public Library; Wade B. Arends Jr., "A Socio-Cultural Study of the Relocated American Indians in Chicago" (master's thesis, University of Chicago, 1958), 8–9, 79.

31. Wade B. Arends Jr., "A Socio-Cultural Study of the Relocated American Indians in Chicago" (master's thesis, University of Chicago, 1958), 103–6; author's personal interview with Edward E. Goodvoice, Sioux, 14 June 1995; author's personal interview with Lucille Spencer, Choctaw, 22 June 1995; minutes of the Joint Indian Committee, 15 July 1957, Church Federation of Greater Chicago Files, 28–4, Manuscript Collections, Chicago Historical Society.

32. "Transition Hard for Indians Here," *Chicago Sun-Times* (20 May 1957), clip file: "Ethnic Groups-Chicago-Indians, American," Harold Washington Public Library; Elaine M. Neils, *Reservation to City: Indian Migration and Federal Relocation* (Chicago: University of Chicago Department of Geography, 1971), 60; Janusz Mucha, "From Prairie to the City: Transformation of Chicago's American Indian Community," *Urban Anthropology* 12 (Fall 1983): 348.

33. Dominic A. Pacyga and Ellen Skerrett, *Chicago, City of Neighborhoods: Histories and Tours* (Chicago: Loyola University Press, 1986), 109–12; David K. Fremon, *Chicago Politics: Ward by Ward* (Bloomington: Indiana University Press, 1988), 303–9; Philip M. Hauser and Evelyn M. Kitagawa, eds., *Local Community Fact Book for Chicago, 1950* (Chicago: Chicago Community Inventory, University of Chicago, 1953), 18; White, "The American Indian in Chicago, 5–6.

34. Biles, *Richard J. Daley*, 7; Hauser and Kitagawa, *Local Community Fact Book*; Evelyn M. Kitagawa and Karl E. Taeuber, eds., *Local Community Fact Book: Chicago Metropolitan Area, 1960* (Chicago: Chicago Community Inventory, University of Chicago, 1963).

35. Madigan, "American Indian Relocation Program," 12; Grace Mary Gouveia, "'Uncle Sam's Priceless Daughters': American Indian Women during the Depression, World War II, and Post-War Era" (PhD diss., Purdue University, 1994), 172–73.

36. Kitagawa and Taeuber, *Local Community Fact Book*.

37. Consolidated Ojibwe Agency report, June 1952, box 2, Narrative Reports, Field Placement and Relocation Office Employment Assistance Records, record group 75, National Archives, Washington, D.C.; Los Angeles FRO Bulletin, 10 March 1953, Robert Rietz Collection, Community Archives, NAES College, Chicago; Alida Bowler, "A Brief Study of Relocation Activities and Results in California," 1 April 1952 through 31 March 1953, Robert Rietz Collection, Community Archives, NAES College, Chicago; Anadarko Area report, October 1952, box 2, Narrative Reports, Field Placement and Relocation Office Employment Assistance Records, record group 75, National Archives, Washington, D.C.; Madigan, "American Indian Relocation Program," 12; Paula Verdet, "Summary of Research on Indians in St. Louis and Chicago" (1961), unpublished manuscript, box 16, American Indian Chicago Conference Records, National Anthropological Archives, Smithsonian Institution, Washington, D.C.; Joan Ablon, "Relocated American Indians in the San Francisco Bay Area: Social Interactions and Indian Identity," *Human Organization* 23 (Winter 1964): 296–304; "National Council of Indian Opportunity Dallas-Fort Worth

Public Forum on the Condition of Urban Indians," 13–14 February 1969, record group 220: Records of the National Council on Indian Opportunity, National Archives II.

38. Interview with Marlene Strouse, Tohono O'odham, 18 July 1983, Chicago American Indian Oral History Pilot Project, #011, Newberry Library, Chicago, and NAES College, Chicago.

39. Scott, White, and Fuchs, *Indians and Their Education in Chicago*, 31–32; undated report, Church Federation of Greater Chicago Files, 32A-1, Manuscript Collections, Chicago Historical Society.

40. Merwyn S. Garbarino, "Indians in Chicago," in *Urban Indians: Proceedings of the Third Annual Conference on Problems and Issues Concerning American Indians Today* (Chicago: Newberry Library, 1981), 57–58.

41. Tony Lazewski takes the position that living in Uptown tended to diminish Indians' adjustment to Chicago. See Lazewski, "American Indian Migrant Spatial Behavior as an Indicator of Adjustment in Chicago," in Jerry N. McDonald and Tony Lazewski, eds., *Geographical Perspectives on Native Americans: Topics and Resources* (Washington, D.C.: Association of American Geographers, 1976), 105–19; Lazewski, "American Indian Migration to and within Chicago, Illinois" (PhD diss., University of Illinois, Urbana-Champaign, 1976), 142.

42. Larry W. Burt, "Roots of the Native American Urban Experience: Relocation Policy in the 1950s," *American Indian Quarterly* 10 (Spring 1986): 89–90; James J. Rawls, *Chief Red Fox Is Dead: A History of Native Americans Since 1945* (Fort Worth: Harcourt, 1996), 50.

43. Madigan, "The American Indian Relocation Program," 8–9.

44. Interview with Ada Powers, Sioux, 19 April 1984, Chicago American Indian Oral History Pilot Project, #012, Newberry Library, Chicago, and NAES College, Chicago.

45. For a more comprehensive analysis of the Native American experience in Chicago during the third quarter of the twentieth century, see James B. LaGrand, *Indian Metropolis: Native Americans in Chicago, 1945–1975* (Urbana: University of Illinois Press, 2002).

11. Blackjack and Lumberjack

Economic Development and Cultural Identity in Menominee Country

BRIAN HOSMER

In February 1997, and at the outset of his latest term on the Menominee Tribal Legislature, Chairman Apesanahkwat announced what probably surprised no one, namely, that the "operation of gaming ventures provides us with the wherewithal to accomplish a lot of things we have in mind." A year later, and this time during a public "debate" with an antigambling activist, he suggested that, while gaming may be a "less than an honorable profession. . . . Poverty is immoral," and so is "the inability of people to have a quality of life that's comparable to what people in the suburbs have." Indeed, the Menominee intention to promote opportunity went beyond the rhetorical. By 1998, the Menominee Nation of Wisconsin boasted two Las Vegas-style casinos, a profitable bingo operation, and over ten years' experience with the gaming business. Their gaming complex, located on state highways 47 and 55 between Keshena and the off-reservation town of Shawano, features parking lots for those cars and buses carrying patrons who expect excitement, if not jackpots. Visitors from near and far also enjoy a fine restaurant, spend the night in the hotel, and maybe even attend concerts, along with boxing matches (sometimes featuring Menominee junior middleweight Jonathan "J. J." Corn) and other events hosted by the tribal gaming corporation.[1]

Farther along Highway 47 stand handsome new buildings housing the College of the Menominee Nation, a tribally operated junior college offering degree programs in management of natural resources, hospitality, and courses delivered via satellite link with other tribal colleges. Along the same road are Menominee public schools, and in Keshena, buildings housing tribal government and the Menominee Historic Preservation department. Past the administrative complex stands Middle Village, with its new homes, senior citizens facility, and freshly planted trees, all on lands recently restored to the tribe. Beyond Middle Village lies Neopit, the location of the tribe's lumber mill, and the headquarters of Menominee Tribal Enterprises; still farther north and west lies Zoar, regarded as home to the most culturally conservative of tribal members.[2]

In one respect or another, gaming affects virtually everything along this highway, and indeed elsewhere across much of today's Menominee reservation. Though it would be an exaggeration to associate gaming with a thorough transformation of the reservation landscape, its tangible benefits are clear enough. Like many Indian nations, Menominees find that the so-called new buffalo can provide a degree of economic security, even with operations decidedly more modest than mega-complexes such as the Mashantucket Pequot's famous Foxwoods. But unlike Foxwoods, Menominee gaming operates within a much broader historical context, a "continuum" of economic activity now one hundred years in the making. The key feature then was logging and lumbering, and this business—ancestor to today's Menominee Tribal Enterprises—also stimulated considerable social, economic, and cultural change.

This chapter seeks to place contemporary Menominee business enterprises, notably gaming, within this broader historical context. It advances the argument that Menominee gaming is best understood as a continuation of a century-long pattern of reaching accommodations between economic change and cultural identity. Over the course of the twentieth century, and driven initially by commercial logging and lumbering, Menominees developed a "tradition" of economic change, a reciprocal interplay between cultural values and introduced elements whose ends affirm a generalized ethnic identity even as certain—perhaps many—of its discrete components appear different. In this case, twentieth- and twenty-first-century Menominee identity has incorporated these accommodations with the capitalist "market" to form an evolving definition of what it means to *be* Menominee. It is a process that has some similarities to Morris Foster's observations among the Comanches and Loretta Fowler's conclusions about Arapahoes and Gros Ventres.[3]

None of this is to suggest that Menominees embrace capitalist economic values wholeheartedly. There are important distinctions between gaming and logging. Their story is more than cultural assimilation just "dressed up" in fancy conceptual clothing. The Menominee situation is far more complex since it involves a multidimensional cultural "dialogue" between change and continuity where the conversation is constructive, indeed transforming, in and of itself. The various "parties" in this dialogue are individuals and groups from all across the tribal community. Moreover, distinctions between logging and gaming have helped to shape this conversation. Obviously, manning a blackjack table differs significantly from operating saws, lathes, and skidders; and like non-Indians, Menominees struggle with possible societal implications of gaming. In Wisconsin and elsewhere, the proliferation of casinos complicates relations between tribes and states, highlighting differences over treaty rights, environmental protection, and the dimensions of tribal sovereignty. In contrast to logging, gaming has engendered discussions of so-called special rights for Indians.[4]

But elements peculiar to gaming should not obscure the potential for fruitful comparison. In the cases of both gaming and the lumber industry, circumstances outside the Menominee community set parameters for the development of these industries. At the same time, Menominees have always shaped the development of their enterprises; debating and deciding any number of locally oriented issues, even if they typically have exerted little influence over matters of economic or Indian policy. Acknowledging this distinction between local and national "agency" (Menominees usually held one and not the other) illustrates how economic growth promoted ideas of self-determination and afforded Menominees some influence over the implementation of policy, if not its formulation. Just how Menominees participated in this process, and the complex cultural and ethical dialogue that emerged, constitute important themes for this chapter.

* * *

The genesis of Menominee casino gaming conventionally is dated to 1987, when on June 5 the tribe opened its first "Las Vegas style" casino. Prompted both by the United States Supreme Court's landmark *Cabazon* decision[5] and the passage of a broadly worded state referendum that legalized a state lottery, the Menominee casino, with its "bingo 21," two "bingolette" tables, twenty-five poker machines, and thirty jobs, stands as the first tribally operated gaming venture in the state of Wisconsin. By 1994, eleven tribes operated twenty-six casinos that generated over $7 million dollars in profits (on some $7.13 billion spent by gamblers), and an additional $60 million from associated ventures (principally lodging, food and beverage service, entertainment, and shopping). What is more, their twelve million patrons helped drive economic growth for nearby, off-reservation towns. At the close of the 1990s, several tribes either had successfully negotiated extensions to their gaming compacts with the state or were well on the way to doing so. Some, in fact, looked forward to expanding operations off reservation, and here again Menominees led the way, purchasing a defunct dog-racing track in the southern Wisconsin city of Kenosha while securing voter approval for what would be their third casino. In retrospect, the initial Menominee embrace of gaming proved not only profitable but also farsighted.[6]

It also engendered controversy. Opening that first casino brought immediate opposition from Wisconsin Attorney General Don Hanaway, who argued that the state's public policy prohibited casino gambling. Tribal Chairman Louise Chapman responded by citing the Supreme Court's *Cabazon* ruling, which seemingly exempted certain types of reservation gaming from state authority. She also pledged to "operate our lawful Casino operation" and welcomed "our many friends and patrons to continue to enjoy the games we offer." Not content with explaining legal issues, Chapman also taunted the attorney general, suggesting in print that while Menominees "understand Mr. Hanaway's desire to preserve a state monopoly over gambling," the tribe "will not step aside merely to accommodate the state's financial interests."[7]

If state officials acted predictably in opposing the casino, perhaps less expected was a challenge from a group of tribal members who also had some experience in the gaming business. These Menominees, who had operated a private "blackjack parlor" until a federal attorney declared the enterprise illegal and ordered its doors shut, threatened to seek an injunction against the tribal casino. They argued that since the tribal casino opened its doors prior to the passage of a business charter by the tribal legislature, it violated the Menominee Tribal Constitution. Chapman and the legislature, however, outflanked the blackjack operators by passing two emergency ordinances, measures that allowed the casino to operate "temporarily," pending action on an official charter. Clearly disappointed, the blackjack operators dropped their case, perhaps bending to the will of a Menominee community that supported its council and legislature—in this matter at least.[8]

Although the Menominee Casino remained open for business, two challenges were significant. On the one hand, Attorney General Hanaway's position proved just the opening salvo in an ongoing contest over gaming, one that touched upon competing tribal and state sovereignties. In this respect the situation in Wisconsin strongly resembles that across the nation. On the other hand, while the dispute with the private blackjack operators turned out to be more a "bump in the road" than a serious impediment to tribal gaming, it is important in at least two respects. It certainly represents an effort on the part of entrepreneurs to protect their interests from what they considered unfair encroachment upon the operation of private enterprise by public officials. In this sense, their concerns were not all that different from those commonly lodged by businessmen against government entities everywhere. But it also revealed an uneasy relationship between entrepreneurial values and those that emphasize group responsibility over individual autonomy, a cultural issue with strong historical antecedents. Menominee businessmen, after all, argued that they held the right to profit privately from a business that, viewed from a tribal perspective, might enrich the tribe generally, if only the tribe were allowed to run it. This is an important issue that resonates strongly in Indian country, where the line between the public and the private is hazy, indistinct, and often contested.[9]

* * *

This contest between the public and private sectors has been part of Menominee history. In June 1890, the United States Congress passed legislation affecting Menominee logging, an enterprise that had existed since the 1870s. An ironic companion to allotment-era legislation, this measure implicitly endorsed Menominee "nationhood" by recognizing logging as a *tribal* venture, while also offering statutory and financial support. In response to a tangle of legal and financial issues, the 1890 act more or less resolved constitutional impediments to selling trust property that had hamstrung tribal lumber operations up to that point. It also limited the annual harvest to 20 million board feet and mandated that sales be conducted via competitive bids submitted to the agent and approved by the Secretary of the Interior. In this sense, the legislation both offered administrative support for Menominee logging and provided access to investment capital to those small, generally family-centered logging companies that typically struggled to secure provisions on credit and at reasonable rates.[10]

In many ways the 1890 act met its objectives. Logging thrived during the final decade of the nineteenth century. More than 270 million board feet of timber were harvested in the 1890s, and deposits of $3 million existed in tribal "log" funds by 1900.[11] Just as important, Menominees escaped allotment, avoided the much maligned "timber fraud" visited upon nearby Ojibwe reservations, and instead derived collective benefit from their resources. The Menominees also avoided the radical denuding of their timber reserves so common where allotment held sway.[12]

Yet many Menominee loggers still found much to dislike in the 1890 act. At a general council held on July 8–9, 1890, some loggers complained that Congress's handiwork effectively transformed Menominee lumberjacks and logging contractors into "employees" of the Indian Office. Rather than concluding their own arrangements with suppliers, merchants, and laborers, and retaining the majority of profits for themselves—the custom previously— contractors now received a set fee based on the quality of logs and difficulty in bringing them to market. Anything over and above wages and expenses reverted to the tribe but was deposited in new funds managed by the United States Treasury. Other Menominee lumbermen complained that the federal regulations limiting the annual harvest at 20 million board feet interfered with entrepreneurs' ability to adjust to favorable market conditions. Some loggers denounced the measure as "an Act to provide for a lot of white politicians and to provide good salaries for some to be paid from the money of the Indians." They also unsuccessfully lobbied for a repeal of the harvest ceiling, but they did secure a one-time exception for an accidental "over cut" of some five million board feet that occurred during the first season under the new legislation. Nevertheless, they argued that the act "left them without means to pay for [their] supplies," and one logger charged that local Indian agents had "threatened . . . that if any Indian refused to obey orders he shall not be permitted to log."[13]

Obviously, Menominee loggers were concerned about federal controls over their operations, but they had never operated autonomously. On several occasions during the 1870s and 1880s, for instance, federal courts had ruled on the legality of selling Menominee trust resources (lumber) for profit, and sometimes federal Indian agents had arbitrarily suspended the operations.[14] Moreover, since Menominee loggers exerted very little control over regional markets, they found themselves subject to larger forces of supply and demand while experiencing firsthand the power of Wisconsin timber merchants over those same markets. In response, some Indian loggers, like Zoar resident Ohopahsa, complained that "we are going to be robed [*sic*]", and called upon officials "to help me and my friends" counteract the activities of merchants. In 1874, Indian agent Thomas Chase responded to what he considered artificially depressed timber prices by withholding from sale some 2 million board feet of Menominee logs—a disastrous gambit that caused Indian lumberjacks to default on some loans. Chase's successor, Joseph Bridgeman, sold those logs in 1875—and at even lower prices.[15]

But more than outside forces constrained the activities of Menominee loggers. In fact, community members engaged in a discussion, generally cordial, regarding control over logging, and more specifically, the distribution, or "ownership," of profits. This conversation proceeded from the very structure of an enterprise in which Menominee contractors operated more or less independent of tribal oversight. Though subject to some administrative control by Indian agents, during the 1870s and 1880s, individual logging "companies" negotiated their own agreements with equipment suppliers and timber merchants, determined where they would log, how much they would take, and generally retained most of the profits.[16] Not surprisingly, kinship played an important role, as logging companies tended to organize around family networks, while contractors generally were leaders of clans or lineage groupings. Logging rolls from the 1880s and 1890s confirm this pattern, with prominent families forming identifiable companies that worked distinct "camps." Other well-placed Menominees operated as middlemen between loggers and non-Indian merchants, and Charles Chickeney, son of chief Mah Chickeney (Ma'tshikine'u) emerged as the most important native merchant-logger. Similarly, principal chief Neo'pit's eldest son, Reginald, a Carlisle student, eventually succeeded his father and earned a reputation as a "modern" leader schooled in the business of logging.[17]

Since logging operated at intersections of kinship and commerce, the industry generated an association between economic and political power. Just as significantly, it did so by rewarding one set of cultural values over another. Sometimes described as an area where "progressives" contested with "traditionalists" (or conservatives), logging was an enterprise that seemed to encourage some individuals or groups to value individuality over responsibilities to the larger tribal community. Undoubtedly, the Menominee timber industry promoted the development of an entrepreneurial "ethos" and differentially rewarded those who embraced individuality. At the same time, however, it would be a mistake to place these modes of behavior in stark opposition to one another, constructing a dichotomy where nothing so neat and easy to measure existed. Rather, a growing body of analysis supports the notion that the comparative importance of these "poles" of behavior and values differed from person to person within a particular community, and typecasting or stereotyping often depended on which "features" of behavior (clothing, religion, etc.) the observer chose to highlight. In reality, each individual likely struggled, in his or her own heart and mind, with this ethical dilemma. For Menominees, there existed no *organized* pro- and anti-logging "parties" or factions. Everyday life was considerably more complex and fluid.[18]

Yet some Menominees clearly embraced behaviors and values that tended to separate them from the group. In doing so, they also formed their own "pressure group," as the consolidation of logging contracts in fewer and fewer hands, and the tendency of loggers to act in concert on issues of broader concern, demonstrates. For example, when the number of separate contractors fell from 133 in 1890–91 to seventy-two in 1892–93, and to sixty-three in 1897–98, it presented the possibility that social fragmentation might accompany the development of an entrepreneurial-oriented "faction."[19] At the same time, established tribal leaders seemed to have understood this danger, for as early as 1882, chief Neo'pit endorsed a plan (supported as well by Indian agent

Ebenezer Stephens) to deduct one dollar from each 1,000 feet of timber cut and sold. Revenues generated from what is known in the industry as a "stumpage fee" were to be deposited into a "poor fund." Clearly conceived as a way to direct a portion of profits to the most needy of Menominees, this logging "tax" put into action a "collectivist" Menominee philosophy that endorsed the proposition that, since Menominees owned the timber collectively, all were entitled to share in profits, irrespective of labor actually performed.[20]

Loggers advanced a different proposition. In 1882 a group of loggers led by Ohopahsa, chief Neo'pit's brother Ahkonemi, and the mixed-blood trader Joseph Gauthier complained that after completing "expensive and hard work," they found that "our Agent, without telling us, went to Washington, and on his return told us that . . . we must pay stumpage."[21] They charged Agent Stephens with "dishonest . . . dealings with the tribe." In response, Neo'pit expressed "great confidence" in Stephens and defended the agent as the Menominees' "true friend and protector."[22] Stephens lost his job (though it remains uncertain if Menominee resistance played any role in his departure), but this exchange of letters illustrates a growing distance between entrepreneurial-minded loggers and established leaders. While the former focused upon protecting their ability "to cut and haul logs to rivers at a fair and reasonable price," Neo'pit sought to derive some collective benefit from an enterprise that rewarded individual initiative.[23]

These diverging interests continued, and the loggers hired St. Louis attorney Fred T. Ledergarber to represent *their* interests in Washington, D.C. These interests included allotment. As one anonymous Menominee explained, the loggers refused to "be dictated [to], by an agent or anyone else." In response, Neo'pit offered to sell the reservation's timber to outside firms—and in turn accept allotments—so long as no land surrenders followed. "We want to sell our timber for a fair price," he explained, and in return "all we ask is to be permitted to keep it [the reservation]," for "our children and grandchildren." Though both Neo'pit and the loggers discussed the possibility of accepting allotment, they did so for different, and instructive, reasons: the loggers because they wanted to free themselves of the influence of old chiefs; Neo'pit out of a determination to mitigate the fractious tendencies of individual enterprise.[24]

* * *

Contemporary Menominees struggle with similar issues. In 1996, tribal councilman Louis Dixon abruptly lost his position as Vice Chairman of the Menominee Tribal Legislature in a dispute over casino management. Dixon publicly objected to the Legislature's vote to disband the independent Menominee Tribal Gaming Corporation and replace it with a single director. The ensuing turmoil revealed details from confidential executive sessions of the legislature. Casting his actions as a matter of conscience, Dixon wrote "I don't feel sad or bad" about doing "the right thing for myself and for the tribe."[25]

Chairman John Teller presented a distinctly different version of the incident. He explained that the Tribal Legislature replaced the five-member gaming board with a single general manager to "streamline the gaming operation and [make] it more responsible to daily business demands." The decision, so Teller explained, followed a meeting that "outlined several problems that existed with the Board." Meanwhile the board took legal action against the tribal legislature, alleging the latter lacked the authority to involve itself in business matters. Dixon also charged the Teller-led majority in the legislature with a "blatant . . . political move to save the job of a friend [meaning the present general manager]," and attempting to disband the board altogether. Teller's policies, according to Dixon, were just the latest in a series of undemocratic moves by a tribal legislature "besieged by members of the Tribe who feel their rights are being denied them."[26]

But what began as a dispute over who held the authority to fire a casino manager soon became a matter of even deeper significance, namely, who, or what body, would control tribally chartered businesses. For his part, Teller argued that, while the Menominee constitution prohibited the tribal legislature from interfering "in the daily operations of a chartered business," it nevertheless retained "all Governmental and Sovereign functions over the tribal business." Therefore, he concluded, "the Gaming Board was appointed by the Tribal Legislature in good faith and trust," but when it violated those conditions, "the action to remove the Gaming Board is a responsibility of the Tribal Legislature." Teller suggested that since Dixon, the former vice chairman "has besmirched the office and has attempted to thwart the laws passed by the legislative body," the legislature had no choice but to impose sanctions. "We are not mavericks, free to maneuver our personal agenda ahead of that which best serves the Menominee Nation," Teller argued. More interestingly, the chairman also pointed out that "the reality of any democracy is that the majority rules and [while] the minority may feel helpless, still the alternative to representative democracy is utter chaos."[27]

Teller's strong endorsement of the principle of majority rule is interesting because it highlights one of the characteristic difficulties faced by tribal governments, particularly when attempting to manage business enterprises. Facing an unclear line between public and private sectors, torn as well by demands from low-income constituents to share the benefits of tribal enterprise equally, tribal governments find themselves at the center of a philosophical, even cultural, battle. Identified by sociologist Stephen Cornell as a distinctively "Indian" definition of "success," and one critically related to a *collective* rather than individualistic ethos, this model nevertheless suggests some important variables when planning or evaluating economic development and change in Indian country.[28]

In reality, Menominee gaming operates under conditions that reflect a clear orientation toward collective needs and values. The tribe's gaming charter, approved in 1993, and in compliance with the Indian Gaming Regulatory Act, mandates that net revenues from tribal gaming are to be used primarily to fund tribal government and programs, to provide for the general welfare of tribal members, and to promote economic development. Moreover, per capita payments can be made only after meeting these first stipulations, and then must not exceed 10 percent of remaining revenues so long as the annual individual distribution does not fall below $100. Operating under these stipulations, tribal officials developed a plan that assigned priority to funding programs and economic development, while reminding constituents that per capita payments would be subject to federal taxation. Just as significantly, the state of Wisconsin likely would consider per capita payments as income for the purposes of assigning public assistance allocations.[29]

A fairly straightforward plan, the Menominee legislature's efforts still generated controversy. Reminding tribal members that "the fact that we have gambling today is no guarantee that it will be allowed to continue," Louis Dixon argued that $72,000 spent to transport patrons from Shawano and surrounding communities to the casino was extravagant and was sufficient for "a per capita to 720 persons." Similarly, $17,000 for a new casino door (since unused) "could have been used to give 170 persons a dividend," and $15,000 on public relations meant that 150 presumably went without their fair shares. Dixon cited other such examples, but more ominously he charged that "our Legislature is doing a lot that is being kept secret from the Tribe." These actions, Dixon claimed, had the effect of undermining the independence (from legislators) of the tribal gaming corporation. He charged that instead of providing "an annual dividend" as promised, the tribal legislature was channeling tribal profits into the hands of the few and well connected. "Don't kid yourselves, Mr. & Mrs. Legislature," Dixon wrote. "The Tribe is watching you and we aren't happy with some of the things you're doing."[30]

Accurate or not, Dixon's claims seem to have found an audience. Laurie Swiney, the manager of the Menominee Nation Casino, rejected any notion of a conflict of interest and assured tribal members "that in whatever role I am carrying out for our tribe, . . . I will always do my very best to assist in the efforts to broaden and sustain our economic self-sufficiency." Tribe member Wanda Guzman addressed payments more directly, warning, "If you tie up your profits in per capita payments, you may create another form of dependency," particularly "if the gaming boom goes bust." Similar letters to the tribal newspaper reflected sentiment in favor of limiting per capita payments in favor of funding development, but the decision to consider a per capita referendum (and the appearance of the issue in the advertisements of candidates for tribal office) demonstrates some difference in perspective.[31]

Swiney was not the only tribal official to feel the sting of Dixon's comments. In 1996, Lawrence Waukau, general manager of Menominee Tribal Enterprises (MTE), and thus the chief executive officer for logging and lumbering, fended off requests for a renewal of dividends drawn from the assessed value of timber, "on the stump." Waukau refused to resurrect stumpage payments, discontinued following the 1973 restoration of Menominee tribal status, and announced "we will not sacrifice long-term profits for short-term gain." His comments also highlighted the tension between an entrepreneurial mindset and a more communal cultural orientation. Waukau remained determined to "operate in a businesslike manner for the best interests of the Tribe and Tribal members." For the MTE manager, this meant conserving scarce capital while also developing more profitable product lines, improving marketing, and making "the commitment to discipline ourselves to be educated in the best business practices available to us."[32]

Waukau's personal decisions reflected an entrepreneurial mindset, but Menominee Tribal Enterprises unequivocally supports the principle that the enterprise exists to benefit the community at large. According to its managers, the mill seeks to maximize job creation, and it manages reservation forests on a "sustained yield basis." According to MTE's "Forest Management Plan," the tribe's "land ethic and management philosophy" is designed "to maximize the quantity and quality of sawtimber grown under sustained yield management principles while maintaining the diversity of native species." This concept, so Menominee managers explain, "is based upon the direction chosen by earlier Menominee leaders who recognized the need to harvest trees for economic survival at a speed (or intensity) under which the forest can replace itself."[33] No idle words: Menominee forest practices have, in fact, preserved the productivity of their woodlands for more than a century, earning the tribe recognition for its efforts. During the mid-1990s, for instance, MTE forestry practices earned a "Presidential Award on Sustained Development" (presented by Vice President Al Gore), a national award from the United States Forest Service, a $30,000 grant from the First Nations Development Institute (in order to expand product lines) and an Environmental Leadership Award from the Wisconsin State Senate. In addition, the tribe itself received a grant from the H. Derkson & Son's Company of Omro, Wisconsin, recognizing it as "an organization that promotes environmental consciousness," and in 1997 the Menominees hosted the twenty-first annual Intertribal Timber Council Symposium."[34]

The upshot is that the Menominee *mill* is an unusual species of enterprise, and its means of operation, not to mention expectations for it, sometimes mirror those of the gaming enterprise. In other words, since Menominees expect something of a *public* orientation for their businesses, and, as casino operations distribute a portion of their profits directly to tribal members, there develops an assumption that MTE will operate similarly. While MTE is a quasi-independent corporation and thus insulated from the vagaries of tribal politics, this phenomenon still indicates a rather close relationship between public and private "sectors." This is particularly notable with regard to gaming, of course, where candidates for the Tribal Legislature take very public stands on the state of, and future for, gaming. It is also illustrated in the tendency, as Louis Dixon's comments indicate, for tribal members to level charges of mismanagement and cronyism at legislators and casino managers alike.[35]

* * *

At the beginning of the twenty-first century gaming sometimes appears to so influence Menominee politics that even when the topic is something else, for instance the MTE, casinos still shape the underlying context. This situation is not uncommon to gaming tribes, but it still obscures the more important historical context—namely, a close association, more than a century old, between Menominee business and politics. By the late 1890s, in fact, loggers had come to dominate tribal politics. Skilled in political organizing and lob-bying, wealthier—and in many cases better educated than their neighbors—Menominee "entrepreneurs" like Mitchell Oshkenaniew took advantage of new opportunities. The Haskell-educated son of a logger, Oshkenaniew pro-moted a message of economic change and Menominee self-determination, and in so doing he emerged as a key spokesman for the entrepreneurs. This brought him into conflict with just about everyone, including tribal leaders, loggers, government officials, and non-Indian timber interests. Oshkenaniew rarely failed to reply in kind, once shrugging off negative comments as simple carping by "officials" who objected to his practice of "criticizing and making remarks concerning the management of our affairs and [for] standing up for our people." Significantly, Oshkenaniew, who served for a time as the business committee's sole representative in Washington, D.C., reminded prominent "friend of the Indian" Herbert Welsh that "the pine belongs to us."[36]

Beyond rhetoric, Oshkenaniew's developing role as spokesman for Menominee loggers indicated a changing political landscape, perhaps even a growing cultural distance between entrepreneurs and those who chose not to participate in the changing Menominee economy. At the same time, however, it would be a mistake to associate Mitchell Oshkenaniew with a message of wholesale economic change, one where the great success of logging rendered obsolete those more "communal" Menominee values. When he declared, "The pine belongs to us," Oshkenaniew also meant to convey a message to Menominees, and particularly nonloggers who held firm to the communal interpretation of enterprise. Taking their concerns into account, in 1891 Oshkenaniew supported a move to deny "mixed bloods who are not and were never members of the tribe" any opportunity to enter into logging contracts. This position, which placed Oshkenaniew at odds with agent Charles S. Kelsey, arose from concerns that white males, intermarried into the tribe, effectively had "crowded out" qualified Menominee workers. Similarly, Oshkenaniew promoted the wider distribution of per capita funds from logging revenues. In this sense, Oshkenaniew honored expectations Menominees held for their leaders, replicating in essence the actions of Neo'pit, a respected chief who had risen to prominence according to accepted conventions.[37]

But there was more to these decisions than fealty to leadership conventions. Some, perhaps many, Menominees evidently perceived in free enterprise a serious threat to community unity, even ethnic identity, and sought means to mitigate its influence. To these Menominees, incidents like a 1905 petition, wherein fifty-three loggers asked to be released from tribal rolls,[38] demonstrated forcefully the uncomfortable possibility that while logging supported material improvements for the many, it might divide community members from one another. In this context, Oshkenaniew's support for per capita payments illustrated his collective orientation in the face of forces that rewarded individuality. He and other Menominees believed that while loggers had a right to the fruits of their labor, the community "owned the trees."

Working out a compromise between these competing philosophies defined Menominee politics between 1890 and 1920. Again, Mitchell Oshkenaniew's career proves instructive. Following a severe windstorm in July 1905 that uprooted thousands of trees, Oshkenaniew maneuvered to the forefront of an effort to reorganize Menominee logging enterprises. Building on what he understood to be Indian Office support, he then devised a plan that centralized logging authority in the hands of a semi-official and logger-dominated Menominee business committee. In a position to award all contracts for work in the "blown down district," the business council succeeded as well in eliminating any promise to hire Menominee laborers, or even, it seems, a requirement that they actually run operations themselves. This effectively transformed the business committee from an interest group to a quasi-governmental entity answerable certainly to the Indian Office but not necessarily to the community at large.[39]

The triumph of the business council marked the apex of Oshkenaniew's career, but as it turns out, the logger/lobbyist's moment in the sun proved transient. Business council activities soon came under harsh scrutiny, and an investigation uncovered mismanagement, corruption, wasteful logging practices, and a preponderance of non-Indian lumberjacks working in the "blown down district." In a stinging commentary, Joseph R. Farr, the Indian Office's General Superintendent of Logging for Wisconsin reservations, wrote in 1907 that "the business committee . . . does not stand for the interests of the tribe, and is controlled by three or four of the most undesirable Indians on the reservation." Reginald Oshkosh, the Carlisle-educated son of Chief Neo'pit, also chimed in and spearheaded a drive to punish his sometimes rival. In fact, it was an Oshkosh-led tribal council that voted to do away with the business committee, and by a tally of 62–0 resolved that "Mitchell Oshkenaniew is forever barred from representing the Menominee Tribe of Indians in any way, shape, or manner in any of their tribal affairs."[40]

This action circumscribed Oshkenaniew's influence and suggested limits to Menominees' embrace of timber entrepreneurs. It also encouraged Congress to pass the landmark 1908 La Follette Act that tightened controls over contracts while enshrining the principle of Menominee preference in hiring. The measure also authorized the construction of a modern sawmill, and this lumber plant, located in the brand new town of Neopit, opened for business in January 1909. Completed at a cost of just over $1 million—all drawn from tribal funds—the mill and town directed Menominees even more toward a commercial orientation as jobs, wages, new homes, and amenities increasingly flowed through Neopit, for better *and* worse. Even those not directly associated with the mill felt its effect, both in terms of services financed by the tribal industry and, perhaps, even a growing isolation from evolving economic, social, and commercial arrangements. Not incidentally, non-Indians and members of the Menominee entrepreneurial elite directed these "arrangements," and it was this trend that seems to have prompted Mitchell Oshkenaniew's return to prominence. In 1912, an Oshkenaniew-led group hired legal council and initiated a lawsuit against the Indian Office. Charging mismanagement of timber reserves and tribal funds, as well as a pattern of denying Menominees access to the best jobs and mistreating native laborers, the Oshkenaniew suit prompted a comprehensive investigation and generated considerable publicity.[41]

While this suit ended without demonstrating "deliberate mismanagement" as alleged by Oshkenaniew's attorneys, it did prompt the Indian Office to inaugurate reforms intended both to improve management of timber stands and to address concerns of Menominee workers.[42] It also boosted Reginald Oshkosh's career and reputation, but at some price to community unity. In 1915, he expressed concerns that although the mill acted "as a center for industrial and social development," it also offers little for "Indian boys learning farming and dairy work," or "old folks," or "young women educated in home making and the women's part on the farm."[43] Reflecting an emerging Menominee "philosophy of economic development" that emphasized a link between industry and broader social responsibilities, Oshkosh's words recognized the Neopit lumbering complex as a turning point for Menominee economics. Not only was the tribe in the business of producing a value-added product (finished lumber from logs), but they were also committed to combining economic growth with cultural, national, and ethnic preservation. Since the town of Neopit featured electric lighting, a hotel, housing for workers, and a variety of entertainment options, the Menominee lumbering enterprise retained its distinctly communitarian emphasis. The mill encouraged Menominees to stay home while it financed schools and all forms of assistance available to everyone. Logging profits also financed a successful settlement of a claim against the Indian Office for mismanaging tribal timber stands. The irony of the tribe's using logging profits to sue that government entity that promoted that very industry compounded when, during the heyday of terminationist sensibilities, Congress linked payment of a substantial cash settlement with Menominee approval for that ill-conceived and ill-fated policy.[44]

* * *

Just as Menominees have attempted to "negotiate" the contours of economic development within their community, they have also entered into dialogues with outside peoples, entities, and economic forces. This is particularly critical since relationships of unequal power intrude into Indian abilities to find ways to operate within the constraints imposed by outside political, economic, and even social and cultural interests. In the final work of a distinguished career, anthropologist Eric Wolf argued that power is distributed unevenly within societies that tend to "construct" and then support these "structural inequities." Indians are aware of this inequality as they labor under systems of unequal access to power, and inequity often remains, despite their demonstrated success at negotiating adequate, if not satisfactory, arrangements with non-Indian institutions.[45]

Logging negotiations proved complex, and indeed frustrating, though generally straightforward. Menominees found themselves subject to the authority of the federal government and marketplace, and so petitioned for legislative remedies. These remedies took the form of procedures for cutting timber and managing profits. Sometimes they reflected Menominee interests, but always as filtered through the overall objectives and perspectives of policymakers—the locus of structural power. Menominees also attempted to "negotiate" *with* the market itself. This proved tricky, since Menominees exerted very little control over the forces of supply and demand; ironically, however, their isolation worked in their favor. Operating at some distance from main currents of American economic and political life, Menominees in the late nineteenth and early twentieth centuries sometimes enjoyed a significant degree of autonomy. Occupying what sociologist Thomas Hall identified as a "region of refuge," Menominees translated this geographical and political isolation into a "space" where they devised any number of small, local accommodations. These decisions sometimes mitigated the influence of those conditions—political, economic, cultural—over which they exerted little influence.[46]

*   *   *

The situation facing contemporary Menominees is rather different. Far from operating in comparative isolation, Indian gaming trends to draw local, regional, and national attention. Notoriety, of course, can be productive and/ or destructive, for while the evident popularity of gaming (and its profits) enhances political potency, a predictable "backlash" threatens not only the industry but also hard-won victories in other areas. Most recently, the U.S. Congress has threatened to reduce its funding to so-called rich tribes (and perhaps across the board as well), rationalizing that gaming profits render social assistance obsolete. Tribes, then, must counter with publicity campaigns and indeed direct involvement in the political process. Both strategies are fueled by gaming dollars and in turn generate still more animosity. This tension, then, surfaces in other ways, from a proposed tax on casino profits to attempts by Congress to abolish tribal sovereign immunity, and to numerous conflicts with states.[47]

In consequence, tribes who sponsor gaming have developed a "sales pitch" to non-Indians. For example, in 1987, when Menominees became Wisconsin's first tribe to open a casino, they sought accommodation with, and support from, businesses and residents of the neighboring town of Shawano. This proved difficult: Louis Dixon encountered such hostility that he publicized the names of uncooperative businesses. Describing his effort to gain support as "an eye-opening experience for me," the outspoken tribal legislator acknowledged that while "a lot of people in Shawano . . . appreciate the economic benefits the tribe brings to the city," some merchants "absolutely refused to help us, and I thought the Tribe ought to know who they are." At the same time, however, it should be remembered that Shawano residents and tourists from farther afield voted with their wallets. The casino survived, even thrived, and by 1989 the Menominees ranked among the first Wisconsin tribes to negotiate ten-year compacts under the provisions of the 1988 Indian Gaming Regulatory Act.[48]

But by the time compacts neared the statutory deadline for renewal, Menominees found a changed landscape, in Wisconsin and across the nation. This necessitated adjustment to negotiating strategies, ones that took into consideration a backlash that influenced the political and cultural dialogue; many non-Indians were concerned about the proliferation of legalized gambling. Even as critics conceded the economic benefits of gaming, they still fretted over its consequences, or, as one editorial writer lamented, "the everlasting pressure to extend gambling's tentacles under the guise of economic expansion." Concerned citizens sometimes echoed these sentiments, with one letter writer (to a Milwaukee newspaper) even arguing that Indian gaming was responsible for the "beauty shops, hardware stores, heating and sheet metal shops, plumbers and even pharmacies" sold "at bargain basement prices or even closed up." The write claimed, "Farms are getting foreclosed not for the loss of 'milk money' but by the farmers' wives spending five days a week at the slots." While the state's major newspapers adopted a more dispassionate stance, one fairly typical editorial from 1997 warned that "turning Wisconsin into a giant Las Vegas is an unacceptable option that should worry the tribes, which would legitimately be held to blame for the inevitable consequences of wide open gambling." Another editorial from that same year asked, "How does it so happen that a state that had prided itself on clean government finds itself enmeshed" in such an enterprise? The fault, so this writer concluded, lay partly with tribes, but also with "voters and politicians who gave us tracks and lotteries and casinos, never bothering to consider the unsavory consequences."[49]

Following suit, a Milwaukee newspaper also commissioned investigative pieces and offered support to politicians who pledged to combat gaming, or at least restrict its growth. Some voters agreed, supporting anti-gaming candidates such as Republican Governor Tommy Thompson and Milwaukee Mayor John Nordquist, a Democrat. In 1993 voters overwhelmingly endorsed a state referendum designed to halt the opening of any more casinos, despite considerable lobbying on the part of tribes.[50] This changed environment affected the Menominees and Wisconsin's other gaming tribes in several ways. It scuttled Menominee plans to help finance a new stadium for the

Milwaukee Brewers baseball club in exchange for the right to open an off-reservation casino contiguous to the ballpark.[51] It also forced tribes to devote more attention to political lobbying and public relations. Either individually or through their trade association, the Wisconsin Indian Gaming Association, the tribes publicized studies documenting gaming's benefits, from tax revenues paid to the state, to job creation on and near reservations. They also highlighted studies discounting associations between reservation gambling and increased crime, and they were quick to counter reports that offered opposite conclusions.[52]

These efforts assumed greater importance with the onset of negotiations to renew gaming compacts, a contentious process because of positions taken by Governor Thompson. An opponent of Indian gaming, Thompson skillfully parlayed the public's ambivalence toward legalized gambling—and not incidentally reports of "rich" Indians purchasing banks and land—into a clever negotiating strategy.[53] Threatening to renegotiate compacts from the ground up (a potential problem for tribes, since the 1993 referendum was understood as prohibiting new compacts allowing tribes to offer blackjack and slot machines—their most profitable games), Thompson proposed to link extension of existing compacts with tribal concessions on treaty rights and claims. He also sought significant changes in tax laws and a prohibition on tribes seeking federal authority to regulate the environment on or near reservations.[54]

Thompson hoped to force Indians to choose between profits and sovereignty. His strategy also fused anti-gaming and anti-treaty rights political forces and drew both to his side. The governor enjoyed some success, and signs were erected outside the reservation reading "Boycott Menominee casinos to protest treaty claim."[55] But Thompson's approach also drew fire. Paul DeMain, editor of *News from Indian Country,* a national newspaper published in Hayward, Wisconsin, calmly responded, "I don't believe the majority of tribal members would ever consider allowing their council to somehow compromise on these rights." Many of Thompson's other critics were more vehement. Some Indian activists called Thompson a "criminal threat to treaty rights," and a non-Indian writing to a Milwaukee newspaper decried the governor's "strong arm tactics," as "blackmail" designed to force tribes "to drop their environmental concerns to save their economic livelihood." Menominee chairman John Teller chimed in as well. Alerting his constituents to "a certain group of Congressmen and Senators, who are dead set against Indian gaming," Teller observed that "nobody complains when Las Vegas or Reno or Atlantic City pulls in the bucks." However, once "some of the tribes are beginning to demonstrate that we can do a good job, the politicians are becoming concerned." He also suggested that if politicians and the public are uncomfortable with tribes "making more in our casinos than they are in their lotteries," why not "let the Indians run the lotteries."[56]

Thompson's strategy also failed to dissuade Menominees from pursuing treaty rights in court or from organizing an energetic protest to the Exxon Corporation's Crandon Mine proposal, a project that threatened to pollute the Wolf River—the reservation's main fishing and recreation corridor. While a federal judge ultimately rejected the treaty rights claim, the Crandon protests forced Thompson to break with his Exxon supporters and sign a mining moratorium bill that Menominees had supported. More important, these activities demonstrated a deep appreciation of the importance of sovereignty, perhaps born of the termination experience, but just as likely a product of a century-old logging and lumbering enterprise.[57]

If Thompson's efforts to link renewal of compacts with concessions on sovereignty proved disappointing, he enjoyed more success in other areas. In 1997, his office declared that his price for renewal for all compacts would be $85 million—*annually*—an astronomical sum by any measure, but particularly so when contrasted with the existing fee of $350,000. Through his assistants, the governor defended the increase as necessary because of gaming's impact on state social services, law enforcement, road and highway maintenance, and revenues lost by competing businesses run by non-Indians (particularly taverns prohibited by law from offering video poker). While widely considered a negotiating figure, it remained alarming since it amounted to one third of casino profits. Moreover, revenue growth showed signs of leveling off, as tribes struggled with growing competition from state lotteries, and from Indian and non-Indian casinos in neighboring states. The irony was that Thompson's financial demands only spurred the tribes' determination to generate income through expanded gaming, regardless, it seems, of the political costs. This price exploded into public view with the controversy over the proposed conversion of a Hudson, Wisconsin, dog-racing track into an Indian-managed casino—a proposal rejected by the Clinton administration and one that generated considerable publicity and an investigation following charges of political favoritism.[58]

Increased competition certainly endangered Menominee profits, and Thompson's negotiation strategy exposed deep differences between the experiences, and objectives, of Wisconsin tribes. According to 1996 estimates, just four tribes (largely because of their proximity to population centers), the Ho-Chunks, Potawatomis, St. Croix Chippewas, and Oneidas, accounted for 70 to 80 percent of Wisconsin Indian gaming revenues.[59] By contrast, the Menominees faced a future where gaming profits were "structurally" limited by location and as a consequence were ill equipped to weather increased state fees. Recognizing the potential peril, tribal chairman John Teller disregarded Governor Thompson's opposition to off-reservation gaming as "just a political position . . . that will change as the politics change," and he initiated a move to open an off-reservation gaming location. His successor, Apesanahkwat, adopted the same position. But while Teller had focused attention on a new baseball facility, Apesanahkwat opened negotiations to purchase a defunct dog-racing track in Kenosha and convert it into a casino. Kenosha, of course, was attractive because of its location astride the interstate highway connecting Chicago with Milwaukee.[60]

Other so-called poor tribes adopted similar strategies, each seeking to open new casinos near major population centers, and while this constituted a sensible approach toward meeting Wisconsin's expectations for increased shares of gaming profits, it also produced a new set of problems. Gaming opponents responded negatively to a further expansion of gambling, arguing that it violated the 1993 referendum. Tribal leaders countered by citing a loophole, namely, that the measure seemingly permits the opening of new casinos so long as the total number of facilities, as well as their allocation among tribes, remains unchanged. With two casinos in Keshena, the Menominee could, under this interpretation, legally open the Kenosha facility simply by closing one of their existing operations. This interpretation did not mollify gaming opponents who sought to prevent the opening of new casinos through local political action.[61]

This strategy, however, also opened divisions between the tribes at the very time they attempted to present a united front in compacting negotiations. In 1998, two tribes, the Potawatomis and the Oneidas negotiated separate compacts with the state.[62] Obviously, the so-called rich tribes saw little benefit in the expansion of off-reservation gaming. On the other hand, poorer tribes considered expansion to be their economic salvation. To complicate matters, tribes also found themselves divided over the comparative importance of treaty rights and environmental protection, a situation that complicated the disagreement.[63]

As unity crumbled, some tribal leaders held firm to the importance of maintaining a united front, but Apesanahkwat argued that, "realistically, there are so many distinctions [between tribes], it's only appropriate to deal with us individually." Apesanahkwat's sentiments may have been influenced by a nasty exchange with Oneida chairperson Deborah Doxtator. Apesanahkwat accused the rich tribes of blocking off-reservation gaming solely to preserve their own profits. This, he argued, demonstrated "a harsh reality about Indian gaming and the behavior of tribes against tribes in their quest to maximize their interests." Further still, Apesanahkwat called for a renewal of "all of our cultural regard for one another" that had, he wrote, "taken a back seat to the greed that intoxicated the leadership."[64]

* * *

This conflict notwithstanding, Menominees still pursued off-reservation gaming and participated in compact talks. Kenosha voters approved the Menominee purchase and conversion plan in 1998, and while negotiations over an operating agreement delayed the casino's opening, it seemed to presage an end to contentious talks over compacting.[65] The end of 1998 also saw a one-year extension of existing compacts, followed by a plan that set tribes' annual contributions to the state at $23 million. Indian gaming, it seems, is secure in Wisconsin.[66] But the process of reaching an accord with the state remains only a part of this story. Just as significant are Menominees' efforts to make gaming work for their community. By the end of the twentieth century, casino profits helped finance broader economic and cultural development and in ways that reflected the efforts of a century before. Where once the tribe had used logging revenues to finance the construction of homes at Neopit, it now directed gaming profits toward building new homes in Middle Village. Where a previous generation of leaders sought to prepare Menominees for the future by financing reservation schools—and indeed sending children to off-reservation schools—the College of the Menominee Nation now has assumed that role. Meanwhile, a new tribal "culture code" encourages language preservation and supports programs aimed at promoting identity and connections with the past. Once Mitchell Oshkenaniew and Reginald Oshkosh sought to extend the reach of economic development beyond logging and toward the production of lumber (and thus jobs); now modern Menominees direct funds and expertise toward a tribal "private sector initiative," featuring a "business incubator" that seeks to promote entrepreneurial activity. And if Mitchell Oshkenaniew once challenged business and political institutions to take Menominees seriously, the current generation of leaders builds upon that tradition of political activism in the service of the intertwined objectives of economic development and cultural renewal.[67]

None of this should be understood as a blanket endorsement—by the author or the Menominees—of economic change generally, or gaming in particular. Yet contemporary events touching upon Menominee economics and cultural life should be considered within a broader historical context. While gaming certainly provides opportunity and poses its own particular challenges, it is a mistake to see the challenges, or Menominees' efforts to resolve them, as unique to the later twentieth century. Indian people—Menominees and others—have a long history of creative engagement with "the market," and it is through these experiences that they devise certain strategies to deal with economic change. It also is possible to argue that, far from finding participation in the marketplace "toxic" to cultural values, Indian peoples have, at some times and in some ways, found that participation in the market might provide opportunities to preserve who, and what, they are.

Notes

1. "Economic Development, Wolf River, Priorities for New Administration," *Menominee Nation News,* vol. 21, no. 4 (21 February 1997): 3; "Tribal Chairman Debates Anti-Casino Leader in Kenosha," Milwaukee *Journal Sentinel,* 24 September 1998; "Menominee Tribal Gaming Corporation," fact sheet provided by the Menominee Tribal Gaming Corporation, ca. 1997; "Reel News," newsletter of the Menominee Casino-Bingo-Hotel, March 1998.

2. College of the Menominee Nation homepage, http://www.menominee.edu; for more on Menominee Tribal Enterprises, see Menominee Tribal Enterprises, "The Menominee Forest Management Tradition: History, Principles and Practices" (Neopit, Wisconsin: MTE, 1997).

3. Foster and Fowler are by no means the only scholars who have considered this phenomenon—namely, change and continuity in the shifting sands of cultural identity—but their work is particularly useful. See Loretta Fowler, *Arapahoe Politics, 1851–1978: Symbols in Crises of Authority* (Lincoln: University of Nebraska Press, 1980), and Morris W. Foster, *Being Comanche: A Social History of an American Indian Community* (Tucson: University of Arizona Press, 1991). For more on this subject, see the introduction to James Clifton, ed., *Being and Becoming Indian: Biographical Studies of North American Frontiers* (Chicago: Dorsey, 1989); Alexandra Harmon, "Lines in the Sand: Shifting Boundaries between Indians and non-Indians in the Puget Sound Region," *Western History Quarterly* 26, no. 4 (Winter 1995): 429–53.

4. For a discussion of the "transformative nature of cultural dialogue," see William Simmons, "Culture Theory in Contemporary Ethnohistory," *Ethnohistory* 35, no. 1 (Winter 1988): 1–14, and Michael Harkin, "Engendering Discipline: Discourse and Counterdiscourse in the Methodist-Heiltsuk Dialogue," *Ethnohistory* 43, no. 4 (Fall 1996): 643–66. The literature on Indian gaming is growing more rapidly than the industry itself. It can be difficult to determine where to begin, but a good place is W. Dale Mason, *Indian Gaming: Tribal Sovereignty and American Politics* (Norman: University of Oklahoma Press, 2000). Mason deals primarily with legal and constitutional issues, so for a different perspective, see Wayne J. Stein, "American Indians and Gambling: Economic and Social Impacts," in Dean Morrison, ed., *American Indian Studies: An Interdisciplinary Approach to Contemporary Issues,* 145–66 (New York: Lang, 1997). For a "nuts and bolts" overview of Indian gaming in Wisconsin, see William Thompson, Ricardo Gazel, and Dan Rickman, "The Economic Impact of Native American Gaming in Wisconsin," *Wisconsin Policy Research Institute Report* 8, no. 3 (April 1995): 1–48.

5. *California v. Cabazon Band of Mission Indians,* 480 U.S. 202, (1987). See also *Seminole Tribe of Florida v. Butterworth,* 491 F. Supp. 1015 (1980), and *Seminole Tribe of Florida v. Butterworth,* 658 F.2d 310 (1981). Mason, *Indian Gaming,* 46–62.

6. "Menominee Nation Casino Opens," *Menominee Tribal News* 11, no. 6 (June 1987); "Menominee Nation Casino Grand Opening Held," *Menominee Tribal News*, vol. 11, no. 7 (July 1987). "Profits Soar for Indian Gaming," *Milwaukee Journal-Sentinel*, 1 August 1997; "Casino Boom Unlikely to Abate Soon," *Milwaukee Journal-Sentinel*, 13 June 1997; W. Thompson, R. Gazel, and D. Rickman, *The Economic Impact of Native American Gaming in Wisconsin* (Madison: Wisconsin Policy Research Institute, 1995), Nos. 3, 8, p. 1. Wisconsin newspapers, and in particular the *Milwaukee Journal-Sentinel*, cover gaming issues rather completely. For a sampling of articles regarding the extension of gaming compacts, see "Progress Reported in Gaming Talks," *Milwaukee Journal-Sentinel*, 22 August 1997; "Thompson, Tribes May Be Near Deal," *Milwaukee Journal-Sentinel*, 4 February 1998; "Lawmakers Seek to Have Final Word on Gaming Compacts," *Milwaukee Journal-Sentinel*, 19 July 1999. For the Menominees' Kenosha deal, see "Tribe Seeks to Buy Kenosha Dog Track," *Milwaukee Journal-Sentinel*, 11 February 1998; "Kenosha Casino on Fast Track after Vote," *Milwaukee Journal-Sentinel*, 5 November 1998; "Approval from Kenosha Voters Makes Casino Plan a Good Bet," *Chicago Tribune*, 5 November 1998; "Kenosha Adlermen Take a Look at Kenosha Deal," *Milwaukee Journal-Sentinel*, 30 June 1999. On the other hand, a similar effort by the Lac du Flambeau Ojibwas to place a casino "off reservation" in the town of New Berlin has run up against considerable opposition. See "Waukesha Area Leaders Take Stand against Gambling," *Milwaukee Journal-Sentinel* 25 May 1999.

7. "Menominee Nation Casino Grand Opening Held," *Menominee Tribal News* 11, no. 7 (July 1987).

8. Ibid.

9. Sociologists Stephen Cornell and Joseph Kalt have explored this question. See Stephen Cornell, "American Indians, American Dreams, and the Meaning of Success," *American Indian Culture and Research Journal* 11, no. 4 (1987): 59–70, and Stephen Cornell and Joseph P. Kalt, "Pathways from Poverty: Economic Development and Institution-Building on American Indian Reservations," *American Indian Culture and Research Journal* 14, no. 1 (1990): 89–125.

10. "An Act to authorize the sale of timber on certain lands reserved for the use of the Menominee tribe of Indians, in the State of Wisconsin," Public Law 153 (26 stats., p. 146). For an official description of the procedures developed for this new act, see *Annual Report of the Commissioner of Indian Affairs* [hereinafter cited as *ARCIA*] 1890, 60–61, 90, 387. For conditions leading up to the act, including the "tangled legal and financial situation," see Brian C. Hosmer, *American Indians in the Marketplace: Persistence and Innovation among the Menominees and Metlakatlans, 1870–1920* (Lawrence: University Press of Kansas, 1999), 36–57.

11. For logging statistics, see "Statistical Supplements," in *ARCIA,* 1881, 85; 1882, 232; 1885, 433; 1886, xlii; 1887, 45–46, 307–8; 1888, 237–38; 1891, 93, 463–64; 1892, 82–84, 513; 1893, 39–42; 1894, 47–48; 1895, 51, 325; 1898, 309; 1902, 71. Also, see Ebenezar Stephens, Menominee Indian Agent, to E. Stevens, 29 December 1881, National Archives, record group 75, Letters Received, Office of Indian Affairs [hereinafter, NA, RG75, LR, OIA], accession 290; Agent Thomas H. Savage to Commissioner D. M. Browning, 30 November 1894, NA, RG75, LR, OIA, accession 48421; Savage to Browning, 7 October 1895, NA, RG75, LR, OIA, accession 41324.

12. Just why Menominees escaped allotment is somewhat of a mystery. Hosmer, in

American Indians in the Marketplace, 34, 51, 56, 61–62, speculates that, while Menominees themselves voted in favor of allotment in 1888, Congress never passed the necessary enabling legislation because commercial timber firms hoped to purchase tribal timberlands. Other explanations certainly are possible. For a contrasting, and disastrous, situation, see Melissa L. Meyer, *The White Earth Tragedy: Ethnicity and Dispossession at a Minnesota Anishinaabe Reservation, 1889–1920* (Lincoln: University of Nebraska Press, 1994).

13. For a description of the July 8–9 council and a discussion of the 1890 act, see Hosmer, *American Indians in the Marketplace*, 60–61. Resolution, dated 6 April 891, NA, RG75, LR, OIA, accession 17395. Mitchell Oshkenaniew to Commissioner John W. Noble, 4 May 1891, NA, RG75, LR, OIA, accession 16867. See also, Hosmer, *American Indians in the Marketplace*, 63–66.

14. Legal problems essentially stemmed from the U.S. Supreme Court's decision in *United States v. Cook*, 19 Wallace, 591 (1873). In this decision, the high court ruled that, absent specific congressional action, it was not lawful to sell resources (like timber) held in trust by the U.S. government. Prior to the act of 1890, this meant that Congress had to authorize Menominee logging each year. For a discussion of this decision and its implications for Menominee logging, see Joseph P. Kinney, *Indian Forest and Range: A History of the Administration and Conservation of the Redman's Heritage* (Washington, D.C.: Forestry Enterprises, 1950), 7–9, and Joseph P. Kinney, *A Continent Lost—A Civilization Won: Indian Land Tenure in America* (Baltimore: Johns Hopkins Press, 1937), 256. Also see Hosmer, *American Indians in the Marketplace*, 31, 37–39.

15. *ARCIA*, 1874, 495; 1875, 872; Ohopasha to Commissioner of Indian Affairs, 7 December 1873, NA, RG75, LR, OIA, accession 22621. For a discussion of Chase's "solution," see Hosmer, *American Indians in the Marketplace*, 30–31; and for Ohopahsa's concerns a decade later, see Hosmer, *American Indians in the Marketplace*, 43–44.

16. For a discussion of logging procedures prior to the 1890 act, see Hosmer, *American Indians in the Marketplace*, 37–41.

17. Ibid., 39–41. Fortunately, some logging rolls survive and can be compared with existing tribal census and petitions signed by Menominee loggers. Stephens to CIA, 23 January 1882, NA, RG75, LR, OIA, accession 1851; Stephens to CIA, 31 January 1882, NA, RG75, LR, OIA, accession 2425; Agent D. P. Andrews to CIA, 11 December 1883, NA, RG75, LR, OIA, accession 22694; Stephens to CIA, 30 May 1882, NA, RG75, LR, OIA, accession 9790; Stephens to E. Scheffels and Son, 26 February 1883, NA, RG75, LR, OIA, accession 9987; A. G. Wescott (attorney) to CIA, 30 October 1883, NA, RG75, LR, OIA, accession 19988; Agent Thomas Jennings to CIA, "Statistics Relating to Logs Banked on the Wolf and Oconto Rivers," 13 June 1889, NA, RG75, LR, OIA, accession 16024; Petition signed by 139 Menominees to CIA, 15 October 1888, NA, RG 75, LR, OIA, accession 13559; Petition signed by 162 Menominees to CIA, 29 January 1890, NA, RG 75, LR, OIA, accession 16024; Agent Charles S. Kelsey to CIA, "Schedule of Logs Cut and Banked by the Menominee Indians, during the Last Winter, on the Wolf and Oconto Rivers and Tributaries," 14 July 1890, NA, RG 75, LR, OIA, accession 21740. Ethnologist Walter James Hoffman produced a useful genealogy of band leaders in "The Menominee Indians," *Fourteenth Annual Report of the Bureau of Ethnology, for the Years 1892–93* (Washington, D.C.: Government Printing Office, 1896), 44–60, as did David Robert Martin Beck in "Siege and Survival: Menominee Responses to an Encroaching World" (PhD diss., University of Chicago, Il-

linois, 1994, 556–94). For more on Reginald Oshkosh see Brian C. Hosmer, "Reflections on Indian Cultural 'Brokers': Reginald Oshkosh, Mitchell Oshkenaniew, and the Politics of Menominee Lumbering," *Ethnohistory* 44 (Summer 1997): 493–507, and Hosmer, *American Indians in the Marketplace*, 88, 90–91, 98–99, 220–21.

18. David Rich Lewis makes this point very eloquently. See Lewis, "Reservation Leadership and the Progressive-Traditional Dichotomy: William Wash and the Northern Utes, 1865–1912," *Ethnohistory* 38, no. 2 (1991): 124–42. Also see Fowler, *Arapaho Politics;* Fowler, *Shared Symbols, Contested Meanings;* and Foster, *Being Comanche.*

19. James I. Cisney, Indian Office inspector, to CIA, 27 April 1891, NA, RG 75, LR, OIA, accession 16867; *ARCIA*, 1892, 513; 1894, 47–56; 1895, 51, 325; 1898, 309. Hosmer, *American Indians in the Marketplace*, 63, 75.

20. Ohopahsa, Louis Oshkenaniew, Joseph F. Gauthier, and Ahkonemi Oshkosh to CIA, 2 June 1882, NA, RG75, LR, OIA, accession 23081; Hosmer, *American Indians in the Marketplace*, 41, 42, 106.

21. Ohopahsa, Louis Oshkenaniew, Joseph F. Gauthier, and Ahkonemi Oshkosh to CIA, 2 June 1882, NA, RG75, LR, OIA, accession 23081; Petition signed by 97 Menominees to CIA, 29 June 1882, NA, RG 75, LR, OIA, accession 10089; Hosmer, *American Indians in the Marketplace*, 41–42.

22. Neo'pit, Mah Chickeney, Ne-ah-tah-wah-puny, Ohopahsa, John Shawanopash, Wytahsha to CIA, 19 January 1883, NA, RG 75, LR, OIA, accession 2308.

23. Petition signed by 187 Menominees to Senator H. L. Dawes, 6 February 1888, NA, RG75, LR, OIA, and accession 4112. Hosmer, *American Indians in the Marketplace*, 42.

24. For Ledergerber's activities, see Hosmer, *American Indians in the Marketplace*, 51–52. For Neo'pit's offer to sell reservation timber, see ibid., 34–35. The quotation is from *ARCIA*, 1881, 235–36.

25. "Menominee Tribal Legislature Enacts Emergency Ordinance," *Menominee Nation News*, vol. 20, no. 15 (9 August 1996); Chairman's Comments, *Menominee Nation News* vol. 20, no. 15 (9 August 1996); "Ousted Vice-Chairman Explains Reasons for Dismissal," *Menominee Nation News*, 6 September 1996.

26. "Ousted Vice-Chairman Explains Reasons for Dismissal," *Menominee Nation News*, 6 September 1996.

27. "Louis Dixon Violated the Spirit of the Constitution," Chairman's Comments, *Menominee Nation News*, vol. 20, no. 23 (6 September 1996); "Chairman Addresses Controversy Surrounding Gaming Corporation," Chairman's Comments, *Menominee Nation News*, vol. 20, no. 23 (6 December 1996).

28. Cornell, "American Indians, American Dreams," 59–70; Cornell and Kalt, "Pathways from Poverty," 89–125.

29. Indian Gaming Regulatory Act Sec. II (2)(b)(B); "The Use of Net Revenues from Tribal Gaming," *Menominee Tribal News*, 11 March 1993.

30. "Tribal Member Expresses Disappointment," *Menominee Tribal News*, 5 August 1993; "Tribal Member Unhappy with New Gaming Venture Charter," *Menominee Tribal News*, 7 October 1993.

31. "Response Made about Positions on the Gaming Boards," *Menominee Tribal News*, 4 November 1993. For commentary on per capitas and candidates' positions, see *Menonimee Tribal News*, 16 November 1995, 19 November 1995, 18 December 1995.

32. "Legislature in Favor of MTE Stipend Payments," *Menominee Nation News*, 20 September 1996; "MTE President: Will Not Sacrifice Long Term Benefits for Short Term Gain," *Menominee Nation News*, 4 October 1996; "MTE to Identify Opportunities in Revitalization and Value-Added Expansion Project," *Menominee Nation News*, 18 May 1995; "MTE Approves Revitalization and Value-Added Expansion Project," *Menominee Nation News*, 8 June 1995.

33. MTE's "Forest Management Plan" is based on three principles: "Forest management practices must be sustainable for multi-use by both current and future generations"; "Management must conserve the productive capacity of the land to produce forest products in order to sustain the Tribe's economy and improve tree quality to maximize the timber value"; and "The forest's diversity must be maintained to ensure environmental health, balance, and productivity." Gary Schnettpeltz, Verna Fowler, and Lawrence Wanka, *The Menominee Forest-Based Sustainable Development Tradition* (Neopit, Wis.: Menominee Tribal Enterprises, 1997), 3–5.

34. "Menominee Tribal Enterprises Wins Presidential Award," *Menominee Nation News*, 14 March 1996; "MTE Awarded First Nations Development Institute Grant," and "MTE President Receives National Award from the U.S. Forest Service," *Menominee Nation News*, 23 January 1997; "MTE Receives Environmental Leadership Award," and "Menominee Tribe Receives $5,000 Donation from H. Derkson & Sons," *Menominee Nation News*, 8 May 1997; "Menominee to Host 21st Annual Timber Symposium," *Menominee Nation*, 22 May 1997.

35. For a typical example of the importance of gaming to tribal politics, see "Candidates Profiles," *Menominee Nation News*, 22 October 1996. For an example of charges of corruption and mismanagement, see "Gaming Venture Is 'Million Dollar Gaming Loss,' Says Menominee Vice-Chairman," *Menominee Nation News*, 21 December 1995. This involved a failed plan to sell Menominee gaming expertise (through an entity entitled "Gaming Venture, Incorporated") to other gaming tribes.

36. Mitchell Oshkenaniew to John W. Noble, NA, RG 75, LR, OIA, accession 17395; Mitchell Oshkenaniew to Herbert Welsh, 31 July 1891, NA, RG 75, LR, OIA, accession 27966. For Mitchell Oshkenaniew's biography and his "rise to prominence," see Hosmer, *American Indians in the Marketplace*, 68–78; and Hosmer, "Reflections on Indian Cultural 'Brokers,'" 497–99.

37. Mitchell Oshkenaniew to E. Whittlesey, 16 October 1891, NA, RG 75, LR, OIA, accession 39569; Oshkenaniew to CIA, 30 November 1892, NA, RG 75, LR, OIA, accession 44684; Charles S. Kelsey to CIA, 2 November 1891, NA, RG 75, LR, OIA, accession 39569. Hosmer, *American Indians in the Marketplace*, 70–73.

38. These loggers requested to be "released" from "the injustice that would be done to [themselves] if they were all held in restraint because of the indisposition or tardiness of a certain portion of their number to acquire civilization." Petition signed by 53 Menominees, 24 January 1905, NA, RG 75, LR, OIA, accession 17261.

39. Hosmer, *American Indians in the Marketplace*, 82–84.

40. J. R. Farr to CIA, 5 November 1907, NA, RG 75, Central Classified Files, Keshena Agency, accession 88433–07; *Conditions of Indian Affairs in Wisconsin: Hearings before the Committee on Indian Affairs*, U.S. Senate, Sen. Res. 263, 60 Cong., 2d. sess. (Washington: GPO, 1910), 857, 865. For more on the troubled 1906–07 logging season and its aftermath,

see Hosmer, *American Indians in the Marketplace*, 84–90. For Reginald Oshkosh, see Hosmer, *American Indians in the Marketplace*, 88–90, and Hosmer, "Reflections on Indian Cultural 'Brokers,'" 493–509.

41. For a detailed discussion of the investigation, the 1908 La Follette Act, the construction of the Neopit plant and town, and Oshkenaniew's suit, see Hosmer, *American Indians in the Marketplace*, 90–106, and Hosmer, "Creating Indian Entrepreneurs: Menominees, Neopit Mills, and Timber Exploitation, 1890–1915," *American Indian Culture and Research Journal* 15, no. 1 (1991): 11–23.

42. Hosmer, "Creating Indian Entrepreneurs," 15–23.

43. Reginald Oshkosh to Edward E. Ayer, 10 February 1915, in Papers Concerning the United States Board of Indian Commissioners, collected by Mr. Edward Everett Ayer, 1913–1919, Newberry Library, Chicago. Hosmer, "Creating Indian Entrepreneurs," 21–23.

44. The best account of Menominee termination remains Nicholas Peroff, *Menominee Drums: Tribal Termination and Restoration, 1954–1974*, (Norman: University of Oklahoma Press, 1982).

45. Eric R. Wolf, *Envisioning Power: Ideologies of Domination and Crisis* (Berkeley: University of California Press, 1999).

46. Thomas D. Hall, "Peripheries, Regions of Refuge, and Nonstate Societies: Toward a Theory of Reactive Social Change," *Social Science Quarterly* 64 (1983): 582–95. For a more recent elaboration of this phenomenon, see Christopher Case-Dunn and Thomas D. Hall, *Rise and Demise: Comparing World Systems* (Boulder, Colo.: Westview, 1997).

47. The politics surrounding Indian gaming continues to be featured in the press. In 1998, Timothy Egan of the *New York Times* explored the topic in some depth. See, "New Prosperity Brings New Conflict to Indian Country," *New York Times,* 8 March 1998, and, "Backlash Grows as Indians Make Stand for Sovereignty," *New York Times,* 9 March 1998. See also Anthony J. Hope, Chairman, National Indian Gaming Commission, "For Indians, Casino Gambling Represents a Self-Help Program," *New York Times,* 14 June 1991; "Wrong Track for Tribes: Casinos Offer a False Promise," *New York Times,* 17 June 1991; "Casinos Are No Economic Cure-All," *New York Times,* 13 June 1993; "Holding the Chips, Tribes Naturally Play Politics" [tribal donations to campaigns in 1996], *New York Times,* 2 November 1998; "As Washington Turns, Gaming Tribes Squirm," *Indian Country Today* 2–9 March 1998; "A Threat to Indian Sovereignty" [re: Senator Slade Gorton's effort to strip tribes of sovereign immunity], *New York Times,* 21 March 1998; "American Indians' Survival Still Endangered, Leader Says" [1998 meeting of the National Congress of American Indians], *Milwaukee Journal Sentinel,* 14 June 1998. Native writer Gerald Vizenor, an opponent of gaming, predicted in 1992 that the backlash against gaming could threaten tribal sovereignty generally. See Gerald Vizenor, "Gambling on Sovereignty," *American Indian Quarterly* 16, no. 3 (Summer 1992): 411–13. For a brief discussion of the 1990s backlash against Indian gaming, see Mason, *Indian Gaming*, 245–59.

48. Louis J. Dixon, "Tribal Casinos under Attack," *Menominee Tribal News*, vol. 12, no. 6, mid-June 1988; Thompson, Gazel, and Rickman, *Economic Impact of Native American Gaming in Wisconsin*, 3–13.

49. "Gambling a Bad Deal for Wisconsin," The Morning Mail, *Milwaukee Journal Sentinel,* 26 November 1997; "Just Say 'No' to More Gaming," *Milwaukee Journal Sentinel,*

23 November 1997; "No Thanks to Potawatomi Gaming," *Milwaukee Journal Sentinel,* 4 November 1997; "State Voters, Lawmakers, Culprits in Casino Mess," *Milwaukee Journal Sentinel,* 2 November 1997.

50. "The New Buffalo," *Milwaukee Magazine* 19 (August 1994): 30–45; "Enemy Territory," *Milwaukee Magazine* 19 (August 1994): 50–61; Wisconsin Tribes Hit the Jackpot," *Milwaukee Journal-Sentinel,* 19 March 1995; "Casinos Help Tribes Create Jobs, Secure Their Future," *Milwaukee Journal-Sentinel,* 20 March 1995; "Study Shows State Economy Improved through Indian Gaming," *Menominee Tribal News,* 25 March 1993; "State Senator Breske in Favor of Casino Gambling," *Menominee Tribal News,* 25 February 1993; "Position on Spring Referenda," *Menominee Tribal News,* 25 March 1993; "Gambling Limits Favored by Wisconsin Voters," *Menominee Tribal News,* 8 April 1993.

51. "Menominee Indian Tribe Backs Vallozzi Stadium Plan," *Menominee Nation News,* vol. 19, no. 13 (7 September 1995); "Chairman's Comments," *Menominee Nation News,* 21 September 1995; "Chairman's Comments," *Menominee Nation News,* 10 October 1995; "Chairman's Comments," *Menominee Nation News,* 6 November 1995. Failure of the Vallozzi-Menominee stadium plan is documented in "Looking Elsewhere: Several Sources Possible," *Milwaukee Journal-Sentinel,* 26 June 1996.

52. "Wisconsin Indian Gaming," special supplement to the *Menominee Nation News,* 5 February 1998; "Gaming Report Contrary to Other Research," *News from Indian Country,* vol. 10, no. 24 (December 1996); "Winnebago Pay $3.4 Million in Taxes," *News from Indian Country,* vol. 9, no. 8 (April 1995); "[Lac Courte Orielles] Tribal Casino Proceeds Used for Many Programs, Chairman Reports," *News from Indian Country,* vol. 9, no. 8 (April 1995); "Ho-Chunk Nation Council Critical of Indian Gambling Study," *News from Indian Country,* vol. 9, no. 8 (April 1995); "[Wisconsin] Tribes Make Hefty Payments under State Gaming Compacts," *Indian Country Today,* August 25–September 1, 1997; "Wisconsin Indian Gaming Association Meeting to Discuss Strategy," *Menominee Tribal News,* vol. 19, no. 20 (July 1995); Wisconsin Tribal Leaders Refute Report on Indian Gaming," *Menominee Tribal News,* vol. 20, no. 20 (22 October 1996); "Study Reveals that Indian Casinos Have No Negative Impact on Crime Rate," *Menominee Tribal News,* vol. 20, no. 21 (August 1996); "Few Crime Problems Found Near Casinos," *Milwaukee Journal Sentinel,* 17 May 1999.

53. For continuing hostility toward gaming, see "Angry Words Exchanged as Tribal Gaming Gets Ripped in Legislation," *News from Indian Country,* vol. 9, no. 15 (August 1995); "[Wisconsin Indian] Gaming Under Growing Scrutiny Says Attorney," *News from Indian Country,* vol. 9, no. 18 (July 1996); "Wisconsin Legislature to See Indian Casino/ Lottery Repeal Drive," *News from Indian Country,* vol. 10, no. 23 (December 1996); "New Plan Would Kill Lottery Faster," *Milwaukee Journal-Sentinel,* 16 April 1997; "Opposing Tribal Sovereignty Is Top Priority for Prosser," *Menominee Nation News,* 6 September 1996; "Oneidas Set Aside Money to Purchase Reservation Land," *News from Indian Country,* vol. 8, no. 8 (April 1994); "Oneida Nation Buys Bancorporation Stock," *News from Indian Country,* vol. 8, no. 22 (November 1993); "Gambling Means $1,200 to Each [Winnebago] Member," *News from Indian Country,* vol. 8, no. 1 (January 1994); [Potawatomi] Casino Seeks $70 Million Expansion," *Indian Country Today,* 13–20 October 1997.

54. For Thompson's strategy, see "Wisconsin Governor Promises to Bring Chippewa Treaty Rights to Casino Compact Renewal Table," *News from Indian Country,* vol. 10, no.

15 (June 1997); "Wisconsin Treaties on the Line for Gambling Compacts," *Indian Country Today*, 5–12 January 1998; "Wisconsin Tribes on Compact Bind," *Indian Country Today*, 11–18 August 1997; "Governor Challenges Tax Immunity," *Indian Country Today*, 19–26 May 1998; "Wisconsin Tribes Fight State over Water," *Indian Country Today*, 26 May–2 June 1997; "Governor Offers to Meet with Tribes," *Milwaukee Journal-Sentinel*, 4 December 1997; "Progress Reported in Gaming Talks," *Milwaukee Journal-Sentinel*, 22 August 1997; "Profits Soar for Indian Gaming," *Milwaukee Journal-Sentinel*, 1 August 1997; "State, Tribes Spar over Money," *Milwaukee Journal-Sentinel*, 13 June 1997; "Tribes' Unity Crumbles in Gaming Talks," *Milwaukee Journal-Sentinel*, 23 November 1997; "Gaming Chief Wants More Staff to Help Regulate Indian Casinos," *Milwaukee Journal-Sentinel*, 23 January 1997.

55. "Treaty Protest Sign Appears along US Highway 41," *Menominee Nation News*, 21 September 1995.

56. "Tribes' Unity Crumbles in Gaming Talks," *Milwaukee Journal-Sentinel*, 23 November 1997; "Activists Call Wisconsin Governor 'Criminal Threat to Treaty Rights,'" *News from Indian Country*, vol. 10, no. 18, (October 1996); "Forcing Unrelated Issues Unfair," *Milwaukee Journal-Sentinel*, 26 November 1996; "Chairman's Comments," *Menominee Nation News*, 18 May 1995, and 7 September 1995.

57. "Menominee Treaty Rights Case Dismissed in District Court," "Menominee Upset by Judge Crabb's Dismissal of Treaty Rights Lawsuit," *Menominee Nation News*, 20 September 1996; "Menominee Treaty Rights Claim To Be Appealed," *News from Indian Country*, vol. 10, no. 17 (October 1996). Ironically, 1999 also brought the Menominees a $32 million settlement for claims arising from the termination period. See "$32 Million Settlement for the Menominee Indians Clears U.S. Senate," *Milwaukee Journal-Sentinel*, 2 July 1999. For more on the Crandon Mine issue, see "Thompson Signs Moratorium Regulating Future Mines," *Milwaukee Journal-Sentinel*, 23 April 1998.

58. "Governor Says State Wants More Casino Profits," *News from Indian Country*, vol. 10, no. 2 (January 1996); "Governor Says He Doesn't Have to Give Tribes Anything," *News from Indian Country*, vol. 10, no. 4 (February 1996); "Thompson Seeks Third of Casino Profits," *Milwaukee Journal-Sentinel*, 30 December 1997. For the Hudson dog track/casino controversy, see "Minnesota Tribes Oppose Hudson Dog Track/Casino Plans," *News from Indian Country*, vol. 8, no. 8 (April 1994); "Wisconsin Tribes May Want More If State Wants More Casino $," *News from Indian Country*, vol. 11, no. 1 (January 1997). For a sampling of opinion regarding the Hudson dog track controversy, one that prompted a congressional investigation that ultimately cleared Interior Secretary Bruce Babbitt, see "Chippewa Tribes Threaten Suit if Casino Is Rejected," *News from Indian Country*, vol. 9, no. 12 (June 1995); "Politics and a Wisconsin Casino: White House Opposed Hudson Gambling Plan, Court Told," *News from Indian Country*, vol. 10, no. 4 (February, 1996); "Tribes Say Hudson Dog Track/Casino Not Over Yet," *News from Indian Country*, vol. 9, no. 14; "Did White House Kill a Casino?" *Milwaukee Journal-Sentinel*, 14 September 1995; "Tribes That Helped Kill Casino Now Urge Approval," *Milwaukee Journal-Sentinel*, 20 December 1997; "Lobbyist Contradicts Top Official Involved in Rejection," *Milwaukee Journal-Sentinel*, 11 March 1998.

59. "Profits Soar for Indian Gaming," *Milwaukee Journal-Sentinel*, 1 August 1997; "Progress Reported in Gaming Talks," *Milwaukee Journal-Sentinel*, 22 August 1997.

60. "Chairman's Comments," *Menominee Nation News,* 22 June 1995; "Tribal Chairman Debates Anti-Casino Leader in Kenosha," *Milwaukee Journal-Sentinel,* 24 September 1998.

61. "Wisconsin Tribes May Want More If State Wants More Casino $," *News from Indian Country,* vol. 11, no. 1 (January 1997).

62. "Thompson, Tribe Reach Casino Deal," *Milwaukee Journal-Sentinel,* 14 February 1998; "Potawatomi Community Signs Gaming Extensions," *Indian Country Today,* 17–24 March 1997.

63. "Negotiations Positive amongst Tribal Leaders," *Menominee Nation News,* 12 June 1997.

64. "Menominee Chair Addresses Oneida's Stand on Future of Off-Reservation Casinos," *Menominee Nation News,* 8 May 1997; "Chairman Shares His Perception on the True Meaning of Being Native American," *Menominee Nation News,* 20 November 1997.

65. "Approval from Kenosha Voters Makes Casino Plan a Good Bet," *Chicago Tribune,* 5 November 1998; "Kenosha Casino on Fast Track after Vote," *Milwaukee Journal-Sentinel,* 5 November 1998; "Group Plans Suit Aimed to Stop Dairyland Casino," *Milwaukee Journal-Sentinel,* 21 July 1999; "Kenosha Aldermen Take Look at Kenosha Deal," *Milwaukee Journal-Sentinel,* 30 July 1999.

66. "Wisconsin Tribes, State, Agree to Extend Compacts," *Indian Country Today,* 2–9 March 1998. Interestingly, Governor Thompson faced controversy when he attempted to direct revenues from tribes toward his own spending priorities and not toward programs agreed to by tribes and municipalities. "Tribes, Counties, Take Issue with Gaming Funds Proposal," *Milwaukee Journal-Sentinel,* 19 May 1999; "Thompson Accused of Shortchanging City of Gambling Cash," *Milwaukee Journal-Sentinel,* 30 March 1999; "Panel Shuffles Governor's Gaming Plan," *Milwaukee Journal-Sentinel,* 22 May 1999.

67. "Brothers Start O'Kimosh Construction, Inc.," *Menominee Nation News,* 22 June 1995; "Menominee Auto Center Opens for Business," *Menominee Nation News,* 7 February 1997; "Menominee Nation College to Pursue Accreditation," *Menominee Nation News,* 21 February 1997; "State Funds Improve Local Economic Development Capacity in Northeast Wisconsin," *Menominee Nation News,* 20 March 1997; "Local Tribal Professional Attends International Business Incubator Conference," *Menominee Nation News,* 6 November 1997.

12 White Earth Women and Social Welfare

MELISSA L. MEYER

In 1891, about a dozen women of all ages assembled for their weekly auxiliary meeting at the Bishop Whipple Hospital on the White Earth Reservation in northern Minnesota. They wore dark cotton dresses with full skirts and loose waists. One had a long braid in back. Older women wore moccasins; others sported brown, "store-bought" shoes. Several young girls who had attended U.S. government boarding schools spoke English and served as interpreters. They all busied themselves making various sorts of handiwork. They sold quilts, sweaters, stockings, and hats to raise money to help fund various social welfare projects undertaken by the Episcopal mission.[1]

When the missionary, Pauline Colby, entered the room, a hush fell over the assembled group as they looked down at their sewing. She had made an outlandish proposition! She had suggested that buildings slated to be abandoned when employees relocated to the new agency be transformed into quarters for the elderly. Anishinaabe (Ojibwe) women, who were accustomed to assuming responsibility for extended families, could not comprehend the motivation behind such a proposal. They feared that the missionaries were "coaxing them into a trap because they are old and useless, and shall . . . dispose of their bodies, when they have succumbed to . . . treatment." Thoroughly flustered, the women put their shawls over their heads and left.[2]

Colby truly worried about the destitute elderly, whom she thought were the "greatest sufferers by this onward sweep of progress," because they could not "adapt themselves to the new order." Not so easily deterred, Colby returned the following week to have "a long and earnest talk with them." She explained that the agent simply wanted to care for the elders, to make them comfortable, warm, and well fed. Still, the women harbored doubts born of decades of unfulfilled promises and social policies that hardly seemed to serve their best interests. They had endured forced land cessions, the abduction of children who were sent to distant boarding schools, and the withholding of food and supplies by Indian agents in their attempts to force Native American people to comply with federal Indian policy. These measures had encouraged many of the women to be distrustful of both Indian agents and their suggestions. Colby's speech was greeted by "dead silence." She warned that if the buildings were closed, they would never reopen. She shifted responsibility for the plight of the elderly on them, saying, "You know they will come if you say it is all right." Since Anishinaabe women long had cared for the people's social needs, Colby knew that earning the trust and respect of these women was critical in implementing successful social programs at the White Earth Reservation. After initiating a short worship service, Colby left the room so the women could discuss what she proposed, knowing that her well-intentioned plan for a home for the aged hung in the balance.[3]

After about twenty minutes she returned to find the women concluding the service by singing "Come Holy Spirit" in the Anishinaabe language. However, instead of the usual bustle associated with their departure, the women sat back down and looked at her. Gemokomaniqua, or Big Butcher Knife Woman, who spoke English well because of her schooling, arose and stated, "The ladies have something what they want to say to you, about that thing what you talk about. . . . They say, why is this done that way, about putting all old people in one house?" Colby admitted that she "felt very much inclined to jump out of . . . [her] skin, but . . . explained for about the hundredth time" that she would do the same thing if she were too old to work and had not saved money to take care of herself. Personalizing it in spiritual terms, she maintained that she would happily go to an "old Ladies' Home . . . and be very glad of such a good home on earth until my heavenly father calls me to that better home on high." Reassured, Gemokomaniqua again stepped forward and replied, "The ladies say all right, they try that way and see if the old people they like that." Relieved, Colby moved ahead with her plans, feeling that someone had "left me a munificent legacy."[4]

Women have always played critical roles in Anishinaabe society, and their involvement in matters of education, health, and administration has continued into the twenty-first century. Documentary evidence, oral tradition, and interviews with Anishinaabe women indicate that they and their grandmothers before them have always contributed to their people's welfare. Oral interviews from the mid- and late twentieth century indicate that modern Anishinaabe women retain a deep commitment to their communities, and like their forbearers they envision their participation in community affairs as a responsibility, not an entitlement. They remember that their mothers respected the gendered roles of the past and drew great power and strength from their ability, "like the Earth," to reproduce and sustain the tribe. (Patricia Hill Collins terms this sort of activism "motherwork.") Moreover, the women persevered through some of the most ill-conceived policies that federal bureaucrats ever devised, and they emerged in the late twentieth century as stewards of their culture.[5]

The White Earth communities that missionary Pauline Colby encountered in the late nineteenth century had evolved through centuries of migrations. Anishinaabe oral traditions recount how the five original clans—Bear, Loon, Crane, Marten, and Catfish—sprang from the Atlantic Ocean to follow the image of a shining *miigis* (a cowry shell) as they made their way through the Great Lakes watershed to northern Minnesota. They evolved culturally as various bands, and interacted with each other and eventually with both Europeans and Euro-Americans who came to trade and then to colonize. Large congregations of people gathered at Sault Ste. Marie, Chequamegon, and La Pointe forged common group identities through diplomatic and trade relationships, intermarriage, and religious ceremonies like the Feast of the Dead and eventually the Midéwiwin or Grand Medicine Society.[6]

The women of White Earth reflected the diversity of these intercultural migration streams. In addition to marrying husbands from the different Anishinaabe bands, the women also married French and later British and Scots traders—conduits for even more diverse intercultural relationships and resources. Their descendants interacted among themselves but also crossed boundaries to intermingle with Americans. In the few decades that the White Earth reservation prospered, ethnic divisions were apparent, but as resources, land, and opportunities dissipated, many left the reservation. The ethnic distinctions blurred among those who remained.[7]

Anishinaabe women also contributed to economic and political life within the tribal communities. Although the villages remained politically autonomous, they shared an interest in common territories and resources. Village leaders determined civil and military leadership, united against common enemies, diplomatically negotiated with other native groups and Euro-Americans, and gathered for religious ceremonies. Sedentary activities took place in villages, from which women regulated usufruct rights over wild rice fields, fishing areas, maple and birch stands, and gardening areas. Families (who so desired) received rights of access to these resources. Hunting and war parties also set forth from and returned to the villages.

During the winter, extended families often left the summer villages to form hunting camps. Hunting bands were "small enough to subsist by hunting and gathering but large enough to furnish protection against hostile war parties and raids." Their movements depended on the habits of the particular animal sought. Yet hunting was not simply a male domain. Women had clear roles in the hunting camps. Some served as skilled hunters themselves, while others helped to carry food, clothing, and equipment. After men had cleared an area of snow, women erected each wigwam, kindled a central fire in each lodge, and dried meat. According to Priscilla Buffalohead, "Women built the lodges, spotted the game, butchered the meat; they processed the hides. . . . [and] fetched the venison and bear's meat from the woods." They also distributed game among relatives and negotiated fair deals with traders.[8]

Women also traditionally distributed meat obtained from the hunt throughout the community. Nicholas Perrot related how a young hunter performing bride service "brought his kill back to the lodge of his mother-in-law," who parceled it out, making sure to give some to his mother. Usually, women feasted the community with the first game taken and then dried what was left. Women also spent considerable time during the winter scraping and tanning hides and furs for bedding, clothing, and trade with Euro-Americans. These tasks escalated as the trade grew in importance. Women also manufactured utilitarian items like nettle-stalk fiber fishnets during the winter. Instead of teaching, elder women and men *storied* children about the proper Anishinaabe way to walk in this world. Tales of Nanabozho, the clever, humorous trickster, conveyed pointed and moral object lessons.[9]

In the spring, people initially returned to the larger villages, and all thoughts turned to the sugar bush. A regular cavalcade of people caravanned to the maple stands. Women led in the sugaring activities and allocated stands of maple trees to families, to which they returned annually. The sugar camp bustled with activity. Women watched over the sap kettles, which boiled constantly until the thick syrup granulated. Birchbark cones and the upper mandibles of duckbills were used to store maple sugar (*zinnzibaakwad*). "Maple sugar days" was one of the most pleasurable times of year.[10]

Spring also brought an upsurge in fishing. Both men and women fished, but in the spring men played a larger role during the "runs" of fish that ascended the streams to spawn. Women sometimes assisted with the spring fishing, but they also fished year round. Pauline Colby observed, "The woman that catches and cures the most fish is esteemed as the best provider, very much as we regard our housekeepers who have the largest store of pickles, preserves, etc."[11]

After the "sugaring" and spring fishing were finished, people returned to the villages so they could plant gardens. Men cleared plots, enabling women (with older children's help) to finish planting "in a few hours" in a "vein of gaity and frolic." Cultivating crops such as maize, squash, and pumpkins to supplement produce from the seasonal round, women again controlled "their own activities" and the fruits of their efforts. They were proud to have "a store of corn" on hand "to exercise . . . hospitality . . . in the entertainment of lodge guests." Sometimes they sold a portion of what they raised, but their primary goal was to shore up their subsistence. Late spring and summer sent women and youngsters gathering all sorts of berries. Though they ate some soon after the picking, they preserved a great many by boiling them down and drying them on birchbark mats. Roots also were a springtime crop, while basswood and birchbark were best taken in the summer. Most medicinal plants blossomed and matured in August. Gathering wild rice, or *manoomin*, dominated the early fall, and women controlled this harvest. Highly nutritious, wild rice was a significant dietary staple. At rice camps, groups gathered together for the last time before the winter dispersal. As with sugar bushes, leaders allocated usufruct rights to certain areas of the rice fields. Women demarcated these areas earlier in the summer by tying together rice sheaves to the designate boundaries.[12]

Women harvested the rice from canoes, bending rice stalks over the gunwales with one stick and gently knocking grains into the canoe with another. Since the rice did not all ripen at once, the harvest encompassed repeated passes through the rice fields. After the rice was harvested it was dried on birchbark mats, parched in kettles, and pounded to loosen the husks. Women then "jigged" on the rice to remove the husks and tossed the mixture up in the air so the wind could winnow out the chaff. Successful harvests yielded sufficient wild rice to provision them through the winter and also provided grain for barter or sale. Surplus kernels were returned to the marsh so that future rice fields could be re-seeded.[13]

Following the "ricing," people returned to their summer villages, where the women harvested their garden produce. Since men usually were absent on their autumn hunt, women fished once the harvest was in. When the men returned, they all departed for the winter hunting camps.

In a typical year, women gathered and cultivated plants more than men. They also frequented lake environments more often. Women's responsibilities for childcare and cooking kept them closer to home, and they tended to cooperate in large groups, often sharing household tasks together. Most tasks were gender specific, but the division of labor was not carved in stone. Women and men sometimes performed separate tasks side by side. For instance, men put canoe frames together, while women sewed birchbark on the frames with spruce roots and used pitch to seal the seams.[14]

Despite the mobile residency, the stability of the timing and direction of the seasonal round gave great continuity to people's lives. In addition, the diversity of foods used by the tribe served as a hedge against the failure of any single source. The whole complex was well suited to Minnesota's north country and served as the cornerstone of the Anishinaabe autonomy.

The fur trade eventually pulled the Anishinaabe's subsistence economy into a commercial arena. Slowly, European-manufactured goods like guns, kettles, hatchets, and cloth replaced native-made counterparts. As they became more dependent on trade goods, Anishinaabe hunters harvested more game than they needed for their own subsistence. Yet the relationship between the Anishinaabeg and traders was more than just an exchange of commodities; it also involved a cultural exchange of the most intimate sort. Traders needed native women to provide entrances into tribal communities. Successful traders usually married native women from high-status families. In turn, these Anishinaabe women served as intercultural brokers, learning European languages and acting as intermediaries between their own people and agents from the outside world.

Children from these unions were even more likely to learn the ways of both parents. Some became truly bicultural and served as intercultural brokers in their own right. After several decades, the numbers of Franco-Anishinaabe people proliferated, and they formed a separate ethnic group. Once their population increased, these children of mixed descent tended to marry among themselves, and true ethnogenesis evolved.[15]

In 1867 the White Earth Reservation was established in western Minnesota, and in the three decades that followed new groups of people arrived at the reservation community. In the 1870s Anishinaabe people from the Mississippi band moved to the reservation, as did Franco-Anishinaabe descendants of fur traders and tribal women from the juncture of the Crow Wing and Mississippi rivers. The latter had extensive experience as intercultural mediators, and many found positions at the Indian Agency, or in assisting merchants who traded with the White Earth people.[16]

Different communities settled at different locations. More conservative band members located on the eastern part of the reservation, a region dotted with lakes and blanketed with coniferous forests. Here, white-tailed deer were plentiful, and people continued the seasonal round of harvesting activities that was the foundation of their subsistence economy. The Franco-Anishinaabe cultural mediators settled more to the west, either at the agency at White Earth Village and other villages in the deciduous midsection of the reservation, or on the western prairies where some tried their hand at agriculture. A few Franco-Anishinaabe merchants operated stores at White Earth Village. After the Minneapolis, St. Paul, and Sault Ste. Marie Railroad (a spur of the Great Northern Railroad) laid a track through the western tier of the reservation, it brought increased business opportunities to towns situated along the railway. People residing in these towns prospered, and their livelihoods did not depend on agency employment, as did most of those who lived near White Earth Village.[17]

As the communities "settled in" on the reservation, the Anishinaabeg learned that American officials (always males) preferred to deal with men, so the Anishinaabeg put their most effective male politicians at the forefront. These men cultivated alliances with Indian agents and influential missionaries such as Episcopal Bishop Henry Whipple, but tribal women continued to exercise considerable influence. *Kitchiogimakwe,* or "queens," the female equivalent of a head chief or *kitchiogima,* continued to function within hereditary lineages. For example, Odubenaunequay, or "Old Mon-i-do-wub," an "old queen" of the Mississippi band, played a conspicuous role at White Earth. Other kitchiogimakwe signed the Nelson Act facilitating the resettlement of their bands at White Earth, and some were listed as "Wahbonequay," or "White Hair," a term designating respect among age-graded societies such as the Aninshinaabeg. According to Indian Agent John Howard, "a great many of them [women] . . . attend . . . councils . . . [and] sometimes they are heard." Women surprised government officials with their vocal role in councils and behind-the-scenes lobbying. Inspector James McLaughlin marveled that "old full blood woman [*sic*] manifest such a deep interest" in tribal affairs and sometimes served as proxies for men, signing formal agreements while men stood on the sidelines. Androcentric U.S. commissioners acquiesced to women signatories "at the request of the chiefs," without recognizing that some of those chiefs indeed were women.[18]

At White Earth, many families continued to follow the seasonal round of hunting and fishing, horticulture, and gathering that had predominated in the pre-reservation era. Erma Vizenor told how "Our family moved with the seasons," harvesting rice in August and September, then traveling to the Red River Valley as farm workers to pick potatoes, carrots, and cabbage, and to top onions. After ricing, Verna Millage's family participated in a big feast and powwow, held annually at Pine Point. Millage's family also had their own "maple-sugar bush about five or six miles from home." Frances Keahna also tapped hundreds of trees "right up the road" for "three good weeks." Berrying, fishing, and hunting also kept them moving, with temporary wigwams to shelter them on their rounds. Maggie Hanks's family netted hundreds of white fish through the ice, which they froze and sold. Naomi Ladue described her father carrying forty mallards on his back to sell at Mrs. Lynch's store. Many, like Ellie Mae Robinson, who "lived in a tarpaper shack," were poor and worked hard to made ends meet; but she proudly remembers that her father "always had a lot of meat on the table because he was a good hunter." Lena Desizlets's father, also "a great deer hunter," knew where the fruit was because of his hunting sojourns, so that "we were great about finding and picking wild fruit" and making jelly and jam. Keahna learned from her mother to harvest certain plants for medicine, once they had blossomed, at the end of the summer. They relieved colds and congestion with pennyroyal because "it would make you sweat and bring the cold right out of you." For headaches, she burned fungus that grew on birch bark, covered her head with a towel and inhaled the smoke. However, she cautioned, "You have to believe . . . that it's going to get you well." Native gatherers also supplied snakeroot and ginseng to local merchants who paid a good price because of its pharmacological value. Merchants bought venison, fish, wild rice, maple sugar, buckskin moccasins, beadwork, and sweetgrass baskets to sell to their regional clientele.[19]

In the 1890s, everyone kept gardens stocked with corn, potatoes, and other vegetables to supplement their gathering efforts. Canning produce helped get them through the winter. Many also raised livestock. Keahna's family "all pitched in and did things together." They fed chickens, slopped hogs, and fed and watered cows and horses. Desizlets's father "raised only enough grain to feed them," which typified subsistence farming efforts. Josephine Lightning Norcross told how those who farmed helped out the needy so that there were "no hard feelings."[20]

People supplemented more traditional economic activities with wage-labor. Women accompanied men to lumber camps and Red River farm fields, cooking and laundering for pay. The agency complex at White Earth Village provided a reliable source of wage income and was located near reservation communities. Local merchants like Ben Fairbanks and Louisa Lynch profited from providing supplies. Men worked as teamsters, hauling supplies and equipment from railroad stations in the junction towns on the western edge of the reservation to the agency headquarters at White Earth.[21]

At the turn of the twentieth century most agency employees were Euro-American, and agency job opportunities for Anishinaabe women were limited. Yet some found employment in the agency's schools and hospitals. Josephine Norcross, whose mother worked as a cook, remembered that "there was quite a few Indians . . . that was educated" who served as matrons in both the boys and girls residences, and as laundresses, seamstresses, assistants, and "night watchmen." Evangeline Critts Fairbanks's mother worked at several jobs. She cooked at various times in the schools, the hospital, a restaurant, and at a camp. She also took in laundry at "Scrappies's Mill," a logging camp, and washed clothes for the nurses at the hospital. Wages earned from these jobs supplemented produce from gathering, gardening, hunting, and fishing and allowed people to purchase other necessities.[22]

Although White Earth women earned individual wages, they retained their strong sense of community and honored their traditional responsibilities of providing for tribal members who needed assistance. As this chapter's opening vignette illustrates, women's church groups especially fulfilled this function. Maggie Hanks recalled how the Women's Auxiliary of the Episcopal Church "used to work quite a lot, sewing, making quilts" to sell "to make money . . . to send in to different places where we were asked." Josephine Norcross explained that the "ladies" would have their own "council meetings" to discuss how to spend the money they earned. The "St. Mary's Society" opened a lunchroom in the Guild Hall when people assembled for the fall annuity payments. Merchants also assembled to take advantage of the sudden influx of cash during this time, but women planned "to help out somebody" who needed food, clothing, or "clothing for their dead." Evangeline Fairbanks's mother was president of the Catholic Church Guild, which raised money through the sale of handmade quilts and dresses and served meals for a modest price on Sundays, holidays, and other festive occasions. Norcross remembered that Jenny Broker "got this woman's club organization from the federal woman's club, to come and organize a women's club over here." Twenty-five women regularly assembled to "sew quilts" and "some would embroider . . . scarfs or anything." They also held square dances to raise money. Funds earned from these activities were used to help the needy, but the women also remembered that they "had a grand old time" in working together.[23]

People also "had a grand old time" dining and socializing with friends at family gatherings and at ceremonies. Ellie Mae Robinson remembered that when she was a girl, "there were trails everywhere, leading to Grandpa's or the neighbors," and her mother appointed her to "watch for company, to see if anybody was coming down the trail . . . so she could get some lunch ready." A prerequisite for welcoming visitors "was to sit down and have tea and a bite of food, whatever we had on hand." Robinson recalled that entertaining visitors was "an honor," and she fondly recalled "those old ladies, how glad they used to be to see each other, how they would laugh and joke and tell stories."[24]

Much of this "socializing," which was the lifeblood of reservation communities, was associated with food. Sharing food is a nearly universal, cross-cultural symbol of familial and community togetherness; in some cases, it has demarcated kinship. Anishinaabe women's role in provisioning feasts was grounded in their lifegiving, nurturing functions, and they took pride in amply supplying such gatherings. In turn, their family and other members of the community regularly praised the women's generosity and their skill as cooks. There were plenty of occasions for women to prepare "a spread." Sundays, both during the day and in the evening, often were devoted to church services and feasting. Naomi Ladue remembered that on Sunday evening, after a dinner, "all the Indian School children would be there and everyone in town." They sang "old time songs . . . the National Anthem, and all those patriotic songs, and some hymns, and oh, we used to have a lot of fun." Feasting, with women directing food preparation, also followed prominent seasonal events, such as making maple sugar and harvesting wild rice. Norcross described the celebrations that followed ricing at Rice Point as "a two day affair," to which visitors, including neighboring Dakotas, were invited. "The reason the Sioux [were] . . . invited to come was they got all the wild rice from friends and relatives." In return, the Anishinaabeg received moccasins, which were "made different from the Chippewa." They also observed that "the Sioux ladies . . . cooked different."[25]

The June 14 Celebration (or later powwow), which commemorated the founding of the reservation, was unique to White Earth. Somewhat resembling a July 4th amalgamation of a parade, a picnic, and games and races, the festivities drew White Earth enrollees from throughout the reservation, visiting Dakota and Nakota tribespeople, and many curious non-Indian observers. Planning for the weeklong event began far in advance. Women assumed responsibilities for hosting the event and solicited donations for the extended feast. The Office of Indian Affairs supplied $1,000. Naomi Ladue told how organizers bought a cow, "and then the day the Siouxs would all get here we'd have a big barbecue up on the hill." Maggie Hanks remembered how "they would decorate the horses real nice and fancy. Oh, that really was the prettiest sight you could see." They symbolically smoked peace pipes and gave talks. "The Indian ladies would make Indian bread" and have meat, coffee, and tea. Hanks added, "If you wanted to eat some meat, you could cut some off it and take it home." Ladue recalled, "The next morning they would have a beautiful parade. My, it used to be so colorful and nice. The Indians in their costumes and singing Indian." They had horse, canoe, and foot races, logrolling contests, and played the moccasin game, baseball, and polo. Everyone retained warm memories of June 14, although some women lamented that it became more like a carnival and seemed to fade in importance in the mid-twentieth century. Describing the celebration as a "big visting time" and "big reunion," Sue Bellefeuille deeply valued that time every year. "The annual White Earth powwow makes me feel connected to think of what went on with our people on those same grounds. . . . It brings back memories of when we were kids. There is dancing . . . and many drummers, from all over the state and Canada. They hold competitions in different categories. There is a big feast on Sunday, and anyone who wants to can eat for nothing. It's nice."[26]

Unfortunately, during the first half of the twentieth century, conditions at

White Earth began to deteriorate. Lands that had been allotted to individual Anishinaabeg were lost through fraudulent sales and tax forfeitures, and the proportion of White Earth land owned by the Anishinaabeg dwindled.[27] Poverty on the reservation increased, and during World War I many Aninishnaabe men enlisted in the armed services. In response, women kept a photo album with pictures of all those who had gone to war. Wives and female relatives who were left behind organized a local Red Cross chapter to raise money for the war effort. Josephine Norcross told how "just about twice a week we used to have dances, making money for the Red Cross, baking cakes and selling them." Ladue remembers, "We knitted socks and khaki scarves that they used to wear." They also "did a lot of work in bandages and surgical things." Twenty to thirty women participated in these activities on a regular basis. When times were tough, people relied on women to provide as much assistance as possible.[28]

Following the war, some men returned to the reservation, and Naomi Ladue told how the town "went all out" for the returning veterans. "They had a big supper for them, banquets and everybody was there, and oh all the music and racket. It was really nice." Led by the Big Bear family, tribespeople at Elbow Lake honored the veterans with a roundhouse dance. Tobacco was distributed to announce the impending celebration, and as usual, women brought an ample supply of food. Ladue remembered, "We were all lined up along the old board sidewalk here. And a lot of people were pounding pans and oh, all the racket you ever heard." Speeches were delivered, dancing (the "Indian two-step") took place, and gifts of food, beads, jewelry, shawls, and even ponies were exchanged. According to Ladue, "The largest dance like this honored the returning vets, then they just kind of kept gradually giving it up."[29]

Conditions at White Earth further deteriorated with the removal of the agency headquarters. Because the agency was located almost twenty miles from the nearest rail line, federal officials complained that it was isolated and expensive to provision and proposed relocating the agency. White Earth residents vociferously opposed the move, but in July 1922 officials opted for removal, and although several Anishinaabe men occupied the agency office and attempted to keep both the offices and the buildings that housed them from being dismantled, federal agents interceded, and the agency was moved to Cass Lake to serve all of the "Consolidated Chippewas." Naomi Ladue lamented that after the agency left White Earth, "everything kind of went down hill here. All of the business places closed and a lot of the people sold their homes here, [which were] torn down." Like many other residents, Evangeline Critts Fairbanks's parents, who had moved to White Earth Village to work in the hospital, lost their employment.[30]

However, things got worse. Josephine Norcross sadly told how, during the Depression, "everything just went down . . . all these lumber camps and saw mills . . . all moved out west." White Earth people used "to work and stay there" where "they had plenty to eat and plenty clothes." Without the employment, "it was awfully hard." Women coped by enlarging their gardens and canning and storing more vegetables, which they shared with people who were too old or infirm to plant gardens. Children were sent to boarding schools, such as Pipestone, Flandreau, Haskell, and Wahpeton, where they would be fed and clothed. Like many others, Norcross "scraped by" by earning a little cash scrubbing the school and washing windows. Even so, Eleanore Robertson remembered, "Someone was always there to take care of us. The community would come together when there was trouble. We were secure."[31]

Nonetheless, the Works Progress Administration (WPA) was a godsend. Most families earned a living through the WPA, building the school, the nursery, roads, and bridges. Ladue told how "the ladies sewed quilts, comforters, made mattresses and gave them out to the people, and clothes, nightgowns, and dresses . . . they really needed it so badly." Norcross sewed quilts on a power machine in the old school building. Naomi Ladue was trained in plumbing, electrical work, and carpentry, while Fairbanks learned to operate power machinery. These skills proved useful later in their lives.[32]

While working for the WPA, three women became eligible to apply to "go on a defense job." After passing a test in which she proved she could efficiently assemble "screws and pegs together," Norcross was offered the chance to go to welding school. At Detroit Lakes, just south of the reservation, she was furnished meals and housing until she completed the training and received a certificate. She then was offered an opportunity to work at jobs in Alameda, California, or in Hawaii. She recalled, "I wanted to see Hawaii so bad . . . still I thought more of my mother and my children."[33]

Then the White Earth community changed overnight. Robertson reminisced, "I'll never forget it. We were all listening to the radio when we heard that Pearl Harbor had been bombed. Everyone left to join the service, Indian and non-Indian." No one complained about contributing. Many men joined the service. Two women joined the WACs, one joined the WAVES, and quite a few left for California to work in the aviation industry.[34]

World War II helped White Earth. Even though much of the remaining population was composed of the elderly and children, Norcross recalled that "there was quite a bit of money circulating around" because women with men in the service "got these allotments." Many "bought homes for themselves." However, when the war ended and the defense work shrank, "thing changed again" and were "quite bad."[35]

Clearly, for most of the first three-quarters of the twentieth century, those Anishinaabe people who remained on the White Earth Reservation often were short of income. Money from the WPA or from benefits paid to military personnel provided only a brief respite to otherwise unrelieved poverty. Employment opportunities constricted, while the Indian-owned allotted land base diminished. The White Earth Anishinaabeg experienced their own diaspora in their desperate efforts to sustain their families. They moved to towns and cities near the reservation, but other people from White Earth also sought new homes across the country.

This diaspora also was influenced by many of the women's boarding school experiences. Historian Brenda Child has discussed the effect of boarding schools on Anishinaabe families, but many of the White Earth women who attended these institutions described their boarding school years as a "mixed blessing"; although some found their time spent in boarding schools pleasurable, they always paid homage to friends and relatives who did not.[36] Most also recognized the destructive aspects of removing children from their families, communities, and culture for years on end. Some of the women believed that children's isolation from their families at the boarding schools contributed to alcoholism. Joan Staples empathized with her alcoholic father when she wondered, "What [would it] do to a child like my father to be taken away from his family and sent to a boarding school for three, eight, twelve years?" She said, "Knowing something about my father's upbringing, I can understand why he had problems with drinking and was an angry, abusive man." For her entire life, Melody LaFriniere felt estranged from her mother who, having been raised in Catholic mission schools, was never hugged and was subjected to harsh, abusive discipline from nuns. If LaFriniere or her siblings dared misbehave, "we had to go out to the lilac bush and cut our own switch" or receive "spankings with the wooden spoon." In church, her mother admonished her to "pay attention or you'll get the hatpin."[37]

Many believed that boarding school incarceration accelerated the loss of their language and culture. Bonnie Wadena knew that "they quit using the language and were discouraged from practicing any Native American traditions." Beverly Warren's grandmother, a boarding school alumnus, retained her knowledge of the Anishnaabe language and songs, but she "always dyed her hair a platinum blond." Beverly said, "[I] never even knew she spoke Indian until I was twenty-two years old." When she questioned her grandmother about why she had never taught her the language, she said, "My girl, I thought it was best for me *not* to teach you." Yvonne Novack surmised, "People lost more than culture and language; they also lost the chance to practice parenting skills because they weren't living with a family." Irene

Auginaush-Turney lamented, "The circle was broken when children were taken away from their parents and raised in schools." Natalie Ann Greenlaw echoed these sentiments, "I consider my generation a 'recovery generation.' Our elders say it will take about five generations for our people to recover from the trauma of the boarding-school era. When the children were taken away, we became lost souls, lost spirits."[38]

Many of the women were convinced that the Anishinaabe diaspora from White Earth and other reservations communities also contributed to alcoholism. Awash in dislocation, grinding poverty, social trauma, and racial discrimination, some Anishinnabeg sought solace in "the bottle." Older women like Naomi Ladue remembered that prior to the massive dispossession, "We never had the drinking problem." Maggie Hanks agreed that at the round houses, "they just simply had a good powwow, no drunks." Ann LaVoy concurred: "When I was growing up, there would be an alcoholic here or there. But now whole families are involved in drugs: users, sellers, or both." Obviously, alcoholism had an adverse influence on the Anishinaabe communities. Delores Rousu bemoaned, "Many young people are kind of lost; there is not much guidance for them because there is so much alcohol abuse around here. These kids feel left out, like no one cares for them." Irene Auginaush-Turney put things into perspective, "Almost all the good memories that the group members come up with have to do with things they did as families—sliding in the snow, going fishing, going on picnics or to the fair. We look at bad memories, too, and almost all of those involve drinking."[39]

The combination of poverty, dysfunction, and cross-cultural misunderstanding provided fertile ground for intervention by well-meaning social workers. Beginning in the 1920s and 1930s, social workers with "the best kind of missionary goals" could only see poverty and neglect when they encountered children living in tarpaper shacks with very mobile families pursuing a seasonal round of subsistence. Aware of growing alcoholism and drug abuse, the social workers attempted to "rescue" the children. Anita Fineday told how "almost every person living on the reservation in the 1950s and 1960s" shared the experience of "having their kids removed by social workers and never knowing what happened to those children. Parental rights were often terminated, and the children were adopted out—something that occurred in a consistent and organized fashion on reservations through the 1960s." She continued, "The number of removals and the number of kids who absolutely disappeared were truly shocking." Naomi Ladue much preferred housing such children in the Indian schools to moving them "around from home to home" because "it just does something to them. They don't know where they belong." Social Services convinced Juanita Blackhawk's father to surrender her to a better life. She went from foster care to an adoptive family where she was sexually abused from age four to fifteen and was forced to be "a virtual slave in that house, a live-in servant." Others remembered the trauma of being torn from their families, lamenting that "many . . . who come back to their homes after having been removed as children don't have any idea what it means to be an Indian person. They've been ripped out of their culture and deprived of their language. They are struggling so hard inside to find out who they really are."[40]

In response to this trauma, some native women turned to higher education. For some, it was a new and challenging path. Melody LaFriniere remembered that traditionally, "school was not encouraged. It was expected, when we reached the age of sixteen, that we'd drop out. We were never expected to graduate." Ann LaVoy recalls her grandfather telling her, "Somebody from here has to go to college. . . . You have to make a hole in the fence so more people can get through." Eleanore Robertson joined the army, served in the Korean War, and went to nursing school on the GI Bill. Some managed to enroll in college through Project Equality, WIN, or other programs for the underprivileged, but enrollment was only the beginning. Retention rates for native students were, and are, very low. Many bounced from one educational institution to another before they realized their goals. Mary Harper explained that many students are "older than average: it takes many people several years to find their way." She called them "stop-outs" rather than drop-outs. Racism continued to plague them even though Yvonne Novack found it "more hidden" in Minnesota. Anne Dunn initially felt overwhelmed in college in Minnesota, so she left for the Indian School of Practical Nursing in Albuquerque, New Mexico, where she was able to realize her goals. She joked, "In New Mexico I was smart; in Minnesota I was dumb. I figured it must have been the sunshine." Others commented on the cultural differences they encountered as college students. Valerie Fox pointed out that, "It's not easy to be very bright and Indian at the same time. The Indians didn't like me answering questions, but the white kids didn't like me no matter how bright I was."[41]

Anishinaabe women also faced major logistical problems in pursuing a degree in higher education. When Natalie Greenlaw, a resident of White Earth, first enrolled at Moorehead State University, she "began five years of commuting a hundred miles each day, raising three kids, and working full-time," she said. "It was brutal, but I knew that in five years I would be where I wanted to be. If I hadn't had the dream to show me the way and motivate me, I never would have been able to do it." Her reward was immense pride and the ability to move ahead with her dream of helping her people. After qualifying to enroll in college through a program for the disadvantaged, Erma Vizenor earned her bachelor's degree, completed a master's program in counseling, and was awarded a Bush Fellowship to the School of Education at Harvard University. Seizing this opportunity, she juggled responsibilities, overcame obstacles, finally wrote her dissertation, and graduated with a doctorate. She remembered the jubilation as her relatives and friends assembled to share in her important day. "It was very exciting. My parents, as poor as they were, my auntie, and many others helped me to believe that all I had to do was go to school and study hard, and nothing would be impossible if I set my mind to it."[42]

During the last quarter of the twentieth century, the concerns of Anishinaabe women for the social and economic welfare of their people have continued to be manifested in a broad spectrum of both traditional and new arenas. Yet regardless of these venues, the women's dedication to serving their kinspeople remains an important part of their lives.

Some have remained focused on education, endeavoring to enlarge the "hole in the fence" so others could make it through like they have. With a bachelor's degree from the University of California at Berkeley, and a master's in education from Harvard, Yvonne Novack was the first American Indian woman to be chosen as a Woodrow Wilson Administrative Fellow. She later became the Director of Indian Education in Minnesota. "Interested in systemic changes in education that will better meet the needs of individual children of all races," Novak wants to keep kids from dropping out of school. Novack was encouraged to apply for the director's position by Ruth Meyers, another native woman who had long been pivotal in American Indian education in Minnesota.

As the coordinator of the Native Americans into Medicine Program at the University of Minnesota at Duluth, Leigh Harper directs students into science and math courses they will need for medical or health-related professions. Kathleen Annette, who directs the Bemidji Area Office of the Indian Health Service, includes mentoring native students pursuing medical careers as one of her top priorities. Before joining the Circle of Life School on the White Earth Reservation to focus on the needs of special education children, Verna Millage served as the coordinator for Moorhead State University's White Earth Program. Designed in response to the "real culture shock (of Indian students) on the campus of a big institution," the program provided extension classes on the reservation and improved retention rates of Indian students at the university. Increasing the number of native students who successfully completed higher education has required a multi-pronged solution. Anishinaabe women have been up to the task.[43]

Like native women across the United States, Anishinaabe women long have been concerned about the removal of children from tribal communities. In 1978 American Indian activists successfully persuaded Congress to pass the Indian Child Welfare Act (ICWA), which addressed this longstanding problem, and Anishinaabe women from White Earth were quick to help implement this legislation. After receiving a law degree from the University of Colorado and working for the Native American Rights Fund (NARF) and Anishinaabe Legal Services, Anita Fineday became tribal attorney for the Leech Lake Reservation. She immediately, "saw the Indian Child Welfare Act as an area of Indian law that had been very much neglected by the all-male tribal councils." She has concentrated "a large part of [her] practice in this area" and has confronted the consequences of the former foster-home program on a daily basis. According to Fineday, "I see many people in their fifties, raised in a non-Indian world, coming back to the reservation to try and figure out who their relatives are. People come into my office and ask me, 'Can you help me find my relatives? I think their names are such-and-such.' They want answers to questions like, 'Who am I? Where did I come from? Who is my family?'" Fineday points out the ICWA was intended to protect children, but if they must be removed from their families, she says, "We look toward placing them on the reservation with relatives—to keep them in Indian homes." Fineday reflected far beyond any one person's needs: "The tribes have been robbed of so much—their land, their children. Without those kids, tribes and culture will cease to exist." She clearly sees the big picture, "We're fighting for our survival by fighting to keep our children. They've got to have that contact with their elders, their families, their communities, and, most important, their tribe."[44]

Thelma Wang is a reunification specialist, trying to smooth the way for children to be rescued from foster care and integrated back into their families. She "wanted to be a social worker to try to save these kids from being in the system so long and ending up in group homes; these experiences left them angry and acting out behaviorally." Wang realizes that "follow-up is so important" because, she says, "There are always problems when a family gets back together. Someone needs to be there to keep an eye on things, to encourage. Parents get overwhelmed."[45]

Like their mothers before them, other modern Anishinaabe women continue to be concerned with the needs of the poor and elderly. While their mothers and grandmothers once worked through kinship groups or institutions associated with missionary organizations (such as the Bishop Whipple Hospital Auxiliary mentioned earlier in this chapter), modern Anishinaabe women continue to labor through organizations established by federal, state, or tribal agencies. Ann LaVoy worked with two programs for the elderly, the Minnesota Board on Aging and the Headwaters Board on Aging. Some like Saraphine Martin, Blanche Turner, and Bonnie Faye Wadena worked for programs that served and delivered meals. Martin related, "We serve anybody who wants to come. We deliver about fifteen trays a day, and about twelve people come into the center." Others provided home care. Sue Bellefeuille assists with physical therapy for people who have had hip or knee replacements. She also bathes bed-ridden patients and helps elderly individuals suffering from diabetes and blindness. Bellefeuille argues, "We need to start taking care of our old people. If we don't take care of our elders, our young will be neglected too."[46]

Other Anishinaabe women have focused their efforts on agencies designed to assist the homeless or to protect battered women. After living in an urban area and observing a "free-clothing business for the needy" called Operation Blessing, Lorraine Lindsay hoped to establish a similar agency at White Earth. "People in the community could come in and take whatever they needed. . . . I would like to set up something like that here on the reservation. I'd like to see us take care of our own." Sharing this dream, Natalie Greenlaw attempted to purchase an old, abandoned school, "so that we can provide anything a family could possibly need—from recreation to spiritual guidance, to school tutoring, to job readiness. We would be like an emergency shelter there for homeless people, as well as transitional housing for those who need it." Realizing that she faced several major challenges, she quickly chimed in, "Our dreams are big, but our vision is clear."[47]

Beverly Warren has always been concerned about women's welfare and maintaining their right to choose. She is the co-director of the Northwoods Coalition for Battered Women in Bemidji and has chaired many other local, state, and national committees focusing on domestic violence. She finds it difficult to work against violence in Indian communities because they are so closely knit, and people try to keep their problems within the family. She wonders, "How do you keep someone safe when everyone knows who you are and where you are?" She hopes her organization will operate a shelter on the reservation "so that our women wouldn't have to leave to get help." She believes that strengthening native spirituality would help battered women with low self-esteem realize, "We are the strong ones. We are the ones who keep the families together. I want women to feel good about that strength."[48]

Some Anishinaabe women have concentrated their efforts on prisons. Marcie Rendon worked in prisons, helping inmates earn their Graduate Equivalency Degree (GED). She also counseled them about acquiring the skills they will need when they are released. Melody LaFriniere also had a job in a reentry program in Minneapolis/St. Paul, "helping people who had been incarcerated for twenty years or more come back into society." Rendon reflected, "The social service part of my career happened because of the idea that Native American women are supposed to give back to the community."[49]

Gladys Ray understood the need for cross-cultural understanding and support more than most people. Working for the Community Action Agency and other economic opportunity programs, she organized the Indian Club and the Indian Center in Fargo, North Dakota. Although public speaking initially made her very nervous, she spoke at the "Communiversity" at Concordia College and received "an offer of a building for an Indian Center—a beautiful old building, standing vacant, that we could use." Ultimately, she was chosen to lead Project Bridge, which was designed "to build bridges between the Indian and non-Indian communities." For this work she received the Fargo-Moorhead Woman of the Year Award in 1973. Gladys reflected on her personal commitment with a spiritual dimension: "I have really spent my life doing work for our people. I feel sometimes that my destiny has been directed."[50]

Anishinaabe women have also continued to serve their communities through careers in medicine and the health sciences. Since Valerie Fox's grandmother was a "medicine woman," she believes that she also is "a lot like my grandmother in her beliefs and spirituality," and she has sought a career in medicine. Kathleen Annette echoed this cultural connection: "My Grandma Big Bear was a medicine woman, so I always knew that we had medicine in our family." This grounding also allowed her to be more sensitive to her native patients' needs. "When I was practicing medicine, the medicine man and I . . . were kind of partners . . . we would cross-refer." If a patient's family was uncomfortable with Western medicine, she referred them to a medicine man because "you don't just treat a patient; you treat the whole family or, in some situations, a whole tribe." She understood cultural differences. Sometimes "there would be twenty people sitting in the waiting room because that's the way it should be." Annette admitted that Anishinaabe values could abet alcohol abuse: "We are great enablers. We are taught to take care of each other." Ellie Mae Robinson recognized the need for a culturally sensitive approach to chemical dependency. Even though she had earned a certificate in chemical dependency treatment at the Hazelden Foundation in Center City, Minnesota, she felt that their confrontational style did not "work well with [her] people" because, she said, "They are very sensitive from having gone through so much in their lives. They have been so intimidated, and you certainly don't want to add to that. They need to feel comfortable with you. Sometimes this takes a long time, but eventually they relate to you." Like many, Annette's ultimate "goal was always to get back home, work for Indian people and Indian health, and be with my family." She dreamed of ministering to her people at the newly opened White Earth clinic.[51]

Others have found both employment and service as health-care administrators or nurses. Initially hired as a hospital nurse-consultant by the Indian Health Service in the Aberdeen, South Dakota, area, Eleanore Robertson soon became its director. She was the first Indian woman hired in this position. She loves to recount a certain story: "A tribal chairman, who reminded me that a woman couldn't do this job, interviewed me. I reminded *him* that men certainly hadn't handled it very well; they had been through three male directors in three years!!" She became director of the Phoenix area office of the Indian Health Service in the late 1990s. Myrna Smith says she *needs* to work as a nurse. Her commitment to her people drives her: "What really keeps me going is that I know the reservation needs more nurses who are Native American. I would like to help improve this situation so that patients would feel more comfortable and relaxed when they come into the clinic."[52]

Several Anishinaabe women have channeled their concerns for social welfare through contributing to tribal government. Some, such as Ann La-Voy and Melody LaFriniere, have attempted to reexamine and revamp tribal enrollment regulations.[53] Others exposed and addressed land fraud and corrupt tribal government. Leah Carpenter enrolled in law school, then worked for the Minnesota Chippewa Tribe, conducting research on White Earth land claims dating from the late nineteenth and early twentieth centuries. After earning her degree, she came home to work for Anishinaabe Legal Services. Her journey has not been easy. She occasionally has been forced to confront judges whom she had faced as a juvenile before she had found her way. "Running into court personnel who remarked about my family or my past in disparaging comments was hard. I don't know if it was because I was an Indian person or just because I was dirt poor. But the classism-type stuff seemed to come up and I heard things that were hard to take on a personal level." Nonetheless, what she had learned about White Earth's past and corruption on the tribal council have strengthened her commitment. "If you don't know your history, you're condemned to repeat it." Leah has worked with other grassroots White Earth activists to right past and present wrongs. For White Earth women, political reform is part of social welfare.[54]

It required considerable courage for White Earth women to investigate malfeasance in tribal government. When Sue Bellefeuille worked in the bingo hall, she remembers witnessing thing that disturbed her. "I was encouraged to go public with what I knew and what I had seen," she said. "I was very troubled by it all, so I quit my job in March 1991." After finishing her graduate coursework at Harvard, a group of people approached Erma Vizenor "to be their spokesperson to protest the corruption in government at White Earth." After she read a statement at a press conference, she realized she had to become further involved. Her doctoral dissertation languished while she "led the movement in White Earth." She traveled all over the country, she said, "telling our story about our fraudulent elections and what kind of corruption we had in government and how the people were suffering." Diana Osborn-King observed sadly, "In our culture we were taught to listen. But . . . I'm not sure if the council is listening to the women, to their voices and their hearts." The movement was peaceful; Vizenor adamantly opposed violence but "did spend one whole summer in jail." Despite the hassle, Bellefeuille remained involved in reform efforts, reflecting, "In most ways, I enjoyed being a part of the changes I thought would be good for the reservation. On the other hand, it caused a lot of conflict among friends and even in my family." Vizenor remained dedicated to reform, despite "doing jail time." "Our offense was to make injustice visible," she said. "My theme was always to unite the tribe and to serve *all* our members, no matter where they are."[55]

As a district representative on the White Earth Tribal Council, Irene Auginaush-Turney was committed to educating people about their right to have a voice and vote. She wanted an open and fair government. In 1996 corrupt tribal leaders were indicted on conspiracy charges and some served prison time. Elizabeth Foster-Anderson was relieved that "after many years of oppression under the old leadership, new voices are finally being heard." Auginaush-Turney hoped that these new voices would be able "to mend that circle of passing on traditions."[56]

While some women turned to politics, others have turned to business. Lorraine Lindsay earned a degree in small-business management from a vocational school in Detroit Lakes. She was offered a position in Mahhomen at the Women's Business Center to work on a three-year demonstration project to help women start their own businesses. Lorraine and her sister had started their own business marketing "jerky-juice meat marinade"; she hoped their example might assist women seeking economic independence, or who wished to make a fresh start.[57]

More recently, some Anishnaabe women have even projected their concerns for the tribe's social welfare toward the most visible (and sometimes controversial) economic activity on the reservations: casinos. Elizabeth Foster-Anderson and Lorna Jean LaGue were attracted to the prospect of working for White Earth's Shooting Star casino because of the "objectives behind the casino: to give Indians preference in hiring and to give them work training and the ability to go on and get other jobs and further education. It was meant to be a stepping-stone." Elizabeth Foster-Anderson always wanted to make a difference for "Native American working people," to help them "get employment, . . . keep their jobs, . . . understand what a payroll check is all about," and "maybe get into the idea of budgeting and being self-supporting." Gaming was only one component; the casino enterprise employed more than a thousand people to operate a 250–room hotel, a five-room conference center, and a cabaret-entertainment facility. The tribe hoped to emphasize family entertainment, not addictive gambling. Profits from the enterprise were earmarked toward improving programs in education, training and employment, social welfare, and cultural preservation. Foster-Anderson explained that they were "trying to change a cycle that has existed for years and years, even for centuries."[58]

Yet the casino has been, at best, a mixed blessing. LaGue, who served as the Shooting Star's human resources manager, admitted, "When you mix a casino industry and tribal government together, you have a heck of a mess on your hands." Former Reservation Business Committee (RBC) Chair Darrell "Chip" Wadena and several other RBC members were indicted, in part, for conspiring to profit from a bogus casino oversight committee that did nothing. Delores Rousu, who supports herself in traditional ways such as harvesting maple sugar, leeching, and cutting wood, exclaimed, "I hate that place; I wish it would blow up. It has wrecked too many families." Sue Bellefeuille agreed: "There is more money because it has provided jobs, but that has made it possible for us to spend more on drinking and gambling." Ronda Sargent-Estey also had "concerns about people gambling away their money." She said, "I think it was too bad that gambling had to be brought to the reservation to provide jobs." Bellefeuille wishes a fund would be set up to benefit the elderly, but she thinks that "we must clean up the elections first, or nothing will change."[59]

In retrospect, perhaps Winona Duke, a prolific and prominent White Earth author, best epitomizes the multi-faceted commitment of modern Anishinaabe women to the social welfare of their tribe. Duke is an advocate for the White Earth Reservation and its people, but she also champions American Indian rights, indigenous women's rights, women's rights in general, and the environment. She has held various positions in Greenpeace, the Indigenous Women's Network, and the Seventh Generation Fund. She also served as Ralph Nader's running mate on the Green Party ticket in the 1996 and 2000 presidential election campaigns. In 1989 she was awarded the International Reebok Human Rights Award, which she used to found the White Earth Land Recovery Project, dedicated to restoring the reservation land base to Indian control. The project has undertaken initiatives to promote native techniques of food production, especially wild rice, maize, maple syrup, raspberries, and strawberries. Project personnel have tried to reintroduce sturgeon into local lakes and have promoted the organic production of native turkeys as an alternative to industrial turkey farms. The project's protests against the genetic engineering of wild rice have been recognized by environmental groups in both the United States and Italy.[60]

The White Earth Land Recovery Project's Mino-Miijim (Good Food) Program hopes to address the diabetes epidemic on the reservation, especially among elders. Each month, "172 diabetic individuals and their families . . . receive buffalo meat, hominy corn, chokecherry or plum jelly (made with honey), maple syrup, wild rice, and mazon (broken wild rice grains good for soup)."[61] The Project also delivers vegetables, fruits, and other healthy food products. They recently opened their Native Harvest facility to process these foods and offer them for sale. "Our new kitchen equipment has made it easier to roast our hominy, can our jellies and jams, and package all of the foods we sell," said Florence Goodman, Native Harvest Food Production Coordinator. "This facility will allow us to take our production to the next level, and hopefully create more jobs for the community."[62]

LaDuke has used her celebrity to spark innovation in all of these areas. In 1994 *Time* magazine named her one of "50 leaders" for the future. Two years later she received the Thomas Merton Award. In 1997 she was the recipient of the Black-Indian-Hispanic-Asian Women in Action Community Service Award, the Ann Bancroft Award for Women's Leadership Fellowship, and was *Ms.* magazine's "Woman of the Year." LaDuke summarized, "One of my core beliefs is that the *whole* community is responsible for its future—not just a tribe, a church, or a certain faction of the community."[63] The title of her first novel, *Last Standing Woman,* expresses the conviction of Anishinaabe women.[64]

At the beginning of the twenty-first century, many Anishinaabe women, like Winona Duke, are persuaded that they must continue to champion the tribe's social welfare. Many believe that the hardships of the twentieth century were particularly difficult for Anishinaabe men, and that many of the traditional male roles no longer were available to them. In turn, Anishinaabe men were forced to cope with a world that provided them with limited or negative role models, and many adopted patterns of behavior that proved dysfunctional, abusive, and disruptive to modern tribal society. Some women blamed the boarding school system, and they expressed empathetic grief over the loss of the men's roles, but most agreed that "women are now the strength" among the people. According to Yvonne Novack, "At least in the

Ojibwe culture, the women had a chance to return (from the boarding school) and continue their roles. They could be strong and still have a voice," while Jane Staples has reiterated, "the woman . . . is the healer, the life giver, and has the power." According to Staples, "it's up to Indian women to keep the ball rolling." This perspective is not unique to White Earth women; it's shared by native women across the country.[65]

In conclusion, there is considerable evidence to support the contention that White Earth women have made a historic and continued contribution to the social welfare of their community. Not all women have taken prominent roles in these procedures, and some White Earth men also have contributed to this process, but historically there has been a nucleus of White Earth women who have assumed the responsibility for this "nurturing," and this responsibility, manifested in many spheres, continues for White Earth women today. Indeed, a concept of "responsibility" remains a key to understanding the White Earth women's commitment. Whereas Western feminists advocate for their "rights," White Earth women accept their "responsibilities." Their dedication to the social welfare of the White Earth community remains strong, even in the face of considerable adversity. As Winona Duke observes, "Seeing Indian women striving to accomplish things that will help our people feeds my soul. It encourages me to see women standing up for their children and what they believe in, resisting government help, and holding on to their beliefs with dignity. That also feeds my soul."[66]

Notes

1. All quotations in the first four paragraphs are from "Reminiscences" in the Pauline Colby Papers, Minnesota Historical Society Archives, 3–5, 80–83.

2. Ibid.

3. Ibid.

4. Ibid.

5. The following discussion of White Earth Anishinaabe women's investment in social welfare will be driven by women's voices but draws on insights from the following: Patricia Hill Collins, "Shifting the Center: Race, Class, and Feminist Theorizing about Motherhood," in *Representations of Motherhood,* ed. Donna Bassin, Margaret Honey, and Meryle Mahrer Kaplan (New Haven, Conn.: Yale University Press, 1994), 59; Lisa J. Udel, "Revision and Resistance: The Politics of Native Women's Motherwork," *Frontiers: A Journal of Women's Studies* 22 (2001): 43–64; Evelyn Nakano Glenn, "Racial Ethnic Women's Labor: The Intersection of Race, Gender and Class Oppression," *Review of Radical Political Economies* 17 (1985); Bonnie Thornton Dill, "Our Mothers' Grief: Racial Ethnic Women and the Maintenance of Families," *Journal of Family History* 13 (1988): 415–31; Nancy A. Naples, *Grassroots Warriors: Activist Mothering, Community Work, and the War on Poverty* (New York: Routledge, 1998); Nancy A. Naples, ed., *Community Activism and Feminist*

Politics: Organizing across Race, Class, and Gender (New York: Routledge, 1998); Kathleen Blee, ed., *No Middle Ground: Women and Radical Protest* (New York: New York University Press, 1998); Alexis Letter, Annelise Orleck, and Diana Taylor, ed., *The Politics of Motherhood: Activist Voices from Left to Right* (Hanover, N.H.: University Press of New England, 1997); Temma Kaplan, *Crazy for Democracy: Women in Grassroots Movements* (New York: Routledge, 1997); Linda Gordon, "Why Nineteenth-Century Feminists Did Not Support 'Birth Control' and Twentieth-Century Feminists Do: Feminism, Reproduction, and the Family," in *Rethinking the Family: Some Feminist Questions,* ed. Barrie Thorne and Marilyn Yalom (Boston: Northeastern University Press, 1992); Paula Gunn Allen, *Off the Reservation: Reflections on Boundary-Busting, Border-Crossing, Loose Cannons* (Boston: Beacon Press, 1998); Rayna Green, "American Indian Women: Diverse Leadership for Social Change," in *Bridges of Power: Women's Multicultural Alliances,* ed. Lisa Albrecht and Rose M. Brewer (Philadelphia: New Society, 1990); Rayna Green, "Review Essay: Native American Women," *Signs: Journal of Women in Culture and Society* 6 (1980): 248–67; Rayna Green, *Women in American Indian Society* (New York: Chelsea House, 1992); Ronnie Farley, ed., *Women of the Native Struggle: Portraits and Testimony of Native American Women* (New York: Orion, 1993); Clara Sue Kidwell, "What Would Pocahontas Think Now? Women and Cultural Persistence," *Callaloo* 17 (1994): 149; Ramona Ford, "Native American Women: Changing Statuses, Changing Interpretations," in *Writing the Range: Race, Class, and Culture in the Women's West,* ed. Elizabeth Jameson and Susan Armitage (Norman: University of Oklahoma Press, 1997); Nancy Shoemaker, "The Rise or Fall of Iroquois Women," *Journal of Women's History* 2 (1991): 39–57; Patricia Albers, "Autonomy and Dependency in the Lives of Dakota Women: A Study in Historical Change," *Review of Radical Political Economics* 17 (1985): 109–34; Patricia Albers, "From Illusion to Illumination: Anthropological Studies of American Indian Women," in *Gender and Anthropology: Critical Reviews for Research and Teaching,* ed. Sandra Gordon (Washington, D.C.: American Anthropological Association, 1989); Beatrice Medicine, "The Hidden Half Lives," in *Cante Ohitika Win (Brave-Hearted Women): Images of Lakota Women from the Pine Ridge Reservation South Dakota,* ed. Caroline Reyer (Vermillion: University of South Dakota Press, 1991); Jo Ann Kauffman and Yvette K. Joseph-Fox, "American Indian and Alaska Native Women," in *Race, Gender, and Health,* ed. Marcia Bayne-Smith (Thousand Oaks: Sage, 1996); Devon A. Mihesuah, "Commonality of Difference: American Indian Women and History," *American Indian Quarterly* 20 (1996); Clara Sue Kidwell, "Indian Women as Cultural Mediators," *Ethnohistory* 39 (1992): 97–107.

6. William Whipple Warren, *History of the Ojibways Based upon Traditions and Oral Statements* (St. Paul: Minnesota Historical Society Press, 1970). *Miigis* (*megis* in many historical sources) translates as "shell; sacred shell." See John Nichols and Earl Nyholm, *Ojibwewi-Ikidowinan: An Ojibwe Word Resource Book* (St. Paul: Minnesota Archaeological Society, 1979), 207. See also Harold Hickerson, *The Southwestern Chippewa: An Ethnohistorical Study* (Memoir 92), American Anthropological Association (Menasha, Wisc.: American Anthropological Association, 1962); Harold Hickerson, *The Chippewa and Their Neighbors: A Study in Ethnohistory* (New York: Holt, Rinehart, and Winston, 1970); Henry Rowe Schoolcraft, *The Indian in His Wigwam; or Characteristics of the Red Race of America* (Buffalo, N.Y.: Graham, 1848).

7. Jacqueline Peterson, "Ethnogenesis: The Settlement and Growth of a 'New People' in the Great Lakes Region, 1702–1815," *American Indian Culture and Research Journal* 6 (1982): 23–64; Jacqueline Peterson, "Many Roads to Red River: Métis Genesis in the Great Lakes Region, 1680–1815," in *The New Peoples: Being and Becoming Métis in North America,* ed. Jacqueline Peterson and Jennifer S. H. Brown (Lincoln: University of Nebraska Press, 1985); Jacqueline Peterson, "Prelude to Red River: A Social Portrait of the Great Lakes Métis," *Ethnohistory* 25 (1978): 41–67; Jacqueline Peterson, "The People in Between: Indian-White Marriage and the Genesis of Métis Society and Culture in the Great Lakes Region, 1702–1815" (PhD diss., University of Illinois, Chicago Circle, 1981); Jennifer S. H. Brown, *Strangers in Blood: Fur Trade Company Families in Indian Country* (Vancouver: University of British Columbia Press, 1980); Sylvia Van Kirk, *"Many Tender Ties": Women in Fur-Trade Society, 1670–1870* (Winnipeg: Watson and Dwyer, 1980).

8. Quotations from Priscilla K. Buffalohead, "Farmers, Warriors, Traders: A Fresh Look at Ojibwa Women," *Minnesota History* 48 (1983): 31, and Emma H. Blair, trans. and ed., *The Indian Tribes of the Upper Mississippi Valley and the Region of the Great Lakes as Described by Nicolas Perrot, French Commandant in the Northwest; Bacqueville e la Potheri, French Royal Commissioner to Canada; Morrell Mareston, American Army Officer; and Thomas Forsyth, United States Agent at Fort Armstrong,* 2 vols. (Cleveland: Clark, 1911) 1:69.

9. Perrot Narrative, in Blair, *Indian Tribes of the Upper Mississippi,* 67–76. For comments about stories to children, also see Kimberley Blaeser, interview, in Vance Vannote, ed., *Women of White Earth: Photographs and Interviews by Vance Vannote* (Minneapolis: University of Minnesota Press, 1999), 5. Hereinafter, citation to interviews in this volume will be cited to the person interviewed and the page number in the volume.

10. Melissa Meyer, *The White Earth Tragedy: Ethnicity and Dispossession at a Minnesota Anishinaabe Reservation, 1889–1920* (Lincoln: University of Nebraska Press, 1994), 25.

11. Ibid. Also see "Reminiscences," in Colby Papers, Minnesota Historical Society Archives, 50.

12. Meyer, *White Earth Tragedy,* 25–26; "Reminiscences," in Colby Papers, Minnesota Historical Society Archives, 53.

13. Meyer, *White Earth Tragedy,* 26–27.

14. Ibid., 27–28.

15. Ibid., 28–35.

16. Ibid., 35–65.

17. Ibid., 69–135.

18. "Report in the Matter of the Investigation of the White Earth Reservation," House Reports 6336, no. 1336, 62 Cong., 3 sess. (1913): 166, 569 (hereinafter "Graham Report"); "Chippewa Indians in Minnesota," House Executive Documents 2747, no. 247, 51 Cong., 1 sess. (1890): 26, 37, 41, 43, 49, 52, 55 (hereinafter "Report of the U.S. Chippewa Commission"); Reverend R. R. Bishop Baraga, *A Dictionary of the Otchipwe Language, Explained in English,* 2 parts (Minneapolis: Ross & Haines, 1966), 291; U.S. General Land Office, Crookston Land District, "Register of Indian Allotment Entries: Nelson Act, 1901," Minnesota State Archives, Minnesota Historical Society Archives (hereinafter MHSA); Meyer, *White Earth Tragedy,* 98–99; Melissa L. Meyer, "'We Can Not Get a Living as We Used To': Dispossession among the White Earth Anishinaabeg, 1889–1920," *American Historical*

Review 96, no. 1 (1991): 368–94; Melissa L. Meyer, "Signatures and Thumbprints: Ethnicity among the White Earth Anishinaabeg, 1889–1920," *Social Science History* 14 (1990): 305–45.

19. Quotes in this paragraph come from interviews with Erma Vizenor (93); Verna Millage (152), Frances Keahna (208), Ellie Mae Robinson (189), and Lena Desizlets (103). All these interviews can be found in Vannote, *Women of White Earth.* Also see "Reminiscences of Maggie Brown Hanks, White Earth Band of the Minnesota Chippewa Tribe," tape 196, no. 23, 4–10; and "Reminiscences of Naomi Warren LaDue, White Earth Band of the Minnesota Chippewa Tribe," tape 221, no. 26, 14, 33. This information can be found in Cynthia Kelsey, rec. and ed., *New York Times* Oral History Program, University of South Dakota American Indian Oral History Project (Sanford N.C.: Microfilming Corporation of America, 1979). These interviews were conducted during the summer of 1968. Hereinafter citations to this collection will be to the individual interview, "South Dakota Oral History Project," tape number, file no., and page. nos. Also see John Rogers, *Red World and White: Reminiscences of a Chippewa Boyhood* (Norman: University of Oklahoma Press, 1996), and Meyer, *White Earth Tragedy,* 72–92.

20. "Keaehna Interview," in Vannote, *Women of White Earth,* 208, 210; "Desizlets Interview," in ibid., 103; "Reminiscences of Josephine Lightning Norcross," South Dakota Oral History Project, tape 226, no. 19, 30.

21. Meyer, *White Earth Tragedy,* 82–86.

22. "Norcross Reminiscences," South Dakota Oral History Project, tape 226, no. 19, 7–8; "Fairbanks's Reminiscences," ibid., tape 234, no. 22, 6, 9, 22, 28.

23. "Hanks's Reminiscences," South Dakota Oral History Project, tape 196, no. 23, 17; "Fairbanks's Reminiscences," ibid., tape 234, no. 22, 16; "Norcross Reminiscences," ibid., tape 226, no. 19, 27–29; "Ladue Reminiscences," ibid., tape, 221, tape 221, no. 26, 14–15.

24. "Robinson Interview," in Vannote, *Women of White Earth,* 192.

25. "Ladue Reminiscences," South Dakota Oral History Project, tape 221, no. 26, 32–33; tape 222, no. 26, 29. Also see "Norcross Reminiscences," ibid., tape 226, no. 19, 43–44.

26. "Ladue Reminiscences," ibid., tape 222, no. 26, 30–33, tape 224, 31–34; "Hanks Reminiscences," ibid., tape 196, no. 23, 31, and tape 233, 1–5. Also see "Sue Bellefeuille Interview," in Vannote, *Women of White Earth,* 110.

27. Meyer, *White Earth Tragedy,* 137–72, 203–24; Thomas D. Peacock and Donald R. Day, "Nations within a Nation: The Dakota and Ojibwe of Minnesota," *Daedalus* 129 (2000).

28. "Norcross Reminiscences," South Dakota Oral History Project, tape 226, 7–8; "Ladue Reminiscences," ibid., tape 222, 30–33.

29. "Ladue Reminiscences," ibid., tape 221, 38, and tape 224, 17, 19–20, 24–28, 37; "Norcross Reminiscences," ibid., tape 226, 24–25.

30. "Ladue Reminiscences," ibid., tape 222, 17; "Fairbank's Reminiscences," ibid., tape 234, no. 22, 10–11.

31. "Norcross Reminiscences," ibid., tape 226, 20–22. Also see "Eleanore Robertson Interview," in Vannote, *Women of White Earth,* 157; M. Inez Hilger, *Chippewa Families: A Social Study of White Earth Reservation* (St. Paul: Minnesota Historical Society Press, 1998).

32. "Norcross Reminiscences," South Dakota Oral History Project, tape 226, 20–22;

"Ladue Reminiscences," ibid., tape 224, 6–7, 10, 12–13: "Fairbanks' Reminiscences," ibid., tape 234, 10–11.

33. "Norcross Reminiscences," ibid., tape 226, 20–22.

34. "Robertson Interview," in Vannote, *Women of White Earth*, 157.

35. "Ladue, "Reminiscences," South Dakota Oral History Project, tape 224, 38–39; "Norcross "Reminiscences," ibid., tape 224, 22–24.

36. Brenda Child, *Boarding School Seasons: American Indian Families, 1900–1940* (Lincoln: University of Nebraska Press, 1998).

37. "Joan Staples Interview," in Vannote, *Women of White Earth*, 149; "Melody LaFriniere Interview," in ibid., 186–87.

38. "Bonnie Wadena Interview," in ibid., 128; "Beverly Warren Interview," in ibid., 204–5; "Yvonne Novack Intervie," in ibid., 17; "Irene Auginaush-Turney Interview," in ibid., 144; "Natalie Greenlaw Interview," in ibid., 165.

39. "Ladue Reminiscence," South Dakota Oral History Project, tape 221, 28; "Hanks Reminiscence," ibid., tape 23, 29; "Lavoy Interview," in Vannote, *Women of White Earth*, 118; "Delores Rousu Interview," in Vannote, *Women of White Earth*, 137; "Irene Auginaush-Turney Interview," in Vannote, *Women of White Earth*, 145.

40. "Anita Fineday Interview," in Vannote, *Women of White Earth*, 114; "Juanita Blackhawk Interview," in ibid., 78; "Leah Carpenter Interview," in ibid., 50–51.

41. "Melody Frinere Interview," in ibid., 184; "Anne LaVoy Interview," in ibid., 118; "Robertson Interview," in ibid., 158; "Diana Osburn-King Interview," in ibid., 20; "Mary Harper Interview," in ibid., 60; "Yvonne Novack Interview," in ibid., 13–15; "Anne M. Dunn Interview," in ibid., 124; "Valerie Fox Interview," in ibid., 164.

42. "Natalie Greenlaw Interview," in ibid., 164; "Erma Vizenor Interview," in ibid., 94–96.

43. "Novack Interview," in ibid., 13–15; "Mary Harper Interview," in ibid., 60; "Kathleen Renee Annette," in ibid., 29; "Millage Interview," in ibid., 154–55.

44. "Fineday Interview," in ibid., 114–16.

45. "Thelma Wang Interview," in ibid., 54–55.

46. "LaVoy Interview," in ibid., 117; "Martin Interview," in ibid., 75; "Turner Interview," in ibid., 46; "Wadena Interview," in ibid., 129; "Bellefeuille Interview," in ibid., 107–9.

47. "Lindsay Interview," in ibid., 85; "Greenlaw Interview," in ibid., 165.

48. "Warren Interview," in ibid., 202–4; "Dunn Interview," in ibid., 122.

49. "Marcie Rendon Interview," in ibid., 132; "LaFriniere Interview," in ibid., 185. Also see "Dunn Interview," in ibid., 122.

50. "Gladys Ray Interview," in ibid., 8–11.

51. "Valerie Fox Interview," in ibid., 71; "Annette Interview," in ibid., 28–31; "Robinson Interview," in ibid., 188–191. See also "Minnesota College Helps American Indians Fight Diabetes," *Community College Week* 16 (April 26, 2004): 22; Christine T. Lowery, "American Indian Perspectives on Addiction and Recovery," *Health and Social Work* 23 (1998); M. J. Braveheart and L. Debruyn, "So She May Walk in Balance: Integrating the Impact of Historical Trauma in the Treatment of Native American Indian Women," in *Racism in the Lives of Women: Testimony, Theory and Guides to Antiracist Practice*, ed. J. Adleman and G. M. Enguidanos (Binghamton, N.Y.: Harrington Park Press, 1995), 345–64; J. T.

Garrett, *Indian Health: Valued, Beliefs, and Practices* (Washington, D.C.: Department of Health and Human Services, 1990 [HHS Publication No. HRS, P-DV-90-4]), 179–191.

52. "Robertson Interview," in Vannote, *Women of White Earth,* 156, 159; "Myrna Joyce Smith Interview," in ibid., 176–77.

53. "LaVoy Interview," in ibid., 120; "LaFriniere Interview," in ibid., 187.

54. "Leah Carpenter Interview," in ibid., 47–50. Also see Louise Erdrich and Michael Dorris, "Who Owns Our Land," *New York Times Magazine,* September 4, 1988, 137.

55. "Bellefeuille Interview," in Vannote, *Women of White Earth,* 110; "Vizenor Interview," in ibid., 95–96; "Osborn-King Interview," in ibid., 21.

56. "Auginaush-Turney Interview," in ibid., 141, 144; "Foster-Anderson Interview," in ibid., 197.

57. "Lorraine Lindsay Interview," in ibid., 85.

58. "Elizabeth Foster-Anderson Interview," in ibid., 194–96; "Lorna Jean LaGue Interview," in ibid., 32–33.

59. "LaGue Interview," in ibid., 32; "Delores Rousu Interview," in ibid., 138; "Bellefeuille Interview," in ibid., 108; "Ronda Sargent-Estey Interview," in ibid., 65.

60. Duke's career as an activist for Anishinaabe, Native American, women's, and environmental rights is well documented. For example, see Winona Duke, "Alaska: Oil and the Natives," *Earth Island Journal* 18 (Autumn 2003); Duke "I Fight Like a Woman: The UN Conference on Women in China, 1995," *Canadian Dimension* 30 (April 1996); Duke, "White Earth," *New Internationalist* 1284 (1996); Tim King, "Native Americans Take Back Land," *Progressive* 58 (1994); Fiona Muldrew, "Winona LaDuke: A Mother Earth Revolt," *Herizons* 10 (Summer 1996); Sonya Paul and Robert Perkinson, "Winona LaDuke," *Progressive* 59 (October 1995); David Van Biema, "Tomorrow: 50 Promising Young Leaders," *Time,* December 5, 1994, 144; Jennifer Baumgardner, "Kitchen Table Candidate: Winona LaDuke," *Ms.,* April–May 2001, 11. Also see http://www.welrp.org/projectdiabetes.html.

61. http://www.welrp.org/projectsdiabetes.html.

62. http://www.welrp.org/nativeharvest/nativeharvest.html.

63. "Winona LaDuke Interview," in Vannote, *Women of White Earth,* 167. For examples of LaDuke's many accomplishments, see the references listed in note 51.

64. Winona LaDuke, *Last Standing Woman* (Stillwater, Minn.: Voyageur, 1997), 5.

65. "Osburn-King Interview," in Vannote, *Women of White Earth,* 20; "Novack Interview," in ibid., 17; "Staples Interview," in ibid., 150.

66. "LaDuke Interview," in ibid., 168.

Contributors

BRADLEY J. BIRZER is the Russell Amos Kirk Chair in History and director of American Studies at Hillsdale College in Michigan. The author of several books, he writes frequently on the American West, mythology, and Christian Humanism. He and his wife Dedra have five children.

BRENDA J. CHILD is an associate professor in the Department of American Studies at the University of Minnesota. She is the author of *Boarding School Seasons: American Indian Families, 1900–1940*. She is Red Lake Ojibwa.

THOMAS BURNELL COLBERT is a professor of social sciences and humanities at Marshalltown Community College in Marshalltown, Iowa. Colbert holds a PhD from Oklahoma State University and has published on midwestern and western history, especially Native American topics.

GREGORY EVANS DOWD is a professor of history and American culture and director of the Program in American Culture at the University of Michigan, Ann Arbor. He is the author of *A Spirited Resistance: The North American Indian Struggle for Unity, 1745–1815*, and *War under Heaven: Pontiac, the Indian Nations, and the British Empire*.

R. DAVID EDMUNDS is Watson Professor of American History at the University of Texas at Dallas and is the author or editor of ten books and more than one hundred essays or articles. He has held fellowships from the Ford Foundation, the Newberry Library, the Guggenheim Foundation, and other scholarly organizations. Edmunds is the past president of the American

Society for Ethnohistory and the Western History Association. His research focuses on Native American biography and on tribal people in the Great Lakes Region and in Oklahoma.

BRIAN HOSMER is an associate professor of history at the University of Illinois at Chicago. From 2002 to 2008 he served as director of the Newberry Library's D'Arcy McNickle Center for American Indian History and the Committee for Institutional Cooperation's American Indian Studies Consortium. His research focuses on intersections between economic change and cultural identity in American Indian communities, and his publications include *American Indians in the Marketplace: Persistence and Innovation among the Menominees and Metlakatlans, 1870–1920,* and *Native Pathways: Economic Development and American Indian Cultures in the Twentieth Century,* co-edited with Colleen O'Neill.

REBECCA KUGEL is an associate professor of history at the University of California, Riverside, has written numerous articles on the Ojibwes, and is the author of *To Be the Main Leader of Our People: A History of Minnesota Ojibwe Politics, 1825–1898.*

JAMES B. LAGRAND is an associate professor of history at Messiah College in Grantham, Pennsylvania. He is the author of *Indian Metropolis: Native Americans in Chicago, 1945–1975* and several articles on American Indian history and modern American history.

MELISSA L. MEYER is a professor of history and American Indian studies at the University of California, Los Angeles. She is the author of *The White Earth Tragedy: Ethnicity and Dispossession at a Minnesota Anishinaabe Reservation, 1889–1920* and *Thicker than Water: The Origins of Blood as a Symbol and Ritual.* Her article "American Indian Blood Quantum: Blood Is Thicker than Family" appears in Valerie Matsumoto and Blake Allmendinger, eds., *Over the Edge: Remapping the American West.* She continues to work on a larger study of American Indian tribal enrollment and blood quantum requirements.

LUCY ELDERSVELD MURPHY is an associate professor of history at Ohio State University, Newark. She is the author of *A Gathering of Rivers: Indians, Me'tis, and Mining in the Western Great Lakes, 1737–1832;* co-editor (with Rebecca Kugel) of *Native Women's History in Eastern North America before 1900: A Guide to Research and Writing;* and co-editor (with Wendy

Hamand Venet) of *Midwestern Women: Work, Community, and Leadership at the Crossroads.* She directs the oral history project, "Discovering the Stories of Native Ohio."

ALAN G. SHACKELFORD is a visiting assistant professor of history at Denison University in Granville, Ohio. He is currently completing a manuscript titled "American Indian Prehistory and History in the Confluence Region."

SUSAN SLEEPER-SMITH is an associate professor of history at Michigan State University. She is the author of *Indian Woman and French Men: Rethinking Cultural Encounter in the Western Great Lakes*; the co-author of *New Faces in the Fur Trade*; and has written articles and essays in many scholarly journals and edited volumes. Her research focuses on the intersection of diverse cultures in the Great Lakes and Upper Mississippi Valley, particularly with regard to how people of mixed ancestry have transcended racism and gender bias to create broad social and economic networks that have affected the development of the region.

STEPHEN WARREN is an assistant professor of history at Augustana College in Rock Island, Illinois. His first book is *The Shawnees and Their Neighbors, 1795–1870.*

Index

The University of Illinois Press
is a founding member of the
Association of American University Presses.

———————————————————————

Composed in 10.5/13 Adobe Minion Pro
by Jim Proefrock
at the University of Illinois Press
Manufactured by Sheridan Books, Inc.

University of Illinois Press
1325 South Oak Street
Champaign, IL 61820-6903
www.press.uillinois.edu